# FIRST-YEAR GERMAN

SECOND EDITION

**ROBERT E. HELBLING**
*University of Utah*

**WOLF GEWEHR**
*Pädagogische Hochschule Münster*

**DIETER JEDAN**
*University of California, Los Angeles*

**WOLFF A. VON SCHMIDT**
*University of Utah*

# FIRST-YEAR GERMAN

SECOND EDITION

HOLT, RINEHART AND WINSTON
*New York   San Francisco   Toronto   London*

Photo Permissions are on page 443

**Library of Congress Cataloging in Publication Data**

Helbling, Robert E
   First-year German.

   Includes index.
   1. German language—Grammar—1950-     I. Gewehr,
Wolf, joint author. II. Von Schmidt, Wolff A., joint
author. III. Title.
PF3112.H4 1978      438'.2'421      78-9859
ISBN 0-03-045171-X (Student Edition)
ISBN 0-03-045176-0 (Instructor's Edition)

# CONTENTS

# INTRODUCTION

In preparing the new edition of *First-year German* we have heeded advice from many collegues at our own and other institutions who have successfully used our original materials, so that this edition is, in many respects, a new text rather than a mere revision. The basic principles of *First-year German*, however, have been maintained. In its methodology, our text allows for flexibility of approach while combining coherent oral and analytical elements to develop simultaneously the four language skills—listening, speaking, reading and writing.

Users of our first edition will find the following significant changes:

—the total number of chapters has been reduced from 22 to 18. This was achieved by omitting some finer points of grammar which are best left for more advanced courses. It is our hope that this shorter text will allow most instructors to complete the program in one year. The remaining grammar points have been reworked so as to make them clearer and more concise.

—an Introductory Chapter has been added. It presents basic vocabulary such as numbers, days of the week, months of the year, expressions of time and weather. It can be used throughout the course as a reference.

—a Chapter Vocabulary is now provided for *each* chapter. Each list is divided according to parts of speech, and there is a separate list of easily recognized words (cognates). The total number of vocabulary words in the text has been substantially reduced. This has been made possible by careful re-entry and strict control of mastered vocabulary. As a reference for word frequency we used Heinz Oehler, *Grundwortschatz Deutsch* (Stuttgart: Ernst Klett, 1966).

—the Useful Phrases section now appears immediately before the Conversation. All words and phrases are completely integrated into the Conversation.

—the Conversations have been rewritten and, where necessary, shortened with a dual purpose in mind: 1) to provide students with examples of the grammar points within a meaningful context, and 2) to give students a glimpse of German as it is actually spoken. We have made every effort to see that the situations are plausible and to tie the topic of the Conversation to that of the subsequent Reading. Content and personalized questions on the Conversations have been added to check student's comprehension and to allow for additional vocabulary manipulation.

—the Readings have been rewritten with an expanded cultural orientation in mind. They now have footnotes, in English, that provide students with cultural information on Germany and German-speaking countries. Marginal notes translate idiomatic expressions or as yet unfamiliar vocabulary.

—throughout the text the exercises have beeen totally reworked. There are now exercises after each major grammar point to allow for immediate check of mastery. The exercises reflect the tighter vocabulary control. Both the new vocabulary within the chapter and previously learned vocabulary are used in all exercises. The Guided Conversation and Guided Composition have been rewritten so as to propose more interesting topics and give more concrete suggestions to the students. Often these topics are accompanied by illustrations.

—the entire illustration program has been revamped. All photographs and cultural realia are recent and show the contemporary German-speaking world and its people. All photographs are integrated with the chapter theme.

—the somewhat mechanical vocabulary exercises that followed the readings in the first edition have been replaced by a Vocabulary Development section that will prove to be an efficient aid in vocabulary building. We have treated those vocabulary problems which are most interesting or troublesome to English speaking students.

—the Supplements which accompany *First-year German* have been totally rewritten. The articles in the two readers, *Current Issues* and *Art and Letters*, have been updated and more closely interrelated with the Conversation and Readings in the corresponding chapter of the basic text. Vocabulary and grammar have been better controlled and students should have no problem reading the texts. The *Laboratory and Exercise Manual* and the *Tape Program* are more closely coordinated in order to provide students with better supplementary oral and written work.

—finally, we now have an *Instructor's Edition*. A detailed introduction precedes this instructor's annotated edition and contains helpful insight into the program, sample lesson plans, sample examinations, listening comprehension passages, questions and dictations from the laboratory program. In addition, we have provided throughout the text additional model sentences, references to previously taught material and to material yet to come, and alternative ways of using the different sections comprising this new edition of *First-year German*.

**CHAPTER ORGANIZATION**

Each of the 18 chapters consists of the following sections:

### Model Sentences

German sentences translated into English introduce each new grammar point to be covered in the chapter. The key phrases are printed in bold face so as to direct attention to them. These model sentences contain previously mastered and new chapter vocabulary in about equal measure. They are re-entered in the grammar explanations and the exercise material.

### Grammar Explanations

No more than three grammar topics are presented within each chapter. They are explained in English, often making use of diagrams and paradigms. All explanations are followed by abundant examples. At strategic intervals, the explanations are followed by brief Check your Comprehension exercises that allow students to test their understanding of the material step by step and before going on to the next point.

### Useful Phrases and Conversation

Preceding each conversation, there is a short series of everyday expressions (exclamations, interjections, or idioms with unusual grammatical structures) with their approximate English equivalents. These phrases are all integrated into the Conversation. The Conversations themselves all revolve around common situations with which students can identify and often are written with a light or humorous touch. They contain examples, in a meaningful context, of the grammar just mastered and their topics relate to those of the Reading which follows. It is our hope that students will find them both interesting and instructive.

The Conversations are followed by a set of Questions testing the students' understanding of the topic and their mastery of vocabulary. A few personalized questions are included to give students a chance to relate the topic to their own experience. The idiomatic English equivalents of the Conversations are included in the Appendix.

A modified version of part of the Conversation is used as one of the two listening comprehension passages in the tape program. This further integrates the program and carries through each concept into each section.

### Practice

This section is made up of a series of exercises ranging from simple drills requiring manipulation of one grammar point, to complex transformation drills requiring assimilation of all the grammar points covered. The new vocabulary of the Conversation, as well as previously mastered vocabulary, is used. This section serves a dual purpose: 1) it allows students an additional opportunity to practice new vocabulary and grammar, and 2) it allows for re-entry of materials in a meaningful context. These exercises can be done either orally or in writing.

## Guided Conversation

The topics in this section are related to that of the Conversation. They enable students to treat the subject matter from a more personal perspective and, at the same time to use the preceding vocabulary and grammar of the chapter. Suggestions are given in English, with some help in German, so as to encourage and guide students to build conversational skills. Often these conversations are based on visual material.

Up to this point, the pedagogic emphasis of the chapter is on grammar, listening and speaking. In the subsequent sections the emphasis shifts to reading and writing without neglecting the other two skills.

## Reading

The Readings have been written to illustrate important aspects of modern life in Germany and the German speaking world, and to show usage of the grammar principles within an appealing context. We have included cultural material on Austria, Switzerland and East Germany as well as on West Germany. The historical references and the cultural material are explained in English footnotes which follow the Reading.

It has been our goal to concentrate on realistic glimpses of every-day life in the German-speaking world. We have attempted to choose situations with which the students can identify. Marginal glosses translate less familiar words or idiomatic expressions not as yet learned. The Questions which follow the Reading can be answered orally or in writing. They test the students' understanding of the topics, and provide an opportunity to practice the new vocabulary and structures. Personalized questions are often included. A modified version of part of the Reading is used as the second listening comprehension passage in the tape program.

## Vocabulary Development

Written in a lighter vein, this section discusses the etymological relationship of words and word groups among themselves, the use of idioms, the recognition of gender in certain word endings, etc. We have tried to concentrate on those areas which pose the greatest problems to English speaking students. This section also provides topics for brief classroom discussion and scenarios that can easily be enacted in class.

## Review Exercises

Still another series of diversified exercises reinforces the application of all the grammar principles and the vocabulary presented in the chapter in combination with those covered in the preceding chapters. A German-English translation passage is included.

## Guided Composition

The topics of the Guided Compositions are largely based on the subject matter of the Readings. Suggestions are made to help students and instructors with the topics. Often visuals are used as a catalyst.

## Chapter Vocabulary

Each Chapter Vocabulary is divided into parts of speech. In addition, there is a separate list of Easily Recognized Words.

## APPENDIX AND VOCABULARY

The *Appendix* is made up of the following elements:
A *Pronunciation Guide* to be used as a quick reference section and as the basis of drills of individual sounds. It can be used throughout the year and/or in conjunction with the Introductory Chapter.
*Translations of all Conversations* appearing in the text. All translations are in idiomatic English.
A *List of all Strong and Irregular Weak Verbs* found in the text.
A *List of Common Weights and Measurements* providing the equivalents between the American system and the metric system.
Four *maps* which provide students with the basic geography of Europe, Germany, Switzerland and Austria.
A complete *German-English end vocabulary*, combining all vocabulary items and idiomatic expressions used throughout the text, and an *English-German end vocabulary* that includes all words and phrases needed to successfully complete the exercise material.

A thorough *Index* to all grammar points covered in the text is also included.

## SUPPLEMENTARY MATERIALS

### Laboratory and Exercise Manual and Tape Program

The following supplementary materials complete the *First-year German* package.
*The Laboratory and Exercise Manual* and the accompanying *Tape Program* follow the chapter structure of the main text. There are two parts for each chapter. Part I, representing approximately twenty minutes of lab work, can most profitably be done after the Practice exercises and the Guided Conversation in the corresponding chapter of the main text. It features pronunciation drills, reinforcement exercises for each point covered in the text and a listening comprehension passage based on the Conversation in the text. Part II, which lasts approximately fifteen minutes, is to be done at the very end of the chapter and consists of one exercise reviewing all the grammatical structures covered, a listening comprehension passage based on the Reading in the text, and a short dictation, also taken from the Reading. The Manual gives all directions

heard on tape, all examples and for approximately half the exercises (aster-isked) the sentences and cues. The latter allows students to prepare for the tape session and/or for the instructor to assign the exercises as additional written work. Other exercises are entirely on tape. All listening comprehension passages as well as the Dictations are included in the Instructor's Edition.

### Instructor's Edition

The *Instructor's Edition* contains chapter by chapter suggestions for classroom presentation of material. A special introduction contains lesson plans, sample examinations, the listening comprehension exercises and the dictations from the tape program.

### Readers

The *First-year German* package includes two readers: *Current Issues*, focusing on problems of contemporary life, and *Arts and Letters*, concentrating on various aspects of the arts in German speaking countries. Both are primarily designed to develop the students' reading comprehension skills and to allow them to read complete articles from the very beginning. Questions checking comprehension and topics for classroom discussion follow, so that the reading experience can be expanded into an oral session. The readings are short with marginal notes to facilitate comprehension. The grammar and vocabulary are carefully controlled so as not to pose a problem for the beginning student. We suggest that the readers be used starting with Chapter 7 of the main text. Although the topics are coordinated with those of the text's conversations and readings, the reader may be used with any other introductory German program.

## ACKNOWLEDGMENTS

We would like to express our gratitude to Ms. Antje Curry, graduate assistant in the Department of Languages, University of Utah, for her expert help in reading and correcting the manuscript copy and in preparing the various vocabularies. Special thanks must go to Mr. Clifford Browder, whose skillful copyediting is responsible for many improvements in the text, and to Ms. Marilyn Hofer, the publisher's special editor, for her professional expertise in coordinating the various parts of the project.

We also gratefully acknowledge the many experts teaching at various institutions throughout the country, whom the publisher called on to give us valuable advice at different stages in our work. A special word of thanks is due to the following reviewers for their most helpful comments:

Patricia Brodsky, *University of Missouri—Kansas City*
Gerald Cerwonka, *Syracuse University*
Frank Donahue, *University of Texas—Austin*
Barbara Eger, *Virginia Commonwealth University*
Alan Galt, *University of Cincinnati*

Henry Geitz, *University of Wisconsin*
Lanthrop P. Johnson, *University of Florida*
Robert L. Kyes, *University of Michigan*
Don Liebersnecht, *Penn State University–York*
Kriemhilde Livingston, *University of Akron*
Margaret Lorman, *California State University–Long Beach*
George Peters, *University of New Mexico*
Fred Piedmont, *Indiana University*
Carroll Reed, *University of Massachusetts*
Claus Reschke, *University of Houston*
Gertrude Shuback, *Arizona State University*
Marjorie Tussing, *California State University–Fullerton*
Helga Van Iten, *Iowa State University*
Reinhard Zollitsch, *University of Maine*

# FIRST-YEAR GERMAN

SECOND EDITION

**Introductory Chapter**

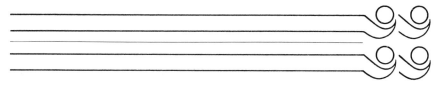

The Introductory Chapter will teach you to say a few common things right away. Study the words and expressions carefully and imitate the pronunciation of your instructor closely. (A guide to the rules of pronunciation is given in the Appendix.)

## I. Cardinal numbers

Cardinal numbers are used for counting and for indicating quantity. Once you know the numbers below, it will be easy to form any other number in German.

| | | | |
|---|---|---|---|
| 0 | null | 6 | sechs |
| 1 | eins (ein–) | 7 | sieben |
| 2 | zwei | 8 | acht |
| 3 | drei | 9 | neun |
| 4 | vier | 10 | zehn |
| 5 | fünf | 11 | elf |

| | | | |
|---|---|---|---|
| 12 | zwölf | 60 | sechzig |
| 13 | dreizehn | 70 | siebzig |
| 14 | vierzehn | 80 | achtzig |
| 15 | fünfzehn | 90 | neunzig |
| 16 | sechzehn | 100 | (ein)hundert |
| 17 | siebzehn | 101 | (ein)hunderteins |
| 18 | achtzehn | 200 | zweihundert |
| 19 | neunzehn | 1000 | (ein)tausend |
| 20 | zwanzig | 1100 | (ein)tausendeinhundert |
| 21 | einundzwanzig | 1101 | (ein)tausendeinhunderteins |
| 30 | dreißig | 2 000 | zweitausend |
| 40 | vierzig | 1 000 000 | eine Million |
| 50 | fünfzig | 2 000 000 | zwei Millionen |

Compound numbers are always written as one word. Notice that the unit number precedes the ten number.

|   | |
|---|---|
| 66 | sechsundsechzig |
| 124 | hundertvierundzwanzig |
| 4210 | viertausendzweihundertzehn |
| 1925 | neunzehnhundertfünfundzwanzig |

## Check your comprehension

1. Count from one to ten.
2. Give all even numbers from one to twenty.
3. Give all odd numbers from eleven to thirty-one.
4. Count by tens to one hundred.
5. Give the number 345.
6. Give the number 1066.
7. Give your age.
8. Give the year.
9. Give the year of your birth.

**USEFUL PHRASES**

Some useful phrases which you will hear from the very beginning are listed below. Memorize them as quickly as possible.

| | |
|---|---|
| **Guten Tag!** | *Good day.* |
| **Guten Morgen!** | *Good morning.* |

| | |
|---|---|
| **Guten Abend!** | *Good evening.* |
| **Auf Wiedersehen!** | *Good-bye.* |
| **Wie geht es Ihnen?** | *How are you?* |
| **Gut!** | *Fine.* |
| **Schlecht!** | *Bad.* |
| **Danke!** | *Thank you.* |
| **Bitte!** | { *Please.* / *You're welcome.* } |
| **Wieviel Uhr ist es?** / **Wie spät ist es?** | *What time is it?* |
| **Es ist acht Uhr.** | *It is eight o'clock.* |
| **Es ist halb neun.** | *It is eight-thirty.* |
| **Es ist viertel vor zwei.** | *It is a quarter to two.* |
| **Es ist viertel nach zwölf.** | *It is a quarter past twelve.* |

## Check your comprehension

*Engage in a conversation with a classmate.*

1. Say good day (morning, evening), and get an answer.
2. Ask each other how you are, and answer.
3. Ask what time it is, and get an approximate answer.
4. Thank the classmate, and get an answer.
5. Say good-bye to each other.

## II. Days of the week

The days of the week are:

| | |
|---|---|
| der Montag | *Monday* |
| der Dienstag | *Tuesday* |
| der Mittwoch | *Wednesday* |
| der Donnerstag | *Thursday* |
| der Freitag | *Friday* |
| der Samstag *or* Sonnabend | *Saturday* |
| der Sonntag | *Sunday* |

| | |
|---|---|
| Was ist heute? | *What is today?* |
| Heute ist Sonntag. | *Today is Sunday.* |
| Was war gestern? | *What was yesterday?* |
| Gestern war Mittwoch. | *Yesterday was Wednesday.* |
| Was ist morgen? | *What's tomorrow?* |
| Morgen ist Freitag. | *Tomorrow is Friday.* |

## *Check your comprehension*

1. Recite the days of the week.
2. Ask a classmate what today is, and get an answer.
3. Ask a classmate what yesterday was, and get an answer.
4. Ask a classmate what tomorrow will be, and get an answer.

## III. Seasons, months, weather

The seasons of the year are:

| | | | |
|---|---|---|---|
| der Frühling | *spring* | der Herbst | *fall* |
| der Sommer | *summer* | der Winter | *winter* |

| | |
|---|---|
| Es ist Frühling. | *It is spring.* |
| Es ist Herbst. | *It's fall.* |

The months of the year are:

| | |
|---|---|
| der Januar | *January* |
| der Februar | *February* |
| der März | *March* |

| | |
|---|---|
| der April | *April* |
| der Mai | *May* |
| der Juni | *June* |
| der Juli | *July* |
| der August | *August* |
| der September | *September* |
| der Oktober | *October* |
| der November | *November* |
| der Dezember | *December* |

| | |
|---|---|
| Es ist Januar. | *It is January.* |
| Es ist Juli. | *It's July.* |

me common expressions of weather are:

| | |
|---|---|
| Wie ist das Wetter? | *What's the weather like?* |
| Es ist schön. | *It's nice (beautiful).* |
| Es ist warm. | *It's warm.* |
| Es ist heiß. | *It's hot.* |
| Es ist kalt. | *It's cold.* |
| Es regnet. | { *It rains.* / *It's raining.* |
| Es schneit. | { *It snows.* / *It's snowing.* |
| Es ist warm und es regnet. | *It's warm and it's raining.* |
| Es regnet oder es schneit. | *It rains or it snows.* |

## Check your comprehension

. Practice the seasons and months with a classmate.

. Ask a classmate what the weather is like, and get an answer.

. Tell a classmate it is a certain season or month, ask what the weather is like, and get an appropriate answer.

AMPLES: Es ist Winter. Wie ist das Wetter?
**Es ist kalt und es schneit.**

Es ist April. Wie ist das Wetter?
**Es ist warm oder kalt. Es regnet.**

**1**

**MODEL SENTENCES**

Study the following sentences carefully. Note the German words in boldface in each set of sentences. Their function and structure will be discussed in the Grammar Explanations.

### I

**Ich** suche das Buch.
*I am looking for the book.*

**Es** ist hier.
*It's here.*

**Wir** studieren Deutsch.
*We are studying German.*

## II

Ulrike **sucht** das Buch.
*Ulrike is looking for the book.*

Was **studieren** Sie, Fräulein Müller?
*What do you study, Miss Müller?*
*What are you studying, Miss Müller?*

Sie **findet** das Buch.
*She finds the book.*

Wie **heißt** das Mädchen?
*What is the girl's name?*

Wie **heißt** du?
*What's your name?*

**Sind** Sie aus Deutschland?
*Are you from Germany?*

Ich **bin** aus Bonn.
*I'm from Bonn.*

Das **ist** interessant.
*That's interesting.*

## III

**Der** Tag ist lang.
*The day is long.*

**Die** Tür ist da drüben.
*The door is over there.*

Hier ist **ein** Buch von Kafka.
*Here's a book by Kafka.*

**Das** Buch heißt „Amerika".
*The book is called Amerika.*

**Das** Mädchen studiert **eine** Sprache.
*The girl is studying a language.*

**Die** Bücher sind interessant.
*The books are interesting.*

**Sie** sind interessant.
*They are interesting.*

## I. Personal pronouns: nominative case

The subject of a sentence is in the *nominative case;* it usually answers the questions *"Who?"* or *"What?"*

| | |
|---|---|
| Ulrike studiert eine Sprache. | Ulrike studies a language. |
| Das Buch ist hier. | The book is here. |

The subject can be a noun, as in the preceding sentences, or a pronoun:

| | |
|---|---|
| Sie studiert eine Sprache. | *She (Ulrike) studies a language.* |
| Es ist hier. | *It (the book) is here.* |

In German as in English, these pronouns can be in the first person (*I, we*), the second person (*you*), or the third person (*he, she, it, they*).

*Personal pronouns: nominative case*

| PERSON | SINGULAR | | PLURAL | |
|---|---|---|---|---|
| 1st | *ich* | *I* | wir | *we* |
| 2nd (familiar) | *du* | *you* | ihr | *you* |
| 3rd | *er* | *he* | | |
| | *sie* | *she* | sie | *they* |
| | *es* | *it* | | |
| 2nd (formal) | *Sie* | *you* | Sie | *you* |

Note these differences between the two languages.

1. The first-person singular, **ich,** is not capitalized in German, except at the beginning of a sentence.

2. The second-person singular and plural have two forms in German, the familiar and the formal. Use the familiar form to address relatives, close friends, and children: in speaking to one person, use **du;** in speaking to more than one, use **ihr.** Use the formal **Sie** to address all other people, especially people you meet for the first time. **Sie** is identical in the singular and plural.

3. In both the second-person singular and plural, the formal **Sie** is always capitalized.

FAMILIAR

| | |
|---|---|
| Peter, **du** bist jung. | *Peter, you are young.* |
| Peter und Doris, **ihr** seid klug. | *Peter and Doris, you are bright.* |

FORMAL

| | |
|---|---|
| Was studieren **Sie,** Fräulein Müller? | *What are you studying, Miss Müller?* |
| Herr und Frau Keller, **Sie** sind aus Amerika?[1] | *Mr. and Mrs. Keller, are you from America?* |

## Check your comprehension

*Complete the sentence with the personal pronoun indicated.*

1. _____ suchen das Buch. (*we*)
2. _____ bist klug. (*you, fam. sing.*)
3. _____ heißt Peter (*he*)
4. _____ heißt Doris. (*she*)
5. _____ studiere hier Deutsch. (*I*)
6. _____ studiert Englisch, Peter und Doris? (*you, fam. pl.*)
7. _____ ist interessant. (*it*)
8. _____ sind Herr und Frau Müller? (*you, formal pl.*)
9. Ja, und _____ sind Herr Meyer? (*you, formal sing.*)

[1] In German, a question may be formed through mere intonation, as in this example. Or it may be formed by inverting the subject and verb: **Sind Sie aus Amerika?**

## II. Present tense of regular verbs and SEIN

**A.** *Formation*

The infinitive is the form of the verb given in vocabulary lists and dictionaries. In English the infinitive consists of *to* + a form of the verb: *to be, to study.* In German it normally ends in **-en,** as in **kommen** (*to come*). In some cases, for phonetic reasons it ends in **-n,** as in **verändern** (*to change*).

| | |
|---|---|
| hoffen | *to hope* |
| kommen | *to come* |
| suchen | *to look for* |
| studieren | *to study* |

The present tense of most German verbs is formed by dropping the infinitive ending **-en** and adding personal endings to the verb stem.

*Present tense: personal endings*

| | SINGULAR | PLURAL |
|---|---|---|
| 1st | **-e** | **-en** |
| 2nd (fam.) | **-st** | **-t** |
| 3rd | **-t** | **-en** |
| 2nd (formal) | **-en** | **-en** |

The present tense of a regular German verb is as follows:

**hoffen** *(to hope)*

| | SINGULAR | | PLURAL | |
|---|---|---|---|---|
| 1st | *ich* | hoff**e** | wir | hoff**en** |
| 2nd (fam.) | *du* | hoff**st** | ihr | hoff**t** |
| 3rd | *er* *sie* *es* | hoff**t** | sie | hoff**en** |
| 2nd (formal) | *Sie* | hoff**en** | Sie | hoff**en** |

If the verb stem ends in a hissing sound, such as **s, ss,** or **ß,**[1] (as in **heißen**), add only **-t** and not **-st** to the stem of the **du** form: **du heißt**

---

[1] **The -ss-** changes to **-ß-** (1) if the preceding vowel is long, (2) at the end of a word, and (3) before a **-t-.**

(*you are called*). Thus the **du, er,** and **ihr** forms are identical: **du heißt, er (sie, es) heißt, ihr heißt.**

If the stem of the verb ends in **-t** or **-d,** as in **arbeiten** (*to work*) or **finden** (*to find*), insert **-e-** between the stem and the endings **-st** and **-t.** This makes it easier to hear and pronounce the endings.

| | | | |
|---|---|---|---|
| du | arbeitest | du | findest |
| ihr | arbeitet | ihr | findet |
| er | | er | |
| sie } | arbeitet | sie } | findet |
| es | | es | |

Also insert **-e-** before these endings when the stem ends in **-n** or **-m,** preceded by a consonant other than **l** or **r,** as in **öffnen** (*to open*).

| | |
|---|---|
| du | öffnest |
| ihr | öffnet |
| er | |
| sie } | öffnet |
| es | |

The verb **sein,** like its equivalent *to be* in English, is the most frequently used verb in German.

**sein** *(to be)*

| | SINGULAR | | | PLURAL | | |
|---|---|---|---|---|---|---|
| *1st* | ich | **bin** | *I am* | wir | **sind** | *we are* |
| *2nd (fam.)* | du | **bist** | *you are* | ihr | **seid** | *you are* |
| *3rd* | er<br>sie }<br>es | **ist** | he<br>she } *is*<br>it | sie | **sind** | *they are* |
| *2nd (formal)* | Sie | **sind** | *you are* | Sie | **sind** | *you are* |

**B.** *Usage*

1. There are no special verbal structures in German that correspond to the forms of the English progressive (*I am hoping*) and emphatic (*I do hope*). The German present tense may therefore have the following meanings in English:

|  |  |
|---|---|
| ich hoffe | *I hope*<br>*I am hoping*<br>*I do hope* |

2.  The present tense can also express an action projected into the near future. This *implied future* is often used with a time phrase such as **heute abend** (*this evening*) or **gleich** (*right away*).

Ich komme gleich.                                   *I'm coming right away.*
Er arbeitet heute abend.                    *He is going to work this evening.*

---

### Check your comprehension

*Supply the appropriate present-tense form of the verb in parentheses.*

1.  Ulrike _____ eine Sprache. (*studieren*)
2.  Herr Meyer _____ das Buch. (*suchen*)
3.  Ihr _____ aus Berlin. (*sein*)
4.  Ich _____ , das Buch ist da. (*hoffen*)
5.  Fritz _____ heute abend. (*arbeiten*)
6.  Wir _____ gleich. (*kommen*)
7.  Wie _____ das Fräulein? (*heißen*)
8.  _____ du aus England? (*sein*)
9.  Ulrike _____ die Tür. (*öffnen*)
10. Fräulein Meyer, Sie _____ aus Deutschland? (*sein*)

---

## III. Article, gender, and number of nouns

German nouns are always capitalized, no matter where they appear in the sentence.

Das Buch ist hier.
Hier ist das Buch.

**A.** *Article and gender of nouns*

In German as in English, a noun may be preceded by either a definite or an indefinite article. A definite article refers to a specific entity: **der Mann** (*the man*). An indefinite article refers to any one of a class of things: **ein Mann** (*a man*).

The article in German indicates the grammatical gender of a noun. Here "gender" is a linguistic rather than a biological term. All German nouns have a gender, even those which do not denote persons.

A German noun is either masculine, feminine, or neuter.

| | | | | | | | |
|---|---|---|---|---|---|---|---|
| *masculine* | der Mann | | *man* | der Tag | | *day* | *Definite article* |
| *feminine* | die Frau | *the* | *woman* | die Tür | *the* | *door* | |
| *neuter* | das Kind | | *child* | das Buch | | *book* | |

|           |           |   |          |          |   |        |
|-----------|-----------|---|----------|----------|---|--------|
| *masculine* | ein Mann  |   | ⎧ man    | ein Tag  |   | ⎧ day  |
| *feminine*  | eine Frau | a | ⎨ woman  | eine Tür | a | ⎨ door |
| *neuter*    | ein Kind  |   | ⎩ child  | ein Buch |   | ⎩ book |

*Indefinite article*

Sometimes biological and grammatical gender are the same, as in **der Mann, die Frau;** but most often there is no way of telling what grammatical gender a noun is: **das Buch, das Kind, das Mädchen** (*girl*). It is therefore necessary to memorize the definite article with each noun.

Nouns are normally preceded by either a definite or an indefinite article. However, when the noun indicates a nationality or occupation, no article is used.

Judy ist Amerikanerin.          *Judy is an American.*
Er ist Student.                 *He's a student.*

## Check your comprehension

*Supply the definite or indefinite article as indicated.*

1. _____ Mädchen heißt Ulrike. (*def.*)
2. Hier ist _____ Tür. (*indef.*)
3. _____ Tag ist lang. (*def.*)
4. Hier ist _____ Buch. (*indef.*)
5. _____Mann ist aus Amerika. (*def.*)
6. _____ Frau ist da. (*indef.*)
7. _____ Kind ist klug. (*def.*)
8. Ich studiere _____ Sprache. (*indef.*)

## B. *Number of nouns*

In German, the article also indicates the number of a noun—that is, whether it is singular or plural. While in English the plural of nouns is normally formed by adding *-s,* in German the plurals vary. Since there is no standard rule for forming the plural of a German noun, it is best to learn a noun's plural along with its singular. In the vocabularies of this book, plural forms are indicated as follows:

| der **Tag,** -e   | *day*  |
|-------------------|--------|
| die **Tür,** -en  | *door* |
| das **Buch,** ¨-er | *book* |
| das **Mädchen,** - | *girl* |

The plural form of the definite article is the same for all three genders: **die.** So the plural forms of the preceding nouns are: **die Tage, die Türen, die Bücher, die Mädchen.**

However, the indefinite article is dropped in the plural.

| | |
|---|---|
| Sie studiert eine Sprache. | *She is studying a language.* |
| Sie studiert Sprachen. | *She is studying languages.* |

---

## Check your comprehension

*Change these sentences to the plural. If you do not know the plural of a noun, look for it in the Chapter Vocabulary.*

EXAMPLE: Das Buch ist interessant.
       **Die Bücher sind interessant.**

1. Der Mann arbeitet heute abend.
2. Das Mädchen ist aus Berlin.
3. Wir studieren eine Sprache.
4. Das Kind ist hier.
5. Der Tag ist lang.
6. Sie suchen ein Buch.
7. Das Fräulein kommt gleich.
8. Die Frau ist klug.
9. Der Student ist aus England.
10. Die Studentin ist jung.

---

**C.** *Use of pronouns*

Be careful to replace a noun by the appropriate pronoun according to grammatical gender and number.

| *noun* | | *pronoun* |
|---|---|---|
| der Tag | → | er |
| die Tür | → | sie |
| das Buch | → | es |
| die Bücher | → | sie |

However, under certain circumstances **sie** or **er** is used in reference to **das Kind, das Mädchen,** or **das Fräulein,** especially when a first or family name is mentioned.

Das Mädchen heißt Ulrike. Sie ist hier.
Das Kind heißt Peter. Er studiert Sprachen.
Fräulein Meyer studiert Sprachen. Sie ist aus Deutschland.

*But:*

Das Kind kommt heute abend. Es ist aus Berlin.

---

## *Check your comprehension*

*Substitute the appropriate personal pronoun for the noun.*

1. *Die Tage* sind lang. _____ sind lang.
2. *Das Kind* ist aus England. _____ ist aus England.
3. *Das Buch* ist interessant. _____ ist interessant.
4. *Fräulein Meyer* studiert in Amerika. _____ studiert in Amerika.
5. *Herr Meyer und Fräulein Keller* arbeiten in Deutschland. _____ arbeiten in Deutschland.
6. *Das Kind* heißt Fritz. _____ heißt Fritz.
7. *Die Amerikanerin* sucht das Institut. _____ sucht das Institut.
8. *Das Mädchen* kommt heute. _____ kommt heute.

---

**USEFUL PHRASES**

Memorize the following everyday phrases.

| | |
|---|---|
| **Wie heißen Sie, bitte?** | *What is your name, please?* |
| **Ich heiße Ulrike Müller.** | *My name is Ulrike Müller.* |
| **Es ist gleich da drüben.** | *It's right over there.* |
| **Viel Glück!** | *Good luck.* |

**CONVERSATION**

Read the following conversation several times, both silently and aloud. Commit to memory the new words, phrases, and structures.

## *Eine Auskunft*

*Judy is an American student who has a scholarship to study at a German university. She stops at the information desk of the library and talks with Mr. Keller, a librarian.*

JUDY Guten Tag! Ich suche das „Institut für deutsche Sprache und Literatur".

HERR KELLER Adenauer[1]-Straße eins. Es ist gleich da drüben. —Sie sind aus Amerika?

JUDY Ja, ich bin aus Buffalo, New York. Ich heiße Judy Miller.

HERR KELLER Und Sie studieren jetzt hier in Deutschland?

JUDY Ja. Ich studiere Deutsch und Soziologie.

HERR KELLER Das ist interessant.

JUDY Ich suche ein Buch von Kafka.[2]

HERR KELLER Wie heißt das Buch?

JUDY Es heißt „Amerika". Ich hoffe, es ist da.

HERR KELLER Ich bin nicht sicher. Der Katalog ist gleich da drüben.

JUDY Danke für die Auskunft. Auf Wiedersehen!

HERR KELLER Bitte! Auf Wiedersehen, Fräulein Miller! Viel Glück!

[1] Konrad Adenauer (1876–1967) was the first chancellor of the Federal Republic of Germany. He presided over Germany's reconstruction after World War II.

[2] Franz Kafka (1883–1924) was one of the most influential writers of the present age. A Czech who wrote chiefly in German, he was the author of three major novels and many short stories.

## *Questions*

*Answer in complete sentences.*

1. Wie heißt die Studentin?
2. Wie heißt der Mann?
3. Was (*what*) sucht die Studentin?
4. Ist sie aus Deutschland?
5. Was studiert sie?
6. Wo (*where*) studiert sie?
7. Wie heißt das Buch von Kafka?
8. Was hofft Judy Miller?
9. Wo ist der Katalog?
10. Wie heißen Sie?
11. Sind Sie aus Deutschland oder Amerika?
12. Sind Sie Student?
13. Studieren Sie Deutsch oder Soziologie?
14. Wo studieren Sie?

**PRACTICE**

**A.** *Supply an appropriate personal pronoun.*

EXAMPLES: _____ seid aus England.
**Ihr seid aus England.**

_____ ist hier. (*Herr Meyer*)
**Er ist hier.**

1. _____ arbeitet in Bonn. (*Fräulein Meyer*)
2. _____ öffnest die Tür.
3. _____ sucht ein Buch. (*Herr Keller*)
4. _____ ist da drüben. (*das Buch*)
5. _____ studieren Deutsch. (*1st person pl.*)
6. _____ heißt Peter.
7. _____ bist aus Deutschland?
8. _____ komme gleich.
9. _____ sind hier. (*die Kinder*)
10. _____ bin aus Hamburg.

**B.** *Complete the definite or indefinite articles.*

EXAMPLES: D_____ Studentin ist aus Deutschland.
**Die Studentin ist aus Deutschland.**

1. D_____ Institut ist da drüben.    2. Ich suche e_____ Buch von Kafka.

3. Er öffnet d_____ Tür.

4. D_____ Mädchen kommen gleich.

5. E_____ Studentin heißt Keller.

6. Wo sind d_____ Bücher?

7. E_____ Herr sucht das Institut.

8. D_____ Auskunft ist da drüben.

9. D_____ Tage sind lang.

10. Wie heißen d_____ Kinder?

**C.** *In the following sentences change everything possible to the plural—nouns, verbs, and pronouns.*

EXAMPLE: Der Mann kommt aus Bonn.
    **Die Männer kommen aus Bonn.**

1. Die Studentin ist aus Deutschland.

2. Sie sucht ein Buch von Kafka.

3. Wo ist der Katalog?

4. Die Straße ist lang.

5. Wie heißt das Kind?

6. Ich studiere eine Sprache.

7. Du arbeitest heute abend?

8. Das Mädchen hofft, du kommst heute abend.

**D.** *Fill in the blanks with the appropriate present-tense form of the indicated verbs.*

EXAMPLE: Der Mann _____ das Institut. (*suchen*)
    **Der Mann sucht das Institut.**

1. Wir _____ sicher. (*sein*)

2. Das Fräulein _____ morgen. (*arbeiten*)

3. Du _____ Fritz? (*heißen*)

4. Wer (who) _____ die Tür? (*öffnen*)

5. Die Kinder _____ gleich. (*kommen*)

6. Was _____ du? (*suchen*)

7. Ihr _____ aus England. (*sein*)

8. Die Studentinnen _____ Sprachen. (*studieren*)

9. Die Mädchen _____ das Buch. (*öffnen*)

10. Wo _____ die Straße? (*sein*)

**E.** *Answer the following questions in complete sentences. Use the cue and replace nouns by pronouns whenever possible.*

EXAMPLE: Wo ist Fräulein Meyer? (*in Hamburg*)
    **Sie ist in Hamburg.**

1. Wie heißt die Studentin aus Amerika? (*Fräulein Miller*)

2. Was ist interessant? (*das Buch*)

3. Wo studieren die Studenten? (*in Köln*)

4. Wer sucht das Institut? (*die Studentin aus Amerika*)

5. Wo ist die Adenauer-Straße? (*in Hamburg*)
6. Was studieren Sie? (*Deutsch*)
7. Ist der Student aus Deutschland? (*aus England*)
8. Was ist Herr Meyer? (*Student*)

**F.** *Give the English equivalents of the following sentences, paying special attention to the various uses of the German present tense.*

1. Du studierst Deutsch in Deutschland.
2. Die Frauen arbeiten heute abend.
3. Wer öffnet die Tür?
4. Was suchen Sie?
5. Ich komme gleich.
6. Er hofft, die Bücher sind da.

## GUIDED CONVERSATION

The following are some suggestions for carrying on a conversation in German, but you need not follow this pattern exactly. Use your own ideas, applying anything you have learned so far. Your conversation should be as natural and free-flowing as possible. Use either the **Sie** or **du** form.

Begin a conversation with the student(s) next to you. Exchange greetings and find out where they are from, what they study, where they live, whether they find a certain book interesting. After that, turn to the class and tell your fellow class members all that you know about the particular student. Here are some sample questions:

Wie heißen Sie? (Wie heißt du?)

Was studieren Sie? (Was studierst du?)

Sie sind aus Berlin? (Du bist aus Berlin?)

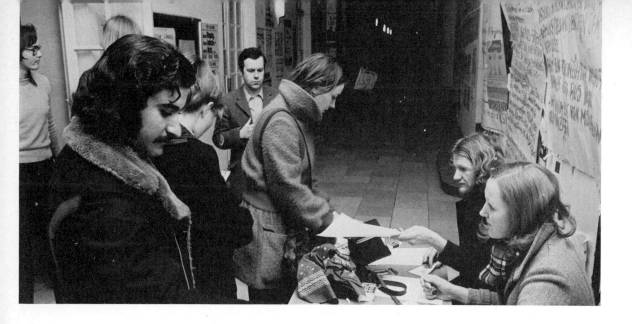

---

*Read the following passage and note all new words, phrases, and structures. When you have finished reading the passage and fully understand what it says, answer the questions that follow it.*

## Das Deutsch-Institut

Herr Keller informiert Judy Miller über das Deutsch-Institut, Adenauer-Straße 1. Judy sucht die Straße. Sie hat Glück.° Sie findet die Adenauer-Straße gleich. Es ist das Deutsch-Institut. — is lucky

Fräulein Miller öffnet die Tür. Ein Student und eine Studentin kommen. Sie verteilen Programme.° Judy hat jetzt ein Programm. Es heißt da:° — distribute leaflets / it says there

informieren

diskutieren

verändern° — change

Judy öffnet das Programm. Es informiert Judy über das Studentenparlament.° Sie findet es wirklich interessant. Der Student heißt Karl. Er informiert Judy jetzt über das Institut. Sie diskutieren über Politik in Deutschland und Amerika. Verändern: Ja oder nein? Was und wie? Der Student und die Amerikanerin diskutieren fast eine Stunde. — student senate

Judy und Karl suchen jetzt das Buch „Amerika" von Kafka. Die Bibliothek ist gleich da drüben. Da ist der Katalog. Sie finden das Buch unter° „K". Es ist in Raum neun unter „Literatur". Karl sagt°: „Auf Wiedersehen." Er hat eine Vorlesung.° — under / says — lecture

Judy öffnet die Tür von Raum neun. Sie hat Glück. Das Buch ist da. Die Amerikanerin öffnet das Buch und arbeitet fast eine Stunde. Sie findet „Amerika" wirklich interessant.

## Questions

*Answer in complete sentences.*

1. Was sucht Judy Miller?
2. Wie heißt die Straße?
3. Wer öffnet die Tür?
4. Wer verteilt Programme?
5. Wie findet sie das Programm?
6. Über was diskutieren der Student und Judy?
7. Wie lange (*how long*) diskutieren sie?
8. Was sucht Judy jetzt?
9. Wo ist die Bibliothek?
10. Wo findet Judy das Buch?
11. Wie lange arbeitet sie?
12. Wie findet sie „Amerika"?

## VOCABULARY DEVELOPMENT

**A.** The masculine singular of nouns indicating nationality is usually formed by adding **-er** to the name of the country. The masculine plural form of the noun is the same.

|  | SINGULAR | PLURAL |
|---|---|---|
| die Schweiz | der Schweizer | die Schweizer |
| *Switzerland* | *the Swiss* | *the Swiss* |
| Österreich | der Österreicher | die Österreicher |
| *Austria* | *the Austrian* | *the Austrians* |
| England | der Engländer | die Engländer |
| *England* | *the Englishman* | *the English, the Englishmen* |

If the name of a country ends in a vowel, it adds **-ner: Amerika, der Amerikaner, die Amerikaner.** But note these exceptions:

| Deutschland | der Deutsche | die Deutschen |
|---|---|---|
| *Germany* | *the German* | *the Germans* |
| Rußland | der Russe | die Russen |
| *Russia* | *the Russian* | *the Russians* |
| Frankreich | der Franzose | die Franzosen |
| *France* | *the Frenchman* | *the French* |

**B.** The feminine singular of nouns denoting persons, including nouns of nationality, is in most cases formed by adding **-in** to the masculine form; for the feminine plural, add **-innen.**

| MASC. SING. | FEM. SING. | FEM. PL. |
|---|---|---|
| der Student | die Studentin | die Studentinnen |
| der Amerikaner | die Amerikanerin | die Amerikanerinnen |
| der Engländer | die Engländerin | die Engländerinnen |
| der Franzose | die Französin | die Französinnen |
| der Russe | die Russin | die Russinnen |

*But:*

| | | |
|---|---|---|
| der Deutsche | die Deutsche | die Deutschen |

Form the feminine singular and plural of **der Schweizer, der Österreicher.**

Practice these nouns by engaging in a short dialogue with your neighbor(s). For instance:

Sylvia, bist du Engländerin?

Nein, ich bin Deutsche.

**REVIEW EXERCISES**

**A.** *Form questions to the following statements, using the cue in parentheses.*

EXAMPLES: Das Fräulein studiert in Berlin. (*wo?*)
**Wo studiert das Fräulein?**

Ich suche ein Buch. (*was?*)
**Was suchst du?**

1. Die Studenten verteilen die Bücher. (*was?*)
2. Ich finde das Institut interessant. (*wie?*)
3. Die Adenauer-Straße ist gleich da drüben. (*wo?*)
4. Die Studentinnen diskutieren über Literatur. (*über was?*)
5. Das Mädchen sucht das Buch von Kafka. (*wer?*)
6. Die Studenten suchen die Bücher von Kafka. (*was?*)
7. Das Deutsch-Programm ist interessant. (*wie?*)

**B.** *Answer the following questions as best you can.*

1. Studieren Sie eine Sprache?
2. Finden Sie die Klasse wirklich interessant?

3. Finden Sie das Buch interessant?
4. Sind Sie sicher?
5. Arbeiten Sie heute abend?

**C.** *Answer the following sentences, using the cue provided.*

EXAMPLE: Wo sind die Kataloge? (*da drüben*)
  **Die Kataloge sind da drüben.**

1. Was studiert die Studentin? (*Englisch*)
2. Wer kommt gleich? (*die Mädchen*)
3. Wie lange studierst du? (*zwei Stunden*)
4. Wer öffnet die Tür? (*die Herren*)
5. Wie heißt sie? (*Luise*)
6. Wer diskutiert über Politik? (*der Franzose und die Schweizerin*)
7. Wo ist das Institut? (*in Köln*)
8. Wer findet die Klasse wirklich interessant? (*die Engländer*)

**D.** *Change the following sentences to the plural.*

EXAMPLE: Wo ist die Tür?
  **Wo sind die Türen?**

1. Ich studiere das Buch.
2. Der Student kommt morgen.
3. Du findest das Institut.
4. Der Mann informiert die Frau.
5. Wo ist das Kind?
6. Sie sucht eine Deutsche.
7. Der Herr findet die Straße.
8. Die Amerikanerin sucht eine Auskunft.

**E.** *Supply the appropriate pronoun.*

1. Fräulein Meyer kommt heute abend? Ja, _____ kommt heute abend.
2. Was findet der Student? _____ findet Bücher.
3. Frau Keller ist aus Bonn? Nein, _____ ist aus Hamburg.
4. Die Engländerin sucht die Bibliothek? Ja, _____ sucht die Bibliothek.
5. Die Auskunft ist interessant? Ja, _____ ist interessant.
6. Das Mädchen heißt Ulrike? Ja, _____ heißt Ulrike.
7. Die Klasse ist lang? Ja, _____ ist lang.
8. Das Kind ist aus Deutschland? Nein, _____ ist aus Amerika.
9. Die Amerikaner diskutieren über Politik? Nein, _____ diskutieren über Soziologie.
10. Die Französinnen sind klug? Ja, _____ sind klug.

**F.** *Express in German.*

1. She is working this evening.
2. We'll come right away.
3. You (*fam. pl.*) are discussing literature.
4. He does study sociology.
5. They are looking for books by Kafka.
6. The room is right over there.
7. What's your name, please?
8. My name is Müller.
9. Good-bye.
10. Good luck.
11. Thank you for the information.
12. You're welcome.
13. He informs the class.
14. The Russians are studying languages.

## GUIDED COMPOSITION

The following are some suggestions for writing a composition in German. You may choose either A or B, but you need not follow the suggestions exactly; rather, use your own ideas and apply whatever vocabulary and grammar constructions you have learned so far. Your composition should be as clear and concise as possible.

**A.** Write a very brief paragraph about yourself, stating your name, where you are from, what you are studying, and if you find it interesting.

**B.** Look at this picture. State what the girl is doing; describe what might be on the title page of the leaflet and the reaction of the male student receiving it.

**CHAPTER
VOCABULARY**

In all chapter vocabularies we will first single out easily recognized words: English-German cognates and loan words that are spelled alike in both languages or involve only minor spelling changes. After these words we will list nouns, then verbs, then other words.

## Easily recognized words

| | | |
|---|---|---|
| (das)[1] | **Amerika** | *America* |
| der | **Amerikaner,** - | *American (male)* |
| die | **Amerikanerin, -nen** | *American (female)* |
| | **diskutieren (über)** | *to discuss* |
| (das) | **England** | *England* |
| (das) | **Englisch** | *English (language, subject)* |
| | **in** | *in* |
| | **informieren (über)** | *to inform (about)* |
| das | **Institut, -e** | *institute* |
| | **interessant** | *interesting* |
| der | **Katalog, -e** | *(card) catalogue* |
| die | **Klasse, -n** | *class* |
| die | **Literatur, -en** | *literature* |
| die | **Politik** | *politics* |
| die | **Soziologie** | *sociology* |
| der | **Student, -en** | *student (male)* |
| die | **Studentin, -nen** | *student (female)* |
| | **studieren** | *to study* |
| die | **Auskunft, ⸚e** | *(piece of) information* |
| die | **Bibliothek, -en** | *library* |
| das | **Buch, ⸚er** | *book* |
| (das) | **Deutsch** | *German (language, subject)* |
| (das) | **Deutschland** | *Germany* |
| die | **Frau, -en** | *woman, wife, Mrs.* |

| | | |
|---|---|---|
| das | **Fräulein,** - | *young lady, Miss* |
| der | **Herr, -en** | *man, gentleman, Mr.* |
| das | **Kind, -er** | *child* |
| das | **Mädchen,** - | *girl* |
| der | **Mann, ⸚er** | *man* |
| der | **Raum, ⸚e** | *room* |
| die | **Sprache, -n** | *language* |
| die | **Straße, -n** | *street* |
| die | **Stunde, -n** | *hour* |
| | **arbeiten** | *to work* |
| | **finden** | *to find* |
| | **heißen** | *to be called* |
| | **hoffen** | *to hope* |
| | **kommen** | *to come* |
| | **öffnen** | *to open* |
| | **sein** | *to be* |
| | **suchen** | *to look for* |
| | **aus** | *from* |
| | **bitte** | *please, you're welcome* |
| | **da** | *there* |
| | **da drüben** | *over there* |
| | **das** | *that* |
| | **fast** | *almost* |
| | **für** | *for* |

See also the nouns of nationality on pp. 21–22.

[1] With some exceptions such as **die Schweiz**, the names of countries do not require an article. In vocabulary lists the article appears in parentheses so as to indicate the gender of a pronoun replacing the noun.

| | | | |
|---|---|---|---|
| **gleich** | right (directly), right away | **nicht** | not |
| **heute abend** | this evening | **sicher** | sure |
| **hier** | here | **über** | about (concerning) |
| **ja** | yes | **von** | by, of |
| **jetzt** | now | **was** | what |
| **jung** | young | **wer** | who |
| **klug** | intelligent, bright | **wie** | how, as |
| **lang; lange** (in respect to time) | long | **wirklich** | really |
| **nein** | no | **wo** | where |

**MODEL SENTENCES**

### I

Ich suche **den** Raum.
*I'm looking for the room.*

Monika findet **einen** Freund.
*Monika finds a friend.*

Er kauft **eine** Platte.
*He buys a record.*

Wir haben **keine** Zeit.
*We have no time.*

Ich habe **ein** Problem.
*I have a problem.*

Sie kaufen **keine** Zigaretten.
*They aren't buying any cigarettes.*

**II**

Du **hast** Probleme.
*You have problems.*

Ihr **habt** ein Telefon.
*You have a phone.*

Sie **hat** ein Kind.
*She has a child.*

**III**

Ja, **den Amerikaner** sucht das Fräulein.
*Yes, the girl is looking for the American.*

**Ist** die Platte neu?
*Is the record new?*

Nein, **neu** ist sie nicht.
*No, it isn't new.*

**Kennst** du die Herren?
*Do you know the gentlemen?*

Was **trinkst** du?
*What do you drink?*
*What are you drinking?*

**GRAMMAR EXPLANATIONS**

### I. Definite and indefinite articles: accusative case

The direct object of a sentence receives the action of the verb directly; often it answers the questions "whom?" or "what?" In German, it is always in the *accusative case.*

| NOMINATIVE | | ACCUSATIVE | |
|---|---|---|---|
| Monika findet | *Monika finds* | einen Freund. | *a friend.* |
| Fritz spielt | *Fritz is playing* | die Platte. | *the record.* |
| Wir rauchen | *We smoke* | Zigaretten. | *cigarettes.* |

In the accusative, the definite and indefinite articles have the same forms as in the nominative, with the exception of the masculine singular: **den Freund, einen Freund.**

As in the nominative, the indefinite article has no plural form in the accusative.

| | |
|---|---|
| Er kauft eine Platte. | *He buys a record.* |
| Er kauft Platten. | *He buys records.* |

<table>
<tr><td>SINGULAR</td><td>NOMINATIVE</td><td>ACCUSATIVE</td></tr>
<tr><td>*masc.*</td><td>{ der<br>ein } Raum</td><td>{ den<br>einen } Raum</td></tr>
<tr><td>*fem.*</td><td>{ die<br>eine } Straße</td><td>{ die<br>eine } Straße</td></tr>
<tr><td>*neut.*</td><td>{ das<br>ein } Buch</td><td>{ das<br>ein } Buch</td></tr>
<tr><td>PLURAL</td><td></td><td></td></tr>
<tr><td>*all genders*</td><td>die { Räume<br>Straßen<br>Bücher</td><td>die { Räume<br>Straßen<br>Bücher</td></tr>
</table>

*Definite and indefinite articles: nominative and accusative cases*

The adjective **kein,** meaning *no, not a,* or *not any,* is used to negate nouns. It takes the same endings as the indefinite article.

| | |
|---|---|
| Ich bin **kein** Student. | *I'm not a student.* |
| Judy findet **keinen** Freund. | *Judy finds no friend.* |
| Er kauft **keine** Bücher. | *He doesn't buy any books.* |

Unlike **ein, kein** has a plural form in both the nominative and accusative cases: **keine Bücher.**

| SINGULAR | NOMINATIVE | ACCUSATIVE |
|---|---|---|
| *masc.* | kein | keinen |
| *fem.* | keine | keine |
| *neut.* | kein | kein |
| PLURAL | | |
| *all genders* | *keine* | *keine* |

**kein:** *nominative and accusative cases*

The accusative of the interrogative **wer** is **wen** (*whom*).

| | |
|---|---|
| Wen suchst du? | *Whom are you looking for?* |
| Wen kennt ihr? | *Whom do you know?* |

## Check your comprehension

**A.** *Supply the appropriate article or* **kein,** *as indicated in parentheses.*

1. Wir suchen _____ Straße. *(def.)*
2. Sie kauft _____ Buch. *(indef.)*
3. Wer hat _____ Telefon? *(def.)*
4. Die Studenten öffnen _____ Bücher. *(def.)*
5. Der Herr hat _____ Zeit. *(kein)*
6. Die Studentinnen suchen _____Bibliothek. *(def.)*
7. Die Mädchen finden _____ Freunde. *(kein)*
8. Der Student sucht _____ Freundin. *(indef.)*
9. Ihr habt _____ Probleme. *(kein)*
10. Das Fräulein findet _____ Klasse. *(kein)*
11. Ich studiere _____ Sprachen. *(indef.)*
12. Die Kinder finden _____ Raum. *(def.)*
13. Kennst du _____ Institut? *(def.)*
14. Findest du _____ Herren? *(def.)*

**B.** *Use* **wer** *or* **wen** *in the following sentences.*

1. _____ sind Sie?
2. _____ sucht der Student?
3. _____ sucht den Amerikaner?
4. _____ kennt er?

## II. Present tense of HABEN

After the verb **sein** (*to be*), the most common verb in German is **haben** (*to have*).

**haben** (*to have*)

|  | SINGULAR | | PLURAL | |
|---|---|---|---|---|
| *1st* | ich | **habe** | wir | **haben** |
| *2nd (fam.)* | du | **hast** | ihr | **habt** |
| *3rd* | er<br>sie<br>es | **hat** | sie | **haben** |
| *2nd (formal)* | Sie | **haben** | Sie | **haben** |

### Check your comprehension

*Supply the appropriate form of* **haben.**

1. Wir _____ einen Freund.
2. Die Studenten _____ keine Freundinnen.
3. Ich _____ keine Bücher.
4. Du _____ kein Telefon.
5. Der Mann _____ keine Zeit.
6. Sie _____ ein Buch. *(you, formal)*
7. Ihr _____ kein Problem.

## III. Word order

Word order is important in languages; each language has its own conventions. In German, there are three basic patterns of word order: normal, inverted, and the word order used in questions.

### A. *Normal word order*

The normal order of the major parts of speech in a German sentence is just like that in English.

| SUBJECT | VERB | DIRECT OBJECT |
|---|---|---|
| **Der Mann** | **hat** | **ein Problem.** |
| *The man* | *has* | *a problem.* |

In a German sentence with normal word order, the adverb is placed between the verb and the direct object, whereas in English it is often placed between the subject and the verb.

| **Der Mann** | **hat** | **wirklich** | **ein Problem.** |
|---|---|---|---|
| *The man* | *really* | *has* | *a problem.* |

### B. *Inverted word order*

For various reasons—meaning, emphasis, and stylistic balance, for example—many German sentences begin with an element other than the subject. In this case, the subject is placed directly *after* the verb. The word order is thus "inverted."

> NORMAL: Er kommt jetzt.
> INVERTED: **Jetzt kommt er.**

In this instance German differs radically from English. In English you simply cannot say, *Now is coming he.* But a German will automatically say, **Jetzt kommt er.**

In the following examples, the verbs and subjects appear in boldface to stress their position in the sentence.

1. Quite frequently an adverb, an adverbial phrase, or an adjective may occupy the first position in a sentence.

| | |
|---|---|
| Jetzt **sucht das Fräulein** einen Freund. | *Now the girl is looking for a friend.* |
| Neu **ist die Platte** nicht. | *The record isn't new.* |

2. For purposes of emphasis or style, the direct object may be in the first position.

> Einen Freund **sucht das Fräulein.**     *The girl is looking for a friend.*

Notice that in normal and inverted word order the verb is fixed in the second position.

The conjunctions **und** (*and*), **aber** (*but*), and **oder** (*or*) do not require inverted word order when placed at the beginning of a clause.

> Ich studiere das Buch, und **es ist**    *I'm studying the book and it's in-*
> interessant.     *teresting.*
>
> Aber **er kommt** heute abend nicht.    *But he's not coming this evening.*

At times an adverb may be placed at the beginning of a sentence for emphasis, and set off by a comma. In this case the rest of the sentence is in normal word order.

> Wirklich, **er kommt** heute abend    *Really, he's not coming this eve-*
> nicht!     *ning.*
>
> Natürlich, **sie arbeitet** viel.     *Naturally she works a lot.*

**C.**   *Word order in questions*

1. With an interrogative word

Interrogative words come first, and are followed by the verb. The most common interrogative words are **wer** (*who?*), **wen** (*whom?*), **was** (*what?*), **wann** (*when?*), **wo** (*where?*), **wie** (*how?*), and **warum** (*why?*).

> Wo **sucht das Fräulein** das Buch?    *Where is the girl looking for the*
>     *book?*

2. Without an interrogative word

Questions requiring a *yes* or *no* answer, such as **Ist er hier?**, do not contain an interrogative word. In this case the verb comes first and is followed by the subject.

> **Sucht das Fräulein** das Buch?     *Is the girl looking for the book?*
> **Kennst du** die Platte?     *Do you know the record?*

In English, most questions are formed with the aid of the verb *to do*: *Do you work? Where do you work?* This is not so in German.

> Arbeitest du? |
> Arbeitet ihr? }     *Do you work?*
> Arbeiten Sie? |
>
> Was trinkst du? |
> Was trinkt ihr? }     *What do you drink?*
> Was trinken Sie? |

Finally, it should be noted that in a negative sentence **nicht** usually comes before the word or phrase that is negated.

Er ist nicht klug. *He isn't smart.*

But if the idea expressed in the whole sentence is negated, **nicht** usually comes at the end.

Ich arbeite heute abend nicht. *I'm not working this evening.*

## Check your comprehension

**A.** *Put the word in italics at the beginning and use the appropriate word order.*

EXAMPLE: Ich kenne *den Amerikaner* nicht.
**Den Amerikaner kenne ich nicht.**

1. Der Amerikaner hat die Platte *sicher* nicht.
2. Die Freundinnen kommen *gleich*.
3. Das Buch ist nicht *neu*.
4. Sie studieren *in Berlin*.
5. Die Frau findet *den Raum* nicht.
6. Das Fräulein öffnet *die Tür*.

**B.** *Form questions which elicit the following responses.*

EXAMPLES: Die Freunde kommen heute abend.
**Wer kommt heute abend?**
*Or:*
**Wann kommen die Freunde?**

Ja, ich komme heute abend.
**Kommst du (Kommen Sie) heute abend?**

1. Der Student studiert in Berlin.
2. Die Studentin heißt Jutta.
3. Claudia kommt morgen nicht.
4. Wir studieren Sprachen.
5. Ja, ich arbeite sehr viel.
6. Nein, ich habe keine Probleme.
7. Die Deutsche sucht das Kind.
8. Ja, die Studentinnen öffnen die Bücher.
9. Die Bibliothek is da drüben.
10. Sie haben keine Klasse.

**USEFUL PHRASES**

| | |
|---|---|
| **Verzeihung!** | { *Excuse me.* <br> { *Pardon me.* |
| **Hast du einen Moment Zeit?** | *Do you have a minute?* |
| **zum Beispiel** | *for example* |
| **Ich habe die Platte wirklich gern.** | *I really like the record.* |
| **Tschüß!** | *So long.* |
| **Bis gleich!** | *See you later.* |

**CONVERSATION**

## Am° Telefon

on the

KLAUS Hier Schönberg.

MONIKA Klaus, hier ist Monika. Verzeihung! Hast du einen Moment Zeit?

KLAUS Sicher.[1] Warum?

MONIKA Wir haben jetzt einen Plattenspieler. Er ist ganz neu.

KLAUS Wirklich? Toll°!

Great!

MONIKA Den Klang finde ich ganz fantastisch. Hast du vielleicht eine Platte von Peter Alexander?

[1] In German, adjectives can also serve as adverbs; **sicher** can mean both *certain* and (as here) *certainly.*

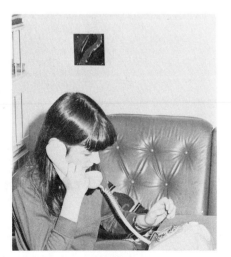

*Udo Jürgens*

KLAUS Von Alexander habe ich leider keine Platte, aber ich habe ein paar Jazz-Platten, zum Beispiel von Louis Armstrong.

MONIKA Toll! Kennst du die Platte ,,Aber bitte mit Sahne''[2] von Udo Jürgens?

KLAUS Nein, ist sie neu?

MONIKA Neu ist sie nicht, aber ich habe die Platte wirklich gern.

KLAUS Prima°! Ich komme gleich. Tschüß, Monika!   *Wonderful!*

MONIKA Tschüß, Klaus! Bis gleich!

## Questions

1. Wer ist am Telefon?
2. Hat Klaus einen Moment Zeit?
3. Was hat Monika jetzt?
4. Wie findet Monika den Klang?
5. Hat Klaus eine Platte von Alexander?
6. Wie findet Monika die Platte von Udo Jürgens?
7. Haben Sie einen Plattenspieler?
8. Ist der Plattenspieler neu?
9. Wie finden Sie den Klang?
10. Haben Sie Jazz-Platten?
11. Haben Sie Platten von Mozart oder Richard Wagner?
12. Welche (*which*) Platten finden Sie ganz fantastisch?
13. Haben Sie die Platten von Louis Armstrong gern?

---

[2] The title means *Please, with whipped cream.* Germans have a marked liking for whipped cream in coffee and on desserts.

**PRACTICE**

**A.** *Restate the following sentences using the word in parentheses to replace the word in italics. Use the appropriate form of the article.*

EXAMPLE: Er hat *ein Buch. (Freund)*
**Er hat einen Freund.**

1. Das Mädchen sucht *das Institut. (Raum)*
2. Ich habe *kein Buch. (Freund)*
3. Das Fräulein öffnet *die Tür. (Katalog)*
4. Peter studiert *eine Sprache. (Sprachen)*
5. *Den Klang* findet Monika fantastisch. *(Platte)*
6. Der Mann findet *die Straße* nicht. *(Bücher)*
7. Ich kenne *keine Studenten. (Studentinnen)*
8. Else hat *einen Freund. (Freundinnen)*
9. Has du *kein Kind? (Kinder)*
10. Habt ihr *ein Telefon? (Probleme)*

**B.** *Form questions which elicit the following answers.*

EXAMPLES: Ja, Ulrike hat einen Freund.
**Hat Ulrike einen Freund?**

Er studiert in England.
**Wo studiert er?**

1. Ja, Monika hat einen Plattenspieler.
2. Ja, Klaus studiert Deutsch.
3. Herr Meyer arbeitet in Berlin.
4. Ja, die Freunde kommen heute abend.
5. Nein, ich kenne die Straße nicht.
6. Ja, die Studenten haben die Platten gern.
7. Die Freundin heißt Barbara.
8. Frau Keller öffnet die Tür.
9. Wir kommen morgen.
10. Ich suche den Deutschen.

**C.** *Put the word in parentheses at the beginning of the sentence. Change the word order, if necessary.*

EXAMPLE: Er kommt. *(Jetzt)*
**Jetzt kommt er.**

1. Ich habe kein Buch von Kafka. *(leider)*
2. Die Engländerinnen kommen. *(heute abend)*
3. Die Studenten haben einen Moment Zeit. *(jetzt)*
4. Peter hat ein paar Platten. *(aber)*
5. Die Studentin studiert Sprachen. *(in Berlin)*
6. Er findet keine Bücher. *(wirklich,)*

**D.**  *Replace the expression in italics with the word in parentheses, and put the new word at the beginning of the sentence. Change the word order, if necessary.*

EXAMPLE: Monika ist *da drüben. (hier)*
**Hier ist Monika.**

1. Ich finde *die Platte* gut. *(Klang)*
2. Das Institut ist *in Frankfurt. (da)*
3. *Leider* habe ich keine Freundin. *(aber)*
4. Das Buch ist nicht *neu. (interessant)*
5. Ihr kennt *die Studentin. (Studenten)*

**E.**  *Construct sentences with the given cues. Start the sentence with the word in italics, use the appropriate word order, and make the necessary changes.*

EXAMPLE: suchen/der Mann/*das Fräulein*
**Das Fräulein sucht den Mann.**

1. kennen/ich/*leider*/das Buch/nicht
2. studieren/die Studentin/*wo?*
3. öffen/die Frau/der Katalog/*jetzt*
4. sein/das Institut/*neu*/nicht
5. kommen/der Amerikaner/*gleich*
6. *finden*/das Kind/die Straße?
7. trinken/ihr/*was?*

*Udo Jürgens*

8. haben/er/keine Freundinnen/*aber*
9. finden/ich/der Tag/*lang*

**F.** *Give the English equivalents of the following sentences, paying special attention to word order in German.*

1. Wo arbeitest du?
2. Kennen Sie die Platte?
3. Heute abend kommen die Freunde.
4. Das Fräulein sucht den Freund.
5. Sucht Klaus die Platte? Nein, das Buch sucht er.
6. Er kennt wirklich fast kein Buch von Kafka.
7. Findet das Kind den Raum?
8. Lang ist die Klasse nicht.

---

**GUIDED CONVERSATION**

**A.** Begin a conversation with two or three persons sitting near you. Ask one another if you have a record player, if it is new or old (**alt**), and how the sound is. Ask one another if you have a few jazz records, or records of Mozart or Beethoven or Wagner, etc. Ask one another how you like the records. Use the **ihr** or **du** forms in speaking with your classmates. When you have finished, tell the rest of the class what you know about your neighbors' record player and records.

**B.** Ask two or three members of your class if they are acquainted with the books of Thomas Mann,[1] or some other author you particularly like. Ask if they find Mann (or another author) interesting, or even fantastic; if they have a book by Mann; and if so, what the book is called and if they believe it is good.

Suggestions:

Hast du Bücher von . . . ?
Wie findest du die Bücher von . . . ?
Kennst du ein Buch von . . . ?
Verzeihung, wie heißt das Buch?

Practice using the formal and familiar forms of address, both in talking to a group and to a single person.

---

[1] Thomas Mann (1875–1955) was the author of many novels, short stories, and essays. A winner of the Nobel Prize in Literature, he left his native Germany in 1933, when Hitler came to power.

## Das Problem

„Fritz, Verzeihung, hast du eine Zigarette?" „Leider nicht." Natürlich, Fritz raucht nicht. Er trinkt auch nicht. Hat er eigentlich° eine     actually
Schwäche? Ja, vielleicht. Er studiert nicht viel, aber er spielt immer
Gitarre.

Sicher habe ich ein Problem. Nein, nein, ich trinke nicht. Wirklich, ich trinke fast keinen Alkohol, nur manchmal ein Bier. Und ich

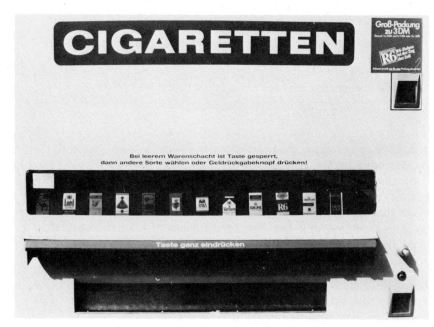

spiele auch nicht immer Gitarre. Aber ich rauche zuviel, besonders
wenn° ich studiere. Und ich studiere viel!     especially when

Ich rauche keine Zigarren, auch keine Pfeife.° Ich rauche mei-     pipe
stens° Zigaretten ohne Filter. Sie kommen aus Deutschland oder Ame-     mostly
rika. In Amerika haben die Zigaretten eine Warnung: Zigaretten sind
gefährlich für die Gesundheit. Aber ich rauche trotzdem.° Andere°     all the same / other
Dinge sind auch gefährlich. Zuviel Zucker, zuviel Kaffee, zum Bei-
spiel.

Aha, Fritz hat wirklich eine Schwäche. Er trinkt immer Kaffee
mit sehr viel Zucker. Das ist sein° Problem!     his

Ist hier ein Automat? Jetzt kaufe ich eine Packung° Roth-Händle.[1]     pack
Eine Schwäche ist so gut wie eine andere.° Und alle Menschen haben     as good as another
eine Schwäche.

[1] A popular brand of rather strong, unfiltered cigarettes.

## Questions

1. Glauben Sie, Fritz hat eine Schwäche?
2. Was ist die Schwäche?
3. Was trinkt der Sprecher (*speaker*)?
4. Spielt er immer Gitarre?
5. Hat er kein Problem?
6. Was haben die Zigaretten in Amerika?
7. Sind andere Dinge gefährlich? Zum Beispiel?
8. Trinken Sie oder rauchen Sie zuviel?
9. Was trinken Sie?
10. Was rauchen Sie?
11. Wenn (*if*) Sie rauchen, rauchen Sie Zigaretten mit oder ohne Filter? Rauchen Sie Zigarren?
12. Glauben Sie, alle Studenten haben eine Schwäche? Alle Professoren? Alle Menschen?

## VOCABULARY DEVELOPMENT

**A.** The adjective of **die Gesundheit** is **gesund** (*healthy*); the opposite is **ungesund** (*unhealthy*) or **krank** (*sick, ill*). A thing or activity is **gesund** or **ungesund**; a person is **gesund** or **krank**.

Ask your neighbor if cigarettes, cigars, alcohol, etc., are healthy or unhealthy, and whether he or she is in good or bad health.

**B.** The adjective of **die Schwäche** is **schwach** (*weak, weakly*); the opposite is **stark** (*strong*).

Now ask a classmate if he or she is strong or weak.

**C. Spielen** may be used with games or instruments.

| | |
|---|---|
| Sie spielt Klavier. | *She plays the piano.* |
| Er spielt Violine. | *He plays the violin.* |
| Wir spielen Karten. | *We play cards.* |
| Ihr spielt Tennis. | *You play tennis.* |

Ask your neighbors whether they play the guitar or another instrument, and if they play tennis. Ask if they play well (**gut**).

**REVIEW EXERCISES**

**A.** *Fill in the blanks with an article as indicated.*

1. D_____ Amerikaner raucht k_____ Zigaretten.
2. Wie finden d_____ Mädchen d_____ Klang?
3. Sind d_____ Kinder stark oder schwach?
4. Hast du e_____ Telefon?
5. D_____ Zigarren haben k_____ Warnung.
6. D_____ Studentin hat e_____ Freund.
7. Wo arbeiten d_____ Männer?
8. Ich hoffe, er findet e_____ Freundin.
9. D_____ Tür ist da drüben.
10. Natürlich habe ich e_____ Plattenspieler.

**B.** *Replace the words in each sentence as indicated, making any necessary changes.*

EXAMPLE: Habt ihr eine Platte? (*kaufen/du*)
      **Kaufst du eine Platte?**

1. Wie heißt die Studentin aus Amerika? (*Studenten/Deutschland*)
2. Findet ihr die Bücher? (*du/Raum*)
3. Er raucht nicht. (*ihr/trinken*)
4. Kennst du eine Studentin aus England? (*haben/Freunde*)
5. Das Bier finden die Männer wirklich gut. (*Kaffee/Frau*)

**C.** *Form sentences with the words supplied. Add any other necessary grammatical elements and start the sentence with the word in italics.*

EXAMPLE: suchen/Institut/Frau/*jetzt*
  **Jetzt sucht die Frau das Institut.**

1. trinken/Alkohol/*der Student*/zuviel.
2. kommen/heute abend/die Freundin/nicht/*leider.*
3. kaufen/Plattenspieler/ich/*vielleicht.*
4. *spielen*/immer/Sie/Gitarre?
5. *kennen*/Studentinnen/ihr/aus Amerika?
6. haben/ein paar/*er*/Freunde/*natürlich.*
7. studieren/zuviel/immer/*wer*?
8. arbeiten/in Berlin/Fräulein/*aber*

**D.** *Answer the following questions in complete sentences. Wherever possible, use pronouns for the subject in the answer.*

1. Wer kennt das Buch von Kafka?
2. Rauchen die Frauen Zigarren?
3. Hat Klaus einen Plattenspieler?
4. Findet das Fräulein den Klang gut?
5. Arbeitet Klaus oder ist er Student?

**E.** *Express in German, paying special attention to word order.*

1. Unfortunately they are ill.
2. Who always drinks too much beer?
3. Do you (*du*) know students from England?
4. No, the record is really not new.
5. Where do you (*ihr*) work?
6. Do the students play tennis?
7. Pardon me, do you (*Sie*) have a moment?
8. Are you (*du*) coming tonight? Great! So long!

## GUIDED COMPOSITION

**A.** Write a few sentences about a particular weakness of one of your friends. Do they smoke, play cards excessively? If they drink, what do they drink? Is their habit a problem? Is it unhealthy or dangerous? In order to practice word order, use expressions such as **leider, vielleicht, manchmal, immer,** etc., at the beginning of several sentences.

**B.** Write a paragraph about what you see in the picture above. Use expressions such as **neu, ein paar,** etc.

---

**CHAPTER VOCABULARY**

### Easily recognized words

| | | | |
|---|---|---|---|
| der | **Alkohol** | *alcohol* | |
| das | **Bier,** -e | *beer* | |
| | **fantastisch** | *fantastic* | |
| die | **Gitarre,** -n | *guitar* | |
| der | **Kaffee** | *coffee* | |
| die | **Karte,** -n | *card* | |
| der | **Moment,** -e | *moment* | |
| das | **Problem,** -e | *problem* | |

| | | | |
|---|---|---|---|
| das | **Telefon,** -e | *telephone* | |
| | **telefonieren** | *to phone* | |
| (das) | **Tennis** | *tennis* | |
| die | **Violine,** -n | *violin* | |
| die | **Warnung,** -en | *warning* | |
| die | **Zigarette,** -n | *cigarette* | |
| die | **Zigarre,** -n | *cigar* | |

| | | | |
|---|---|---|---|
| das | **Beispiel,** -e | *example* | |
| das | **Ding,** -e | *thing* | |
| der | **Freund,** -e | *friend (male)* | |
| die | **Freundin,** -nen | *friend (female)* | |
| die | **Gesundheit** | *health* | |
| der | **Klang,** ⸚e | *sound* | |
| das | **Klavier,** -e | *piano* | |
| der | **Mensch,** -en | *human being, man* | |
| die | **Platte,** -n | *record* | |
| der | **Plattenspieler,** - | *record player* | |
| die | **Schwäche,** -n | *weakness, vice* | |
| die | **Zeit,** -en | *time* | |
| der | **Zucker** | *sugar* | |

| | | |
|---|---|---|
| **glauben** | *to believe, think* |
| **haben** | *to have* |
| **kaufen** | *to buy* |
| **kennen** | *to know (someone or something), be acquainted with* |
| **rauchen** | *to smoke* |
| **spielen** | *to play* |
| **trinken** | *to drink* |

| | |
|---|---|
| **aber** | *but* |
| **alt** | *old* |
| **auch** | *also* |
| **ein paar** | *a few* |
| **ganz** | *quite, completely* |
| **gefährlich** | *dangerous* |
| **gesund** | *healthy* |
| **immer** | *always* |
| **kein** | *no; not a; not any* |
| **krank** | *sick, ill* |
| **leider** | *unfortunately* |
| **manchmal** | *sometimes, once in a while* |
| **natürlich** | *naturally* |
| **neu** | *new* |
| **nur** | *only* |
| **ohne** | *without* |
| **schwach** | *weak, weakly* |
| **sehr** | *very* |
| **stark** | *strong* |
| **ungesund** | *unhealthy* |
| **viel** | *much, a lot* |
| **vielleicht** | *perhaps, maybe* |
| **wann** | *when* |
| **warum** | *why* |
| **zuviel** | *too much* |

## I

**Nimmst** du den Bus?
*Are you taking the bus?*

Nein, ich **nehme** ein Taxi.
*No, I'm taking a cab.*

Ich **fahre** nach Frankfurt, und Hilde **fährt** nach Hannover.
*I'm driving to Frankfurt, and Hilde is driving to Hannover.*

**Liest** du das Programm?
*Are you reading the program?*

Nein, ich **lese** ein Buch.
*No, I'm reading a book.*

## II

**Steigen** Sie bitte **ein**!
*Step in, please.*

Franz, **mach** die Tür **zu**!
*Franz, close the door.*

Der Taxifahrer **hält an**.
*The cab driver stops.*

Wo **fährst** du heute abend **hin**?
*Where are you going tonight?*

Fräulein Heller **geht** die Treppe **hinauf**.
*Miss Heller is going upstairs.*

## III

**Komm** schnell, Peter!
*Come quickly, Peter.*

**Geht** weiter, Peter und Monika!
*Go on, Peter and Monika.*

Herr Kunz, **nehmen Sie** bitte Platz!
*Mr. Kunz, please have (take) a seat.*

## GRAMMAR EXPLANATIONS

### I. Present tense: stem-vowel changes

In the second- and third-person singular of the present tense, the stem vowel **e, a,** or **au** of many common verbs undergoes a change known as "vowel variation."

    **e** changes to **i** or **ie**
    **a** changes to **ä** (umlaut)[1]
    **au** changes to **äu** (umlaut)

---

[1] For a discussion of the umlaut, see the Guide to Pronunciation section in the Appendix, pps. 380–382.

|  | **sprechen**<br>*(to speak)* | **sehen**<br>*(to see)* | **fahren**<br>*(to drive)* | **laufen**<br>*(to run)* |
|---|---|---|---|---|
| SINGULAR |  |  |  |  |
| *1st* | ich spreche | ich sehe | ich fahre | ich laufe |
| *2nd (fam.)* | du sprichst | du siehst | du fährst | du läufst |
| *3rd* | er spricht | er sieht | er fährt | er läuft |
| PLURAL |  |  |  |  |
| *1st* | wir sprechen | wir sehen | wir fahren | wir laufen |
| *2nd (fam.)* | ihr sprecht | ihr seht | ihr fahrt | ihr lauft |
| *3rd* | sie sprechen | sie sehen | sie fahren | sie laufen |
| SINGULAR/PLURAL |  |  |  |  |
| *2nd (formal)* | Sie sprechen | Sie sehen | Sie fahren | Sie laufen |

*Present tense: stem-vowel changes of strong verbs*

Other common verbs with vowel variation include:

| INFINITIVE | 2ND PERSON<br>SINGULAR | 3RD PERSON<br>SINGULAR |
|---|---|---|
| **a > ä** |  |  |
| halten (*to stop*) | du hältst | er hält |
| lassen (*to let*) | du läßt[1] | er läßt |
| verlassen (*to leave*) | du verläßt[1] | er verläßt |
| **e > i** or **ie** |  |  |
| essen (*to eat*) | du ißt[1] | er ißt |
| nehmen (*to take*) | du nimmst | er nimmt |
| lesen (*to read*) | du liest[1] | er liest |
| sprechen (*to speak*) | du sprichst | er spricht |
| vergessen (*to forget*) | du vergißt[1] | er vergißt |

The verb **nehmen,** in addition to changing **e > i,** undergoes a consonant change:

| | |
|---|---|
| ich nehme | wir nehmen |
| du ni**mm**st | ihr nehmt |
| er ni**mm**t | sie nehmen |

[1] Note that verbs with a stem ending in a hissing sound have the same form in the second- and third-person singular. The **ihr** form is different, since it has no vowel variation: **ihr laßt, ihr eßt,** etc.

This book's vocabularies and most dictionaries indicate the vowel variation of a verb by listing the third-person singular after the infinitive: **halten, hält.**

---

*Check your comprehension*

*Complete the sentence with the correct form of the verb in parentheses.*

1. Fräulein Lang _____ sehr gut Englisch. (*sprechen*)
2. _____ du ein Buch von Thomas Mann? (*lesen*)
3. Der Student _____ zuviel. (*essen*)
4. Die Amerikanerin _____ da drüben. (*sein*)
5. Ihr _____ immer den Kaffee. (*vergessen*)
6. _____ Sie Deutsch? (*sprechen*)
7. Peter _____ heute nach Salzburg. (*fahren*)
8. Was _____ du? (*kaufen*)
9. Er _____ das Taxi nicht. (*sehen*)
10. Das Mädchen _____ nicht schnell. (*laufen*)
11. _____ ihr das Institut? (*verlassen*)
12. Wo _____ der Bus? (*halten*)

---

## II. Present tense: verbs with separable prefixes

Many German verbs consist of the verb itself and a particle known as a prefix. This particle is placed directly in front of the infinitive to form a unit: **einsteigen,** *to get in (a vehicle).*

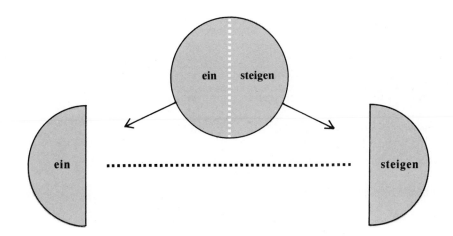

In the present tense some prefixes are detached from the verb and placed at the end of the clause. These are the *separable prefixes.*

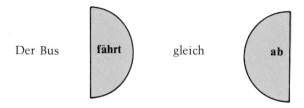

Der Bus **fährt** gleich **ab**

*The bus is departing right away.*

Robert **steigt** in ein Taxi **ein**

*Robert is getting in a taxi.*

Er **geht** die Treppe **hinauf**

*He's going upstairs.*

In pronunciation the separable prefix receives the stress accent: **ein-steigen; er steigt ein.**

A separable prefix adds an important nuance to the meaning of a verb. Sometimes the meaning may be changed altogether. In the beginning of your studies, you cannot easily anticipate a separable prefix when you see a verb. So to understand the verb correctly, be sure to glance at the end of the clause or sentence.

| | |
|---|---|
| Er kommt aus Amerika. | *He comes from America.* |
| Er kommt in Deutschland **an.** | *He arrives in Germany.* |
| Wir fahren nach Frankfurt. | *We're driving to Frankfurt.* |
| Wir fahren **ab.** | *We're leaving.* |

These are the most common separable prefixes:

| ab | ab·fahren *to depart, drive off* |
|---|---|
| an | { an·halten *to stop* <br> an·kommen *to arrive* |
| aus | aus·steigen *to get out (of a vehicle), get off* |
| ein | ein·steigen *to get in* |
| weiter | { weiter·fahren *to drive on* <br> weiter·gehen *to go on* |
| zu | zu·machen *to close* |
| zurück | zurück·laufen *to run back* |

In dictionaries and vocabularies, a separable prefix is indicated by a dot (·), as in **ein·steigen.** However, the dot is not part of the spelling; it is merely an aid to the student.

---

*Check your comprehension*

*Answer the following sentences in the affirmative, then translate your answers into English.*

EXAMPLE: Fährt der Bus ab?
**Ja, der Bus fährt ab.**
*Yes, the bus is leaving.*

1. Kommt das Taxi an?
2. Fahren die Herren weiter?
3. Steigt Hilde in das Auto ein?
4. Machst du die Tür zu?
5. Läuft der Student in die Bibliothek zurück?
6. Steigt ihr hier aus?
7. Geht Franz immer weiter?
8. Hält der Bus hier an?
9. Fahren die Russen ab?
10. Steigst du ein?

---

A special group of separable prefixes are constructed with **hin** (or **hinein, hinauf, hinunter,** etc.), suggesting a movement *away from* the position of the speaker, and with **her** (or **herein, herauf, herunter, heran,** etc.), suggesting a movement *toward* the speaker.

| AWAY FROM THE SPEAKER | TOWARD THE SPEAKER |
|---|---|
| hin·fahren *to drive (there)* | her·fahren *to drive (here)* |
| hinein·lassen *to let in (there)* | herein·lassen *to let in (here)* |
| hinauf·gehen *to go up (there)* | herauf·kommen *to come up (here)* |
| hinunter·gehen *to go down (there)* | herunter·kommen *to come down (here)* |

AWAY FROM                                   TOWARD

Er geht **hin**auf.                            Sie kommt **her**unter.
*He's going up there.*                        *She's coming down here.*

Notice that **gehen** and **kommen** inherently express *movement toward* and *movement away from;* the separable prefix expresses the direction more specifically.

    **Hin** and **her** should not be confused with **hier** (*here*) and **dort** or **da** (*there*), which indicate fixed position only and not movement:

POSITION

Fritz ist **hier.**                    *Fritz is here.*
Monika arbeitet **dort.**            *Monika works there.*

MOVEMENT

Er kommt gleich **her.**          *He's coming here right away.*
Wir fahren gleich **hin.**         *We'll drive there right away.*

With verbs of movement, *where?* is expressed by either **wohin,** *(to) where?*, or **woher,** *from where?* **Wo** (*where*) is used when no movement is implied.

| | | |
|---|---|---|
| | Wohin fahren Sie? | *Where are you driving?* |
| | Woher kommt er? | *Where is he coming from?* |
| *But:* | Wo sind wir? | *Where are we?* |
| | Wo arbeitest du? | *Where do you work?* |

## Check your comprehension

**A.** *Form the questions to which the following statements are the answers, then translate the answers into English.*

EXAMPLE: Ich gehe die Treppe hinauf. (*du*)
**Gehst du die Treppe hinauf?**
*Are you going upstairs?*

1. Wir gehen die Treppe hinunter. (*Sie*)
2. Herr Kunz fährt hin.
3. Ich lasse die Studenten herein. (*du*)
4. Das Fräulein geht schnell hinauf.
5. Karl kommt jetzt herunter.
6. Wir lassen die Amerikanerin hinein. (*ihr*)
7. Die Männer fahren auch hin.
8. Sie kommt die Treppe herauf.

**B.** *Form the questions to which the following statements are the answers. Use* **wo, wohin,** *or* **woher.**

EXAMPLE: Sie geht in das Institut.
**Wohin geht sie?**

1. Die Studenten fahren nach Salzburg.
2. Da arbeitet er.
3. Sie kommt aus England.
4. Sie studieren in Berlin.
5. Fritz geht in die Bibliothek.
6. Die Frauen fahren nach Hamburg.

## III. The imperative

The imperative form of the verb is used to give a command or make a suggestion. German distinguishes between three forms of direct address in the imperative: the **Sie, du,** and **ihr** forms. Usually they are followed by an exclamation mark.

The formal or **Sie** form of the imperative is identical with the present-tense form, except that pronoun and verb are inverted.

| | |
|---|---|
| Kommen Sie, bitte! | *Please come.* |
| Gehen Sie, bitte! | *Please go.* |
| Lesen Sie, bitte! | *Read, please.* |

The imperative of the plural familiar or **ihr** form is identical with the present-tense form, except that the pronoun is dropped.

| | |
|---|---|
| Kommt, bitte! | *Please come.* |
| Geht, bitte! | *Please go.* |
| Lest, bitte! | *Read, please.* |

The imperative of the singular familiar or **du** form consists of the stem of the second-person singular of the present tense; the ending **-st** is dropped. However, if the stem ends in **-s** or **-ß,** only the **-t** is dropped.

| PRESENT TENSE | IMPERATIVE |
|---|---|
| du kommst | komm! |
| du gehst | geh! |
| du sprichst | sprich! |
| du liest | lies! |
| du nimmst | nimm! |
| du fährst | fahr! |
| du läßt | laß! |

Note that verbs with the vowel variation **a > ä** or **au > äu** do not carry the umlaut into the singular imperative.

In all three forms of the imperative, the separable prefixes always move to the end of the imperative clause.

| | | |
|---|---|---|
| **du** form: | Steig bitte ein! | *Get in, please.* |
| **ihr** form: | Lauft bitte weiter! | *Run on, please.* |
| **Sie** form: | Gehen Sie bitte zurück! | *Go back, please.* |

The verb **sein** (*to be*) has the following irregular imperative forms:

| | | |
|---|---|---|
| **du** form: | Sei so gut! | |
| **ihr** form: | Seid so gut! | *Be so kind (good).* |
| **Sie** form: | Seien Sie so gut! | |

The infinitive may be used as an impersonal imperative form to give instructions to the public. A bus driver, for instance, might call out the following:

| | |
|---|---|
| Bitte, einsteigen! | *Please step in.* |
| Weitergehen, bitte! | *Please move on.* |
| Bitte, aussteigen! | *(Everybody) out, please.* |

## Check your comprehension

*Use the appropriate imperative form of the verb in parentheses. Watch the position of the separable prefix.*

EXAMPLE: Klaus, _____ gleich! (*herunterkommen*)
**Klaus, komm gleich herunter!**

1. Peter und Lotte, _____ die Bücher nicht! (*vergessen*)
2. Herr Meyer, bitte _____! (*einsteigen*)
3. Richard, _____ nicht so schnell! (*sprechen*)
4. Fräulein Schmidt, bitte _____! (*heraufkommen*)
5. Fritz, _____ schnell in die Klasse! (*zurücklaufen*)
6. Ulrike, _____ die Tür! (*zumachen*)
7. Franz, _____ hier nicht! (*anhalten*)
8. Karl, _____ bitte Platz! (*nehmen*)
9. Anna, _____ die Treppe! (*hinuntergehen*)
10. Herr Wegner, _____ die Mädchen! (*hereinlassen*)

## USEFUL PHRASES

| | |
|---|---|
| **Er bittet um Auskunft.** | *He asks for information.* |
| **alle (fünfzehn) Minuten** | *every (fifteen) minutes* |
| **Ich habe keine Eile.** | *I'm not in a hurry.* |
| **Vielen Dank!** | { *Thank you very much.* / *Thanks a lot.* |
| **das nächste Mal** | *next time* |
| **Moment mal!** | *Just a moment.* |

## Bus oder Taxi?

*Flugplatz Berlin-Tempelhof. Robert kommt gerade in West-Berlin an. Er nimmt das Gepäck und verläßt die Halle.° Draußen° stehen Taxis. Er bittet einen Taxifahrer um Auskunft.*  —  *terminal | outside*

ROBERT Guten Tag! Verzeihung! Fährt ein Bus von hier zum° Kurfürstendamm?[1]  —  *to the*

TAXIFAHRER Nicht direkt° von hier. Aber sehen Sie die Bus-Haltestelle da drüben? Nehmen Sie den Bus Nummer acht!  —  *directly*

*Dort fährt gerade ein Bus Nummer acht ab.*

ROBERT Wie oft fährt der Bus zum Kurfürstendamm?

TAXIFAHRER Moment mal, ich glaube, alle fünfzehn Minuten.

ROBERT Wirklich?

TAXIFAHRER Aber nehmen Sie doch ein Taxi! Da, steigen Sie ein!

ROBERT Danke, ich habe keine Eile und auch nicht genug Geld für ein Taxi. Vielen Dank für die Auskunft.

TAXIFAHRER Bitte.

*Nach fünfzehn Minuten kommt ein Bus Nummer acht an und Robert steigt ein. Der Bus ist voll.°*  —  *full*

ROBERT Fahren Sie zum Kurfürstendamm?

[1] The main shopping street in West Berlin, called "Kudamm" by the Berliners.

BUSFAHRER  Nein, nein. Steigen Sie schnell wieder aus und nehmen Sie
Bus Nummer fünfzehn.—Einsteigen, bitte. Gehen Sie weiter! Wei-
tergehen, bitte!

*Der Busfahrer macht die Tür zu.*

ROBERT (*zu sich*)° Das nächste Mal nehme ich ein Taxi.                    *to himself*

## Questions

1. Wo kommt Robert an?
2. Wen bittet er um Auskunft?
3. Fährt Bus Nummer acht oder fünfzehn zum Kurfürstendamm?
4. Nimmt er den Bus oder das Taxi? Warum?
5. Wie oft fährt der Bus zum Kurfürstendamm?
6. Steigt Robert in den Bus ein?
7. Was sagt der Busfahrer zu Robert?
8. Hast du Eile?
9. Nimmst du heute einen Bus? Wohin?
10. Hast du genug Geld für ein Taxi?
11. Kennst du West-Berlin?
12. Bittest du oft Taxifahrer oder Busfahrer um Auskunft?

## PRACTICE

**A.** *Substitute the appropriate form of each verb in parentheses for the
verb in the sentence.*

1. Friederike nimmt das Auto. (*sehen/verlassen/anhalten/fahren*)
2. Du fährst sehr schnell, Angelika. (*laufen/sprechen/lesen/essen*)
3. Herr Steiner, fahren Sie bitte ab! (*einsteigen/heraufkommen/weitergehen/
   anhalten*)

**B.** *Use the appropriate form of the verb in parentheses. Watch the position of the separable prefix.*

EXAMPLE: Albert, _____ nicht so schnell! (*laufen*)
**Albert, lauf nicht so schnell!**

1. Else, _____ Deutsch, nicht Englisch! (*sprechen*)
2. Wo _____ die Busse? (*anhalten*)
3. _____ ihr den Bus oder das Taxi? (*nehmen*)
4. Bitte, Herr Schmidt, _____! (*aussteigen*)
5. Erich, _____ das Buch nicht! (*vergessen*)
6. _____ du oft Bücher von Thomas Mann? (*lesen*)
7. Er _____ manchmal. (*hinuntergehen*)
8. Wer _____ die Treppe? (*heraufkommen*)
9. Der Freund _____ heute abend in Berlin. (*ankommen*)
10. Viktor und Thomas, bitte _____ die Tür. (*zumachen*)
11. _____ ihr die Bus-Haltestelle da drüben? (*sehen*)
12. Der Student _____ viel zuviel. (*essen*)
13. _____ du den Bus oder das Taxi? (*nehmen*)
14. Hans, _____ den Mann! (*hereinlassen*)
15. Die Frau _____ gleich den Flugplatz. (*verlassen*)

**C.** *In the following sentences use the appropriate separable prefix with the verb given in parentheses, and place it in the appropriate position. The direction is indicated by the arrow, and the position of the speaker by* **o**.

EXAMPLE: Die Studentin _____ die Treppe. (_____ *kommen* → o)
**Die Studentin kommt die Treppe herauf.**

1. Wo _____ ihr morgen? (_____ *fahren* o →)
2. Wo _____ du? (_____ *kommen* → o)

3. Hier _____ wir die Treppe. (_____ *gehen* o ↘)

4. _____ du den Freund nicht? (_____ *lassen* → o)

5. Herr Frisch _____ in das Haus (_____ *gehen* o →)

**D.** *Construct sentences with the following cues. Watch the punctuation to determine whether the sentence is a statement, question, or command.*

EXAMPLE: weiterfahren/bitte/Herr Bunzle!
    **Fahren Sie bitte weiter, Herr Bunzle!**

1. fahren/Fräulein Heller/nach Frankfurt?

2. anhalten/der Bus/hier?

3. zumachen/Paul/die Tür!

4. abfahren/wir/heute abend.

5. heraufkommen/wer/die Treppe?

6. fahren/Herr Müller/immer/sehr schnell.

7. zurücklaufen/die Studentin/in das Institut.

8. aussteigen/ich/hier.

9. essen/Hans/zuviel/Zucker.

10. vergessen/Dieter/das Gepäck/nicht!

**E.** *Use the appropriate imperative form of the verbs in parentheses. Watch the position of the separable prefix.*

EXAMPLE: Arnold, _____ so gut und _____ den Raum! (*sein, verlassen*)
    **Arnold, sei so gut und verlaß den Raum!**

1. Fräulein Ottinger, _____ bitte die Warnung! (*lesen*)

2. Joachim, _____ doch nicht so schnell! (*essen*)

3. Monika und Jürgen, _____ so gut und _____ das Geld! (*sein, suchen*)

4. Herr Brandt, bitte _____! (*hinfahren*)

5. Willy, _____ bitte die Treppe und _____ die Tür! (*hinaufgehen, öffnen*)

**F.** *Give the English equivalents of the following sentences.*

1. Oskar, halt hier nicht an; fahr weiter!

2. Bitte, Herr Müller, laufen Sie in die Halle zurück!

3. Er ist krank, ißt nicht genug und vergißt sehr viel.

4. Vielleicht kommt Gretchen heute abend an.

5. Robert hat keine Eile und nimmt den Bus.

6. Der Bus fährt alle zwanzig Minuten ab.

7. Moment mal! Warum steigt ihr hier aus?

8. Wer kommt die Treppe herauf?

9. Er läßt die Frauen nicht hinein.

10. Das nächste Mal vergessen Sie das Gepäck nicht!

In the image the signs read:

Hier keine
Netz-u.Bezirkskarten.
Monats- u. Wochenkarten.
Gruppenfahrten.
(Ausgabe: Schalter 9 - 11)

Auslandsfahrkarten
gegenüber
(Ausgabe: Schalter 16 - 21)

An den Schaltern 8 - 11 erhalten Sie Ausflugskarten für
Brannenburg, Kampenwand,
Wendelstein,

**A.** Look at this picture of a woman asking for some information and reconstruct the possible dialogue, for instance:

> Wo fährt der Bus ab?
> Wann fährt der Bus ab?
> Wie oft fährt der Bus zum (*to the*) Flugplatz?

Ask your neighbor to give the answers.

**B.** Tell your neighbor(s) to do something, then give them the opposite command. Here's a start:

> Öffne die Tür! Nimm den Bus! Lassen Sie das Gepäck hier!

Vary the commands between the **du, ihr,** and **Sie** forms.

## *Zimmer Nummer dreizehn*

Robert verläßt das Hotel „Adler". Es ist fünf Uhr. Er sieht einen Kiosk°, kauft eine Zeitung und geht in ein Café. Aber er geht nicht hinein. Er findet einen Platz auf dem Bürgersteig° und bestellt eine Tasse Kaffee. Dann kommt eine Studentin an und fragt: „Ist hier noch ein Platz frei?"[1] „Oh ja, natürlich, nehmen Sie bitte Platz!" sagt er. Sie bestellt eine Tasse Tee und ein Stück Kuchen. Dann öffnet sie ein Buch, liest und spricht nicht. „Na, schön",° denkt Robert, „dann lese ich die Zeitung und trinke den Kaffee."

Plötzlich hört er eine Sirene. Ein Feuerwehrwagen° kommt heran. Alle Autos fahren nach rechts und halten an. Robert sieht Rauch aufsteigen.° „Ist das möglich?" denkt er. „Ist das nicht das Hotel Adler?"

*newsstand*

*on the sidewalk*

*well, then*

*fire truck*

*smoke rising*

[1] In Germany it is customary to sit down at a partially occupied table in a crowded restaurant or café.

Er läuft schnell zurück, aber die Polizei läßt Robert nicht hinein. „Halt! Nicht hineingehen!" hört er. Er protestiert. Vergeblich.° End-    in vain
lich ist das Feuer unter Kontrolle. Robert geht schnell die Treppe hin-
auf und öffnet die Tür von Zimmer Nummer dreizehn. Das Federbett,[2]
das Gepäck, alles ist ganz naß.° Er macht die Tür wieder zu und geht    wet
langsam die Treppe hinunter. „Heute habe ich wirklich kein Glück",
denkt er. „Das nächste Mal nehme ich kein Zimmer Nummer dreizehn!"

## Questions

1. Was macht Robert um (*at*) fünf Uhr?
2. Was kauft er?
3. Wohin geht er?
4. Was bestellt er?
5. Wer kommt an?
6. Was fragt sie?
7. Kennt Robert die Studentin?
8. Was macht dann die Studentin?
9. Was denkt Robert?
10. Was hört er plötzlich?
11. Was machen alle Autos?
12. Wohin läuft Robert schnell?
13. Wer läßt Robert nicht in das Hotel?
14. Was ist in Zimmer dreizehn ganz naß?
15. Was denkt Robert?

**VOCABULARY DEVELOPMENT**

**A.** German is versatile in combining separable prefixes with verbs. For instance:

| | |
|---|---|
| weiter·lesen | *to go on reading* |
| weiter·machen | *to go on doing* |
| weiter·sprechen | *to go on talking* |

[2] Eiderdown. This is standard bedding in Germany.

Give some commands with these compounds, such as: **Sprich weiter!**
Here are some compounds with **mit** (*with*):

| | |
|---|---|
| mit·fahren | *to travel along with* |
| mit·lesen | *to read along with* |
| mit·nehmen | *to take with* |

Form a few questions or commands with these verbs, such as: **Nimmst
du die Zeitung nicht mit? Rudolf, lies mit!**

**B.** The opposite of **rechts** is **links** (*left*), which also occurs frequently
with **nach**; for instance:

| | |
|---|---|
| Fahren Sie nach links! | *Drive to the left.* |

Construct a few short sentences with the two expressions, using the
verbs **fahren** and **gehen.**

**C.** German uses many "flavoring particles," such as **doch** and **mal,**
which must be understood within a given context; there is no one
translation for all instances.

| | |
|---|---|
| Nehmen Sie Platz! | *Have a seat.* |
| Nehmen Sie doch Platz! | *Do sit down.* |
| Nehmen Sie ein Taxi! | *Take a taxi.* |
| Nehmen Sie doch ein Taxi! | *Well then, take a taxi!* |

The particle **mal** can be combined with numerals: **einmal, zweimal, dreimal,** etc. (*once, twice, three times,* etc.) It may also be used
as a noun: **das nächste Mal** (*next time*). As a flavoring particle it takes
on the sense of *just* or *even:*

| | |
|---|---|
| Moment mal! | *Just a moment.* |
| Sie sieht den Mann nicht mal an. | *She doesn't even look at the man.* |

**REVIEW EXERCISES**

**A.** *Construct sentences with the following cues; watch the punctuation
to decide whether the sentence is a statement, question, or command.
Start the sentence with the word in italics, where so indicated. Watch
the word order.*

EXAMPLE: ankommen/der Freund/morgen früh/*sicher*
    **Sicher kommt der Freund morgen früh an.**

1. sein/Zucker/gefährlich/für die Gesundheit?
2. essen/du/sehr viel/Kuchen?
3. nehmen/Adolf/das Buch/und/lesen/das Beispiel!
4. arbeiten/der Freund/sehr viel/aber/weiterkommen/er/nicht.
5. spielen/Monika/die Platte/von Louis Armstrong!
6. ankommen/Fräulein Ohlendorf/heute/nicht/*leider.*
7. zurücklaufen/Ernst/doch/und/kaufen/eine Zeitung!
8. nehmen/Herr Schwarzkopf,/doch/bitte/Platz!
9. hinfahren/er/morgen/*vielleicht.*
10. sprechen/er/viel/zu langsam/*immer.*

**B.** *Fill in each blank with a form of the appropriate verb listed at the right.*

1. Adalbert, du _____ viel zu schnell; das _____ nicht gut für die Gesundheit.
2. Der Student _____ immer das Deutschbuch.
3. Die Polizei _____ die Studentin nicht in das Hotel.
4. Sie (Sing.) _____ das Institut.

    a. *verlassen*
    b. *sein*
    c. *essen*
    d. *lassen*
    e. *vergessen*

**C.** *Express in German.*

1. Please have a seat.
2. We're getting out here. Thanks a lot.
3. Mrs. Ottinger, when are you going downstairs?
4. We aren't in a hurry.
5. Ulrike eats too much cake.
6. The police let Robert in.
7. He asks the taxi driver for information.
8. The children are coming up again.
9. Now the men are leaving the hotel.
10. The bus stops every twelve minutes.
11. Erika, please drive slowly!
12. Where is Hilde running?

## GUIDED COMPOSITION

In a few sentences, describe a street scene involving yourself or a friend, as for instance leaving the house, taking a bus, buying something, sitting down in a café, drinking and eating something, going home, studying German.

## CHAPTER VOCABULARY

### Easily recognized words

| | | |
|---|---|---|
| das | **Auto,** -s | *car, automobile* |
| der | **Bus,** -se | *bus* |
| das | **Café,** -s | *café, coffeehouse* |
| das | **Hotel,** -s | *hotel* |
| die | **Minute,** -n | *minute* |
| die | **Nummer,** -n | *number* |
| | **oft** | *often* |
| | **protestieren** | *to protest* |
| das | **Taxi,** -s | *taxi, cab* |
| der | **Tee** | *tea* |
| | | |
| der | **Busfahrer,** - | *bus driver* |
| das | **Feuer,** - | *fire* |
| der | **Flugplatz,** ⸚e | *airport* |
| das | **Geld,** -er | *money* |
| das | **Gepäck** | *luggage* |
| die | **Haltestelle,** -n | *(bus or train) stop* |
| der | **Kuchen,** - | *cake* |
| der | **Platz,** ⸚e | *place, seat;* **Platz nehmen** *to take (have) a seat* |
| die | **Polizei (sing.)** | *police* |
| das | **Stück,** -e | *piece* |
| die | **Tasse,** -n | *cup* |
| der | **Taxifahrer,** - | *taxi driver* |
| die | **Treppe,** -n | *stairs* |
| die | **Zeitung,** -en | *newspaper* |

| | | |
|---|---|---|
| das | **Zimmer,** - | *room* |
| | **ab·fahren (fährt)** | *to leave, depart, drive off* |
| | **an·halten (hält)** | *to stop* |
| | **an·kommen** | *to arrive (at a place)* |
| | **aus·steigen** | *to get out (of a vehicle), get off* |
| | **bestellen** | *to order* |
| | **bitten (um)** | *to ask (for)* |
| | **denken** | *to think* |
| | **ein·steigen** | *to get in or into (a vehicle)* |
| | **essen (ißt)** | *to eat* |
| | **fahren (fährt)** | *to drive, go (by vehicle)* |
| | **fragen** | *to ask (a question)* |
| | **gehen** | *to go* |
| | **halten (hält)** | *to stop* |
| | **hören** | *to hear* |
| | **lassen (läßt)** | *to let, let go* |
| | **laufen (läuft)** | *to run, go (by foot)* |
| | **lesen (liest)** | *to read* |
| | **machen** | *to do* |
| | **nehmen (nimmt)** | *to take* |
| | **sagen** | *to say* |
| | **sehen (sieht)** | *to see* |
| | **sprechen (spricht)** | *to speak* |

| | | | |
|---|---|---|---|
| **stehen** | *to stand* | **gerade** | *just now, just then* |
| **vergessen (vergißt)** | *to forget* | **langsam** | *slow(ly)* |
| **verlassen (verläßt)** | *to leave (behind)* | **links** | *left, on the left;* **nach links** *to the left* |
| **weiter· + *verb*** | *to (do) further, to go on (doing)* | **mit** | *with* |
| **zu·machen** | *to close* | **möglich** | *possible* |
| **zurück·laufen (läuft)** | *to run back* | **plötzlich** | *suddenly* |

See also the **hin** and **her** verbs on p. 51.

| | | | |
|---|---|---|---|
| | | **rechts** | *right, on the right;* **nach rechts** *to the right* |
| **alles** | *all, everything* | **schnell** | *quickly, fast* |
| **dann** | *then* | **von** | *of* |
| **dort** | *there* | **wieder** | *again* |
| **einmal** | *once* | **woher** | *where, from what place* |
| **endlich** | *finally* | **wohin** | *where, to what place* |
| **frei** | *free, vacant* | **zu** | *to* |
| **genug** | *enough* | | |

### I

Das Kind bringt **dem Mann** einen Schlüssel.
*The child brings the man a key.*

Der Taxifahrer zeigt **den Frauen** den Bahnhof.
*The taxi driver shows the railroad station to the women.*

Das Mädchen bezahlt **dem Busfahrer** das Geld.
*The girl pays the bus driver the money.*

**Wem** gibst du die Zeitung?
*To whom do you give the newspaper.*

### II

Wir kommen gerade **aus dem Hotel.**
*We're just coming out of the hotel.*

Die Herren gehen **zur Haltestelle.**
*The gentlemen are going to the bus stop.*

Die Freundinnen fahren **mit dem Auto.**
*The girlfriends are traveling by car.*

Heute abend bin ich **zu Hause.**
*I'll be home tonight.*

### III

Ich zeige **dem Studenten** die Stadt.
*I show the student the city.*

Gib **dem Herrn** die Adresse!
*Give the address to the gentleman.*

**GRAMMAR EXPLANATIONS**

### I. Dative case

Another important part of a sentence is the *indirect object*, which tells to whom or for whom something is done. For instance, in the act expressed by the verb **geben** (*to give*), three elements are involved:

the one who gives = subject
the one to whom something is given = indirect object
the thing that is given = direct object

The case of the indirect object is called the *dative*.

Thomas gibt     dem Mann     das Buch.

*Thomas gives the man the book.*

In German, if the two objects are nouns, the dative normally precedes the accusative. But for emphasis the indirect object can be placed at the beginning or the end of the sentence: **Dem Mann gibt Thomas das Buch. Thomas gibt das Buch dem Mann.**

In English the indirect object is recognized by the prepositions *to* or *for*, expressed or understood. In German the indirect object occurs without a preposition, and is indicated by special forms of the definite and indefinite articles and the negative **kein.**

| | |
|---|---|
| Thomas bringt **der** Frau einen Schlüssel. | *Thomas brings the woman a key.* |
| Thomas öffnet **einem** Freund die Tür. | *Thomas opens the door for a friend.* |
| Thomas zeigt **keinem** Kind die Zeitung. | *Thomas doesn't show the paper to any child.* |
| Thomas bezahlt **den** Männern das Geld. | *Thomas pays the men the money.* |

In the plural of the dative, all nouns add **-n** (for phonetic reasons, at times **-en**), unless their nominative plural form already ends in **-n.**

| | | NOMINATIVE PLURAL | DATIVE PLURAL |
|---|---|---|---|
| *masc.* | | die Männer | den Männer**n** |
| *fem.* | | die Städte | den Städte**n** |
| *neut.* | | die Kinder | den Kinder**n** |
| | *But:* | die Studentinnen | den Studentinnen |
| | | die Frauen | den Frauen |

---

*Articles,* **kein,** *and* nouns: *dative case*

| SINGULAR | DEF. ARTICLE | INDEF. ARTICLE | **kein** |
|---|---|---|---|
| *masc.* | de**m** Mann | ein**em** Mann | kein**em** Mann |
| *fem.* | de**r** Frau | ein**er** Frau | kein**er** Frau |
| *neut.* | de**m** Kind | ein**em** Kind | kein**em** Kind |

| PLURAL | | | |
|---|---|---|---|
| *masc.* | | — Männer**n** | |
| *fem.* | **den** { Männer**n** / Frauen / Kinder**n** | — Frauen | **keinen** { Männer**n** / Frauen / Kinder**n** |
| *neut.* | | — Kinder**n** | |

---

Foreign words like **das Auto, das Café,** and **das Hotel,** which end in **-s** in the nominative plural, do not add **-n** in the dative plural:

| | |
|---|---|
| *nom. sing.* | das Auto |
| *nom. pl.* | die Auto**s** |
| *dat. pl.* | den Auto**s** |

| SINGULAR | NOMINATIVE | ACCUSATIVE | DATIVE |
|---|---|---|---|
| *masc.* | der | den | dem |
| | ein | einen | einem |
| | kein | keinen | keinem |
| *fem.* | die | die | der |
| | eine | eine | einer |
| | keine | keine | keiner |
| *neut.* | das | das | dem |
| | ein | ein | einem |
| | kein | kein | keinem |
| PLURAL | | | |
| *all genders* | die | die | den |
| | — | — | — |
| | keine | keine | keinen |

*Articles and* **kein:** *nominative, accusative, and dative cases*

The interrogative word **wer** (*who*) also has a dative form: **wem** (*to whom*).

**Wem** gibt er das Geld?

*To whom does he give the money?*
*Whom does he give the money to?*

*Salzburg*

---

## Check your comprehension

**A.** *Fill in the appropriate accusative or dative of the noun indicated in parentheses. Determine first whether the noun is a direct or indirect object, singular or plural.*

1. Karl öffnet _____. (*eine Tür*)
2. Geben Sie _____ da drüben das Buch. (*das Fräulein*)
3. Die Frau zeigt _____ das Gepäck. (*der Taxifahrer*)
4. Heute essen wir _____. (*ein Kuchen*)
5. Sie bringt _____ ein Bier. (*der Mann*)
6. Wir zeigen _____ die Platte. (*eine Freundin*)
7. Warum öffnest du _____ die Tür nicht? (*die Kinder*)
8. Hans sieht _____. (*die Freundin*)
9. Er bringt _____ die Karten. (*die Studentinnen*)

**B.** *Use* **wer, wen,** *or* **wem** *in the following sentences.*

1. _____ ist da?
2. _____ bringst du das Buch?
3. _____ kennst du gut?
4. _____ gibst du eine Zeitung?
5. _____ öffnet sie die Tür?
6. _____ bringt den Tee?

---

## II. Prepositions with the dative

A preposition is usually followed by a noun or a pronoun. In German, a preposition governs a specific case, most often the dative or accusative.

The following is a list of prepositions that are always followed by an object in the dative case. Memorize them, for they occur frequently. The English translations given here are general and flexible; sometimes they must be adjusted to the context of the sentence.

**aus** *out of, from*
Er kommt **aus dem Hotel.**
*He is coming out of the hotel.*

Jürgen kommt **aus** Köln.
*Jürgen comes from Cologne.*

**außer** *except, besides*
Helga ißt alles **außer Kuchen.**
*Helga eats everything except cake.*

**bei** *near, at (the place of)*
Sie steht **bei der Tür.**
*She is standing near the door.*

Heinz wohnt **bei Frau Becker.**
*Heinz lives at Mrs. Becker's (place).*

**mit** *with, by (means of)*

Sie spricht **mit den Kindern.**
*She's talking with the children.*

Wir fahren **mit dem Auto.**
*We're traveling by car.*

**nach** *after, to (referring to cities and countries)*

**Nach dem Abendessen** liest er die Zeitung.
*After dinner he reads the newspaper.*

Sie gehen **nach Deutschland.**
*They are going to Germany.*

**seit** *since, for (in reference to time)*

**Seit dem Feuer** ißt er hier.[1]
*(Ever) since the fire he has been eating here.*

Sie ist **seit Tagen** krank.[1]
*She has been ill for days.*

**von** *from, by, of, about*

Kommt ihr **von der Haltestelle?**
*Are you coming from the bus stop?*

Wir sprechen gerade **von dem Feuer.**
*We're just now talking about the fire.*

**zu** *to (referring to persons and public places), at*

Die Frau geht **zu den Kindern.**
*The woman is going to the children.*

Er geht **zu der Haltestelle.**
*He is going to the (bus) stop.*

The prepositions **bei, von,** and **zu** are often contracted with the definite article in the singular:

WITH **dem** (MASC. AND NEUT.)
bei + dem = **beim**
von + dem = **vom**
zu + dem = **zum**

WITH **der** (FEM.)
zu + der = **zur**

Die Herren stehen **beim** Fenster.
Die Freundin kommt **vom** Bahnhof.
Heidi geht **zum** Hotel.
Frau Strauß fährt **zur** Haltestelle.

Two phrases using prepositions governing the dative have special meanings: **zu Hause** indicates a fixed position, *at home;* **nach Hause** indicates movement *toward home.*

Das Gepäck lasse ich **zu Hause.**
*I'll leave the luggage at home.*

Wir gehen jetzt **nach Hause.**
*We're going home now.*

---

[1] Note that **seit** is used with the present tense in German.

The interrogative **wem** may occur with a dative preposition.

**Mit wem** fahren Sie nach Köln?     *With whom are you driving to Cologne?*

---

## Check your comprehension

**A.** *Complete the sentence with the cue in parentheses.*

1. Herr Müller kommt _____. (*out of the house*)
2. Heute fahren wir _____ ab. (*to Germany*)
3. Die Mädchen gehen _____. (*to the bus stop*)
4. Robert wohnt _____. (*at Mrs. Lang's*)
5. Die Studenten sprechen _____. (*about the fire*)
6. Werner, spiel jetzt nicht _____! (*with the children*)
7. Er kennt Frau Klein _____. (*since July*)
8. Der Bus fährt _____. (*from Cologne to Dortmund*)
9. Wir gehen gleich _____. (*home*)

**B.** *Complete the sentence by using either* **zu Hause** *or* **nach Hause.**

1. Ich bin heute abend _____.
2. Das Kind geht gerade _____.
3. Der Student ißt vielleicht _____.
4. Heute abend fahre ich _____.

---

## III. Special noun declensions

Although most nouns do not add any endings in the nominative, accusative, and dative singular, certain masculine nouns add **-en** to all cases *except* the nominative singular. These nouns maintain the **-en** ending throughout the plural. In this group are **der Student, der Mensch, der Präsident** (*president*), **der Tourist** (*tourist*), and **der Junge**[1] (*boy*).

|  | SINGULAR | PLURAL |
|------|-----------------|------------------|
| *nom.* | der Student | die Studenten |
| *acc.* | den Studenten | die Studenten |
| *dat.* | dem Studenten | den Studenten |

*Special masculine declension*

---

[1] A frequently used plural of **der Junge** is **die Jungens** (*boys*); **die Jungen** nowadays primarily means *the young.*

The common noun **der Herr** deviates slightly from this special declension; it adds **-n** in the accusative and dative singular, and **-en** in all plural forms.

*Declension:* **der Herr**

|  | SINGULAR | PLURAL |
|------|----------|--------|
| *nom.* | der Herr | die Herren |
| *acc.* | den Herr**n** | die Herren |
| *dat.* | dem Herr**n** | den Herren |

## Check Your Comprehension

*Use the appropriate case of the noun in parentheses.*

1. Wir bringen _____ die Gitarre. (*der Student*)
2. Kennst du _____? (*der Mensch*)
3. Wo sind _____? (*die Herren*)
4. Sag _____, ich gehe nach Hause. (*der Junge*)
5. Fräulein Schell sucht _____. (*der Student*)
6. Renate, gib _____ das Geld! (*der Busfahrer*)
7. Er spricht mit _____. (*die Touristen*)
8. Wir sehen _____ nicht. (*der Präsident*)

## USEFUL PHRASES

| | |
|---|---|
| **Bitte sehr?** | { *What can I do for you?* <br> { *May I help you?* |
| **Moment bitte!** | *One moment, please.* |
| **Das ist nicht gerade billig.** | *That is not particularly cheap.* |
| **zu Hause sein** | *to be (at) home* |
| **nach Hause gehen** | *to go home* |
| **Wie ist es mit . . . ?** | *How about . . . ?* |

## CONVERSATION

## *Das Studentenzimmer*

*Heinz ist in Köln zu Hause, aber er studiert in Marburg. Er sucht ein Zimmer. Er liest die Zeitung und geht dann zum Vermittlungsbüro.°* ° *rental agency*
*Dort spricht er mit Fräulein Schell.*

FRL.[1] SCHELL Guten Morgen! Bitte sehr?
HEINZ Ich bin Student hier in Marburg und suche ein Zimmer.
FRL. SCHELL Wieviel möchten° Sie monatlich bezahlen? *would like to*
HEINZ Ungefähr zweihundert Mark monatlich.
FRL. SCHELL Moment bitte! Wie ist es mit einem Zimmer direkt bei der Universität? Es kostet zweihundertvierzig Mark mit Heizung.° *heat*
HEINZ Das ist nicht gerade billig! Ist das mit einer Kochgelegenheit?° *cooking facilities*
FRL. SCHELL Ja, ich bin sicher.
HEINZ Hat das Zimmer auch eine Dusche oder ein Bad?
FRL. SCHELL Nein, aber es hat ein Waschbecken.

---

[1] **Frl.** is the abbreviation for **Fräulein.**

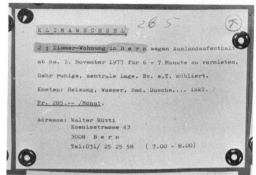

HEINZ Und wie ist es mit der Toilette?

FRL. SCHELL Sie ist direkt beim Zimmer.

HEINZ Nicht schlecht! Wie ist die Adresse, bitte?

FRL. SCHELL Frau Becker, Lindenstraße fünf. Beim Hindenburg-Platz.[2]

HEINZ Danke! Was kostet das?

FRL. SCHELL Acht Mark. (*Sie bringt dem Studenten ein Formular.°*) Unter-   *form (sheet)*
schreiben° Sie bitte das Formular und geben Sie es Frau Becker!   *sign*

*Heinz unterschreibt und bezahlt.*

HEINZ Vielen Dank! Auf Wiedersehen!

*Heinz geht nach Hause.*

---

[2] Named for Paul von Hindenburg (1847–1934), a famous general who became president
of the German Republic in 1925, but was unable to stem the rising tide of Nazism.

## QUESTIONS

1. Wo ist Heinz zu Hause?
2. Was liest Heinz?
3. Was sucht er?
4. Wohin geht Heinz, und mit wem spricht er dort?
5. Wieviel möchte Heinz monatlich bezahlen?
6. Hat das Zimmer bei der Universität Heizung?
7. Was ist direkt beim Zimmer?
8. Wieviel bezahlt Heinz beim Vermittlungsbüro?
9. Wo sind Sie zu Hause?
10. Haben Sie ein Zimmer mit Heizung?
11. Ist es billig oder teuer?
12. Wieviel bezahlen Sie monatlich?
13. Hat das Zimmer eine Dusche oder ein Bad oder ein Waschbecken?
14. Ist es direkt bei der Universität?

 **PRACTICE**

**A.** *Substitute the items in parentheses for the noun in italics and make the necessary changes. Note that some substitutions are singular and some plural.*

1. Bringt ihr *der Frau* das Gepäck?
   (*Fräulein/Freundin/Mädchen, pl./Studenten/Junge*)
2. Zeigst du *dem Fräulein* das Haus?
   (*Busfahrer, pl./Kinder/Freund/Herren/Mädchen, sing./Polizei*)
3. Wir öffnen *einem Studenten* immer die Tür.
   (*Mädchen, sing./Studentin/Freund/Frauen/Kinder/Freundinnen*)

**B.** *Form sentences with the following elements. Be careful to use the right case ending. First form a question and then an answer.*

EXAMPLE: er/geben/der Herr/das Geld.
       **Gibt er dem Herrn das Geld?**
       **Ja, er gibt dem Herrn das Geld.**

1. das Mädchen/bestellen/die Freunde (*or* die Freundin)/ein Buch.
2. der Busfahrer/zeigen/die Studentin (*or* der Student)/die Haltestelle.
3. das Kind/bringen/der Mann (*or* der Herr)/die Zeitung.
4. der Herr/öffnen/die Frauen (*or* das Fräulein)/die Tür.
5. der Student/geben/die Studentinnen (*or* die Männer)/das Geld.

**C.** *Substitute the noun in parentheses for the noun in italics, and make the necessary changes.*

1. Außer *der Zeitung* bringt er Paul ein Buch. (*Geld*)
2. Ich gehe sicher *zur Polizei*. (*Café*)
3. Der Freund fährt mit *dem Bus*. (*Auto*)
4. Er kommt aus *der Bibliothek*. (*Zimmer*)
5. Sie wohnt nicht bei *der Universität*. (*Flugplatz*)

**D.** *Supply the appropriate expression, either* **zu Hause** *or* **nach Hause.**

1. Heute abend sind wir _____.
2. Kommt ihr bald _____?
3. Fahren wir jetzt _____?
4. Das Mädchen ist _____.
5. Herr und Frau Müller sind heute nicht _____.

**E.** *Substitute or add each phrase as it is introduced into the previous sentence and make any necessary structural changes.*

Öffnen Sie bitte dem Fräulein die Tür!
_____ Herr _____!
_____ das Zimmer!
_____ Junge _____!
_____ das Buch!
Bringen _____!
_____ einen Kaffee!
Gib _____!

**F.** *Answer the following questions.*

1. Bei wem wohnen Sie?
2. Wohnen Sie direkt bei einer Bus-Haltestelle?
3. Fahren Sie oft mit dem Bus? Wohin?
4. Gehen Sie heute abend nach Hause?
5. Kommen Sie morgen zur Universität?
6. Mit wem kommen Sie zur Universität?
7. Studieren Sie oder essen Sie nach der Klasse?
8. Gehen Sie oft zur Bibliothek? Was finden Sie da?
9. Geben Sie manchmal Freunden Geld?

**G.** *Now ask your neighbor the same questions in the* **du** *form and get an answer.*

**H.** *Give the English equivalent of the following sentences.*

1. Geht ihr jetzt mit dem Studenten nach Hause?
2. Bezahlen Sie bitte das Geld monatlich!

*Salzburg*

3. Beim Bahnhof finden Sie ein Zimmer mit Bad.
4. Er bestellt den Touristen kein Bier.
5. Wir suchen den Herren ein Hotel.

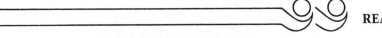

**GUIDED CONVERSATION**

Ask your neighbor to describe his or her living quarters. Ask whether there is a bath or shower or wash basin. Ask for the location in terms of what is near. Inquire with whom he or she shares quarters, what means of transportation is available to go to the university, and what the monthly rent is.

**READING**

## „Zum weißen Rößl"[1]

Susan und Lynn wohnen in Amerika und reisen seit Juni in Europa. Sie kommen mit dem Zug aus München in Salzburg (Österreich) an. Da finden sie viele Touristen, denn° in Salzburg sind das Geburtshaus° von Mozart, Schloß° Mirabell, die Feste° Hohensalzburg und Kirchen aus dem Barock.°

for
the house of birth / castle / fortress
in the baroque style

[1] The name of the hotel means "At the Little White Horse."

Zuerst suchen sie ein Hotel. Es gibt viele Hotels in Salzburg, aber sie sind nicht gerade billig. Der Herr bei der Zimmervermittlung° sagt den Amerikanerinnen, das Gasthaus „Zum weißen Rößl" ist nicht zu groß oder zu teuer. Es liegt nicht zu weit von der Stadtmitte beim Mozart-Platz. Susan und Lynn fahren mit dem Bus vom Bahnhof zum Gasthaus.

    *room accommodation service*

    Nach ein paar Minuten kommen sie beim Gasthaus an. Sie sehen ein Schild bei der Tür—„Zimmer frei". Lynn liest die Worte „Zimmer frei" laut° und Susan sagt sofort: „Nein, nein, das bedeutet nicht, es kostet nichts; das bedeutet, ein Zimmer ist noch frei". Das Haus ist hübsch, es hat auch einen Garten.

    *aloud*

Die Besitzerin°, eine Frau Strauß, empfängt° die Studentinnen bei der Tür. Susan und Lynn unterschreiben die Formulare°. Dann fragen sie nach dem Schlüssel und gehen die Treppe hinauf. Sie haben Zimmer Nummer neun.

owner / receives
forms

Das Zimmer ist nicht groß aber sehr hübsch. Beim Fenster stehen ein Tisch mit zwei Stühlen und ein Sessel. Rechts von der Tür steht ein Doppelbett, es ist sehr groß und alt. Links von der Tür ist das Waschbecken. Susan denkt, außer dem Bad und der Toilette ist alles hier. Sie stellen das Gepäck in die Ecke und öffnen die Koffer.

Dann verlassen sie das Zimmer und machen die Tür zu. Rechts von Zimmer Nummer neun sehen sie das Badezimmer mit Dusche. Bei dem Badezimmer ist ein Telefon. Die Toilette ist auch da, mit einem Schild bei der Tür—„WC".[2] Das Gasthaus hat nur ein Badezimmer und eine Toilette pro Etage°, aber das ist genug.

per floor

Sie gehen die Treppe hinunter und geben Frau Strauß den Zimmerschlüssel. Dann verlassen sie das Gasthaus und gehen zum Abendessen.

## Questions

1. Seit wann reisen Susan und Lynn in Europa?
2. Wohin fahren sie?
3. Wo liegt Salzburg?
4. Was suchen die zwei Studentinnen zuerst?
5. Was sagt der Herr von der Zimmervermittlung?
6. Wo liegt das Gasthaus?
7. Nehmen die Mädchen einen Zug oder einen Bus zum Gasthaus?
8. Was bedeutet das Schild „Zimmer frei"?
9. Wer empfängt die zwei Studentinnen?
10. Wie ist das Zimmer?
11. Was finden sie da?
12. Wie ist das Bett?

[2] Derived from the English *watercloset*; pronounced *veh-tseh*.

13. Was stellen sie in die Ecke?
14. Wohin gehen sie jetzt?
15. Wem geben die Studentinnen den Schlüssel?

---

**VOCABULARY DEVELOPMENT**

**A.** The adverb derived from **der Monat** (*month*) is **monatlich** (*monthly*). Similar constructions:

| | |
|---|---|
| die Stunde (*hour*) | stündlich |
| der Tag (*day*) | täglich |
| die Woche (*week*) | wöchentlich |
| das Jahr (*year*) | jährlich |

Ask your neighbor how much he or she pays for a room per day, per week, per month, per year.

**B.** The expression **es gibt,** meaning *there is, there are,* is used frequently.

| | |
|---|---|
| In Salzburg gibt es viele Gasthäuser. | *In Salzburg there are many inns.* |
| In München gibt es viel Bier. | *In Munich there is lots of beer.* |

But by itself the question **Was gibt es?** (often abbreviated as **Was gibt's?**) means *What's the matter? What's happening?* What then would be the meaning of: **Was gibt's heute zum Abendessen?**

The shades of meaning of this expression have to be carefully observed through context.

**C.** The word for *meal* in German is **das Essen.** Here are the names of the three main meals:

| | |
|---|---|
| das Frühstück, -e | *breakfast* |
| das Mittagessen, - | *lunch, dinner* |
| das Abendessen, - | *dinner, supper* |

**Der Mittag** means *noon,* therefore **das Mittagessen** is the midday meal, whether one calls it lunch or dinner. Similarly, **der Abend** means *evening,* so **das Abendessen** is the evening meal, whether one calls it dinner or supper.

The prepositions **bei** and **zu** are often used with these words, meaning *at* and *for,* respectively.

> **Beim** Frühstück liest er die Zeitung.     *He reads the paper at breakfast.*
>
> **Zum** Frühstück essen die Deutschen Brötchen und trinken Kaffee.     *For breakfast the Germans have rolls and coffee.*

Ask some classmates if they read books or papers or talk a lot at breakfast. Ask them what they have for breakfast, lunch, or dinner. In addition to other words that you have had, these words will help in the answers.

| | | | |
|---|---|---|---|
| das Brot, -e | *bread* | die Kartoffel, -n | *potato* |
| das Brötchen, - | *roll* | die Milch | *milk* |
| das Ei, -er | *egg* | das Obst | *fruit* |
| der Fisch, -e | *fish* | der Salat, -e | *salad* |
| das Fleisch | *meat* | die Suppe, -n | *soup* |
| das Gemüse, - | *vegetable* | | |

## REVIEW EXERCISES

**A.** *Express in German.*

1. Karl drives from Hamburg to Berlin.
2. The girls give the key to Mr. Klein.
3. We have no rooms today.
4. Are you (*du*) going home tonight?
5. Please, give (*du*) the address to the boy.
6. Order Mr. Schmidt a beer, please.
7. First we'll talk with the tourists.
8. Are you (*Sie*) coming from the railroad station?
9. The girls live at Mr. and Mrs. Braun's.
10. There is everything here except hotels and an airport.
11. Show (*Sie*) the (girl) students the garden.
12. When are you (*ihr*) home?

**B.** *Use the following sentence elements in a question and an answer. Watch the word order and the case endings and use the right pronoun for the subject in the answer:*

EXAMPLE: das Mädchen/geben/der Brief/der Herr
   **Gibt das Mädchen dem Herrn den Brief?**
   **Ja, es gibt dem Herrn den Brief.**

1. der Freund/bezahlen/viel Geld/der Busfahrer.
2. du/sehen/die Busfahrerin (*pl.*).
3. die Mädchen/sprechen/von/die Amerikanerin (*pl.*).
4. Barbara/zeigen/das Auto/der Freund.
5. ich/geben/die Zeitung/das Fräulein.
6. du/kennen/der Herr.
7. Herr Meyer/lesen/ein Buch.
8. ihr/fahren/zu/der Flugplatz.

**C.** *Complete the following sentences with the appropriate form of the suggested definite or indefinite article or* **kein.** *Make any contractions that are possible.*

1. D———— Fräulein gibt d———— Mann e———— Schlüssel.
2. E———— Busfahrer fährt d———— Bus zu d———— Flugplatz.
3. D———— Frau öffnet e———— Koffer.
4. Franz kauft d———— Freundin k———— Gitarre.
5. Er gibt e———— Taxifahrer e———— paar Zigaretten.
6. Außer d———— Bad findet d———— Mädchen alles.
7. D———— Mädchen da drüben kennen d———— Bücher nicht.
8. Bei d———— Bett steht k———— Tisch.
9. D———— Herren kommen d———— Treppe herunter.
10. E———— Studenten zeigt d———— Fräulein d———— Stadt.
11. Links von d———— Fenster steht e———— Doppelbett.
12. Leider liegen d———— Gasthäuser weit von d———— Kirche.

**GUIDED COMPOSITION**

Write a few sentences about how you would look for a hotel room. Also describe in detail what kind of accommodations you would expect. Should the room be cheap or expensive, and what should its location be?

## Easily recognized words

| | | |
|---|---|---|
| die | **Adresse, -n** | *address* |
| (das) | **Europa** | *Europe* |
| das | **Gasthaus, ⸚er** | *inn, small hotel* |
| das | **Haus, ⸚er** | *house* |
| die | **Mark** | *mark: the unit of German currency* |
| der | **Präsident, -en** | *president* |
| der | **Tourist, -en** | *tourist* |
| die | **Universität, -en** | *university* |

| | | |
|---|---|---|
| das | **Abendessen, -** | *supper, dinner* |
| das | **Bad, ⸚er** | *bath* |
| das | **Badezimmer, -** | *bathroom* |
| der | **Bahnhof, ⸚e** | *railroad station* |
| das | **Bett, -en** | *bed* |
| das | **Doppelbett, -en** | *double bed* |
| die | **Dusche, -n** | *shower* |
| die | **Ecke, -n** | *corner* |
| das | **Fenster, -** | *window* |
| der | **Garten, ⸚** | *garden* |
| das | **Jahr, -e** | *year* |
| der | **Junge, -ns** | *boy* |
| die | **Kirche, -n** | *church* |
| der | **Koffer, -** | *suitcase* |
| der | **Monat, -e** | *month* |
| das | **Schild, -er** | *sign* |
| der | **Schlüssel, -** | *key* |
| der | **Sessel, -** | *armchair* |
| die | **Stadt, ⸚e** | *city* |
| die | **Stadtmitte** | *city center* |
| der | **Stuhl, ⸚e** | *chair* |
| der | **Tisch, -e** | *table* |
| die | **Toilette, -n** | *lavatory, toilet* |
| das | **Waschbecken, -** | *wash basin, sink* |
| die | **Woche, -n** | *week* |
| das | **Wort, -e** | *word* |

See also the words for meals and food on pp. 82–83.

| | | |
|---|---|---|
| der | **Zug, ⸚e** | *train* |

| | |
|---|---|
| **bedeuten** | *to have the meaning, mean* |
| **bezahlen** | *to pay* |
| **bringen** | *to bring* |
| **fragen nach** | *ask for* |
| **geben, gibt** | *to give;* **es gibt** *there is, there are* |
| **kosten** | *to cost* |
| **liegen** | *to lie, be situated* |
| **reisen** | *to travel* |
| **stellen** | *to put, set* |
| **unterschreiben** | *to sign* |
| **wohnen** | *to reside, live* |
| **zeigen** | *to show* |

| | |
|---|---|
| **billig** | *cheap* |
| **direkt** | *directly, right* |
| **groß** | *big, large* |
| **hübsch** | *attractive, pretty* |
| **jährlich** | *yearly* |
| **monatlich** | *monthly, per month* |
| **nichts** | *nothing* |
| **noch** | *yet, still* |
| **sofort** | *at once* |
| **stündlich** | *hourly* |
| **täglich** | *daily* |
| **teuer** | *expensive* |
| **ungefähr** | *approximately* |
| **viele** | *many* |
| **weit** | *far* |
| **wieviel** | *how much;* **wieviele** *how many* |
| **wöchentlich** | *weekly* |
| **zu** | *too (in excess of)* |
| **zuerst** | *first of all, at first* |

See also the prepositions on pp. 71–72.

5

## I

Ich **habe** ein Auto **gekauft.**
*I have bought a car.*

Ich **habe** Kaffee **getrunken.**
*I drank coffee.*

Der Zug **hat angehalten.**
*The train stopped.*

Du **hast** alles wieder **vergessen.**
*You forgot everything again.*

Warum **ist** er nicht **gekommen**?
*Why didn't he come?*

Kürzlich **ist** bei uns viel **passiert.**
*A lot has happened to us recently.*

**Seit** Montag **arbeitet** er wieder.
*He's been working again since Monday.*

**II**

Hast du **ihn** vergessen?
*Did you forget him?*

Ich kenne **dich.**
*I know you.*

Gib **mir** eine Antwort!
*Give me an answer.*

Kennst du **mich**?
*Do you know me?*

**III**

Ich kenne ihn **nicht.**
*I don't know him.*

Das Auto ist **nicht** neu.
*The car isn't new.*

Frl. Schell ist **nicht** zu Hause.
*Miss Schell isn't at home.*

Die Kinder fahren **nicht** ab.
*The children are not leaving.*

Sind die Männer **nicht** angekommen?
*Haven't the men arrived?*

Frau Steinhoff hat die Schlüssel **nicht.**
*Mrs. Steinhoff doesn't have the keys.*

**GRAMMAR EXPLANATION**

### I. Present perfect tense

German and English have several tenses to express past time; these tenses are used differently in the two languages and must be studied with care. This chapter introduces the present perfect tense.

**A.** *Formation*

The present perfect tense consists of two parts: (1) the present tense of an auxiliary verb, and (2) the past participle of the principal verb. For this reason, it is often called a compound tense. For most verbs, the auxiliary is **haben.**

|  | SINGULAR | PLURAL |
|---|---|---|
| *1st* | ich habe gekauft | wir haben gekauft |
| *2nd (fam.)* | du hast gekauft | ihr habt gekauft |
| *3rd* | er<br>sie } hat gekauft<br>es | sie haben gekauft |
| *2nd (formal)* | Sie haben gekauft | Sie haben gekauft |

*Present perfect:* **kaufen**
*(to buy)*

Ich habe ein Auto gekauft.　　　{ *I have bought a car.*
　　　　　　　　　　　　　　　{ *I bought a car.*

Notice that the past participle is placed at the end of the clause.

German verbs can be classified as weak, irregular weak, or strong. These three types form the past participle differently.

1. *Weak verbs* form the past participle by placing the unchanged verb stem within the frame **ge—t.**

| INFINITIVE | PAST PARTICIPLE |
|---|---|
| kaufen *to buy* | gekauft *bought* |
| haben *to have* | gehabt *had* |
| sagen *to say* | gesagt *said* |

Note that **haben** is conjugated with itself:

**Er hat viel Gepäck gehabt.**　　　*He had a lot of luggage.*

If the stem of a weak verb ends in **-d** or **-t,** as in **arbeiten** (*to work*), or in **-m** or **-n** when preceded by a consonant other than **l** and **r**, as in **öffnen** (*to open*), **-e-** is inserted between the stem and the **-t** of the participle to make the word easier to pronounce: **gear**beit**et, ge**öffn**et.** Verbs ending in **-ieren** do not add **ge-** to the past participle, but always take the suffix **-t.**

| INFINITIVE | PAST PARTICIPLE |
|---|---|
| studieren *to study* | studiert *studied* |
| passieren *to happen* | passiert *happened* |

2. *Irregular weak verbs* form the past participle by placing a changed form of the stem within the frame **ge—t.** These verbs are few in number, and include:

| INFINITIVE | | PAST PARTICIPLE | |
|---|---|---|---|
| brennen | *to burn* | gebrannt | *burned* |
| bringen | *to bring* | gebracht | *brought* |
| denken | *to think* | gedacht | *thought* |
| kennen | *to know* | gekannt | *known* |

In the chapter and end vocabularies, the past participles of all irregular weak verbs are indicated.

## Check your comprehension

**A.** *Form the past participles of the following weak verbs:*

1. zeigen
2. hören
3. protestieren
4. fragen
5. suchen
6. rauchen
7. diskutieren
8. kosten
9. wohnen
10. spielen

**B.** *Answer the following questions affirmatively in the present perfect tense.*

EXAMPLE: Haben Sie ein Auto gekauft?
**Ja, ich habe ein Auto gekauft.**

1. Hast du eine Zigarette geraucht?
2. Hat er viel protestiert?
3. Habt ihr ein Problem gehabt?
4. Haben Sie den Schlüssel gebracht?
5. Haben sie bei einem Flugplatz gewohnt?
6. Hast du manchmal über Politik diskutiert?
7. Hat er den Mann gekannt?
8. Hat sie oft Karten gespielt?

3. *Strong verbs* form the past participle by placing a changed form of the stem, or occasionally the unchanged stem, within the frame **ge—en: trinken** (*to drink*), **getrunken** (*drunk*); **geben** (*to give*), **gegeben** (*given*).

Since the stem changes are not predictable, you must memorize the past participle of each verb when you learn the infinitive. Here are some strong verbs that you have already encountered.

| INFINITIVE | | PAST PARTICIPLE | |
|---|---|---|---|
| bitten (um) | *to ask (for)* | gebeten | *asked* |
| essen | *to eat* | gegessen | *eaten* |
| finden | *to find* | gefunden | *found* |
| geben | *to give* | gegeben | *given* |
| halten | *to stop* | gehalten | *stopped* |
| heißen | *to be called* | geheißen | *been called* |
| lassen | *to let* | gelassen | *let* |
| lesen | *to read* | gelesen | *read* |
| liegen | *to lie, be situated* | gelegen | *lain* |
| nehmen | *to take* | genommen | *taken* |
| sehen | *to see* | gesehen | *seen* |
| sprechen | *to speak* | gesprochen | *spoken* |
| stehen | *to stand* | gestanden | *stood* |
| trinken | *to drink* | getrunken | *drunk* |

In the chapter and end vocabularies, the past participles of all strong verbs are indicated.

## Check your comprehension

*Change the following sentences to the present perfect tense. Pay special attention to the position of the past participle.*

EXAMPLE: Wir trinken Milch.
**Wir haben Milch getrunken.**

1. Wir nehmen ein Taxi.
2. Er sieht das Feuer.
3. Ich bitte um Auskunft.
4. Findest du ein Zimmer?
5. Warum spricht sie mit dem Busfahrer?
6. Eßt ihr viel Fleisch?
7. Wir geben dem Herrn das Geld.
8. Sie lesen Bücher von Thomas Mann.
9. Warum hält der Zug?
10. Wo steht das Bett?

**B.** *Past participles of verbs with prefixes*

German has two types of prefix verbs: (1) the verbs with a separable prefix discussed in Chapter 3: **abfahren, einsteigen,** etc.; and (2) the verbs with an inseparable prefix, such as **be-, emp-, ent-, er-, ge-, ver-,** and **zer-: bestellen, vergessen,** etc. Inseparable prefixes always remain attached to the verb.

| *separable prefix* | zu·machen | Er **macht** das Fenster **zu.** |
| *inseparable prefix* | bestellen | Sie **bestellt** eine Tasse Tee. |

Verbs with separable prefixes are stressed on the prefix: **éinsteigen.** But verbs with inseparable prefixes are stressed on the stem: **bestéllen, vergéssen.**

Both separable and inseparable prefix verbs are found among the weak, irregular weak, and strong verbs. The formation of their past participle differs from the normal pattern.

1. *Verbs with separable prefixes* insert the **ge-** of the past participle between the separable prefix and the stem.

| | INFINITIVE | PAST PARTICIPLE |
|---|---|---|
| *weak* | zu·machen *to close* | zugemacht |
| *irreg. weak* | herein·bringen *to bring in* | hereingebracht |
| | an·halten *to stop* | angehalten |
| *strong* | weiter·lesen *to go on reading* | weitergelesen |
| | weiter·sprechen *to go on speaking* | weitergesprochen |

Der Zug hat angehalten.　　　　　*The train stopped.*

2. *Verbs with inseparable prefixes* do not add **ge-** to the past participle.

| | INFINITIVE | PAST PARTICIPLE |
|---|---|---|
| *weak* | bezahlen *to pay* | bezahlt |
| *irreg. weak* | erkennen *to recognize* | erkannt |
| | bekommen *to get, receive* | bekommen |
| *strong* | vergessen *to forget* | vergessen |
| | verlassen *to leave* | verlassen |

Du hast alles vergessen.　　　　　*You forgot everything.*

## Check your comprehension

**A.** *Form the past participles of the following prefix verbs.*

1. erkennen
2. zumachen
3. hereinbringen
4. bekommen
5. anhalten

6. verlassen
7. bedeuten
8. weiterlesen
9. bezahlen
10. vergessen

**B.** *Change the following sentences to the present perfect tense. Pay special attention to the position of the past participle.*

EXAMPLE: Wir bestellen eine Tasse Kaffee.
**Wir haben eine Tasse Kaffee bestellt.**

1. Er vergißt die Adresse.
2. Die Studentin liest weiter.
3. Der Busfahrer erkennt die Männer.
4. Was bedeutet das Schild?
5. Wann verlassen sie das Hotel?
6. Hier hält der Zug an.
7. Anna macht die Fenster zu.
8. Was bringt sie herein?
9. Fräulein Lerner bezahlt dem Herrn sechs Mark.

## C. *Verbs taking* **sein** *as an auxiliary*

Though most verbs use the auxiliary **haben** to form the present perfect tense, some verbs use the auxiliary **sein.** To use **sein** as the auxiliary, a verb must meet two criteria: (1) it must not take a direct object (that is, it must be intransitive), and (2) it must indicate a change in the position or condition of the subject.

|  | SINGULAR | PLURAL |
|---|---|---|
| *1st* | ich bin gekommen | wir sind gekommen |
| *2nd (fam.)* | du bist gekommen | ihr seid gekommen |
| *3rd* | er<br>sie } ist gekommen<br>es | sie sind gekommen |
| *2nd (formal)* | Sie sind gekommen | Sie sind gekommen |

*Present perfect:*
**kommen** *(to come)*

Warum ist er gekommen? { *Why did he come?* { *Why has he come?*

Prefix verbs that take **sein** form the past participle in the same way as prefix verbs that take **haben: ab·fahren** (*to depart*), **ist abgefahren.**

Verbs taking **sein** include the following:

| INFINITIVE | | PAST PARTICIPLE |
|---|---|---|
| ab·fahren | *to depart* | ist abgefahren |
| an·kommen | *to arrive* | ist angekommen |
| aus·steigen | *to get out* | ist ausgestiegen |
| ein·steigen | *to get in* | ist eingestiegen |
| fahren | *to drive* | ist gefahren |
| gehen | *to go* | ist gegangen |
| herunter·kommen | *to come down* | ist heruntergekommen |
| hinunter·gehen | *to go down* | ist hinuntergegangen |
| kommen | *to come* | ist gekommen |
| laufen | *to run* | ist gelaufen |
| passieren | *to happen* | ist passiert |
| reisen | *to travel* | ist gereist |
| weiter·fahren | *to drive on* | ist weitergefahren |
| weiter·gehen | *to move on* | ist weitergegangen |
| zurück·laufen | *to run back* | ist zurückgelaufen |

Though they do not indicate movement or change, the auxiliary verb **sein** (*to be*), when used as a principal verb, and the verb **bleiben** (*to stay*) are both conjugated with **sein.**

Ich bin dort gewesen.     *I have been there.*
Er ist hier geblieben.     *He's stayed here.*

To avoid asking oneself constantly whether to use **sein** or **haben,** memorize the auxiliary along with the past participle. In the vocabularies of this book, verbs taking **sein** have their past participles indicated thus: **fahren, ist gefahren.** Verbs taking **haben** do not have the auxiliary indicated: **trinken, getrunken.**

## Check your comprehension

**A.** *Answer the following questions affirmatively in the present perfect tense.*

EXAMPLE: Bist du kürzlich angekommen?
  **Ja, ich bin kürzlich angekommen.**

1. Sind Sie sofort weitergegangen?
2. Bist du ungefähr vier Wochen geblieben?
3. Ist Herr Müller mit dem Zug gefahren?
4. Seid ihr endlich hinuntergegangen?
5. Sind wir auch dort gewesen?
6. Ist Jürgen schnell zurückgelaufen?
7. Bist du zuerst ausgestiegen?
8. Sind die Busse gerade abgefahren?

**B.** *Change the following sentences to the present perfect tense. Pay special attention to the choice of the auxiliary verb.*

EXAMPLE: Wir fahren ab.
  **Wir sind abgefahren.**

  Wieviel bezahlt das Mädchen?
  **Wieviel hat das Mädchen bezahlt?**

1. Wo essen Sie?
2. Ich fahre sofort nach links.
3. Leider hält der Zug an.
4. Die Menschen kommen von der Stadtmitte.
5. Plötzlich erkennt sie die Amerikanerin.
6. Hans geht direkt zum Bahnhof.
7. Frau Keller findet kein Gasthaus.
8. Immer bittet er um Geld.

## D. Use of the present perfect tense

In German the present perfect is most often used as a "conversational past" in the spoken language and in informal writing, such as a letter to a friend. It denotes an action that was completed at a point in the past, and is rendered by the English past tense.

Ich habe das Auto gesehen.  *I saw the car.*
Ich bin schnell nach links gefahren.  *I quickly drove to the left.*

The present perfect may also emphasize a stretch, rather than a point, of time in the past. This occurs when an action or situation starting in the past lasts or has an effect right up to the more recent past or the present. In this case the present perfect carries the same connotation in German as in English.

Kürzlich ist bei uns viel passiert.     *A lot has happened to us recently.*

When such a stretch of time is expressed, the present perfect is often used with **schon** (*already*) in the affirmative and **noch nicht** (*not yet*) in the negative.

Haben Sie schon gegessen?     *Have you already eaten?*
Nein, ich habe noch nicht geges-     *No, I have not yet eaten.*
sen.

Compare the two uses of the present perfect:

PAST TIME
*Point of time:* ●     PRESENT TIME
   Ich **habe** das Auto **gesehen.**
   *I saw the car.*

*Stretch of time:* ━━━▶
   Kürzlich **ist** bei uns viel **passiert.**
   *A lot has happened to us recently*

In many instances the time span expressed stretches through the present into the future. In that case, German uses the present tense, often with the preposition **seit,** whereas English uses the present perfect tense.

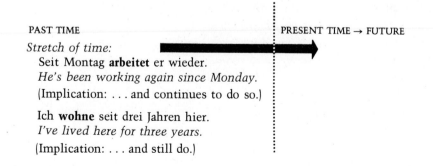

PAST TIME
*Stretch of time:*     PRESENT TIME → FUTURE
   Seit Montag **arbeitet** er wieder.
   *He's been working again since Monday.*
   (Implication: . . . and continues to do so.)

   Ich **wohne** seit drei Jahren hier.
   *I've lived here for three years.*
   (Implication: . . . and still do.)

*Check your comprehension*

*Express in German.*

1. We found a hotel.
2. You (*du*) forgot the newspaper.
3. I have already read the book.
4. What happened here?
5. The children recognized the man.
6. The students have lived here for four years.
7. Paul has been reading for ten minutes.
8. Where did the gentlemen get off?

## II. Personal pronouns: accusative and dative cases

The personal pronouns, introduced in the nominative case in Chapter 1, also have accusative and dative case forms.

SINGULAR

| | | |
|---|---|---|
| *Acc.* | Er kennt **mich** nicht. | *He doesn't know me.* |
| *Dat.* | Sie hat oft mit **mir** gesprochen. | *She often talked with me.* |
| *Acc.* | Er hat **dich** nicht gesehen. | *He didn't see you.* |
| *Dat.* | Sie schreibt **dir** oft. | *She writes (to) you often.* |
| *Acc.* | Er findet **ihn** nicht. | *He doesn't find him.* |
| *Dat.* | Sie hat { **ihm** / **ihr** } den Brief gegeben. | *She gave { him / her } the letter.* |

PLURAL

| | | |
|---|---|---|
| *Acc.* | Er sieht **uns** nicht. | *He doesn't see us.* |
| *Dat.* | Sie schreibt **uns** oft. | *She writes (to) us often.* |
| *Acc.* | Er hat **euch** nicht gesehen. | *He didn't see you.* |
| *Dat.* | Sie spricht oft mit **euch.** | *She talks with you often.* |
| *Acc.* | Er kennt **sie** nicht. | *He doesn't know them.* |
| *Dat.* | Sie trinken oft mit **ihnen.** | *They often drink with them.* |
| *Acc.* | Er kennt **Sie** nicht. | *He doesn't know you.* |
| *Dat.* | Sie schreibt **Ihnen** oft. | *She writes (to) you often.* |

Notice that in the first- and second-person plural, the pronouns are the same in the dative and accusative: **uns, euch.**

*Personal pronouns:
nominative, accusative,
and dative cases*

| SINGULAR | NOMINATIVE | ACCUSATIVE | DATIVE |
|---|---|---|---|
| *1st* | ich | mich | mir |
| *2nd (fam.)* | du | dich | dir |
| *3rd* | er<br>sie<br>es | ihn<br>sie<br>es | ihm<br>ihr<br>ihm |

| PLURAL | | | |
|---|---|---|---|
| *1st* | wir | **uns** | **uns** |
| *2nd (fam.)* | ihr | **euch** | **euch** |
| *3rd* | sie | sie | ihnen |

| *SINGULAR/PLURAL* | | | |
|---|---|---|---|
| *2nd (formal)* | Sie | Sie | Ihnen |

To determine the position of dative and accusative nouns and pronouns, the simplest rule is as follows: the dative precedes the accusative unless the accusative is a pronoun.

|  |  | DAT. | ACC. |
|---|---|---|---|
|  | Jürgen bezahlt | dem Mann | das Geld. |
|  | Jürgen bezahlt | ihm | das Geld. |
| *But:* |  | ACC. | DAT. |
|  | Jürgen bezahlt | es | dem Mann. |
|  | Jürgen bezahlt | es | ihm. |

## Check your comprehension

**A.** *Substitute the appropriate personal pronouns for all nouns. Watch the word order.*

1. Karl gibt dem Herrn die Zigarre.
2. Herr und Frau Schmidt bringen den Studenten den Tisch.
3. Der Busfahrer zeigt den Studentinnen die Haltestelle.
4. Gib dem Herrn die Adresse!
5. Bei Frau Schell wohnen drei Mädchen.
6. Wir haben den Mädchen den Koffer gebracht.

**B.** *Use the appropriate form of the pronoun for the nouns or pronouns given in parentheses.*

1. Ich kenne _____ nicht. (*das Gasthaus*)
2. Die Studentin sieht _____ nicht mal an. (*der Herr*)
3. Albert, zeig _____ _____! (*das Zimmer, die Frau*)
4. Kürzlich haben die Freunde _____ geschrieben. (*wir*)
5. Hans, spiel doch mit _____! (*die Kinder*)
6. Ich habe _____ _____ gegeben. (*der Schlüssel, der Student*)
7. Haben Sie _____ gelesen? (*die Zeitung*)

## III. Position of NICHT

The position of **nicht** (*not*) varies considerably in German. It should be gradually learned through careful observation. Here are a few useful guidelines.

1. **Nicht** is usually placed at the end of a sentence.

| | |
|---|---|
| Er kommt heute nicht. | *He's not coming today.* |
| Er verläßt sie nicht. | *He isn't leaving her.* |

But it precedes
(a) parts of verbs—that is, separable prefixes, and the past participle in the present perfect tense.

| | |
|---|---|
| Wir steigen nicht ein. | *We aren't getting in.* |
| Er ist gestern nicht angekommen. | *He didn't arrive yesterday.* |

(b) predicate adjectives and predicate nouns.

| | |
|---|---|
| Das Auto ist nicht neu. | *The car is not new.* |
| Er ist nicht Student. | *He isn't a student.* |

(c) prepositional phrases.

| | |
|---|---|
| Wir gehen nicht nach Hause. | *We aren't going home.* |

2. **Nicht** can also be placed before any element in the sentence that one wants to emphasize.

| | |
|---|---|
| Die Party ist nicht heute, sie ist morgen. | *The party isn't today, it's tomorrow.* |

## Check your comprehension

*Place* **nicht** *in the correct position within each sentence.*

1. Er hört.
2. Die Betten sind alt.
3. Die Studentinnen sind zu Hause.
4. Ich finde die Adresse.
5. Sie spricht sehr schnell.
6. Wir zeigen ihm die Kirche.
7. Wir arbeiten heute.
8. Hier steigen wir aus.
9. Haben Sie das Wort vergessen?
10. Ist er abgefahren?

## USEFUL PHRASES

| | |
|---|---|
| **Ich glaube, ja.** | *I think so.* |
| **Wie ist das passiert?** | *How did it happen?* |
| **Ich habe keine Ahnung.** | *I have no idea.* |

## CONVERSATION

### Vor Gericht°

STAATSANWALT° Herr Steinhoff, jetzt sagen Sie uns bitte: Wie ist der Unfall passiert?

STEINHOFF Ja, ich habe eine Party bei Freunden besucht.°

STAATSANWALT Was haben Sie denn[1] getrunken?

STEINHOFF Wir haben Wein, Bier oder Orangensaft getrunken.

STAATSANWALT Aha! Und Sie haben natürlich Orangensaft getrunken.

STEINHOFF Ich glaube, ja.

*in court*

*district attorney*

*went to*

---

[1] **Denn** is a "flavoring particle" that cannot be translated directly. It is frequently used to give a question more emphasis.

STAATSANWALT  Wie bitte?° Ich verstehe Sie nicht. Die Polizei hat Sie   *How is that?*
angehalten und eine Blutprobe° gemacht.   *blood test*

STEINHOFF  Das ist richtig.

STAATSANWALT  Haben Sie wirklich nur Orangensaft getrunken?

STEINHOFF  Jemand hat mir vielleicht etwas Wodka° hineingemischt,   *vodka*
aber ich habe nichts gemerkt.

STAATSANWALT  Herr Steinhoff, haben Sie es schon vergessen? Sie ha-
ben Staatseigentum° beschädigt!°   *public property | damaged*

STEINHOFF  Ach, Sie meinen den Baum?

STAATSANWALT  Ja, wie ist das eigentlich passiert?

STEINHOFF  Ein Volkswagen hat mich überholt, und ich bin schnell
nach links gefahren.

STAATSANWALT  Herr Steinhoff, aber der Baum hat rechts gestanden!

STEINHOFF  Dann habe ich ihn wahrscheinlich nicht gesehen.

STAATSANWALT  Warum nicht, Herr Steinhoff?

STEINHOFF  Ich habe keine Ahnung.

STAATSANWALT  Dann gebe ich Ihnen die Antwort. Sie haben leider
etwas zuviel Orangensaft im Blut° gehabt!   *in your blood*

## Questions

1. Wen hat Herr Steinhoff besucht?
2. Was hat er getrunken?
3. Was haben die Freunde von Herrn Steinhoff getrunken?
4. Wer hat Herrn Steinhoff angehalten?
5. Was hat jemand mit dem Orangensaft von Herrn Steinhoff gemacht?
6. Was hat Herr Steinhoff beschädigt?
7. Warum ist er schnell nach links gefahren?
8. Wo hat der Baum gestanden?
9. Hat Herr Steinhoff den Baum eigentlich gesehen?

10. Was hat er zuviel im Blut gehabt?
11. Haben Sie auch schon einen Unfall gehabt?
12. Trinken Sie viel Orangensaft?
13. Mischen Sie manchmal etwas Wodka hinein?

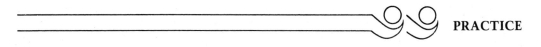 **PRACTICE**

**A.** *Change the sentences into the present perfect.*

1. Wie passiert der Unfall?
2. Ich besuche eine Party bei Freunden.
3. Was trinken Sie denn dort?
4. Wir trinken da Wein, Bier und Orangensaft.
5. Die Polizei hält Sie an.
6. Sie macht eine Blutprobe.
7. Ich merke nichts.
8. Da kommt plötzlich ein Volkswagen von rechts und überholt mich.
9. Trinken Sie den Wein wirklich nicht?
10. Mischt jemand etwas Wodka hinein?
11. Ich sehe den Baum nicht.
12. Sprechen Sie mit der Polizei?

**B.** *Substitute a personal pronoun for every noun in boldface.*

1. **Die Party** ist bei **den Freunden** in Hamburg gewesen.
2. Sprechen Sie Deutsch mit **der Studentin?**
3. **Die Polizei** hat **den Autofahrer** dort angehalten.
4. Sie gibt **den Kindern die Antwort.**
5. Was bedeuten **die Worte?**
6. Ich habe **die Bäume** gesehen.
7. Haben Sie **den Wein** wirklich getrunken?
8. Herr Klein ist bei **Karl** gewesen.
9. **Der Freund** hat **Heidi die Adresse** gegeben.
10. Hat **der Herr den Unfall** schon vergessen?

**C.** *Rewrite the sentences in B by inserting* **nicht.**

**D.** *Answer the following questions, substituting appropriate pronouns for nouns (or other pronouns) wherever possible.*

EXAMPLES: Sind die Freunde gestern bei Ihnen gewesen?
**Ja, sie sind gestern bei uns gewesen.**

Wohnt Sylvia bei Frau Meyer?
**Nein, sie wohnt nicht bei ihr.**

1. Hast du dem Herrn das Buch bezahlt?
2. Habt ihr Fräulein Müller das Zimmer gezeigt?
3. Sind die Freunde schon bei Ihnen angekommen?
4. Haben Sie die Adresse vergessen?
5. Kauft Fritz die Gitarre?
6. Sehen Sie die Kirche da drüben?
7. Hat Robert der Frau den Schlüssel gegeben?
8. Habt ihr den Salat schon gegessen?

**E.** *Change the sentences into the present perfect tense.*

1. Wir bleiben zu Hause.
2. Ein Volkswagen überholt uns.
3. Sehen Sie den Baum da drüben?
4. Wo passiert der Unfall von Herrn Steinhoff?
5. Trinken Sie keinen Orangensaft mit Wodka?
6. Das Auto kommt sehr schnell von links.
7. Der Student fährt heute abend nach Hause.
8. Ich besuche Freunde in Berlin.
9. Wir geben ihm eine Tasse Kaffee.
10. Wo bist du gerade?

**F.** *Complete the following text by supplying the appropriate personal pronoun in either the accusative or the dative case.*

Herr Steinhoff, jetzt sagen Sie es _____ (wir) endlich! Sie sind bei Freunden gewesen. Was haben Sie bei _____ (sie, pl.) gemacht? Die Freunde haben Sie doch gut gekannt. Ist der Wodka vielleicht von _____ (sie) gewesen? Ist das möglich? Sie kennen _____ (sie) besser als wir. Glauben Sie mir doch! (Sie) passiert wahrscheinlich nicht viel! Verstehen Sie _____ (iich)? Die Polizei hat _____ (Sie) angehalten und bei _____ (Sie) eine Blutprobe gemacht. Was ist das Resultat? Hier, lesen Sie _____ (es)! Sie sagen: „Ein Volkswagen hat _____ (ich) von rechts überholt." Ich sage _____ (Sie): Das ist nicht möglich!

**G.** *Answer the following questions in reference to yourself.*

1. Haben Sie gestern eine Party besucht?
2. Was haben Sie getrunken?
3. Mit wem haben Sie gesprochen?
4. Sind Sie mit dem Auto nach Hause gefahren?
5. Hat ein Volkswagen Sie überholt?
6. Hat die Polizei Sie angehalten?
7. Sind Sie sehr schnell gefahren?
8. Wer ist mit Ihnen gefahren?

**H.** *Now ask your neighbor the same questions in the* **du** *form and get an answer.*

**I.** *Give the English equivalent.*

1. Bei uns ist kürzlich sehr viel passiert.
2. Hast du das nicht gemerkt?
3. Ich arbeite seit zwei Jahren hier in Berlin.
4. Wie ist der Unfall eigentlich passiert?
5. Wahrscheinlich haben sie es ihr noch nicht geschrieben.

## GUIDED CONVERSATION

Exchange greetings with someone in your class, and ask if he or she has ever (**einmal**) had an accident. If so, ask what happened: where the accident happened, how it happened, why it happened. You might ask if he or she was driving a Volkswagen, went to a party, had anything to drink; also, if the police came and if they administered a blood test. You might tell about an accident you had or one that a friend of yours had.

## READING

## *Ein Brief*

Bonn, den 19. März

Liebe Elke, lieber Hans,

Schon lange habe ich Euch[1] keinen Brief geschrieben. Leider habe ich nie genug Zeit, und ich schreibe nicht gern.

Bei uns ist viel passiert. Anfang Februar ist Peter zwei Wochen krank gewesen. Er ist beim Skilaufen° hingefallen.° Resultat: Gehirnerschütterung.° Fünf Woehen hat er nicht gearbeitet. Aber seit Montag arbeitet er wieder. Außerdem hat Gisela Masern° bekommen. Deshalb habe ich natürlich viel Arbeit gehabt. Aber jetzt geht es auch ihr wieder besser.

Das Wetter bei uns ist furchtbar. Seit zwei Wochen regnet es. Wir sind oft zu Hause geblieben und haben Karten gespielt. Peter hat nicht gut gespielt. Er hat immer verloren. Er sagt, es ist die Gehirnerschütterung. Hoffentlich ist das Wetter bald wieder schön.

Aber die Nachrichten von uns sind nicht nur schlecht. Kürzlich

*(margin glosses:)* while skiing/fell — brain concussion — measles

---

[1] All second-person pronouns in a letter are capitalized.

sind wir bei Müllers gewesen. Dort haben wir die Kapps getroffen. Sie sind wirklich nett! Bei° viel Wein und Bier haben wir lange geredet. Er ist gerade aus Amerika zurückgekommen. Dort ist er in New York und Washington gewesen und hat schnell Boston besucht. Er hat sehr interessant erzählt. Leider hat er sonst° nicht viel gesehen, aber er glaubt, er kennt Amerika. Wir sind bis sehr spät bei Müllers geblieben. Peter und ich sind dann noch mit dem Auto nach Hause gefahren; das ist bei° dem Wetter gefährlich gewesen. Wir haben aber keinen Unfall gehabt.

    Noch eine° Nachricht: wir haben gerade Möbel für das Schlafzimmer und Wohnzimmer gekauft. Sehr schön, aber natürlich ist alles furchtbar teuer gewesen. Leider ist heutzutage nichts billig.

    Hoffentlich seid Ihr alle gesund geblieben. Ich habe lange nichts von Euch gehört. Schreibt mir bald mal wieder.

Seid herzlich gegrüßt

P.S. Grüße auch von Peter.

*Jutta*

*Margin glosses:* While drinking · otherwise · because of · another

## Questions

1. Wer hat den Brief geschrieben?
2. Wo hat Jutta den Brief geschrieben?
3. Was ist Peter beim Skilaufen passiert?
4. Was ist das Resultat gewesen?
5. Was macht Peter seit Montag?
6. Was hat Gisela bekommen?
7. Wie ist das Wetter in Bonn gewesen?

8. Was haben Peter und Jutta zu Hause gemacht?

9. Wer hat immer verloren?

10. Wo sind Peter und Jutta kürzlich gewesen?

11. Wen haben Peter und Jutta bei Müllers getroffen?

12. Wo ist Herr Kapp gerade gewesen?

13. Was hat Herr Kapp in Amerika gesehen?

14. Was haben sie bei Müllers getrunken?

15. Was haben Peter und Jutta gerade gekauft?

16. Sind die Möbel teuer oder billig gewesen?

**VOCABULARY DEVELOPMENT**

**A.** When used by itself, the adverb **gern** means *gladly*. For instance, in a short reply to a request: Hans, gib mir doch bitte den Schlüssel!— Ja, gern. But most often **gern** is used with a verb, and should be translated as *to like to (do something)*.

| | |
|---|---|
| Ich lese gern. | *I like to read.* |
| Er studiert nicht gern. | *He doesn't like to study.* |
| Herr Steinhoff trinkt gern Orangensaft. | *Mr. Steinhoff likes to drink orange juice.* |

Ask your neighbor some questions with **gern** and a verb. For instance, **Schreiben Sie gern?** or **Schreibst du gern?** An answer: **Nein, ich schreibe nicht gern.** Other possibilities: Auto fahren, Freunde besuchen, Wodka trinken, bis sehr spät mit Freunden reden, etc.

**B.** The verb **gehen** occurs with **es** in one of the most frequently used expressions in German:

| | |
|---|---|
| Wie geht es? | { *How's it going?* |
| | { *How are you?* |

Often the expression is shortened to **Wie geht's?**

If a pronoun or noun is used with this expression, it is in the dative case.

| | |
|---|---|
| Wie geht es dir? } | *How are you?* |
| Wie geht es Ihnen? } | |
| Danke, es geht mir gut. | *Thanks, I'm fine.* |
| | |
| Wie geht es den Kindern? | *How are the children?* |
| Leider geht es ihnen nicht so gut. | *Unfortunately they don't feel so good.* |

Notice that **es** is the grammatical subject; therefore the verb is third-person singular: **geht.**

In this context the opposite of **gut** is **schlecht.**

| | |
|---|---|
| Wie geht es Frau Müller? | *How is Mrs. Müller?* |
| Es geht ihr leider schlecht. | *She's not well, unfortunately.* |

Quite often one encounters **besser** with **es geht:**

| | |
|---|---|
| Es geht ihm wieder besser. | *He's better again.* |

Ask your neighbors how they or friends of theirs are.

**REVIEW EXERCISES**

**A.** *Express in German.*

1. Have you been in Salzburg recently?
2. How did the accident happen?
3. A car passed me on the left.
4. Have you forgotten the letter?
5. I drank a cup of coffee and ate a piece of cake.
6. He found it (the hotel) right away.
7. The bathroom was on the left of room number nine.
8. I paid two hundred marks a month.
9. Was the furniture attractive?
10. The fire was not very dangerous.

**B.** *Answer the following questions in complete sentences. Use pronouns wherever possible.*

1. Sind die Schmidts bei Frau Becker gewesen?
2. Hat Elke dem Amerikaner den Brief geschrieben?
3. Hast du Peter das Buch gebracht?
4. Seid ihr bei den Studentinnen gewesen?
5. Gibst du den Kindern die Platten?
6. Wohin sind Sie gestern gefahren?
7. Was hat Frau Wegner Ihnen gezeigt?
8. Wer hat euch oft besucht?
9. Wem hat sie die Briefe geschrieben?

**C.** *First add* **nicht** *to each sentence. Then change all nouns in the sentence to pronouns.*

EXAMPLE: Thomas hat das Haus erkannt.
**Thomas hat das Haus nicht erkannt.**
**Er hat es nicht erkannt.**

1. Ich kenne das Resultat.
2. Frau Ottinger redet gern.
3. Gestern hat sie das Hotel verlassen.
4. Klaus hat den Touristen verstanden.
5. Wir bringen die Möbel herein.
6. Lotte hat die Kinder gegrüßt.
7. Ich habe dem Taxifahrer die Koffer gegeben.
8. Die Antworten sind richtig.

**D.** *Change the following sentences into the present or present perfect, whichever is applicable.*

1. Ich habe nichts gemerkt.
2. Der Student kommt zu Hause an.
3. Die Frau hat dem Taxifahrer den Koffer gegeben.
4. Peter hat immer alles vergessen.
5. Der Mann bringt das Kind nach Hause.
6. Wo ist die Zeitung?

## GUIDED COMPOSITION

Write a short letter to a friend, telling what has happened to you recently. If you had an accident or if you were sick, give some details about your misfortune. If you took a trip, mention where you went and whom you visited. If you gave a party, tell who came and who did not. Mention any other recent news that your friend might find interesting.

Before you write your letter, notice how the form of a German letter differs from that of a letter in English. Note how the date is given; note that you address a male friend with **Lieber . . .** and a female friend with **Liebe . . .** ; and that all second-person pronouns (familiar and formal, singular and plural) are capitalized.

You might close your letter with one of the following expressions:

**Sei herzlich gegrüßt** (addressing one person)
**Seid herzlich gegrüßt** (addressing more than one person)
**Dein(e) Freund(in)**
**Dein(e)**
**Viele Grüße**

CHAPTER
VOCABULARY

## Easily recognized words

| | | |
|---|---|---|
| die | **Party, -ies** | *party* |
| das | **Resultat, -e** | *result* |
| der | **Volkswagen, -** | *VW* |

| | | |
|---|---|---|
| der | **Anfang, ⸚e** | *beginning* |
| die | **Antwort, -en** | *answer* |
| die | **Arbeit, -en** | *work* |
| der | **Baum, ⸚e** | *tree* |
| der | **Brief, -e** | *letter* |
| der | **Gruß, ⸚e** | *greeting* |
| die | **Möbel** (*pl.*) | *furniture* |
| die | **Nachricht, -en** | *news* |
| der | **Orangensaft, ⸚e** | *orange juice* |
| das | **Schlafzimmer, -** | *bedroom* |
| der | **Unfall, ⸚e** | *accident* |
| der | **Wein, -e** | *wine* |
| das | **Wetter** | *weather* |
| die | **Woche, -n** | *week* |
| das | **Wohnzimmer, -** | *living room* |

| | |
|---|---|
| **bekommen (bekommen)** | *to get, receive* |
| **besuchen** | *to visit* |
| **bleiben (ist geblieben)** | *to stay* |
| **brennen (gebrannt)** | *to burn* |
| **erkennen (erkannt)** | *to recognize* |
| **erzählen** | *to tell (stories)* |
| **grüßen** | *to greet* |
| **herein·bringen (hereingebracht)** | *to bring in* |
| **hinein·mischen** | *to mix in* |
| **meinen** | *to mean* |
| **merken** | *to notice* |
| **passieren (ist passiert)** | *to happen* |

| | |
|---|---|
| **reden** | *to talk* |
| **regnen** | *to rain* |
| **schreiben (geschrieben)** | *to write* |
| **treffen (trifft, getroffen)** | *to meet* |
| **überholen** | *to pass* |
| **vergessen (vergißt, vergessen)** | *to forget* |
| **verlieren (verloren)** | *to lose* |
| **verstehen (verstanden)** | *to understand* |

| | |
|---|---|
| **außerdem** | *besides, in addition* |
| **bald** | *soon* |
| **besser** | *better* |
| **deshalb** | *therefore* |
| **eigentlich** | *actually* |
| **einmal** | *ever; once* |
| **etwas** | *a little, something* |
| **furchtbar** | *awful* |
| **gern** | *gladly;* **etwas gern haben** *to like* |
| **herzlich** | *cordial(ly)* |
| **heutzutage** | *these days, nowadays* |
| **hoffentlich** | *hopefully* |
| **jemand** | *someone* |
| **kürzlich** | *recently* |
| **lange** | *for a long time* |
| **lieb** | *dear* |
| **nett** | *pleasant* |
| **nie** | *never* |
| **richtig** | *right, correct* |
| **schon** | *already* |
| **spät** | *late* |
| **tatsächlich** | *indeed* |
| **wahrscheinlich** | *probably* |

## I

Das Mädchen **bezahlte** den Taxifahrer.
*The girl paid the taxi driver.*

Klaus **ging** die Treppe **hinunter.**
*Klaus went downstairs.*

Ich **kannte** ihn nicht.
*I didn't know him.*

Wir **hatten** kein Geld bei uns.
*We had no money with us.*

Du **fuhrst** zu schnell.
*You drove too fast.*
*You were driving too fast.*

Da **kam** ein Polizist.
*A policeman came (on the scene).*

Wir **gingen** nach Hause.
*We went home.*

Karl **war** krank.
*Karl was sick.*

Die Studentin **brachte** ihm ein Buch.
*The student brought him a book.*

## II

Peter **will** nicht hier bleiben.
*Peter doesn't want to stay here.*

**Können** Sie Deutsch (sprechen)?
*Do you know German?*

Ich **möchte** nach Hause (gehen).
*I would like to go home.*

**Durften** Sie mit dem Auto kommen?
*Were you allowed to come by car?*

Viktor **mußte** zu Hause arbeiten.
*Viktor had to work at home.*

Renate **weiß** es noch nicht.
*Renate doesn't know it yet.*

**Wußtet** ihr es?
*Did you know it?*

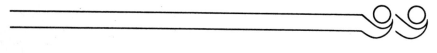

**GRAMMAR
EXPLANATION**

### I. Past tense

As discussed in Chapter 5, the present perfect tense is generally preferred in conversation. The past tense, on the other hand, is used primarily in writing as the so-called "narrative past," when the narrator enumerates step by step the events that form part of a sequence, as in a story. Yet the past tense may be used in the spoken language, too, when the speaker turns narrator.

. . . Ich suchte lange einen Parkplatz und konnte keinen finden . . .  *. . . I looked for a parking place for a long time and couldn't find one . . .*

. . . Schließlich parkte ich den Wagen auf dem Bürgersteig . . .  *. . . Finally I parked the car on the sidewalk . . .*

**A.** *Formation*

Like the present, the past tense is a "simple" tense, because it does not need an auxiliary. In this tense the difference in conjugation between the weak and strong verbs is particularly apparent.

|  | INFINITIVE | PAST |
|--|-----------|------|
|  | machen | machte |
|  | studieren | studierte |
| *But:* | gehen | ging |
|  | trinken | trank |

1. *Weak verbs* form the past tense by inserting **-t-** between the unchanged stem and a personal ending.

*Past tense:* **sagen** *(to say)*

| SINGULAR | | PLURAL | |
|----------|--------|--------|--------|
| ich | sagte | wir | sagten |
| du | sagtest | ihr | sagtet |
| er sie es | sagte | sie | sagten |
| Sie | sagten | Sie | sagten |

In English the equivalent of the weak-verb ending is *-ed,* as in *to play, played.*

In German, since the **-t-** of the past tense must be clearly audible, verbs with a stem ending in **-d** or **-t** insert **-e-** between the stem and the ending.

Ich arbeit**e**te heute.          *I worked today.*

The same is true for verbs with a stem ending in **-m** or **-n** preceded by a consonant other than **l** and **r.**

Du öffn**e**test die Tür.          *You opened the door.*

Remember that these verbs also insert **-e-** in the present tense and in the past participle: **du öffnest, geöffnet.**

The verb **haben,** otherwise weak, shows an irregularity in its past forms.

| INFINITIVE | PAST | PAST PARTICIPLE |
|-----------|------|-----------------|
| haben | **hatte** | gehabt |

| SINGULAR | | PLURAL | | *Past tense:* **haben** |
|---|---|---|---|---|
| ich | hatte | wir | hatten | |
| du | hattest | ihr | hattet | |
| er | | sie | hatten | |
| sie | hatte | | | |
| es | | | | |
| Sie | hatten | Sie | hatten | |

2. *Irregular weak verbs* take the same past-forming element **-t-** and the same personal endings as weak verbs, but feature a stem-vowel change similar to the strong verbs.

| INFINITIVE | PAST | PAST PARTICIPLE |
|---|---|---|
| brennen *to burn* | **brannte** | gebrannt |
| bringen *to bring* | **brachte** | gebracht |
| denken *to think* | **dachte** | gedacht |
| kennen *to know* | **kannte** | gekannt |

In the chapter and end vocabularies, the past and past participle forms of all irregular weak verbs are indicated.

## Check your comprehension

*Supply the appropriate past-tense form of the verb in parentheses.*

1. Die Autofahrer _____ einen Parkplatz. (*suchen*)
2. Der Student _____ zu Hause. (*arbeiten*)
3. Du _____ wirklich Probleme. (*haben*)
4. Wir _____ ihm kein Geld. (*bringen*)
5. Ich _____ dich. (*meinen*)
6. Er _____ uns immer. (*grüßen*)
7. Er _____ ihn nicht. (*kennen*)

3. *Strong verbs*, instead of using **-t-**, change their stem vowel and add to the changed stem different personal endings.

*Past tense:* **fahren**

| SINGULAR | | PLURAL | |
|---|---|---|---|
| ich | fuhr | wir | fuhren |
| du | fuhrst | ihr | fuhrt |
| er<br>sie } fuhr<br>es | | sie | fuhren |
| Sie | fuhren | Sie | fuhren |

| INFINITIVE | PAST | PAST PARTICIPLE |
|---|---|---|
| halten | **hielt** | gehalten |
| nehmen | **nahm** | genommen |
| bleiben | **blieb** | ist geblieben |
| kommen | **kam** | ist gekommen |

Note that the stem change in the past tense is not necessarily the same as that in the past participle.

Since the stem changes are not predictable, you must memorize the past of each verb along with the infinitive and past participle. In the chapter and end vocabularies, the past and past participle forms are indicated for all strong verbs. The strong verbs without prefixes that you have already encountered include those listed on page 90, plus **bleiben, fahren, gehen, kommen, laufen, schreiben,** and **treffen.**

Just as for the past participle, the verb **sein** has a special form for the past tense: **war** plus the usual endings for strong verbs.

| INFINITIVE | PAST | PAST PARTICIPLE |
|---|---|---|
| sein | **war** | ist gewesen |

*Past tense:* **sein**

| SINGULAR | | PLURAL | |
|---|---|---|---|
| ich | war | wir | waren |
| du | warst | ihr | wart |
| er<br>sie } war<br>es | | sie | waren |
| Sie | waren | Sie | waren |

## Check your comprehension

*Change the following sentences to the past tense.*

1. Peter ist furchtbar krank.
2. Er schreibt mir einen Brief.
3. Wir bitten um Wein.
4. Karl findet keinen Platz.
5. Spricht Maria mit euch?
6. Frau Scholz nimmt ein Taxi.
7. Wir fahren nach Köln.
8. Sie bleibt zu Hause.
9. Er trifft uns bei Friedrich.

**B.** *Past forms of verbs with prefixes*

*1. Verbs with separable prefixes* have their prefixes detached from the verb and placed at the end of the clause. This applies no matter whether the verb is weak, irregular weak, or strong.

|  | INFINITIVE | PAST | PAST PARTICIPLE |
|---|---|---|---|
| *weak* | zu·machen *to close* | **machte zu** | zugemacht |
| *irreg. weak* | herein·bringen *to bring in* | **brachte herein** | hereingebracht |
| *strong* | an·halten *to stop* | **hielt an** | angehalten |

Die Polizei hielt uns an.     *The police stopped us.*

*2. Verbs with inseparable prefixes,* such as **be-, emp-, ent-, er-, ge-, ver-,** and **zer-,** are governed by the respective rules for weak, irregular weak, and strong verbs in the past tense.

|  | INFINITIVE | PAST | PAST PARTICIPLE |
|---|---|---|---|
| *weak* | bezahlen *to pay* | **bezahlte** | bezahlt |
| *irreg. weak* | erkennen *to recognize* | **erkannte** | erkannt |
| *strong* | bekommen *to get, receive* | **bekam** | bekommen |

Er bekam keine Antwort.     *He got no answer.*

Infinitive, past, and past participle are called the *three principal parts of the verb.* From this point on, you should memorize the three principal parts of strong and irregular weak verbs, and then add the necessary personal endings. As a matter of convention, the past-tense form is indicated by the third-person singular. In verbs with vowel variation in the present tense, the third-person singular will also be listed. If the present perfect is formed with **sein, ist** will precede the past participle.

| denken | dachte | gedacht |
| lesen (liest) | las | gelesen |
| kommen | kam | ist gekommen |

The forms of weak verbs, however, need not be memorized individually, since they can easily be derived from the infinitive stem.

In the Appendix on pp. 401–405 you will find a list of the most important strong and irregular weak verbs with all their principal parts. Look there for verbs whose forms you do not know; if a verb does not occur there, it is weak.

## Check your comprehension

*Supply the appropriate past-tense form of the verb in parentheses.*

1. Herr Klein _____ die Zeitungen. (*vergessen*)
2. Erika _____ das Auto. (*anhalten*)
3. Der Polizist _____ die Treppe. (*hinaufgehen*)
4. Wir _____ bei der Haltestelle. (*aussteigen*)
5. Wen _____ Karl? (*hereinbringen*)
6. Die Herren _____ die Kinder. (*erkennen*)
7. Leider _____ ich den Brief. (*verlieren*)
8. Er _____ nach Köln. (*weiterfahren*)
9. Anna _____ keinen Brief. (*bekommen*)
10. Natürlich _____ Jürgen gleich. (*zurücklaufen*)
11. _____ du nichts? (*bezahlen*)
12. Wann _____ ihr den Flugplatz? (*verlassen*)

## II. Modals and WISSEN (to know)

### A. *Modal Auxiliaries*

In German as well as in English, certain verbs function as *modal auxiliaries*, describing how an action is viewed. In the sentences *I must go home now* and *You may leave now*, for instance, the verbs *must* and *may* show how the speaker feels (his *mode* or manner of feeling) about going or leaving.

German has six modal auxiliaries: **dürfen, können, mögen, müssen, sollen,** and **wollen,** expressing permission, ability, desire or preference, necessity, obligation, and intention. Remember their basic meanings, rather than any direct word-for-word translations.

| MODAL | SAMPLE SENTENCE | APPROXIMATE TRANSLATION | BASIC MEANING |
|---|---|---|---|
| **dürfen** | Du **darfst** heute hier bleiben. *You may (are allowed to) stay here today.* | to be allowed to | permission |
| **können** | Ich **kann** Deutsch. *I can (speak) German.* | to be able to, can | ability |
| **mögen** | Ich **mag** nicht hier bleiben. *I don't like to stay here.* | to like to | desire, preference |
| | Ich **möchte** hier bleiben. *I would like to stay here.* | would like to | |
| **müssen** | Ich **muß** nach Hause gehen. *I must (have to) go home.* | to have to, must | necessity, compulsion |
| **sollen** | Ich **soll** nach Köln fahren. *I am supposed to go to Cologne.* **Sollen** wir nach München gehen? *Shall we go to Munich?* | to be supposed to, ought to, shall | imposed obligation (in questions: suggestion) |
| **wollen** | Ich **will** hier bleiben. *I want (intend to) stay here.* | to want to, intend to | intention, strong desire |

Modals most often occur with the infinitive of another verb. Sometimes the infinitive is understood, as in **Ich kann Deutsch** or **Ich muß nach Hause.** Infinitives used with modals do not take a word comparable to the English *to* (*I want to go*), and are placed at the end of the clause.

Ich **will** morgen nach Frankfurt **fahren.**   *I want to drive to Frankfurt tomorrow.*

**Möchten,** a special form of **mögen,** is used frequently. It has the meaning *would like to,* and expresses a statement or request more politely.

Ich möchte kommen.                    *I would like to come.*

In the present tense, the modals undergo considerable vowel changes in their conjugation and need to be memorized carefully.

|  | **dürfen** | **können** | **mögen** | **müssen** | **sollen** | **wollen** | |
|---|---|---|---|---|---|---|---|
| *ich* | darf | kann | mag/möchte | muß | soll | will | *Present tense: modals* |
| *du* | darfst | kannst | magst/möchtest | mußt | sollst | willst | |
| *er* | | | | | | | |
| *sie* | darf | kann | mag/möchte | muß | soll | will | |
| *es* | | | | | | | |
| *wir* | dürfen | können | mögen/möchten | müssen | sollen | wollen | |
| *ihr* | dürft | könnt | mögt/möchtet | müßt | sollt | wollt | |
| *sie* | dürfen | können | mögen/möchten | müssen | sollen | wollen | |
| *Sie* | dürfen | können | mögen/möchten | müssen | sollen | wollen | |

Except for **möchten,** which adds **-e-** in the first- and third-person singular, the modals do not add endings in the present tense of the first- and third person singular.

In the past tense, the modals add **-t-** and the weak verb endings to a slightly changed stem.

|  | **dürfen** | **können** | **mögen** | **müssen** | **sollen** | **wollen** | |
|---|---|---|---|---|---|---|---|
| *ich* | durfte | konnte | mochte | mußte | sollte | wollte | *Past tense: modals* |
| *du* | durftest | konntest | mochtest | mußtest | solltest | wolltest | |
| *er* | | | | | | | |
| *sie* | durfte | konnte | mochte | mußte | sollte | wollte | |
| *es* | | | | | | | |
| *wir* | durften | konnten | mochten | mußten | sollten | wollten | |
| *ihr* | durftet | konntet | mochtet | mußtet | solltet | wolltet | |
| *sie* | durften | konnten | mochten | mußten | sollten | wollten | |
| *Sie* | durften | konnten | mochten | mußten | sollten | wollten | |

In the past tense the umlaut of the infinitive is dropped, and the **-g-** of **mögen** changes to **-ch-**.

To express a situation in the past, a modal followed by an infinitive requires the past tense, not the present perfect.

Ich **wollte** wirklich pünktlich sein.   *I really wanted to be on time.*

Ich **konnte** keinen Parkplatz finden.   *I couldn't find a parking place.*

## B. WISSEN *(to know)*

The verb **wissen,** meaning *to know* in the sense of knowing facts, is highly irregular in the present tense and must therefore be memorized separately.

*Present tense:* **wissen**

| SINGULAR | | PLURAL |
|---|---|---|
| ich | weiß | wir wissen |
| du | weißt | ihr wißt |
| er | | |
| sie | weiß | sie wissen |
| es | | |
| Sie | wissen | Sie wissen |

Er weiß nichts.      *He knows nothing.*

The principal parts of this verb are **wissen (weiß), wußte, gewußt.**

**Wissen** behaves like the irregular weak verbs in the past and present perfect tenses.

Ich wußte es nicht.     *I didn't know it.*

Das hast du leider nicht gewußt.     *Unfortunately you didn't know that.*

## *Check your comprehension*

**A.** *Supply the correct present-tense form of the modal in parentheses, then translate into English.*

1. Der Herr _____ keine Zigaretten rauchen. (*dürfen*)
2. Der Amerikaner _____ die Zeitung nicht lesen. (*können*)
3. Ich _____ keinen Kuchen. (*mögen*)
4. _____ du mit uns kommen? (*möchten*)
5. Die Studenten _____ heute abend arbeiten. (*müssen*)
6. Wir _____ mit ihr nach Bonn fahren. (*sollen*)
7. Wer _____ den Brief schreiben? (*wollen*)

**B.** *Supply the correct past-tense form of the modal in parentheses, then translate into English.*

1. Heinrich _____ nicht viel essen. (*dürfen*)
2. Wir _____ hier nicht studieren. (*können*)
3. Ich _____ nach Hause gehen. (*müssen*)
4. Das Mädchen _____ schnell zurückfahren. (*sollen*)
5. Sie (*pl.*) _____ uns verlassen. (*wollen*)

**C.** *Supply the indicated tense of* **wissen.**

1. Ich _____ nichts, und Helga _____ alles. (*present*)
2. _____ Sie es auch? (*past*)
3. Das _____ ich lange nicht _____. (*present perfect*)
4. _____ du die Antwort nicht? (*present*)
5. Das _____ wir schon _____. (*present perfect*)

---

## USEFUL PHRASES

| | |
|---|---|
| **Es tut mir leid.** | *I'm sorry.* |
| **Ich wollte wirklich pünktlich sein.** | *I really wanted to be on time.* |
| **Das ist nichts Neues.** | *That's nothing new.* |
| **Na und dann?** | { *Well?* <br> *Go on!* |

---

## CONVERSATION

## *Die Brötchen*

*Georg und Sibille hatten eine Verabredung° für neun Uhr morgens in*   date
*einer Kaffee-Bar.¹ Georg kommt fünfzehn Minuten zu spät.*

SIBILLE Da bist du ja² endlich! Wo bist du so lange gewesen?
GEORG Tag,³ Sibille! Es tut mir leid. Ich wollte wirklich pünktlich sein.
SIBILLE Was ist denn wieder passiert?
GEORG Ich suchte lange einen Parkplatz und konnte keinen finden.

---

¹ A stand-up bar where one can drink a quick cup of coffee (now very popular in Europe).

² **Ja** is another flavoring particle that cannot be directly translated. It is frequently used to give more emphasis to an affirmative statement, just as **denn** gives more emphasis to a question.

³ Short for **Guten Tag.**

SIBILLE Das ist nichts Neues.

GEORG Schließlich parkte ich den Wagen auf dem° Bürgersteig vor    *on the*
der Bäckerei.°    *in front of the bakery*

SIBILLE Na und dann?

GEORG Ich wollte gerade aussteigen, da kam ein Polizist heran. „Sie
dürfen hier nicht parken. Fahren Sie weiter", sagte er.

SIBILLE Aber du weißt doch, da kannst du nicht parken.

GEORG „Nur für ein paar Minuten", bat ich. Aber der Kerl blieb uner-
bittlich° und wollte mir gleich ein Strafmandat° geben.    *pitiless / ticket*

SIBILLE Warum wolltest du denn zur Bäckerei gehen?

GEORG Ich sollte doch Brötchen mitbringen!

SIBILLE Und wo sind die Brötchen?

GEORG Die Brötchen? Ach, jetzt habe ich sie ganz vergessen!

## Questions

1. Wann und wo hatten Georg und Sibille eine Verabredung?
2. Warum konnte Georg nicht pünktlich sein?
3. Wo parkte Georg den Wagen?
4. Wer kam da plötzlich zu ihm heran?
5. Was sagte der Polizist zu Georg?
6. Wie lange wollte Georg da parken?
7. Was wollte der Polizist Georg geben?
8. Warum wollte Georg zur Bäckerei gehen?
9. Was hat Georg leider vergessen?

**PRACTICE**

**A.** *Change the sentence from the present to the past tense.*

1. Wo bist du denn?
2. Ich will wirklich pünktlich sein.
3. Ich soll noch ein paar Brötchen mitbringen.
4. Du kannst keinen Parkplatz finden?
5. Georg findet keinen Parkplatz.
6. Ich parke den Wagen auf dem Bürgersteig.
7. Ein Polizist kommt heran.
8. Der Polizist will mir ein Strafmandat geben.
9. Ich will zur Bäckerei gehen.
10. Georg vergißt leider die Brötchen.

**B.** *Supply the appropriate present-tense form of the modal in parentheses.*

1. Ich _____ keinen Kaffee trinken. (*dürfen*)
2. _____ du zu Hause bleiben? (*möchten*)
3. Was _____ er studieren? (*wollen*)
4. Georg _____ keine Antwort finden. (*können*)
5. Wir _____ morgen nach Bonn fahren. (*sollen*)
6. Ihr _____ jetzt zur Arbeit gehen. (*müssen*)

**C.** *Change the sentence from the present perfect to the past tense.*

1. Ich habe viel Zeit gehabt.
2. Wir sind pünktlich gewesen.
3. Habt ihr die Zeitung vergessen?
4. Hat der Baum rechts gestanden?
5. Herr Steinhoff ist schnell aus dem Haus gegangen.
6. Sibille hat nichts gesagt.
7. Die Studentinnen haben heute gearbeitet.
8. Der Polizist hat mich angehalten.
9. Ich habe es wirklich nicht gewußt.
10. Bist du gleich zurückgelaufen?

**D.** *Change the sentences in exercise C from the present perfect to the present.*

**E.** *Supply the appropriate past-tense forms of the verbs in parentheses.*

Freitag abend _____ (*sollen*) Herr Steinhoff nach Mannheim fahren. Er _____ (*besuchen*) eine Party bei Frau Schumacher. Frau Schumacher _____ (*grüßen*) ihn herzlich. Bei ihr _____ (*treffen*) er die Kapps. Frau Kapp _____ (*sein*) wirklich nett. Herr Steinhoff _____ (*glauben*) sie zu kennen. Herr Kapp _____ (*erzählen*) sehr interessant von einer Reise (*trip*) nach Amerika. Sie _____ (*bleiben*) bis sehr spät bei Frau Schumacher, und _____ (*diskutieren*) über Politik. Natürlich _____ (*wollen*) Herr Steinhoff nur Orangensaft trinken, aber jemand _____ (*hereinmischen*) etwas Wodka. Herr Steinhoff _____ (*merken*) es nicht. Endlich _____ (*müssen*) er die Party verlassen. Er _____ (*zurückfahren*) sehr schnell nach Hause. Plötzlich _____ (*überholen*) ihn ein Volkswagen. Herr Steinhoff _____ (*fahren*) sofort nach rechts. Leider _____ (*sehen*) er den Baum nicht. Das Resultat _____ (*sein*) ein Unfall. Moral: Für die Gesundheit ist Orangensaft manchmal gefährlich!

**F.** *Change the sentence from the present to the past tense.*

1. Können Sie Deutsch?
2. Dürft ihr das?
3. Mögen Sie Wodka mit Orangensaft?
4. Wir müssen nach Hause.
5. Ich will das Buch nicht.

**G.** *Answer the following questions.*

1. Kamen Sie heute pünktlich zur Klasse?
2. Können Sie immer einen Parkplatz finden?
3. Haben Sie einmal einen Wagen auf dem Bürgersteig geparkt?
4. Bekamen Sie dann ein Strafmandat?
5. Müssen Sie manchmal viel studieren?
6. Haben Sie wirklich fast alles vergessen?
7. Wollten Sie heute abend Brötchen essen?
8. Wollen Sie morgen zu Hause bleiben?
9. Möchte eine Freundin zu Ihnen kommen?
10. Dürfen Sie zu Hause rauchen und Alkohol trinken?
11. Möchten Sie morgens Orangensaft oder Kaffee trinken?
12. Müssen Sie nach der Klasse nach Hause?

**H.** *Now ask your neighbor the same questions in the* **du** *form and get an answer.*

**I.** *Give the English equivalents of the following sentences.*

1. Wolfgang kann kein Englisch.
2. Ich möchte gern eine Tasse Kaffee.
3. Herr Klein weiß nicht immer alles.
4. Durftest du mit dem Auto nach Hause fahren?
5. Der Unfall passierte bei der Thomas-Kirche.
6. Wo warst du kürzlich mit Frau Kapp?

**GUIDED CONVERSATION**

Begin a conversation with someone in your class. Pretend you just arrived in a café to meet a friend. After a short greeting explain why you are late and how you forgot to bring along a book you had promised to buy the friend. Ask your friend whether he or she would like a cup of coffee and rolls.

**READING**

## Das Radfahren

Heutzutage fährt man° in Deutschland, wie überall in Europa und Amerika, wieder Rad. Natürlich fährt man immer noch mit dem Auto und dem Zug. Aber seit einigen° Jahren ist das Fahrrad wieder populär. Vor° dem Krieg fuhr man mit dem Rad oder der Straßenbahn. Autos und Benzin waren zu teuer. Auch jetzt ist das Benzin wieder teuer. Aber seit dem Krieg verdienen die Deutschen viel Geld und können Autos kaufen. Aber leider haben die Autos die Luft verschmutzt. Wer weiß das nicht? Das Radfahren verschmutzt die Luft nicht und ist auch gesund. Man kann auch beim Radfahren viel Spaß haben!

    *one*
    *several*
    *before*

Viele Menschen fahren deshalb wieder mit dem Rad zur Arbeit oder machen kurze Ferienreisen° mit dem Rad. Es gibt sogar Fahrradwege.° Das gab es vor dem Krieg nicht. Es war nicht nötig. Das Radfahren war nicht so gefährlich; es gab nicht so viele Autos.

    *vacation trips*
    *bicycle paths*

Aber nicht nur die Luft ist schmutzig. Seit einigen Jahren sind auch die Seen und Flüsse von den Abwässern° schmutzig. Deshalb sind zweihundert Radfahrer und Radfahrerinnen aus der Schweiz, der Bundesrepublik,[1] Frankreich und Holland kürzlich in Schaffhausen zusammengekommen. Sie wollten gegen° die Verschmutzung des Rheins° protestieren. Schaffhausen liegt beim Rheinfall° in der Schweiz. Der Rheinfall ist in Europa so bekannt wie zum Beispiel der Niagarafall in Amerika.

    *sewage*

    *against*
    *of the Rhine / Rhine falls*

Die zweihundert Radfahrer kündigten° die Fahrt in vielen Zeitungen an. Sie fuhren mit dem Rad tief° nach Deutschland hinein, bis zur

    *announced*
    *deep*

---

[1] The official German term for West Germany is (**die**) **Bundesrepublik Deutschland (BRD)**. Frequently just the term **Bundesrepublik** is used. The term for East Germany is (**die**) **Deutsche Demokratische Republik (DDR)**.

Lorelei,[2] und zurück in die Schweiz. Überall haben sie angehalten, mit
vielen Menschen gesprochen und Programme verteilt.° Die Journa-          distributed leaflets
listen haben viele Berichte über die zweihundert Radfahrer geschrie-
ben, aber auch über die Verschmutzung des Rheins. Einige Berichte
waren satirisch.° „Der Rhein ist nicht mehr voll Gold, er ist voll          satirical
Schmutz", las man zum Beispiel in Berichten mit Bezug auf° die Oper          with regard to
von Richard Wagner.[3] Tatsächlich fließen° die Abwässer von Indu-          to flow
strie und Städten in den Rhein, und jetzt muß man den Rhein wieder
säubern.

Das Radfahren kann das natürlich nicht erreichen. Aber die zweihundert Radfahrer haben wenigstens das Publikum auf das Problem
aufmerksam gemacht. Deshalb war die Fahrt kein Reinfall!°

Aber was denken Sie, was haben die Fahrer beim Fahren getrunken? Rheinwasser, speziell° vom Wasserwerk° in Zürich (Schweiz)
gesäubert!

[2] A rock on the right bank of the Rhine, noted for the danger it caused navigation. From
this originated the legend of the siren who lured boatmen to destruction. The poet
Heinrich Heine (1797–1856) celebrated this rock in his famous poem "Lorelei."

[3] Richard Wagner (1813–1883) was one of the most influential composers of the nineteenth century. **Das Rheingold** is the first part of his impressive opera tetralogy, **Der
Ring des Nibelungen.**

## Questions

1. Was fährt man heutzutage wieder?
2. Was fährt man meistens (*mostly*) in Europa und Amerika?
3. Sind Autos und Benzin in Europa billig?
4. Was verschmutzen die Autos?
5. Warum gab es vor dem Krieg keine Fahrradwege?
6. Wo liegt der Rheinfall?
7. Wie bekannt ist der Rheinfall in Europa?
8. Gegen was wollten die zweihundert Radfahrer protestieren?
9. Wo kündigten die Radfahrer die Fahrt an?
10. Wer hat Berichte über die Radfahrer geschrieben?
11. In *Das Rheingold* von Richard Wagner gibt es Gold im Rhein. Was gibt es heutzutage wirklich im Rhein?
12. Was haben die Radfahrer beim Fahren getrunken?

**VOCABULARY DEVELOPMENT**

**A. Man** is a frequently used and versatile word. It can be rendered in English by *people, one,* or the indefinite *they,* depending on context.

| | |
|---|---|
| Man sagt, die Schweiz ist schön. | *People say Switzerland is beautiful.* <br> *They say Switzerland is beautiful.* |
| Beim Studieren muß man aufmerksam sein. | *When studying, one must be attentive.* |

In the Reading, underline **man** wherever it is used, and translate the sentences in which it occurs.

**B.** At times a verb may be used as a *neuter noun*, as for instance **Ski-laufen** (*to ski*):

Das Skilaufen ist hier sehr populär.    *Skiing is very popular here.*

The verbal noun may be used with a preposition, as in the sentence under A above: **Beim Studieren muß man aufmerksam sein.** Form a few sentences with **lesen, schreiben, (Karten) spielen,** and **(Rad) fahren,** using them as nouns.

**C.** In building a vocabulary it is useful to observe *word families*. In this and earlier lessons, for instance, you have seen the following words involving **fahren** and **Rad: das Fahren, das Radfahren, die Fahrt, der Radfahrer, die Radfahrerin, der Busfahrer, der Taxifahrer.** Take **Auto** and combine it with **fahren** in similar fashion, then use each word in a sentence.

**D. Wissen, kennen,** and **können** can all mean *to know.* **Wissen** means *to know* in the sense of knowing a fact.

Ich weiß das.    *I know that.*

Wir wissen, Claudia kommt mor-gen.    *We know Claudia is coming to-morrow.*

**Kennen** means *to know* in the sense of knowing about or being acquainted with a person or thing.

Ich kenne Herrn Meyer seit Jahren.    *I have known Mr. Meyer for years.*

Er kennt München sehr gut.    *He knows Munich very well.*

The modal **können** may also mean *to know*, but in the sense of having know-how, of having mastered something that one has studied or has a talent for.

Herr Müller kann gut Englisch.    *Mr. Müller knows English well.*

Fritz kann gut Gitarre spielen.    *Fritz knows how to play the guitar well.*

*In the following sentences, use the appropriate present-tense form of either* **wissen, kennen,** *or* **können.**

1. I know he's at home.
2. Do you (*du*) know the gentleman?
3. He can play the piano very well.
4. They know the answer.
5. Do you (*Sie*) know Berlin?
6. He knows German well.

**REVIEW EXERCISES**

**A.** *Form sentences by combining each item on the left with an item on the right. Make sure your sentences make sense.*

EXAMPLE: Wir müssen    mit vielen Menschen sprechen
**Wir müssen mit vielen Menschen sprechen.**

1. Wir müssen
2. Viele Menschen möchten
3. Ich will
4. Die Studenten können
5. Die Industrie muß
6. Man soll

gegen die Verschmutzung
  protestieren
nichts tun
die Städte säubern
mit dem Rad zur Arbeit fahren
das Publikum aufmerksam machen
die Luft und das Wasser nicht
  verschmutzen
Spaß beim Radfahren haben
die Seen und die Flüsse säubern
mit vielen Menschen sprechen
die Probleme manchmal vergessen

**B.** *Now eliminate the modal auxiliaries and restate your sentences in the past tense.*

EXAMPLE: Wir müssen mit vielen Menschen sprechen.
**Wir sprachen mit vielen Menschen.**

**C.** *Now restate in the present perfect tense the sentences thus obtained.*

EXAMPLE: Wir sprachen mit vielen Menschen.
**Wir haben mit vielen Menschen gesprochen.**

**D.** *Change the following sentences into the present, past, and present perfect. Omit the tense given.*

1. Karl trifft die Freundin beim Bahnhof.
2. Die Möbel waren leider teuer.
3. Die Kinder haben den Brief nicht bekommen.
4. Hoffentlich merkt der Kerl nichts.
5. Peter fuhr morgens mit der Straßenbahn.
6. Der Student schreibt einen Bericht über die Verschmutzung.
7. Der Unfall passierte in Köln.
8. Der Journalist hat mir die Adresse gegeben.
9. Das Hotel liegt weit von der Stadtmitte.
10. Wieviel kostet das Fahrrad?

## GUIDED COMPOSITION

Imagine that you were one of the two hundred cyclists who protested the pollution of the Rhine. Write a brief composition telling where you went, what you did, and why you did it. These verbs may prove useful: **zusammenkommen, protestieren, ankündigen, verschmutzen, säubern, erreichen.**

## CHAPTER VOCABULARY

### Easily recognized words

| | | |
|---|---|---|
| (das) **Holland** | *Holland* | |
| die **Industrie, -n** | *industry* | |
| der **Journalist, -en** | *journalist* | |
| die **Oper, -n** | *opera* | |
| **parken** | *to park* | |
| **populär** | *popular* | |
| **so** | *so* | |

| das **Benzin** | *gasoline* |
|---|---|
| der **Bericht, -e** | *news report, account* |
| das **Brötchen, -** | *roll (bread)* |
| die **Bundesrepublik Deutschland (BRD)** | *West Germany, Federal Republic of Germany* |
| der **Bürgersteig, -e** | *sidewalk* |
| das **Fahren** | *driving* |
| der **Fahrer, -** | *driver* |
| das **Fahrrad, ⁼er** | *bicycle* |
| die **Fahrt, -en** | *trip* |
| der **Fluß, ⁼sse** | *river* |
| der **Kerl, -e** | *guy, fellow* |
| der **Krieg, -e** | *war* |
| die **Luft** | *air* |
| der **Parkplatz, ⁼e** | *parking place* |
| der **Polizist, -en** | *policeman* |
| das **Publikum** | *public, people* |
| das **Rad, ⁼er** | *bicycle, wheel* |

| das **Radfahren** | *cycling* |
|---|---|
| der **Schmutz** | *pollution, dirt* |
| der **See, -n** | *lake* |
| der **Spaß** | *fun* |
| die **Straßenbahn, -en** | *streetcar* |
| die **Verschmutzung** | *pollution* |
| der **Wagen, -** | *car* |
| das **Wasser** | *water* |

| **erreichen** | *to achieve* |
|---|---|
| **mit·bringen, brachte, mitgebracht** | *to bring along* |
| **säubern** | *to cleanse, clean up* |
| **tun, tat, getan** | *to do* |
| **verdienen** | *to earn* |
| **verschmutzen** | *to pollute* |
| **wissen (weiß), wußte, gewußt** | *to know (a fact)* |
| **zusammen·kommen, kam, (ist) zusammengekommen** | *to gather (come together)* |

See also the modal auxiliaries on pp. 116–118.

| **aufmerksam** | *alert;* **aufmerksam machen** *to alert (someone)* |
|---|---|

| | | | | |
|---|---|---|---|---|
| **bekannt** | *well known* | | **schließlich** | *finally* |
| **immer noch** | *still, yet* | | **schmutzig** | *dirty* |
| **man** | *one, you, we, they, people* | | **so . . . wie** | *as . . . as* |
| **mehr** | *more* | | **sogar** | *even* |
| **morgens** | *in the morning(s)* | | **überall** | *everywhere* |
| **nicht mehr** | *not any more* | | **voll** | *full (of)* |
| **nötig** | *necessary* | | **wenigstens** | *at least* |
| **pünktlich** | *on time, punctual* | | | |

# 7

### I

Wir gingen **durch den Garten.**
*We went through the garden.*

Wir haben nicht genug Geld **für den Urlaub.**
*We don't have enough money for vacation.*

Ich habe nichts **gegen dich.**
*I have nothing against you.*

Der Junge ist **ohne einen Koffer** angekommen.
*The boy arrived without a suitcase.*

Fahrt **um die Ecke!**
*Drive around the corner.*

### II

**Wilfrieds** Freund heißt Jakob.
*Wilfried's friend is called Jacob.*

Hier ist die Adresse **der Studentin.**
*Here's the student's address.*

Ferien befreien uns von der Routine **des Alltags.**
*Vacations liberate us from the routine of everyday life.*

**Anstatt des Autos** nehme ich das Fahrrad.
*Instead of the car I'll take the bicycle.*

**Wegen eines Unfalls** ist er zu spät angekommen.
*Due to an accident he arrived late.*

**Trotz des Regens** sind sie schon abgefahren.
*In spite of the rain they have already left.*

## III

Beim Autofahren **wird** man **müde.**
*In driving one gets tired.*

Ferien innerhalb des Landes **sind** auch **teuer geworden.**
*Vacations within the country have also become expensive.*

Eine Stadt kann nicht **zu einem Garten werden.**
*A city cannot become a garden.*

Was **werden** Sie **mitnehmen**?
*What will you take along!*

## GRAMMAR EXPLANATION

### I. Prepositions with the accusative

The *accusative* case must be used after certain prepositions.

| | |
|---|---|
| **durch** *through* | Wir gingen **durch den Garten.** <br> *We went through the garden.* |
| **für** *for* | Ich habe eine Nachricht **für dich.** <br> *I have news for you.* |
| **gegen** *against* | Elfriede hat nichts **gegen ihn.** <br> *Elfriede has nothing against him.* |
| **ohne** *without* | Robert ist **ohne einen Koffer** ange- kommen. <br> *Robert arrived without a suitcase.* |
| **um** *around, at* (with time of day) | Sie machen eine Reise **um die Welt.** <br> *They are taking a trip around the world.* |
| | Der Bus fährt **um neun Uhr** zurück. <br> *The bus returns at nine o'clock.* |
| **bis** *until, as far as* | Claudia arbeitete **bis neun Uhr.** <br> *Claudia worked until nine o'clock.* |

When referring to a place, **bis** usually occurs in combination with **zu.**

| | |
|---|---|
| Die Radfahrer fuhren **bis zum** Flugplatz. | *The bicyclists rode as far as the airport.* |

Notice that **zum** is a contraction of **zu** and **dem; zu** requires the dative, and the last preposition governs the case of the object.

With proper names, however, **nach** is used with **bis.**

| | |
|---|---|
| Wir reisen **bis nach** Paris. | *We'll travel as far as Paris.* |

Some of these prepositions are contracted.

| | |
|---|---|
| durch + das = **durchs** | Er geht für sie **durchs** Feuer. *He will go through fire for her.* |
| für + das = **fürs** | Walter macht alles nur **fürs** Geld. *Walter does everything merely for money.* |
| um + das = **ums** | Albert lief schnell **ums** Haus. *Albert ran quickly around the house.* |

## Check your comprehension

*Use the appropriate form of the noun or pronoun indicated on the right. Pay attention to the case and use contractions where possible.*

1. Ich habe eine Platte für _____ gekauft. (*er*)
2. Gehst du bis zu _____? (*der See*)
3. Hermann ist ohne _____ nach Berlin gereist. (*die Kinder*)
4. Was hat sie eigentlich gegen _____? (*du*)
5. Herr Weber hat lange bei _____ gewohnt. (*die Universität*)
6. Erwin fuhr immer zu schnell durch _____. (*die Stadtmitte*)
7. Das Café war gleich um _____. (*die Ecke*)
8. Er hat das Zimmer ohne _____ verlassen. (*ein Gruß*)
9. Frau Mann kommt gerade von _____. (*der Flugplatz*)
10. Seit _____ ist sie krank. (*die Fahrt nach Salzburg*)

## II. Genitive case and prepositions

**A.** *Nouns and the definite article*

The fourth case in German, the *genitive case,* usually denotes the possessive relationship of one noun to another, or corresponds to many English expressions with *of.*

With proper names—names of particular people and places—the

German genitive is expressed by adding **-s** to the name, without an apostrophe.

| | |
|---|---|
| Werners Fahrrad ist neu. | *Werner's bicycle is new.* |
| Der Süden Frankreichs ist sehr schön. | *The South of France is very beautiful.* |

If no proper name is involved, a genitive phrase must be used.[1] A genitive phrase consists of an article followed by a noun; both are in the genitive case.

*Definite article: genitive case*

| SINGULAR | | PLURAL | |
|---|---|---|---|
| *masc.* | des | *all genders* | der |
| *fem.* | der | | |
| *neut.* | des | | |

1. Masculine and neuter nouns of more than one syllable usually add **-s** in the genitive singular.

| | |
|---|---|
| Das Zimmer **des Mädchens** ist sehr groß. | *The girl's room is very big.* |
| Ich habe die Adresse **des Hotels** nicht. | *I don't have the address of the hotel.* |

2. Masculine and neuter nouns that have only one syllable, or that end in **-s** or another hissing sound, usually add **-es** in the genitive singular.

| | |
|---|---|
| Der Koffer **des Mannes** ist da drüben. | *The man's suitcase is over there.* |
| Der Garten **des Gasthauses** ist schön. | *The garden of the hotel is lovely.* |

3. Feminine nouns in the singular, and all nouns in the plural, take no special endings in the genitive.

| | |
|---|---|
| Hier ist die Adresse **der Frau.** | *Here's the woman's address.* |
| Die Luft **der Städte** ist verschmutzt. | *The air of the cities is polluted.* |
| Wo hast du die Fahrräder **der Kinder** gefunden? | *Where did you find the children's bicycles?* |

4. Some nouns denoting human beings, which form their plurals by adding **-n** or **-en**, do not add **-s** or **-es** in the genitive singular. Instead, they take **-en.** Such nouns include **der Student, der Polizist, der Präsident, der Tourist, der Journalist,** and **der Mensch.**

---

[1] Certain phrases are exceptions: *a glass of beer* = **ein Glas Bier;** *a piece of cake* = **ein Stück Kuchen;** etc.

|       | SINGULAR       | PLURAL        |
|-------|----------------|---------------|
| *nom.* | der Student   | die Studenten |
| *acc.* | den Studenten | die Studenten |
| *dat.* | dem Studenten | den Studenten |
| *gen.* | **des** Stud<br>**ten** | **der** Studen**ten** |

*Declension:* **der Student**

| Die Polizei hat den Wagen des Studenten gesucht. | *The police looked for the student's car.* |
|---|---|

## Check your comprehension

**A.** *Restate in the genitive.*

1. der Schlüssel
2. der Baum
3. die Antwort
4. der Spaß
5. das Benzin
6. der Polizist
7. die Straßenbahn
8. der Mensch
9. das Jahr
10. die Unfälle

**B.** *Use the appropriate form of the noun indicated at the right.*

1. Wo ist _____ Adresse? (*Viktor*)
2. Ich las die Berichte _____. (*der Journalist*)
3. Die Möbel _____ haben viel gekostet. (*die Familie Kapp*)
4. Sind die Seen _____ verschmutzt? (*Amerika*)
5. Die Kirchen _____ sind alt. (*die Stadtmitte*)
6. Die Gärten _____ beim Hotel sind hübsch. (*die Häuser*)

## B. The indefinite article and **kein**

The indefinite article and **kein** also have special genitive forms that are used with nouns in the genitive.

| SINGULAR | INDEFINITE ARTICLE | KEIN |
|----------|--------------------|------|
| *masc.* | eines | keines |
| *fem.* | einer | keiner |
| *neut.* | eines | keines |
| **PLURAL** | | |
| *all genders* | — | keiner |

*Indefinite article and* **kein:** *genitive case*

| | |
|---|---|
| Er gab mir die Adresse eines Ho-tels. | *He gave me the address of a hotel.* |
| Ich habe die Adresse keines Hotels. | *I have the address of no hotel.* |

With the inclusion of the genitive, the list of forms of the definite and indefinite articles and **kein** is complete.

*Declension: definite and indefinite articles,* **kein**

|  | SINGULAR | | | | | | | | | PLURAL |
|---|---|---|---|---|---|---|---|---|---|---|
|  | MASCULINE | | | FEMININE | | | NEUTER | | | ALL GENDERS |
| nom. | der | ein | kein | die | eine | keine | das | ein | kein | die —keine |
| acc. | den | einen | keinen | die | eine | keine | das | ein | kein | die —keine |
| dat. | dem | einem | keinem | der | einer | keiner | dem | einem | keinem | den—keinen |
| gen. | des | eines | keines | der | einer | keiner | des | eines | keines | der —keiner |

## Check your comprehension

**A.** *Restate in the genitive.*

1. keine Industrie
2. ein Fluß
3. ein Fahrrad
4. kein Gasthaus
5. keine Häuser
6. ein Brief
7. keine Oper
8. kein Waschbecken

**B.** *Use the genitive form of the noun in parentheses.*

1. Zeigen Sie uns das Zimmer _____. *(eine Studentin)*
2. Er fand die Adresse _____ für mich. *(ein Gasthaus)*
3. Sie hat eine Gehirnerschütterung; es ist das Resultat _____. *(ein Unfall)*
4. Wir suchen das Zimmer _____. *(ein Freund)*

**C.** *Prepositions*

A number of prepositions always demand the genitive in the word that follows.

| | |
|---|---|
| **außerhalb** *outside of* | **Außerhalb der Stadt** gab es noch viel Land. *Outside of the city there was still much land.* |
| **innerhalb** *inside of, within* | **Innerhalb der Städte** gibt es keinen Platz mehr für Gärten. *Within the cities there is no more room for gardens.* |
| **(an)statt** *instead of* | Oskar, nimm doch die Straßenbahn **statt des Autos!** *Oskar, why don't you take the streetcar instead of the car!* |
| **trotz** *in spite of* | **Trotz des Wetters** fuhr Peter mit dem Auto nach Hause. *In spite of the weather Peter drove home by car.* |
| **während** *during* | **Während der Ferien** fahre ich nach München. *During the vacation I'll drive to Munich.* |
| **wegen** *because of, due to* | **Wegen eines Unfalls** konnte er nicht arbeiten. *Because of an accident he couldn't work.* |

## Check your comprehension

*Use the appropriate form of the noun in parentheses. Analyze the case carefully.*

1. Außerhalb _____ gab es nicht viele Taxis. (*die Stadt*)
2. Ich habe nicht genug Geld für _____. (*der Urlaub*)
3. Siegfried bleibt während _____ zu Hause. (*die Ferien*)
4. Trotz _____ ist der Journalist pünktlich angekommen. (*der Regen*)
5. Frau Keller kommt gerade aus _____. (*das Haus*)
6. Das Wasser _____ ist verschmutzt. (*die Seen*)
7. Wegen _____ hat er die Brötchen vergessen. (*die Polizistin*)
8. Fahrt nicht durch _____! (*die Stadtmitte*)
9. Schließlich kaufte sie ein Fahrrad statt _____. (*ein Auto*)
10. Innerhalb _____ gibt es keine Parkplätze. (*die Universität*)

## III. WERDEN and the future tense

**A. WERDEN** *used with adjectives or nouns*

The verb **werden** (*to become*) has many uses in German. For instance, it may occur with an adjective.

| | |
|---|---|
| Beim Studieren wird man müde. | *In studying one gets tired.* |
| Ferien sind teuer geworden. | *Vacations have become expensive.* |

It may also be used with a noun, often with the preposition **zu.**

| | |
|---|---|
| Eine Stadt kann nicht zu einem Garten werden. | *A city cannot become (turn into) a garden.* |
| Klaus wird Polizist. | *Klaus is becoming a policeman.* |

**B. Werden** *used as an auxiliary for the future tense*

Followed by the infinitive of another verb, **werden** is used as an auxiliary to form the *future tense.* In German, the future tense suggests a rather vague future.

| | |
|---|---|
| Er **wird** sehr spät ankommen. | *He will arrive very late.* |
| **Wirst** du mir nicht schreiben? | *Won't you write to me?* |

Notice that the separable prefix in **an·kommen** stays with the verb, since it is in the infinitive.

But the immediate future, especially in connection with an expression of time, is expressed by the present tense (see Chapter 1).

| | |
|---|---|
| Er kommt heute abend. | *He's coming tonight.* |

Memorize the irregular forms of **werden.**

| | PRESENT | PAST | PRESENT PERFECT |
|---|---|---|---|
| *ich* | werde | wurde | bin geworden |
| *du* | wirst | wurdest | bist geworden |
| *er* *sie* *es* | wird | wurde | ist geworden |
| *wir* | werden | wurden | sind geworden |
| *ihr* | werdet | wurdet | seid geworden |
| *sie* | werden | wurden | sind geworden |
| *Sie* | werden | wurden | sind geworden |

## Check your comprehension

**A.** *Give the English equivalent.*

1. Fritz wurde plötzlich krank.
2. Wann werdet ihr Urlaub haben?
3. Das Reisen innerhalb der Schweiz ist teuer geworden.
4. Der Parkplatz wird zum Garten.
5. Was wirst du ihm schreiben?
6. Wir gehen morgen zur Universität.
7. Was wollen Sie werden?

**B.** *Put the following sentences into the future tense.*

1. Die Polizei gibt dem Fahrer ein Strafmandat.
2. Anstatt des Autos nahm ich das Fahrrad.
3. Endlich ist Thomas zurückgekommen.
4. Er parkte den Wagen auf dem Bürgersteig.
5. Wir haben keine Zeitungen gekauft.

**USEFUL PHRASES**

| | |
|---|---|
| **Hör mal!** | *Listen!* |
| **Das hat doch noch Zeit.** | *There's still (ample) time for that.* |
| **Nicht doch!** | *No! Certainly not! (Said in contradiction.)* |
| **(Das) stimmt.** | *(That's) right.* |
| **Nicht wahr?** | *Isn't that so?* |
| **Was hältst du von Südfrankreich?** | *How do you feel about Southern France?* |

**CONVERSATION**

## Die Ferienreise

*Jutta und Kurt sind seit fünfzehn Jahren verheiratet und haben zwei Kinder, Walter, 12, und Claudia, 10. Sie machen Pläne für den Urlaub der Familie.[1] Sie möchten zusammen mit den Kindern eine Ferienreise machen.*

JUTTA Kurt, hör mal, wir müssen jetzt Pläne für die Ferien machen.

KURT (*liest die Zeitung*) Das hat doch noch Zeit!

JUTTA Nicht doch! In zwei Monaten wirst du schon Urlaub haben.

KURT (*läßt die Zeitung fallen*) Stimmt. Aber wohin sollen wir fahren? Wir haben leider kaum noch Geld für den Urlaub.

JUTTA Aber wir können doch nicht zu Hause bleiben. Die Kinder möchten zum Beispiel den Süden Frankreichs sehen.

KURT Was? Den Süden Frankreichs? Das wird zu teuer. Warum fahren wir nicht zur Nordsee°, vielleicht nach Westerland.[2]    *North Sea*

JUTTA Aber du weißt doch, das Reisen innerhalb Deutschlands ist auch nicht billig. Außerdem wird es da oben° wieder regnen.    *up there*

KURT Dann nehmen wir Regenschirme statt der Badehosen mit.

[1] German workers receive a special allowance for their vacation, the **Urlaubsgeld.** In most cases it is the same for unmarried and married persons, with or without children.

[2] Westerland is a resort on the Isle of Sylt, a long, narrow island near the Danish border. It is popular with Germans as a summer resort, although it has a somewhat windy and rainy climate.

JUTTA Sei doch nicht so zynisch°! Wir müssen doch schließlich auch etwas für die Kinder tun.    *cynical*

KURT Natürlich. Aber während der Ferien möchte ich etwas Ruhe haben. Südfrankreich ist so weit, und beim Autofahren wird man so müde.

JUTTA Ich kann doch schließlich auch fahren, nicht wahr? Also°, was hältst du von Südfrankreich?    *so*

## Questions

1. Seit wann sind Jutta und Kurt verheiratet?
2. Wofür (*for what*) machen die zwei Pläne?
3. Wohin möchten die Kinder reisen?
4. Warum will Kurt nicht in den Süden Frankreichs fahren?
5. Wohin will er fahren?
6. Wie ist das Wetter da oben?
7. Was möchte Kurt während der Ferien haben?
8. Sind Sie auch verheiratet? Wenn ja, seit wann? Wieviele Kinder haben Sie?
9. Was machen Sie während der Ferien?
10. Haben Sie genug Geld für die Ferien?
11. Werden Sie beim Autofahren auch manchmal müde?
12. Nehmen Sie einen Regenschirm oder Badehosen in die Ferien mit? Sind Sie dann Optimist oder Pessimist?

**PRACTICE**

**A.** *Fill in the appropriate form of the noun or pronoun in parentheses; use contractions where possible.*

1. Der Zug fährt schnell durch _____. (*das Land*)
2. Die Nachricht ist für _____. (*wir*)
3. Während _____ sagte er nichts. (*die Fahrt*)
4. Ich fahre nur bis zu _____. (*die Stadtmitte*)
5. Was hast du eigentlich gegen _____? (*ich*)
6. Wegen _____ bin ich mit _____ gefahren. (*der Regen/die Straßenbahn*)
7. Ist das Reisen innerhalb _____ teuer? (*Deutschland*)
8. Habt ihr genug Geld für _____? (*ein Wagen*)
9. Wegen _____ muß Erich zu Hause bleiben. (*ein Unfall*)
10. Die Familie ist ohne _____ abgefahren. (*er*)
11. Statt _____, hat er nur Wasser getrunken. (*der Wein*)
12. Innerhalb _____ ist es billig zu reisen. (*kein Land*)
13. Robert stieg aus _____ und ging durch _____. (*das Taxi/der Garten*)
14. Trotz _____ ist die Industrie nötig. (*die Verschmutzung*)

**B.** *Construct sentences in the present tense with the following cues. Watch the punctuation to determine whether it is a statement, question, or command. Use contractions where possible.*

EXAMPLE: gehen/ich/gleich/zu/die Polizei.
**Ich gehe gleich zur Polizei.**

1. können/kommen/wegen/ein Unfall/Fritz/nicht.
2. laufen/schnell/das Kind/durch/der Garten.
3. treffen/der Freund (subj.) /ich/bei/der Bahnhof?
4. merken/sie (sing.) /nichts/trotz/die Warnung.
5. fragen (sing.) /der Busfahrer/nach/die Straße!

**C.** *Answer each question, using the words in parentheses.*

EXAMPLE: Woher sind Sie gekommen? (*von/der Bahnhof*)
**Ich bin vom Bahnhof gekommen.**
*Or:* **Vom Bahnhof bin ich gekommen.**

1. Woher kommt Kurt gerade? (*aus/das Haus*)
2. Wann kann man Ruhe finden? (*während/die Ferien*)
3. Was möchtest du jetzt tun? (*durch/der Garten/gehen*)
4. Wo wohnen Sie? (*außerhalb/die Stadt*)
5. Gehst du durch die Stadtmitte? (*ja, trotz/die Autos*)
6. Wohin ist Erich gegangen? (*zu/die Polizei*)
7. Haben die Leute protestiert? (*ja, gegen/der Krieg*)
8. Haben sie nichts getan? (*nein, trotz/die Warnung*)

**D.** *Fill in the blanks, where necessary, with the appropriate ending of the noun, the suggested article or* **kein,** *or the indicated pronoun.*

1. Frau Zeller _____ Haus liegt sehr schön.
2. Bitte, geben Sie _____ (ich) e_____ Glas Bier_____!
3. Kennen Sie d_____ Adresse e_____ Student_____?
4. Thomas, sprich doch mit _____ (sie, sing.).
5. Max, kauf schnell e_____ Zeitung für _____ (ich).
6. Jakob_____ Fahrrad ist schmutzig.
7. Hast du k_____ Brötchen (plural) für _____ (wir)?
8. D_____ Kinder möchten d_____ Süden Deutschland_____ sehen.
9. Wir fahren bis zu _____ Kirche.

**E.** *Put the following sentences into the future tense.*

1. Dann nehmen wir Regenschirme mit.
2. In drei Monaten habt ihr Urlaub.
3. Während der Ferien bleibt die Familie nicht zu Hause.
4. Die Polizei gibt dem Fahrer ein Strafmandat.
5. Elfriede schreibt dem Freund keine Briefe mehr.
6. Trotz der Krankheit geht er zur Universität.

**F.** *Give the English equivalent.*

1. Beim Lesen wird man müde.
2. Das Kind ist groß geworden.
3. Die Gärten sollen nicht zu einem Parkplatz werden.
4. Wann wirst du endlich Urlaub nehmen?
5. Stimmt. Er kommt schon morgen an.
6. Die Fahrt ist lang. Werdet ihr nicht müde werden?
7. Die Studentin wurde plötzlich krank.
8. Das Kind wird zum Mann.

 **GUIDED CONVERSATION**

Team up with a fellow student and make plans for a mutual vacation or weekend trip. Ask each other where you would like to go. Ask other questions such as: When will we go? What means of transportation will we use? Will it be expensive? Will we go even if it rains? Do you like to cycle a lot? Or do you prefer to read books, find relaxation, do nothing, and forget the world? Do you eat and drink much during a trip? Etc.

## Die Freizeit

    Die Ferien und die Beschäftigung während der Freizeit sind für die Deutschen wie auch für die Europäer im allgemeinen° sehr wichtig geworden. Man sagt, Ferien und Freizeitbeschäftigung befreien den Menschen von der Routine des Alltags.° Aber „Hobbies"[1] und Ferien sind durch° die Inflation, aber auch wegen der Überbevölkerung°, teuer geworden.

    Zum Beispiel, seit Jahren ist der Gartenbau° in Deutschland sehr populär.[2] Heute gibt es in Deutschland über dreizehn Millionen Freizeit-Gärtner. Außerhalb der Stadt kaufen oder mieten sie ein Stück Land und pflanzen Gemüse, Obst und Blumen. Das Gemüse und das Obst aus dem Privatgarten sind gut für die Gesundheit, sagt man, denn° sie haben keine Chemikalien.°

    Aber es wird schwierig, einen Platz zu finden und billig zu mieten. Innerhalb der Städte gibt es fast keinen Platz mehr für Gärten und außerhalb ist der Boden zu teuer geworden. Was soll man da tun? Stadtparks in Gärten für Privatleute° umwandeln?° Das tut man tat-

*in general*

*everyday life*
*due to / overpopulation*

*horticulture*

*since / chemicals*

*private individuals / to transform*

---

[1] The English *hobby* is now commonly used in German-speaking countries, although **das Steckenpferd** (*hobby-horse, fad*) can still be heard.

[2] The so-called **Schrebergärten,** small garden plots within the city limits, have been rather popular with city-dwellers in German-speaking countries ever since the second half of the nineteenth century. They are named after a certain Dr. Daniel G. M. Schreber, who in the 1860s created the first playgrounds for children. These "children-gardens" later on became "garden-house colonies" for adults.

sächlich in Städten wie Dortmund, Hamburg und Bremen.[3] Aber es gibt nicht genug Parks innerhalb der Städte. Und schließlich kann nicht eine ganze Stadt zum Gemüsegarten werden!

Vielleicht muß der Staat intervenieren, den Boden um die Stadt aufkaufen° und dann billig an° die Freizeit-Gärtner vermieten.° Alle Einwohner müssen dann mehr Steuern bezahlen. Natürlich sind die Nicht-Gärtner gegen diese Lösung.° „Etwas mehr Chemikalien können wir noch verdauen,° aber kaum mehr Steuern", sagen sie. „Trotz der Steuern müssen wir Platz für Gärten machen", antworten die Gärtner. „Gärten verbessern die Qualität des Lebens. Was ist besser: Steuern bezahlen oder Chemikalien essen?" Wer hat recht?

Aber nicht nur der Gartenbau ist populär als Freizeitbeschäftigung. Trotz der Popularität des Fernsehens lesen die Deutschen, wie auch die Österreicher und Schweizer noch sehr oft Bücher während der Freizeit. Und wie in Amerika, macht man jetzt auch in Deutschland Reparaturen° außerhalb und innerhalb des Hauses selbst°. Nach° Statistiken der Regierung wird man in Zukunft° noch viel mehr Geld für die Freizeit ausgeben als jetzt. So wird die Freizeit einer Person zur Beschäftigung einer anderen!°

*buy up / to / rent out*

*this solution*
*to digest*

*repairs / oneself / according to*
*in the future*

*of another (person)*

[3] In Bremen, for instance, there are 23,000 small gardeners who within the city cultivate roughly 3,000 acres of "green areas" open to the public.

## Questions

1. Was ist heutzutage für die Deutschen sehr wichtig geworden?
2. Wovon (*from what*), sagt man, befreien die Ferien und die Freizeitbeschäftigung den Menschen?

3. Was machen die Freizeit-Gärtner außerhalb der Stadt?
4. Was wird schwierig für die Freizeit-Gärtner?
5. Was tut man in Städten wie Dortmund, Hamburg und Bremen?
6. Was muß der Staat vielleicht tun?
7. Was sagen die Nicht-Gärtner?
8. Was antworten ihnen die Gärtner?
9. Wer hat recht, die Gärtner oder die Nicht-Gärtner?
10. Was machen die Deutschen noch trotz des Fernsehens?
11. Was wird man wahrscheinlich in Zukunft für die Freizeit tun?

## VOCABULARY DEVELOPMENT

### A. Nicht wahr?

This phrase, literally meaning *not true?*, is often added to a statement. It usually expresses a desire to have one's opinion confirmed.

| | |
|---|---|
| Ich kann doch auch fahren, nicht wahr? | *I can also drive, can't I?* |
| Die Kinder wollten nicht nach Norddeutschland gehen, nicht wahr? | *The children didn't want to go to Northern Germany, did they?* |

Note that **nicht wahr?** can be added to a positive or a negative statement. It is much easier to handle than its many equivalents in English (*is it?, isn't it?, didn't you?,* etc.).

### B. Wie ist das Wetter?

In the Introductory Chapter you learned certain expressions referring to the weather; here are more. While they are used impersonally (that is, the subject is always **es**), the verbs **regnen** (*to rain*), **schneien** (*to snow*), **donnern** (*to thunder*), and **blitzen** (*to lighten*) are regular weak verbs. On the other hand, **scheinen** (*to shine*) is a strong verb, and it is not impersonal.

| | |
|---|---|
| Gestern hat es viel geregnet. | *Yesterday it rained a lot.* |
| Leider schneite es. | *Unfortunately it snowed.* |
| Es donnert. | *It's thundering.* |
| Es blitzt. | *There is lightning.* |
| Die Sonne scheint. | *The sun is shining.* |

Learn also the nouns **der Regen** (*rain*) and **der Schnee** (*snow*).

Now ask a classmate **Wie ist das Wetter heute?** and have him or her describe the weather in two or three sentences.

## C. *Compound nouns*

English offers the possibility of gathering up words into compound nouns like *Midsummernight's Dream,* but it does this much less than German, where compound nouns abound.

| | |
|---|---|
| **frei** (*free*) + **Zeit** (*time*) | = **Freizeit** (*free time, leisure*) |
| **Freizeit** + **Beschäftigung** (*activity, occupation*) | = **Freizeitbeschäftigung** (*leisure-time activity*) |

Notice that the last noun in the compound determines the gender: **die** Stadt + **der** Park = **der** Stadtpark.

Some words may also be combined with the aid of a hyphen: **Freizeit-Gärtner, Nicht-Gärtner, Hindenburg-Platz.** At times an **-s-** is used to connect the two nouns: **Urlaubsgeld.**

No easy rules can be formulated for combining words; learn through observation. Note, however, that all kinds of words may be involved in combinations; noun + noun, adjective + noun, preposition + noun, adverb + noun.

Go back to the Conversation and Reading and single out and dissect a few more compound nouns.

A mindteaser: figure out the meaning of this name, which really exists: **Vierwaldstättersee-Dampfschiffahrtsgesellschaft.** Hints: the **Vierwaldstättersee** is a lake in Switzerland. **Dampf** = *steam.* **Gesellschaft** = *company.*

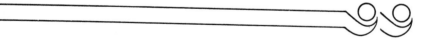

**REVIEW**

**A.** *Construct sentences with the following cues. Use the tense indicated in parentheses. Use contractions where possible. Watch the punctuation.*

1. werden/die Ferien/für/die Europäer/wichtig. (*present perfect*)
2. sein/das Gemüse/aus/der Privatgarten/für/die Gesundheit/gut. (*future*)
3. Geben/doch/die Kinder/Fahrräder/statt/ein Auto! (*imperative*)
4. machen/wann/du/endlich/Urlaub? (*future*)
5. werden/das Wasser/plötzlich/schmutzig. (*past*)
6. werden/der Boden/in/Deutschland/teuer. (*present perfect*)

**B.** *Fill in the blanks with the ending or pronoun indicated. Then answer the questions. Use contractions where possible.*

Jutta machte e_____ Reise zu d_____ Freund_____ (*pl.*) in Österreich. Während d_____ Fahrt las sie e_____ Buch. Der Zug fuhr schnell durch d_____ Städte. Nur in München hielt _____ (*it*) an. Sie stieg schnell aus d_____ Zug und kaufte e_____ Zeitung. „Ich muß schnell wieder einsteigen oder d_____ Zug fährt ohne _____ (*me*) ab", dachte sie. Außerhalb d_____ Stadt regnete es. Nach e_____ Stunde konnte sie durch_____ Fenster trotz d_____ Regen_____ die Alpen (*the Alps*) sehen. In Innsbruck schien d_____ Sonne. Jutta stieg aus d_____ Zug und suchte d_____ Freunde. Sie waren schon da. Sie fuhren zusammen mit e_____ Taxi zu_____ Hotel. „Für_____ Skilaufen (*skiing*) ist d_____ Wetter nicht gut", sagten sie während d_____ Fahrt, „hoffentlich schneit _____ (*it*) morgen."

1. Zu wem fuhr Jutta?
2. Wann las sie ein Buch?
3. Hielt der Zug in vielen Städten an?
4. Was kaufte Jutta in München?
5. Fuhr der Zug ohne Jutta ab?
6. Wo regnete es?
7. Wann konnte sie die Alpen sehen?
8. Wie war das Wetter in Innsbruck?
9. Wohin fuhren sie mit dem Taxi?
10. Was sagten sie während der Fahrt?

**C.** *Answer either set of questions, as directed.*

(1) Für die Gärtner:

1. Pflanzen Sie Gemüse, Obst, Bäume oder Blumen?
2. Glauben Sie, der Gartenbau (*horticulture*) befreit den Menschen von der Routine des Alltags?

(2) Für die Nicht-Gärtner:

1. Möchten Sie einen Garten haben?
2. Wenn ja, was möchten Sie pflanzen? Wenn nein, warum nicht? Was haben Sie gegen den Gartenbau (*horticulture*)? (*Possibilities*: zuviel Arbeit, keine Zeit, müde werden.)
3. Was tun Sie während der Freizeit statt des Gartenbaus? Ist das gesund, populär? Verbessert das die Qualität des Lebens?
4. Geben Sie viel Geld für die Freizeit aus? Warum?

**D.** *Express in German.*

1. I always get tired while driving the car.
2. Despite the taxes we must make room for gardens.
3. I had nothing against you (*du*).
4. Heinrich stayed home on account of the rain.

5. Unfortunately I can do nothing for the students.
6. Hans, run quickly around the corner and buy me a newspaper.
7. She will stay with us for two months.
8. They went as far as the bus stop.
9. There are not enough parks within the cities.
10. Where will you (*Sie*) go during the vacation?

## GUIDED COMPOSITION

**A.** Describe in a few short paragraphs what you do in your leisure time or what hobbies you have. Do you work in the garden? If so, what do you plant? Do you play an instrument? Do you go bicycle riding? Do you read a lot? If so, what kind of books? Do you like to travel? Where do you go?

**B.** Look at the picture below and describe what the boy is doing and whether he seems to enjoy himself.

**CHAPTER
VOCABULARY**

## Easily recognized words

| | | |
|---|---|---|
| der | **Europäer,** - | *European* |
| das | **Glas,** ⸚er | *glass* |
| | **illustrieren** | *to illustrate* |
| die | **Inflation** | *inflation* |
| | **intervenieren** | *to intervene* |
| das | **Land,** ⸚er | *land, country* |
| der | **Park,** -s | *park* |
| die | **Person,** -en | *person* |
| der | **Plan,** ⸚e | *plan* |
| die | **Popularität** | *popularity* |
| die | **Qualität,** -en | *quality* |
| die | **Routine,** -n | *routine* |
| die | **See** | *sea; ocean* |

| | | |
|---|---|---|
| die | **Steuer,** -n | *tax* |
| der | **Urlaub** | *leave, vacation* |
| die | **Welt,** -en | *world* |

| | | |
|---|---|---|
| die | **Badehose,** -n | *bathing trunks* |
| die | **Beschäftigung,** -en | *activity, occupation* |
| die | **Blume,** -n | *flower* |
| der | **Boden,** ⸚ | *ground, soil, land* |
| der | **Einwohner,** - | *resident, inhabitant* |
| die | **Familie,** -n | *family* |
| die | **Ferien** (*always pl.*) | *vacation(s)* |
| das | **Fernsehen** | *television* |
| die | **Freizeit** | *leisure (time)* |
| der | **Gärtner,** - | *gardener* |
| das | **Leben** | *life* |
| die | **Leute** (*pl.*) | *people* |
| der | **Platz,** ⸚e | *space, room, place* |
| der | **Regenschirm,** -e | *umbrella* |
| die | **Regierung,** -en | *government* |
| die | **Reise,** -n | *trip, journey* |
| die | **Ruhe** | *rest, peace* |
| der | **Staat,** -en | *state* |
| der | **Stadtpark,** -s | *municipal park* |

| | |
|---|---|
| **antworten** (+ *dat.*) | *to answer* |
| **aus·geben (gibt), gab, ausgegeben** | *to spend (money)* |
| **befreien** | *to free, liberate* |
| **halten von (hält), hielt, gehalten** | *to think about, feel about* |
| **mieten** | *to rent* |
| **mit·nehmen (nimmt), nahm, mitgenommen** | *to carry with, along* |
| **pflanzen** | *to plant* |
| **scheinen, schien, geschienen** | *to shine* |
| **verbessern** | *to improve* |
| **werden (wird), wurde, (ist) geworden** | *to become, get* |

| | |
|---|---|
| **als** | *than* |
| **kaum** | *hardly* |
| **müde** | *tired* |
| **recht haben** | *to be right* |
| **schwierig** | *difficult* |
| **so** | *thus* |
| **verheiratet** | *married* |
| **wenn** | *if* |
| **wichtig** | *important* |
| **wie** | *like* |
| **zusammen** | *together* |

See also the prepositions on pp. 135–136, and the weather expressions on pp. 145–146.

**I**

Sie halten **auf der Straße** an.
*They are stopping on the street.*

Kinder, geht nicht **auf die Straße!**
*Children, don't go into the street!*

Die Leute warten **in der Bahnhofshalle.**
*The people are waiting in the entrance hall of the railway station.*

Max, lauf schnell **in die Bahnhofshalle!**
*Max, run quickly into (the entrance hall of) the railway station.*

Das Auto steht **vor dem Haus.**
*The car is (standing) in front of the house.*

Der Vater stellt das Fahrrad **vor das Haus.**
*The father puts the bicycle in front of the house.*

Die Eltern warten **auf den Zug.**
*The parents are waiting for the train.*

Das Mädchen hört nicht **auf die Eltern.**
*The girl doesn't listen to her parents.*

**II**

Ich **möchte** das Matterhorn **besteigen.**
*I would like to climb the Matterhorn.*

Ich habe vergessen, dir **zu** schreiben.
*I forgot to write you.*

Die Tochter ging in die Stadt, **um** Einkäufe **zu** machen.
*The daughter went downtown shopping (lit., in order to make purchases).*

**(An)statt** zu Fuß **zu** gehen, fahren wir oft im Auto.
*Instead of walking (lit., going on foot), we often ride in the car.*

Man kann Sport treiben, **ohne** Mitglied eines Sportklubs **zu** sein.
*One can engage in sports without being a member of a sports club.*

**GRAMMAR EXPLANATIONS**

### I. Prepositions with the dative or accusative

Apart from the dative and accusative prepositions discussed earlier, German also has some prepositions that may take *either* the dative *or* the accusative. The determining factor is not the preposition itself, but the meaning of the preceding verb.

The *dative* is used after these prepositions when the verb denotes the location in which an action takes place. The prepositional phrase then answers the question *where?* or *in what place?*

Peter wartet in der Bahnhofshalle.

*Peter is waiting in the entrance hall of the railway station.*

Peter geht in der
Bahnhofshalle auf und ab.

*Peter is pacing up and down in the
entrance hall of the railway station (but not going anywhere).*

The *accusative* is used after these prepositions when the verb
denotes a motion toward a place. In this case the prepositional phrase
answers the question *where to?*

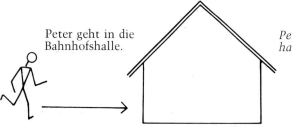

Peter geht in die
Bahnhofshalle.

*Peter is going into the entrance
hall of the railway station.*

In German the questions answered by these statements are:

| | | |
|---|---|---|
| Wo wartet Peter? | Er wartet in der Bahnhofshalle. | |
| Wo geht er auf und ab? | Er geht in der Bahnhofshalle auf und ab. | *dative* |
| *But:* Wohin geht er? | Er geht in die Bahnhofshalle. | *accusative* |

The prepositions in this category—at times called the "two-way
prepositions"—are:

**an** *at, on, to*  Die Mutter steht **am (an dem) Fen-
ster.**
*The mother is standing at the win-
dow.*
Das Kind geht **ans (an das) Fenster.**
*The child goes to the window.*

**auf** *on, upon*  Der Kuchen ist **auf dem Tisch.**
*The cake is on the table.*
Stell den Kuchen **auf den Tisch!**
*Put the cake on the table!*

| | |
|---|---|
| **hinter** *behind* | Der Park ist **hinter der Kirche.**<br>*The park is behind the church.*<br>Ich fuhr schnell **hinter die Kirche.**<br>*I drove quickly behind the church.* |
| **in** *in, into* | Der Vater arbeitet **im (in dem) Garten.**<br>*The father is working in the garden.*<br>Der Sohn läuft **in den Garten.**<br>*The son runs into the garden.* |
| **neben** *beside* | Der Regenschirm steht **neben dem Stuhl.**<br>*The umbrella is (standing) next to the chair.*<br>Sie stellte den Regenschirm **neben den Stuhl.**<br>*She put the umbrella next to the chair.* |
| **über** *above, over, about* | Siehst du die Sonne **über dem Berg?**<br>*Do you see the sun above the mountain?*<br>Karl fährt **über den Berg.**<br>*Karl is driving over the mountain.* |
| **unter** *below, under, among* | Ich parkte den Wagen **unter einem Baum.**<br>*I parked the car under a tree.*<br>Ich lief **unter einen Baum.**<br>*I ran under a tree.* |
| **vor** *in front of, before* | Herr Müller hielt **vor dem Hotel** an.<br>*Mr. Müller stopped in front of the hotel.*<br>Herr Müller fuhr **vor das Hotel.**<br>*Mr. Müller drove in front of the hotel.* |
| **zwischen** *between* | Der Koffer ist **zwischen den Stühlen.**<br>*The suitcase is between the chairs.*<br>Stell den Koffer **zwischen die Stühle.**<br>*Put the suitcase between the chairs.* |

Again, some of these prepositions may be contracted with the definite article.

| DATIVE | ACCUSATIVE |
|---|---|
| an + dem = **am** | an + das = **ans** |
| in + dem = **im** | in + das = **ins** |
| | auf + das = **aufs** |

Some of these prepositions plus the accusative may be used with certain verbs that do not denote physical motion toward a place.

| | |
|---|---|
| Ich denke oft an dich. | *I often think of you.* |
| Das Kind hört nicht auf die Mutter. | *The child doesn't listen to his (her) mother.* |
| Wir sprechen über den Unfall. | *We are talking about the accident.* |
| Die Leute warten auf den Zug. | *The people are waiting for the train.* |

If you used **warten auf** + dative, as in the phrase „die Leute warten auf dem Zug," it would express the unlikely situation of people waiting on top of the train. But it is possible to say:

| | |
|---|---|
| Die Leute warten im Zug. | *The people are waiting on the train.* |

Note also these common expressions with **an:**

| | |
|---|---|
| am Morgen | *in the morning* |
| am Nachmittag | *in the afternoon* |
| am Abend | *in the evening* |
| am Montag | *on Monday* |

---

## Check your comprehension

*Fill in the appropriate form of the indicated article. Use contractions wherever possible.*

EXAMPLE: Ich denke oft *an* d_____ Geld.
   **Ich denke oft ans Geld.**

1. Die Mutter liest die Zeitung in d_____ Garten hinter d_____ Haus.
2. Der Schlüssel liegt auf d_____ Tisch.
3. Heute abend gehen wir in d_____ Stadt.
4. Fritz sprach über e_____ Reise.
5. Wir fahren mit d_____ Fahrrädern auf d_____ Land.
6. Sehen Sie den Wagen zwischen d_____ Garten und d_____ Haus?
7. Stell den Regenschirm neben d_____ Koffer!
8. Der Vater hat das Auto unter e_____ Baum geparkt.
9. Siehst du das Schild über d_____ Tür?
10. Wollt ihr in e_____ Café gehen?
11. Der Unfall passierte auf d_____ Straße nach Düsseldorf.
12. Oskar wartete lange auf d_____ Bürgersteig vor e_____ Hotel.
13. Wir haben lange in d_____ Hotel auf e_____ Freundin gewartet.
14. Wohin läuft er so schnell? Zu d_____ Polizei?
15. Essen die Europäer an d_____ Abend sehr viel?

## II. Infinitive clauses

**A.** *Clauses with* **zu**

In German as in English, the infinitive is often used with the preposition **zu** (*to*).

| | |
|---|---|
| Es wird schwierig, einen Parkplatz zu finden. | *It's getting difficult to find a parking place.* |

When the infinitive phrase has an object and/or an adverb, it is set off by a comma.

| | |
|---|---|
| Wir versuchen, wenigstens einmal in der Woche Sport zu treiben. | *We try to engage in sports at least once a week.* |
| Wir werden versuchen, schnell zu parken. | *We'll try to park quickly.* |
| *But:* Er vergaß zu schreiben. | *He forgot to write.* |

If the verb has a separable prefix, **zu** is placed between the prefix and the infinitive, and the whole is written as one word.

| | |
|---|---|
| Er hat vergessen, am Bahnhof aus-**zu**steigen. | *He forgot to get off at the railway station.* |

Three prepositions discussed earlier—**um, ohne,** and **(an)statt**—may be used as conjunctions with **zu** to introduce an infinitive clause.

| | |
|---|---|
| **um . . . zu** *in order to* | Er ging in die Stadt, **um** Einkäufe **zu** machen. *He went shopping downtown.* |
| **(an)statt . . . zu** *instead of* | **(An)statt** zu Fuß **zu** gehen, nehmen wir oft das Auto. *Instead of walking, we often take the car.* |
| **ohne . . . zu** *without* | Die Tochter sah mich an, **ohne** mich **zu** grüßen. *The daughter looked at me without greeting me.* |

When introducing an infinitive clause with these conjunctions, commas must be used.

Notice also that in all these infinitive clauses the infinitive is at the end of the clause, immediately preceded by **zu.**

## B. *Clauses without* **zu**

The modals (see Chapter 6) and a few other verbs, such as **lassen,
hören, sehen,** and **bleiben,** do not require **zu** in front of an infinitive
that follows.

| | |
|---|---|
| Ich möchte das Matterhorn besteigen. | *I would like to climb the Matterhorn.* |
| Die Frau ließ ihn weiterreden. | *The woman let him go on talking.* |
| Ich hörte ihn Gitarre spielen. | *I heard him play(ing) the guitar.* |
| Wir sahen den Sohn das Zimmer verlassen. | *We saw the son leave the room.* |
| Der Polizist blieb vor dem Hotel stehen. | *The policeman remained standing in front of the hotel.* |

## *Check your comprehension*

*Supply the appropriate form of the infinitive clause given in parentheses.*

1. Die Kinder sind in die Stadt gegangen, _____. (*in order to buy a bicycle*)
2. Es ist schwierig, _____. (*to rent a house*)
3. Fritz spielte Gitarre, _____. (*instead of studying*)
4. Ich versuchte, _____. (*to close the door*)
5. Franz ist zu mir gekommen, _____. (*without bringing along a record*)
6. Albert ließ sie _____. (*talk about the accident*)
7. Sie sahen Emma _____. (*leave the park*)
8. Wir hörten dich _____. (*arrive in the car*)
9. Sie vergassen _____. (*to come*)
10. Er blieb lange auf dem Boden _____. (*to lie*)

**USEFUL PHRASES**

| | |
|---|---|
| **aus Richtung Bielefeld** | *from the direction of Bielefeld* |
| **in Richtung Bahnhof** | *in the direction of the railroad station* |
| **Kommen wir da beim Dom vorbei?** | *Will we pass the cathedral?* |
| **Das geht nicht.** | *That's no good.* / *That doesn't (won't) work.* |
| **jemand anders** | *someone else* |
| **Bitte schön!** | *You're welcome.* |

**CONVERSATION**

## *Auf der Suche nach° der Universität*

*looking for*

*Fritz und Rudi, zwei Freunde und Universitätsstudenten, kommen in einem Volkswagen aus Richtung Bielefeld in Münster/Westfalen[1] an. Sie fahren in Richtung Bahnhof. Auf einer Straße halten sie an und bitten einen Passanten um Auskunft.*

FRITZ Verzeihung, wie kommen wir von hier zur Universität?

PASSANT Zur Universität? Das ist ganz einfach. Sehen Sie den Brunnen da vorne° am Ende des Parkplatzes?

*up ahead*

FRITZ Oh ja.

PASSANT Da fahren sie gleich nach rechts bis zur Klosterstraße.

FRITZ Sie meinen gleich da vorne hinter dem Brunnen?

PASSANT Hm, ja. Aber passen Sie auf! Auf der Klosterstraße müssen Sie nach links fahren.

RUDI (*studiert einen Stadtplan*) Kommen wir da beim Dom[2] vorbei?

PASSANT Nein, der Dom ist geradeaus. Aber das geht nicht. Es ist eine Fußgängerstraße.[3]

FRITZ Aber auf der Klosterstraße fahren wir nach links.

PASSANT Das müssen Sie. Sie werden sehen, es ist eine Einbahnstraße. Dann kommen Sie an eine Kreuzung.

[1] Bielefeld and Münster are both cities in Westphalia, an historic region of northwest Germany now incorporated in the **Land** (*state*) of **Nordrhein-Westfalen,** one of the eleven states constituting the German Federal Republic.

[2] Münster has a well-known cathedral dating back to the period of late Romanesque and early Gothic architecture.

[3] Many cities in Germany and other European countries now have pedestrian malls, especially in the older sections of towns with narrow streets.

FRITZ Gut.

PASSANT Aber nach der Kreuzung fahren Sie weiter bis zum Ende der Schützenstraße.

FRITZ Und dann?

PASSANT Dann fragen Sie vielleicht jemand anders.

FRITZ Vielen Dank.

PASSANT Bitte schön.

FRITZ (*zu Rudolf*) Du, sagte er nun nach rechts oder geradeaus da vorne an der Ecke?

RUDI Keine Ahnung. Fahr doch mal geradeaus. Wir werden die Uni° schon finden. Man sagt, es ist ein Palast.[4]     Universität

[4] The main building of the University of Münster (**Westfälische Wilhelms-Universität**) is indeed a former episcopal palace.

## Questions

1. Aus welcher (*which*) Richtung kommen die zwei Freunde?
2. Wo halten Sie an, und warum?
3. Ist es einfach, die Universität zu finden?
4. Wo steht der Brunnen?
5. Welche Straße erreichen die Freunde an der Ecke?
6. Warum dürfen sie nicht geradeaus zum Dom fahren?
7. Wen sollen die Freunde am Ende der Schützenstraße um Auskunft bitten?
8. Haben die Freunde die Auskunft gut verstanden?
9. Wen fragst du um Auskunft auf einer Fahrt durch eine Stadt?
10. Gibt es bei dir auch Fußgängerstraßen oder Einbahnstraßen? Wenn ja, warum?
11. Gibt es bei dir Dome oder Paläste? Bist du jemals (*ever*) hineingegangen?

**PRACTICE**

**A.** *Fill in the appropriate form of the indicated article or pronoun. Use contractions wherever possible (for instance:* **in + dem = im***).*

1. Der Bus hält vor d_____ Bahnhof, aber Moritz fährt mit d_____ Taxi hinter d_____ Bahnhof.

2. Helen nahm d_____ Regenschirm und verließ d_____ Zimmer, ohne _____ (*er*) anzusehen.

3. Der Polizist ging an d_____ Fenster und sah auf e_____ Parkplatz hinunter.

4. Was gibt es denn eigentlich zwischen _____ (*du*) und _____ (*sie*)? Ihr seht _____ (*ihr*) kaum an.

5. Auf d_____ Reise in d_____ Schweiz wurde _____ (*er*) plötzlich krank.

6. Sehen Sie d_____ Schild über d_____ Tür? Da gehen Sie durch d_____ Tür und d_____ Treppe hinauf.

7. Geh nicht in d_____ Park hinein, bleib hier neben d_____ Wagen stehen und warte auf _____ (*ich*); ich gehe schnell bis zu d_____ Kreuzung.

8. Sie warteten auf d_____ Bürgersteig vor d_____ Bahnhof auf e_____ Freund. Er kam spät an d_____ Abend mit e_____ Freundin an.

9. Trotz d_____ Regens ist Herr Weiß schon früh an d_____ Morgen mit d_____ Fahrrad zu d_____ Arbeit gefahren.

10. Er kam spät aus d_____ Gasthaus und wollte bis zu d_____ Haltestelle gehen, aber blieb an d_____ Ecke stehen.

**B.** *Answer the following questions in complete sentences with the phrases provided. Be careful to use the right case. Employ pronouns and contractions where possible.*

EXAMPLE: Wo ist die Universität? (an/der Schloßplatz)
   **Sie ist am Schloßplatz.**

1. Wohin gehen die Leute? (zu/der Bahnhof)
2. Auf wen wartet ihr? (auf/ein Freund)
3. Wo werdet ihr auf mich warten? (vor/das Hotel/unter/der Baum)
4. Aus welcher (which) Richtung kommen die Studenten? (aus/Richtung/Münster)
5. Wo seht ihr einen Brunnen? (da vorne/an/die Ecke)
6. Auf wen hörten die Kinder immer? (auf/die Mutter)
7. Wohin werden die Studenten reisen? (mit/der Zug/in/der Süden/Deutschland)
8. Worüber (about what) sprechen die Leute? (über/die Regierung)
9. Wo geht er auf und ab? (in/das Wohnzimmer)
10. An wen denkt sie? (an/ein Student/in/die Schweiz)

**C.** *Complete the sentences with the correct form of the phrases provided. Be careful of word order.*

EXAMPLES: Ich möchte immer _____. (bleiben/hier)
   **Ich möchte immer hier bleiben.**

   Es ist einfach, _____. (fahren/zu/die Universität)
   **Es ist einfach, zur Universität zu fahren.**

1. Man muß Geld haben, _____. (reisen/weit/um)
2. Ich hörte ihn früh am Morgen _____. (gehen/auf und ab/in/das Schlafzimmer)
3. Der Student ließ alles _____. (liegen/auf/der Boden)
4. Ich studierte sechs Stunden, _____. (essen/etwas/ohne)
5. Er hat vergessen, _____. (anhalten/vor/das Hotel)
6. Das Mädchen las weiter, _____. (antworten/anstatt)
7. Ich konnte heute nicht _____. (fahren/auf/das Land)
8. Wir sahen ihn früh am Morgen _____. (einsteigen/in/der Bus)

**D.** *Give the English equivalent.*

1. Anstatt mit dem Auto zu fahren, hat er den Zug genommen.
2. Elfriede ist nicht aufmerksam genug, um auf die Kinder aufzupassen.
3. Es ist sehr gefährlich, im Auto schnell über eine Kreuzung zu fahren.
4. Man muß zuerst anhalten, nach rechts und links sehen, und dann weiterfahren.
5. Sie warteten auf dem Bürgersteig vor dem Hotel auf einen Freund aus der Schweiz.
6. Die Studenten baten den Passanten um eine Auskunft über die Universität.

7. Es ist schwierig für ihn, in der Stadt anstatt auf dem Land zu leben.

8. Der Volkswagen kam um die Ecke und fuhr schnell weiter auf der Einbahnstraße in Richtung Bahnhof.

9. Kinder, geht nicht auf die Straße, bleibt hier und spielt im Garten!

10. Herr Stolz ließ das Geld für den Kaffee liegen und verließ den Raum, ohne auf die Frage zu antworten.

## GUIDED CONVERSATION

Look at the city map below. In your mind, position yourself at a certain street corner and determine where you want to go. Then ask your neighbor to tell you how to get there.

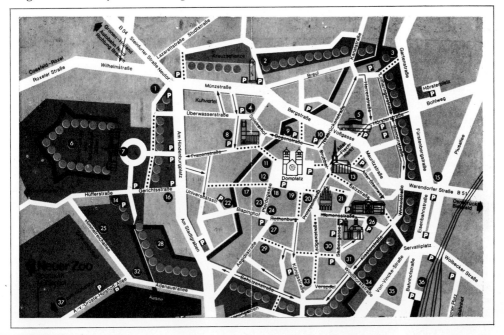

Zeichen: ──▶ Einbahnstraße • • • • Fußgängerstraße
Ⓟ Parkplatz ⓘ Information des Verkehrsvereins

Die Zahlen sind nach gedachten waagerechten Linien von Norden nach Süden angeordnet:
1 I. Korps der Bundeswehr 2 Buddenturm 3 Zwinger
4 Observantenkirche 5 St. Martini/Stadttheater
6 Schloßgarten 7 Schloß (Universität) 8 Überwasserkirche 9 Kiepenkerldenkmal 10 Apostelkirche
11 Bischöfliches Palais (Generalvikariat)
12 Fürstenberghaus der Universität/Archäologisches Museum/Studiobühne 13 St. Lamberti/Krameramtshaus/Dominikanerkirche 14 Mineralogisches Museum
15 Landeshaus (Landschaftsverband Westfalen)
16 Amts- und Landgericht 17 Petrikirche
18 Landesmuseum für Kunst und Kulturgeschichte

19 Postamt am Domplatz 20 Regierung 21 Rathaus/Stadtweinhaus/Stadtverwaltung 22 Universitätsbibliothek 23 Geologisch-Paläontologisches Museum
24 Landesmuseum für Vor- und Frühgeschichte
25 Landesmuseum für Naturkunde 26 Erbdrostenhof/Clemenskirche 27 Oberverwaltungsgericht NRW
28 Stadtbad/Turnierplatz Westerholtsche Wiese
29 Aegidiikirche 30 Landesamt für Agrarordnung NRW
31 Raphaelsklinik 32 Zoo-Tropenhaus 33 St. Ludgeri
34 Industrie- und Handelskammer
35 Landesversorgungsamt NRW 36 Hauptbahnhof/Bundesbahndirektion/Zimmertheater
37 Richtung Mühlenhof
38 Handwerkskammer 39 Landwirtschaftskammer
40 Kreishaus 41 Jugendherberge
42 Halle Münsterland/Stadthafen

## Sport und Leibesübungen

„Im Westen ißt man zu viel. Wir sind zu dick und zu faul geworden. Wir brauchen mehr Körperbewegung, um gesund zu bleiben!"
liest und hört man oft in der Presse. Man hört Argumente wie:

„Statt zu Fuß zu gehen, um Einkäufe zu machen, auch nur° um    *even just*
die Ecke, fahren wir im Auto." Oder: „Viele Menschen sitzen den
ganzen° Tag im Büro, gehen nach Hause, essen und trinken gut und    *whole*
sitzen dann noch ein bis zwei Stunden vor dem Fernsehapparat bevor°    *before*
sie ins Bett gehen. Sie haben zu wenig Körperbewegung."

Aber der Mensch von heute treibt auch sehr viel Sport oder versucht, wenigstens einmal oder zweimal in der Woche Leibesübungen
zu machen. In Deutschland gibt es zum Beispiel über 43000 Sportclubs
mit ungefähr 14 Millionen Mitgliedern. Man braucht kein Athlet zu
sein, um Mitglied zu werden. Im Club kann man turnen°, schwim-    *do gymnastics*
men, auch Fußball° und Tennis spielen oder mit Mitgliedern des    *soccer*
Clubs Fußwanderungen machen. Es gibt viele Möglichkeiten.

In den letzten° Jahren hat man auch außerhalb der Städte „Vita    *recent*
Parcours" [1] eingerichtet°, besonders in der Schweiz. Da sieht man oft    *installed*
an einem Sonntag oder während der Woche früh am Morgen oder spät

[1] These are publicly maintained physical fitness courses, with facilities for gymnastic
exercises or simple jogging. **Vita** = Latin for *life;* **parcours** = French for *track.* In Germany they are often called **"Trimm [Dich] Kurse"** = *trim [yourself] courses*

am Nachmittag eine ganze Familie—Vater, Mutter, Söhne und Töchter—durch einen Wald laufen, über Hindernisse° springen und Turnübungen machen. Sie springen nicht immer graziös° wie die Gazellen°, aber sie haben viel Spaß, atmen gute Luft ein und kommen hungrig und durstig nach Hause.

obstacles<br>gracefully<br>gazelles

Auch während der Ferien sucht man Körperbewegung in der Natur. Aber der Stadtmensch möchte auch den Lärm des Stadtlebens vergessen und auf dem Lande und in den Bergen Ruhe finden. Deshalb ist das Bergsteigen unter den Europäern sehr populär. Am Matterhorn² in der Schweiz, zum Beispiel, hat man bis zu 200 Bergsteiger an einem Tag gesehen! Aber viele erreichen den Gipfel° nicht. Leider stürzen einige ab°. Andere werden müde und geben es auf. Aber zu Hause sagen sie: „Ich habe das Matterhorn bestiegen!" Die Wahrheit ist: Sie sind auf dem Matterhorn herumgestiegen.° Natürlich haben sie den Gipfel nicht erreicht, aber wenigstens Bewegung,° wenn nicht Ruhe gefunden.

peak<br>fall off<br><br>climb around<br>exercise

² *The Matterhorn is in southern Switzerland; the Swiss-Italian border runs across its peak.*

## Questions

1. Was brauchen wir, um gesund zu bleiben?
2. Wo sitzen viele Menschen den ganzen Tag?
3. Wo sitzen sie dann zu Hause, bevor sie ins Bett gehen?
4. Muß man Athlet sein, um Mitglied eines Sportclubs zu werden?
5. Was macht man im Club?
6. Was macht die ganze Familie auf dem Vita Parcours?
7. Was atmet man dort ein?
8. Warum ist das Bergsteigen unter den Europäern sehr populär?
9. Warum erreichen viele Bergsteiger den Gipfel nicht?
10. Was sagen sie zu Hause?
11. Was haben sie tatsächlich am Matterhorn gefunden?

## A. Die Familie

The German words for the members of the family are:

| | |
|---|---|
| der Vater, ∺ | *father* |
| die Mutter, ∺ | *mother* |
| die Eltern *(pl.)* | *parents* |
| die Tochter, ∺ | *daughter* |
| der Sohn, ∺ | *son* |
| der Bruder, ∺ | *brother* |
| die Schwester, -n | *sister* |
| der Großvater, ∺ | *grandfather* |
| die Großmutter, ∺ | *grandmother* |
| der Onkel, - | *uncle* |
| die Tante, -n | *aunt* |
| der Neffe, -n | *nephew* |
| die Nichte, -n | *niece* |

Describe your family briefly. Tell how many brothers and sisters, etc., you have. State whether your parents or grandparents are still alive (**am Leben**) or dead (**gestorben**), and whether you have or would like to have children.

## B. *The gender of nouns and their endings*

As we said in the beginning of this course, it is best to memorize the gender and plural of nouns. Nonetheless, in some instances it is possible to determine from certain features of the noun its gender and plural.

For instance, all nouns ending in **-heit, -keit,** and **-ung** are feminine and take **-en** in the plural. Often they are derived from an adjective or verb.

| | | | |
|---|---|---|---|
| krank | *sick* | die Krank**heit,** -en | *sickness* |
| möglich | *possible* | die Möglich**keit,** -en | *possibility* |
| bewegen | *to move* | die Bewe**gung,** -en | *movement* |
| | | | *exercise* |
| üben | *to practice* | die Ü**bung,** -en | *practice* |

Go back to the last three Readings, locate at least three more nouns with these endings, and find their derivation.

Give the nouns derived from **gesund, schwierig,** and **wahr.**

Other feminine noun endings with a plural in **-en** are:

| die Part**ei**, -en | *(political) party* |
|---|---|
| die Nat**ion**, -en | *nation* |
| die Mann**schaft**, -en | *team (especially in sports)* |
| die Universi**tät**, -en | *university* |
| die Indust**rie**, -n | *industry* |

However, these are not derived from adjectives or verbs. Some are in fact of foreign origin.

**REVIEW EXERCISES**

**A.** *A sports enthusiast is addressing a group of students. Fill in the blanks as indicated.*

1. Die Menschen von heute _____ *(have become too fat)*.
2. Statt _____ *(walking)*, fahren sie immer _____ *(by car)*.
3. Und Sie, liebe Studenten, müssen den ganzen Tag _____ *(sit in the library)*, oder Sie liegen _____ *(under trees)* und _____ *(read books)*.
4. Und am Abend _____ *(after work)* sitzen Sie zwei oder drei Stunden _____ *(in front of the television set)*.
5. Das ist kein Leben! Statt _____ *(sitting at home)*, gehen Sie doch _____ *(to the Vita Parcours)*, springen Sie _____ *(over obstacles)* und laufen Sie _____ *(through forests)*!
6. Sie brauchen nicht _____ *(to be athletes)*, _____ gute Luft _____ *(in order to breathe in)*, und Sie _____ *(will have much fun)*.

**B.** *Fill in the appropriate form of the indicated article or* **kein,** *and in some cases the ending of the noun, then add the appropriate form of the infinitive clause with the cues given in parentheses. Use contractions where possible.*

EXAMPLE: Er versucht, zweimal in d_____ Woche _____.*(machen/ eine Leibesübung, pl.)*
  **Er versucht, zweimal in der Woche Leibesübungen zu machen.**

1. Ihr müßt durch d_____ Stadtmitte _____. *(fahren/erreichen/um/ die Universität)*
2. Vor k_____ Haus sehe ich _____. *(stehen/ein Wagen)*
3. Anstatt d_____ Zeitungen sollen wir _____. *(mitnehmen/ein Buch, pl.)*
4. Fahr weiter bis zu d_____ Kreuzung und bleib nicht _____! *(stehen/ auf/die Einbahnstraße)*
5. Sie möchten d_____ Lärm d_____ Stadtleben _____ vergessen und _____. *(finden/Ruhe/auf/das Land)*

6. Wir brauchen mehr Körperbewegung, _____. (*werden/nicht/zu/dick/um*)

**C.** *Fill in the blanks with the appropriate forms of the cues given in parentheses.*

EXAMPLE: Geh schnell in _____, da liegt das Buch auf _____.
(*das Wohnzimmer/der Tisch*)
**Geh schnell ins Wohnzimmer, da liegt das Buch auf dem Tisch.**

1. Frau König lief aus _____ auf _____. (*das Hotel/die Straße*)
2. Wir sahen _____ in _____ über _____ springen. (*ein Mann/der Wald/ Hindernis, pl.*)
3. Nach _____ gingen sie in _____ und sprachen über _____. (*das Abendessen/das Wohnzimmer/der Unfall*)
4. Während _____ hat sie immer mit _____ geredet. (*die Fahrt/ der Student*)
5. Siehst du _____ nicht? Er liegt gerade vor _____ auf _____. (*der Schlüssel/du/der Boden*)
6. An _____ haben Sie _____ geschrieben? (*wer/ein Brief*)

**D.** *Express in German.*

1. You needn't be an athlete (in order) to engage in sports.
2. During vacations the city dweller seeks quiet and exercise in the country.
3. How do we get (**kommen**) to the railroad station from here?
4. Turn left there at the corner.
5. Then drive straight ahead as far as the intersection.
6. Behind the fountain, drive around the corner.
7. Drive on to the end of the street.
8. Be careful of the one-way streets.
9. They have been waiting for some time (**schon lange**) at the bus stop for a friend.
10. Whom are you waiting for?

# GUIDED COMPOSITION

**A.** Describe what you do for physical exercise and how often you do it, if at all. Do you swim, play tennis, run, hike, go mountain climbing? Tell when you do these things, and where—in the city or the country, at the university, in parks, woods, mountains, lakes, rivers. Do you do them with friends or alone (**allein**). Tell also what sports and physical activities you would like to do (**ich möchte ...**). But if you'd rather stay home and play records, or drink beer and discuss politics, or lie under a tree reading a book, don't be afraid to say so.

**B.** In the pictures below describe briefly what these people are doing and whether they seem to do it well.

# CHAPTER VOCABULARY

## Easily recognized words

| | | |
|---|---|---|
| der | **Athlet,** -en | *athlete* |
| das | **Ende,** -n | *end* |
| die | **Natur** | *nature* |
| der | **Sport** | *sport(s)* |
| der | **Sportclub,** -s | *sportsclub* |
| | | |
| der | **Berg,** -e | *mountain* |
| das | **Bergsteigen** | *mountain climbing* |
| der | **Bergsteiger,** - | *mountain climber* |
| der | **Brunnen,** - | *fountain* |
| das | **Büro,** -s | *office* |
| der | **Dom,** -e | *cathedral* |
| die | **Einbahnstraße,** -n | *one-way street* |
| der | **Einkauf,** ⸚e | *purchase, errand* |
| die | **Eltern** (*pl. only*) | *parents* |
| der | **Fernsehapparat,** -e | *television set* |
| der | **Fußgänger,** - | *pedestrian* |
| die | **Fußwanderung,** -en | *hike;* **Fußwanderungen machen** *to go on hikes* |
| das | **Hindernis,** -se | *obstacle* |
| die | **Körperbewegung,** -en | *physical activity* |
| die | **Kreuzung,** -en | *intersection, crossroads* |
| der | **Lärm** | *noise* |
| die | **Leibesübung,** -en | *physical exercise;* **Leibesübungen machen** *to do physical exercise* |
| das | **Mitglied,** -er | *member (of a club, etc.)* |
| die | **Möglichkeit,** -en | *possibility* |
| die | **Mutter,** ⸚ | *mother* |
| der | **Nachmittag,** -e | *afternoon* |
| der | **Palast,** ⸚e | *palace* |
| der | **Passant,** -en | *passer-by* |
| die | **Richtung,** -en | *direction* |
| der | **Sohn,** ⸚e | *son* |
| die | **Tochter,** ⸚ | *daughter* |
| die | **Turnübung,** -en | *gymnastic exercise* |
| der | **Vater.** ⸚ | *father* |

| | | |
|---|---|---|
| die | **Wahrheit** | *truth* |
| der | **Wald,** ⸚er | *forest* |

See also the words for members of the family on p. 164.

| | |
|---|---|
| **auf·geben (gibt), gab, aufgegeben** | *to give up* |
| **auf·passen (auf** + *acc.*) | *to pay attention (to); to be careful (of)* |
| **besteigen, bestieg, bestiegen** | *to climb* |
| **brauchen** | *to need* |
| **ein·atmen** | *to breathe (in)* |
| **erreichen** | *to reach attain* |
| **gehen: zu Fuß gehen** | *to go on foot, walk* |
| **hören (auf** + *acc.*) | *to listen to* |
| **schwimmen, schwamm, (ist) geschwommen** | *to swim* |
| **sitzen, saß, gesessen** | *to sit* |
| **springen, sprang, (ist) gesprungen** | *to jump* |
| **treiben, trieb, getrieben** | *to practice, work at;* **Sport treiben** *to engage in sports, go in for sports* |
| **versuchen** | *to try* |
| **warten (auf** + *acc.*) | *to wait (for)* |
| | |
| **besonders** | *especially* |
| **dick** | *fat* |
| **durstig** | *thirsty* |
| **einfach** | *simple* |
| **einmal** | *once;* **einmal in der Woche** *once a week* |
| **faul** | *lazy* |
| **geradeaus** | *straight ahead* |
| **hungrig** | *hungry* |
| **leicht** | *easy* |
| **wenig** | *little, not much* |

See also the prepositions on pp. 152–153.

# 9

MODEL SENTENCES

### I

Sonja ist gerade angekommen, **aber** sie kommt leider etwas spät.
*Sonja just arrived, but unfortunately she's a little late.*

Peter geht nicht zu Fuß in die Stadt, **sondern** fährt mit dem Fahrrad.
*Peter doesn't walk downtown but goes by bike.*

Willst du zu Hause bleiben, **oder** sollen wir ins Theater gehen?
*Do you want to stay home, or shall we go to the theater?*

### II

Ich weiß, **daß** sie eine Tochter **hat.**
*I know that she has a daughter.*

Wir besuchen euch, **sobald** die Ferien **beginnen.**
*We will visit you as soon as vacations begin.*

Du vergißt, **daß** der Vater den ganzen Tag im Büro **sitzen muß.**
*You forget that father has to sit in an office all day.*

**Wenn** du Lust **hast,** können wir heute abend in ein Restaurant gehen.
*If you're in the mood, we can go to a restaurant tonight.*

Margret konnte nichts sagen, **weil** Oskar die ganze Zeit **redete.**
*Margret couldn't say anything because Oskar talked all the time (the whole time).*

**Als** das Mädchen **anrief,** war ich leider nicht zu Hause.
*When the girl called, unfortunately I wasn't home.*

**GRAMMAR
EXPLANATION**

## I. Coordinating conjunctions

Instead of merely juxtaposing words or phrases, we often wish to show their mutual relationship. Conjunctions make it possible to do this. In the following example, note the use of the conjunction **denn:**

Ich kann nicht ins Kino gehen. Ich muß heute abend studieren.

Ich kann nicht ins Kino gehen, **denn** ich muß heute abend studieren.

*I can't go to a movie, for I must study tonight.*

There are two kinds of conjunctions: *coordinating conjunctions* like **denn** connect clauses of equal value, whereas *subordinating conjunctions* introduce a clause that is dependent on another clause. In German, the word order of a clause is determined by the kind of conjunction that introduces it.

The *coordinating conjunctions* do not affect the word order of the clause. They leave it in its original sequence, whether normal or inverted. The most important of these conjunctions are:

aber[1] *but*
denn[1] *for, because*
oder *or*
sondern *but, on the contrary*
und *and*

Sie kommt gerade an, **aber** sie kommt leider etwas spät.

*She's just arriving, but unfortunately she's a little late.*

Ich gehe nicht ins Kino, **denn** jetzt bin ich zu müde.

*I'm not going to the movies, because now I'm too tired.*

[1] These conjunctions may also be used as "flavoring particles," as explained earlier.

Sollen wir zu Hause bleiben, **oder** willst du ins Theater gehen?     *Shall we stay home, or do you want to go to the theater?*

Peter fährt nicht mit dem Auto zur Universität, **sondern** mit dem Fahrrad.     *Peter doesn't drive to the university but goes by bike.*

Der Vater arbeitet im Garten, **und** die Tochter liest im Wohnzimmer.     *The father works in the garden, and the daughter reads in the living room.*

**Aber** means *but* in the sense of *nevertheless;* it can be used after a positive clause or a negative clause containing **kein. Sondern** means *but* in the sense of *on the contrary;* it contradicts a preceding negative statement, and is used only after a negative clause containing **nicht.**

Notice also that the word order of the clause following the conjunction may be normal or inverted, or a question, depending on the position of other elements in the sentence.

Ich gehe nicht ins Kino, denn **ich bin** jetzt zu müde.

Ich gehe nicht ins Kino, denn jetzt **bin ich** zu müde.

Sollen wir zu Hause bleiben, oder **willst du** ins Theater gehen?

## Check your comprehension

*Combine each pair of sentences into one by using the conjunction indicated.*

EXAMPLES: Moritz braucht mehr Körperbewegung. Er ist zu dick geworden. (*for*)
**Moritz braucht mehr Körperbewegung, denn er ist zu dick geworden.**

Er war nicht im Haus. Er war im Garten. (*but*)
**Er war nicht im Haus, sondern im Garten.**

1. Er war kein Athlet. Er war Mitglied eines Sportclubs. (*but*)
2. Gehen wir beim Baum um die Ecke? Gehen wir geradeaus? (*or*)
3. Der Vater wollte den Gipfel erreichen. Er gab es auf. (*but*)
4. Wir schwammen nicht im Fluß. Wir schwammen im See. (*but*)
5. Die Schwester lief durch den Wald. Ich blieb zu Hause. (*and*)
6. Er fand die Adresse nicht. Die Passanten konnten ihm keine Auskunft geben. (*for*)
7. Fahren Sie nicht nach links. Fahren Sie bis Sie zu einem Brunnen kommen. (*but*)

## II. Subordinating conjunctions and dependent word order

Unlike the coordinating conjunctions, the *subordinating conjunctions* affect the word order of the clause they introduce. They require the dependent or subordinate word order. This means that the inflected part of the verb phrase stands at the very end of the clause. One must therefore watch carefully whether the verb is in a simple or compound tense, as in the following examples with **daß** (*that*).

| | |
|---|---|
| Du weißt doch, daß ich Ferien **habe.** | *You know that I have a vacation.* |
| Du vergißt, daß ich keine Ferien **hatte.** | *You forget that I had no vacation.* |
| Ich wußte nicht, daß du keine Ferien **gehabt hast.** | *I didn't know that you'd had no vacation.* |
| Ich glaube, daß er bald Ferien **haben wird.** | *I think that he'll have a vacation soon.* |

The sentence may of course involve a verb with a separable prefix. In that case, prefix and verb are united even in the simple tenses.

| | |
|---|---|
| Ihr wißt doch, daß sie bald **abfährt.** | *You know that she's leaving soon.* |
| Wir wissen nicht, ob sie schon **abgefahren ist.** | *We don't know whether she has already left.* |

Or the clause may contain a modal, which must be placed at the end:

| | |
|---|---|
| Du wußtest doch, daß ich am Freitag nicht ins Kino gehen **konnte.** | *You knew that on Friday I couldn't go to the movies.* |

With certain conjunctions such as **wenn** (*if*), the subordinate clause often stands at the beginning. In that case, the main clause which follows is in the inverted word order.

| | |
|---|---|
| **Wenn** du Lust hast, **können wir** in einem Restaurant essen. | *If you like, we can eat in a restaurant.* |

Notice that clauses introduced by a subordinating conjunction are always set off from the main clause by a comma.

There are many subordinating conjunctions. Here are some of those frequently used.

| | |
|---|---|
| als *when, as* | obwohl *although* |
| bevor *before* | seit, seitdem *since* (time) |
| daß *that* | sobald *as soon as* |
| nachdem *after* | weil[1] *because* |
| ob *whether, if* | wenn *if, when* |

[1] At times **da** is used instead of **weil**.

| | |
|---|---|
| **Als** er ankam, lasen wir die Zeitung. | *When he arrived, we were reading the paper.* |
| Sie machte die Tür zu, **bevor** sie die Treppe hinaufging. | *She closed the door before she went upstairs.* |
| Er wußte, **daß** Karl oft Berge bestieg. | *He knew that Karl often climbed mountains.* |
| **Nachdem** wir die Nachrichten gehört haben, sitzen wir immer lange vor dem Fernsehapparat. | *After we've heard the news, we always sit a long while in front of the television set.* |
| Ich weiß nicht, **ob** er gern Bücher liest. | *I don't know if he likes to read books.* |
| Er redete noch lange weiter, **obwohl** wir alle müde waren. | *He kept on speaking a long time, although we were all tired.* |
| **Seitdem** sie aus den Ferien zurückgekommen ist, habe ich sie nicht mehr gesehen. | *Since she got back from vacation, I haven't seen her any more.* |
| **Sobald** du gegessen hast, fahren wir ab. | *As soon as you have eaten, we'll depart.* |
| Ich konnte es dir nicht sagen, **weil** du die ganze Zeit redetest. | *I couldn't tell you, because you talked all the time.* |
| Wir gehen nach Hause, **wenn** er nicht bald kommt. | *We'll go home if he doesn't come soon.* |

**Als** and **wenn** can both be translated by *when*, but they cannot be used interchangeably. **Als** is used to express a single action in the past.

| | |
|---|---|
| **Als** er uns anrief, waren wir gerade beim Essen. | *When he called us, we were eating.* |

**Wenn** is used to express an action in the present (or in the future).

| | |
|---|---|
| **Wenn** er anruft, gehe ich sofort hin. | *When he calls, I'll go there right away.* |

**Wenn** is also used to express a repeated action in the past, especially in conjunction with **immer.**

| | |
|---|---|
| **Immer wenn** sie anrief, war ich nicht zu Hause. | *Whenever she called, I was not at home.* |

Compare now the various kinds of word order in German:

| | |
|---|---|
| NORMAL | Sie ist in die Stadt gegangen. |
| INVERTED | Heute morgen ist sie in die Stadt gegangen. |
| QUESTION | {Wann ist sie in die Stadt gegangen?<br>{Ist sie in die Stadt gegangen? |
| DEPENDENT | Ich weiß nicht, ob sie in die Stadt gegangen ist. |

## *Check your comprehension*

*Combine each pair of sentences into one by using the conjunction indicated. Be careful of word order and punctuation.*

EXAMPLE: Er bezahlt. Er steigt aus. (*bevor*)
**Er bezahlt, bevor er aussteigt.**

1. Wir lasen die Zeitung. Die Mutter rief aus Düsseldorf an. (*als*)
2. Er ist Mitglied eines Sportclubs geworden. Er ist kein Athlet. (*obwohl*)
3. Ich werde dich anrufen. Ich habe das Gepäck geholt. (*sobald*)
4. Mach die Tür zu. Du gehst ins Bett. (*bevor*)
5. Er grüßt uns nicht mehr. Er verdient so viel Geld. (*seitdem*)
6. Die Eltern gehen nicht ins Theater. Sie sind sehr spät aus der Stadt zurückgekommen. (*weil*)
7. Kommt doch zu uns. Ihr habt gegessen. (*nachdem*)
8. Wir wissen nicht. Sie werden bald nach Stuttgart abfahren. (*ob*)
9. Man muß sehr viel Übung (*practice*) im Bergsteigen haben. Man will das Matterhorn besteigen. (*wenn*)
10. Sie verließen den Raum. Er spielte Klavier. (*immer wenn*)

**USEFUL PHRASES**

| | |
|---|---|
| **vor einer Stunde** | *an hour ago* |
| **Hast du Lust, ins Kino zu gehen?** | *Do you feel like going to the movies?* |
| **Mach mir nichts vor!** | { *Come on!* { *Don't kid me!* |

| | |
|---|---|
| **interessiert sein (an + *dat.*)** | *to be interested in* |
| **Alles schön und gut.** | *That's all fine and dandy.* |
| **Ganz recht!** | *That's right.* |
| **Einverstanden?** | *Agreed?* |
| **die ganze Zeit** | *the whole time, all the time* |
| **Viel Vergnügen!** | *Have fun!* |

**CONVERSATION**

## Sollen wir ins Kino gehen?

*Heinz ist ein Film-Enthusiast. Er ruft einen Freund, Karl Zimmermann,
an und versucht, ihn zu überreden, mit ihm am Abend ins Kino zu gehen.*

KARL Zimmermann.

HEINZ Hallo Karl! Hier Heinz. Endlich bist du zu Hause. Vor einer
Stunde rief ich dich schon an, aber ich erhielt keine Antwort.

KARL Ich war doch heute im Seminar bei Professor Dietrich. Zum
Schluß ließ er einen Studenten noch lange reden, obwohl wir
alle fast am Einschlafen° waren.                                    *asleep*

HEINZ Das ist nichts Neues. Als ich vor einem Jahr bei ihm im Seminar saß, geschah das jede° Woche. Aber hör mal, hast du Lust,   *every*
ins Kino zu gehen?

KARL Lust habe ich sicher, aber ich habe schon eine Verabredung.

HEINZ Mach mir nichts vor! Den Faßbinder[1] Film im „Odeon" mußt
du unbedingt sehen, wenn du wirklich an der Filmkunst interessiert bist.

---

[1] Rainer-Maria Faßbinder, a German film maker whose social commentaries and artis-
tic sense have caught the attention of the German and even an international public.

KARL Alles schön und gut, aber ich kann doch nicht gleichzeitig an zwei Orten sein.

HEINZ Ganz recht! Also, ich hole dich ab, sobald du gegessen hast. Einverstanden?

KARL Aber Heinz, heute abend gehe ich mit Margret ins Theater zu einer Faust²-Vorstellung. Verstehst du?

HEINZ Aber warum hast du denn das nicht gleich gesagt?

KARL Weil du die ganze Zeit redest.

HEINZ Na, gut. Viel Vergnügen! Aber mach keine Gretchen-Tragödie³ aus deiner° Verabredung!

        *your*

² *Faust*, by Johann Wolfgang Goethe (1749–1832), is probably the most eminent work of German literature. It is a dramatic poem in two parts, only the first of which is widely known abroad.

³ **Gretchen** is the diminutive of **Margarete** or **Margret**. The **Gretchentragödie** is an episode in the first part of *Faust* where Gretchen, seduced and abandoned by Faust, is driven to madness.

## Questions

1. Wen ruft Heinz an?
2. Was versucht er zu tun?
3. Warum hat er Karl nicht erreicht, als er anrief?
4. Wann will Heinz den Freund abholen?
5. Warum kann Karl nicht mit Heinz ins Kino gehen?
6. Warum hat Karl das nicht gleich gesagt?
7. Haben Sie Lust, heute abend ins Kino zu gehen?
8. Gehen Sie oft ins Kino oder ins Theater?
9. Mit wem gehen Sie meistens ins Kino oder Theater?
10. Sind Sie ein Film-oder Theater-Enthusiast? Wenn nein, was für ein (*what kind of a*) Enthusiast sind Sie?

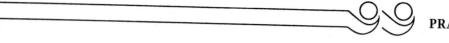

**PRACTICE**

**A.** *Complete each sentence with the item following it. Be careful of word order.*

1. Rudi gab das Bergsteigen auf. Er wird leicht müde. (*denn*)
2. Es regnete. Ich konnte keinen Parkplatz beim Hotel finden. (*und*)
3. Herr Dietrich geht zum Vita Parcours. Er ist kürzlich krank gewesen. (*obwohl*)
4. Du vergißt. Ich kann nicht gleichzeitig an zwei Orten sein. (*daß*)
5. Nichts Neues ist geschehen. Die zweihundert Radfahrer sind in Schaffhausen zusammengekommen. (*seitdem*)

6. Hör doch auf zu reden. Wir schlafen alle ein. (*bevor*)

7. Ich weiß nicht. Ferien befreien den Menschen von der Routine. (*ob*)

8. Passen Sie auf. Die Polizei hält Sie an. (*oder*)

9. Sie sah uns nicht an. Wir fragten nach dem Schlüssel. (*als*)

10. Frau Heller hat die Polizei angerufen. Sie hörte den Lärm im Schlafzimmer. (*sobald*)

**B.** *Combine the two sentences with the conjunction listed on the right, and put the verb in parentheses in the indicated tense. Watch word order and punctuation.*

EXAMPLE: Sie/noch nicht ins Bett (*gehen, pres. perf.*)
es/erst neun Uhr (*sein, pres.*) denn
**Sie sind noch nicht ins Bett gegangen, denn es ist erst neun Uhr.**

1. Die ganze Familie/immer gern in die Berge (*reisen, pres. perf.*)
man/da gute Luft (*einatmen können, pres.*) weil

2. Wir/erst heute (*hören, pres. perf.*)
Herr Meyer/so lange krank (*sein, past*) daß

3. Er/Mitglied eines Sportclubs (*werden, pres. perf.*)
er/kein Athlet (*sein, pres.*) obwohl

4. Er/das Haus wieder (*vermieten, future*)
es/frei (*werden, pres. perf.*) sobald

5. Die Schwester/lange in Hamburg (*leben, past*)
der Bruder/außerhalb der Stadt (*wohnen, past*) und

**C.** *Form sentences with the given cues and combine them first with* **denn** *and then with* **weil** *in the indicated tenses. Watch the word order and punctuation.*

EXAMPLE: sein/die Schwester/noch/sehr schwach (*pres.*) sein/sie/lange/krank. (*pres. perf.*)
**Die Schwester ist noch sehr schwach, denn sie ist lange krank gewesen.**
**Die Schwester ist noch sehr schwach, weil sie lange krank gewesen ist.**

1. haben/wir/jetzt/kein/Geld (*pres.*)
ausgeben/zuviel/für die Möbel. (*pres. perf.*)

2. Können/fahren/du/nicht/auf/die Klosterstraße/geradeaus (*pres.*)
sein/eine Einbahnstraße. (*pres.*)

3. trinken/ich/viel (*pres. perf.*)
sein/sehr/durstig. (*past*)

4. abholen/ich (*subject*)/er/an/der Bahnhof (*future*)
haben/er/immer noch/kein Wagen. (*pres.*)

**D.** *Fill in the asterisked blank with* **aber** *or* **sondern***. Also fill in the indicated articles, contracted where possible.*

1. Der Bruder lebt nicht in d_____ Stadt _____* auf d_____ Land.

2. Der Vater hat in d_____ Garten hinter d_____ Haus viel Gemüse _____* auch viele Blumen gepflanzt.

3. An d_____ Kreuzung da vorne müssen Sie nach links fahren, _____*
passen Sie auf, denn sie werden auf e_____ Einbahnstraße kommen.

4. Sie wartet nicht auf d_____ Vater _____* auf d_____ Freunde.

5. Er hielt bei d_____ Fußgängerstraße an, _____* er stieg nicht aus
d_____ Wagen.

6. Der Parkplatz ist nicht vor d_____ Bahnhof _____* neben d_____
Bushaltestelle.

**E.** *Fill in the blanks with* **als** *or* **wenn**. *Fill in also the appropriate form
of the indicated article, contracted where possible.*

1. _____ ihr k_____ Leibesübungen macht, werdet ihr zu dick.

2. _____ er in d_____ Stadt fuhr, hatte er e_____ Unfall.

3. Immer _____ wir in d_____ Restaurant gingen, vergaß er, Geld
mitzubringen.

4. _____ sie nach Westerland in d_____ Ferien reisten, hatten sie viel
Spaß.

5. _____ ihr gute Luft einatmen wollt, geht auf d_____ Land!

**F.** *Having used certain subordinating conjunctions in dependent word
order, you will readily understand sentences and phrases containing
other subordinating conjunctions, such as:*

falls   *in case, if*          sooft   *as often as, whenever*
so daß  *so that*              während   *while*
solange  *as long as*          wie   *as*

*Now give the English equivalents of the following sentences.*

1. Falls du wirklich an dem Problem interessiert bist, kannst du das Buch
mitnehmen.

2. Wie ich gerade in den Nachrichten im Fernsehen hörte, ist auf der Straße
vor dem Theater ein Autounfall geschehen.

3. Sooft er versuchte, mich zu überreden, hörte ich nicht auf ihn.
4. Während der Student weiterredete, schliefen wir fast alle ein.
5. Elfriede treibt sehr viel Sport, so daß sie nicht oft krank ist.
6. So lange man gesund ist, macht man oft keine Leibesübungen.

**GUIDED
CONVERSATION**

Look at the film ads below, select the film you would like to see, and then try to convince your neighbor(s) to come with you to the movie. Give them reasons why you think they should come. They may or may not agree to come with you. If not, they should give you a good reason in turn.

READING

## Theater, Film und Fernsehen

Man hört oft, daß der Film das Theater ersetzt hat und das Fernsehen bald den Film ersetzen wird. Aber das ist natürlich eine Übertreibung.° Man kann das Problem nicht so einfach ausdrücken, sondern man muß viele Faktoren betrachten. Zum Beispiel darf man sagen, daß das Theater eine lange Tradition hat und seit den Anfängen tief° in der Kultur des Volkes verwurzelt° ist. Obwohl es später oft zum Unternehmen° einer Elite wurde, ist das Theater auch heute noch, besonders in Europa, sehr populär. In Deutschland, Österreich und der Schweiz gibt es viele „Stadttheater" oder „Staatstheater". Das sind Theater, die° von der Stadt oder vom Staat Subventionen° erhalten. Das heißt, man verwendet° einen Teil der Steuern, das Theater zu unterstützen. So wird das Theater fast zum Eigentum° des Publikums.

> exaggeration

> deep / rooted
> undertaking

> which / subsidies
> uses
> property

Auch im Theater selber°, während der Vorstellung, hat man das Gefühl, ein Teil des Geschehens° zu sein, denn oft kennt man das Theaterstück oder auch die Schauspieler, und man weiß, wenn sie es gut machen oder nicht. Während der Pause geht man ins Foyer, trinkt Sekt¹, ißt Kuchen und spricht mit Freunden über die Vorstellung. Man ist da, nicht nur um zu sehen, sondern auch, um gesehen zu werden.° Deshalb geht man sehr oft im besten Anzug ins Theater.

> itself
> event

> to be seen

Man will im Gespräch auch zeigen, daß man etwas vom Theaterstück versteht. Manchmal ist zum Beispiel der erste° Teil von Goethes „Faust"² auf dem Programm. Aber die Interpretation des Stückes läßt viele Möglichkeiten offen, und meistens glaubt das Publikum, „Faust" gut zu verstehen. So hörte man kürzlich bei einer Faust-Vorstellung im Residenztheater³ in München Gespräche wie: „Du, Fritz, zum Teufel noch mal°, der Mephistopheles⁴ schien mir am Anfang doch etwas zu kriecherisch".° „Ja, vielleicht, aber der Teufel braucht ja nicht immer so selbstsicher° zu sein. Er hat schließlich auch Probleme mit Gott". „Du bist aber zynisch° heute."

> first

> what the devil
> fawning
> self-assured
> cynical

Man trinkt noch schnell einen Schluck° und geht dann in den Theatersaal zurück.

> sip

Im Film ist der Intellekt vielleicht nicht so stark beschäftigt. Viele

¹ German champagne.

² Usually only the first part of *Faust* is performed on the stage. Most directors consider the second part, almost five times as long as the first, to be too immense for a stage performance.

³ A well-known state theater in Munich, situated in part of the former residence of the Bavarian kings.

⁴ Mephistopheles, the devil in Goethe's *Faust,* is a clever schemer who contends with God for Faust's soul and is ultimately defeated.

Leute sagen, daß der Film das Auge ebenso° beschäftigen soll wie den   as much as
Intellekt. Es ist richtig, daß im Film die Kunst des Photographierens°—   photography
Licht, Farben, Bewegungen°—sehr wichtig ist. Aber viele Filme ver-   light, colors, action
binden die Kunst des Photographierens mit einem ernsten° Thema. In   serious
Deutschland haben einige Filmproduzenten° diese Kunstform sehr ge-   film producers
fördert,° und der Staat unterstützt sie auch.   promoted

    Im Fernsehen muß man aber mit dem Thema vorsichtig sein.
Viele Fernsehfilme sind in Deutschland sehr lehrhaft.° Sie drücken   instructional
etwas über ein Problem aus, wie zum Beispiel die Emanzipation der
Frau oder die Unterdrückung° von Randgruppen.° Aber, wie in Ame-   oppression / minorities
rika, sind „Krimis", Shows und Quizzes⁵ sehr populär, denn wenn man
am Abend nach Hause kommt, will man die Probleme des Tages vergessen.

---

⁵ **Krimis** (from **Kriminal**) is an abbreviation for murder mysteries and detective stories.
The terms **Shows** and **Quizzes** are now commonly used in Germany.

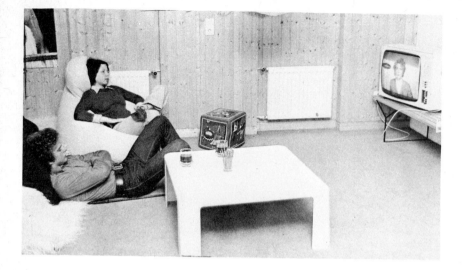

## Questions

1. Was hört man oft?
2. Warum kann man das Problem nicht so einfach ausdrücken?
3. Was darf man über das Theater sagen?
4. Wer unterstützt ein Stadttheater? ein Staatstheater?
5. Was tut man im Theater in Deutschland während der Pause?
6. Was will man im Gespräch über das Theaterstück zeigen?
7. Was ist im Film sehr wichtig?
8. Was verbinden viele Filme?
9. Was drücken viele Fernsehfilme in Deutschland aus?
10. Warum wollen viele Leute solche (*such*) Filme am Abend nicht sehen?

**VOCABULARY
DEVELOPMENT**

## A. Wortfamilien

If you are observant, you will develop a certain flair in detecting relationships between words and in making deductions from the known to the unknown. It can be fun. For instance:

1. drücken = *to press*
   aus·drücken = *to express*
   > der Ausdruck, ⸚e = *expression*
   unterdrücken = *to suppress or oppress*
   > die Unterdrückung = *suppression, oppression*

But watch out! If you use **ein·** instead of **aus·**, there is trouble ahead.

|  |  |  |
|---|---|---|
| | ein·drücken | = *to press or push in, or break* (a window, for instance) |
| *But:* | beeindrucken | = *to impress (make an impression)* |
| | | > der Eindruck, ¨e = *impression* |

So when somebody has made an impression on you, be careful to say:

|  |  |  |
|---|---|---|
| | Er hat mich sehr beeindruckt. | *He impressed me very much.* |
| *Or:* | Sie hat einen guten Eindruck auf mich gemacht. | *She made a good impression on me.* |

2. In this lesson you have had **ab·holen,** meaning *to go or come get somebody* (at the airport, for instance), and **holen,** meaning *to fetch.* But **wiederholen** means *to repeat*—literally, to fetch again and again.

|  |  |
|---|---|
| Wiederholen Sie die Übung! | *Repeat the exercise once more!* |

So what would a **Wiederholungsübung** be?
   **Wieder** (*again*) could of course occur as an adverb with **holen:**

|  |  |
|---|---|
| **Hol** mir das Buch **wieder,** bitte! | *Please fetch me that book again.* |

3. With **schlafen** (*to sleep*) you must also be careful: **ein·schlafen** doesn't mean *to sleep in,* but *to go to sleep;* **aus·schlafen** means *to completely rest up by sleeping, to get a good night's sleep.*
   Use these three verbs in a few sentences.

## B. Clothing

**Der Anzug** (*suit*) is derived from **an·ziehen, zog, angezogen,** which means *to pull or put on (clothes).* Here now are some German words for clothing. (You have already had **die Badehose** in Chapter 7.)

|  |  |
|---|---|
| die Hose, -n | *trousers, pants* |
| das Kleid, -er | *dress* |
| die Jacke, -n | *jacket* |
| der Mantel, ¨ | *overcoat* |
| das Hemd, -en | *shirt* |
| die Socke, -n | *sock* |
| der Schuh, -e | *shoe* |
| die Krawatte, -n | *tie* |
| der Rock, ¨e | *skirt* |
| die Bluse, -n | *blouse* |
| die Weste, -n | *vest* |

das Kopftuch, ⁼er       *scarf*

die Sandale, -n       *sandal*

der Pulli, -s   }
der Pullover, - }       *sweater*

---

**REVIEW**

**A.** *Combine each pair of sentences into one by using the conjunction indicated.*

EXAMPLE: Ich gehe heute nicht ins Kino. Ich muß noch sehr viel studieren. (*for*)
**Ich gehe heute nicht ins Kino, denn ich muß noch sehr viel studieren.**

1. Wir haben keinen Brief von ihm erhalten. Er kennt die Adresse nicht. (*for*)
2. Es war nicht möglich einzuschlafen. Die Studenten machten so viel Lärm auf der Straße. (*because*)
3. Man weiß nicht. Das Fernsehen wird bald den Film ersetzen. (*whether*)
4. Das Publikum weiß. Die Schauspieler machen es gut. (*if*)
5. Er sprach mit Freunden über die Vorstellung. Er ging während der Pause ins Foyer. (*when*)
6. Wir trinken Sekt. Wir gehen in den Theatersaal zurück. (*before*)
7. Ich habe ihn nicht gesehen. Wir sind zusammen ins Theater gegangen. (*since*)
8. Man sagt. Man muß mit dem Thema vorsichtig sein. (*that*)

**B.** *Form sentences with the given cues in the indicated a./b. sequence. Watch the word order and punctuation.*

EXAMPLE: a. sprechen/der/Professor/obwohl/lange über das Problem (*past*)
         b. verstehen/ich/nichts (*pres. perf.*)
**Obwohl der Professor lange über das Problem sprach, habe ich nichts verstanden.**

1. a. unterstützen/die Regierung/obwohl/es (*pres.*)
   b. sein/das Theater/teuer.
2. a. können/ausdrücken/man/das Problem/nicht/so einfach (*pres.*)
   b. müssen/betrachten/man/denn/viele Faktoren. (*pres.*)
3. a. anrufen/er (*subject*)/sobald/ich (*pres. perf.*)
   b. abholen/ich (*subject*)/er. (*future*)
4. a. sagen/ich/nichts (*past*)
   b. reden/er (*subject*)/weil/die ganze Zeit. (*past*)
5. a. zurückgehen/das Theater/bis zu/die Anfänge/die Kultur (*pres.*)
   b. sein/die Filmkunst/aber/neu. (*pres.*)
6. a. wissen/du (*pres.*)
   b. verwenden/man/in Deutschland/daß/Steuern/für/das Theater? (*pres.*)

**C.** *Put the second clause at the beginning of the sentence and adjust the word order of the other clause. At the same time fill in the blanks with the appropriate forms and endings, using contractions where possible.*

1. Er ging lange in d_____ Zimmer auf und ab, weil er nicht einschlafen konnte.

2. Ich werde nicht in d_____ Theater gehen, wenn ihr nicht mitkommt.

3. Er sah _____ (*wir*) nur an, während wir versuchten, _____ (*er*) zu überreden.

4. Sie sind nicht an d_____ Film interessiert, obwohl der Film zu e_____ Kunstform geworden ist.

5. Er hat _____ (*ich*) nicht geschrieben, seitdem er bei d_____ Freunden wohnt.

6. Wir werden _____ (*ihr*) anrufen, sobald wir gegessen haben.

**D.** *Express in German.*

1. Although I like to go to the theater, I can't go there (*hin·gehen*) very often.

2. It is said that television will soon replace the film.

3. Are you in the mood to go to a movie, or do you wish to stay home?

4. I don't know whether she has already arrived.

5. Don't try (*ihr*) to convince us.

6. One may say that the art of the film does not have a long tradition.

7. While they were talking about God and the devil, we fell asleep.

8. Although the play is very good, the performance was bad.

9. I can't go with you this evening, because I already have a date.

10. When he called on the phone an hour ago, we were sitting in front of the television set.

**GUIDED COMPOSITION**

First, state whether you are interested in the theater, cinema, or television, or all three, and why. Then describe briefly a visit to a theater or movie house. Where was it? Were there many people there? Were you interested in the theme of the play or movie? Are you interested in the photography of the film? Was there an intermission? What did people say and do during intermission? Did you go home directly or did you go to a café or restaurant first? With whom did you go? Are you in a mood to go with that person again?

## Easily recognized words

| | | |
|---|---|---|
| der | **Enthusiast,** -en | *enthus* |
| der | **Film,** -e | *film, movie* |
| die | **Form,** -en | *form* |
| der | **Intellekt** | *intellect* |
| | **interessiert** (**an** + *dat.*) | *interested (in)* |
| die | **Interpretation,** -en | *interpretation* |
| die | **Kultur,** -en | *culture* |
| das | **Restaurant,** -s | *restaurant* |
| das | **Theater,** - | *theater* |
| das | **Thema,** *pl.* **Themen** | *theme* |
| die | **Tradition,** -en | *tradition* |

| | | |
|---|---|---|
| der | **Anzug,** ̈e | *suit (clothes)* |
| das | **Auge,** -n | *eye* |
| das | **Foyer,** -s | *lobby* |
| das | **Gefühl,** -e | *feeling* |
| das | **Gespräch,** -e | *conversation, discussion* |
| der | **Gott,** ̈er | *god* |
| das | **Kino,** -s | *movie theater;* **ins Kino gehen** *to go to the movies* |
| die | **Kunst,** ̈e | *art* |
| die | **Lust** | *desire, joy;* **Lust haben** *to be in the mood, feel like (doing something)* |
| der | **Ort,** -e | *place, spot* |
| die | **Pause,** -n | *intermission* |
| der | **Saal,** *pl.* **Säle** | *hall, large room* |
| der | **Schauspieler,** - | *actor* |
| der | **Teil,** -e | *part* |
| der | **Teufel,** - | *devil* |
| das | **Theaterstück,** -e | *play* |
| die | **Verabredung,** -en | *date, appointment* |
| das | **Vergnügen** | *pleasure* |
| das | **Volk,** ̈er | *people* |
| die | **Vorstellung,** -en | *performance* |

See also words for clothes on pp. 183–184.

| | |
|---|---|
| **ab·holen** | *to come or go for, come or go get* |
| **an·rufen, rief, angerufen** | *to call (by phone)* |
| **aus·drücken** | *to express* |
| **beschäftigen** | *to occupy* |
| **betrachten** | *to consider* |
| **ein·schlafen (schläft), schlief, (ist) eingeschlafen** | *to go to sleep* |
| **erhalten (erhält), erhielt, erhalten** | *to receive* |
| **ersetzen** | *to replace* |
| **geschehen (geschieht), geschah, (ist) geschehen** | *to happen* |
| **holen** | *to fetch, get* |
| **scheinen** (+ *dat.*), **schien, geschienen** | *to seem* |
| **überreden** | *to persuade* |
| **unterstützen** | *to support* |
| **verbinden, verband, verbunden** | *to join, unite, combine* |
| **wiederholen** | *to repeat* |

| | |
|---|---|
| **also** | *therefore* |
| **gleichzeitig** | *at the same time* |
| **nachmittags** | *in the afternoon* |
| **offen** | *open* |
| **sondern** | *but, on the contrary* |
| **später** | *later on* |
| **unbedingt** | *absolutely, definitely* |
| **vor** + *dat.* | *ago* |
| **vorsichtig** | *careful* |

See also the conjunctions on pp. 170–173.

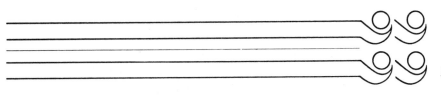

**MODEL SENTENCES**

### I

**Dieses** Gespräch war interessant.
*This conversation was interesting.*

**Welchen** Film möchtet ihr sehen?
*Which film would you like to see?*

Ich suche **meinen** Anzug.
*I'm looking for my suit.*

Wo habt ihr **eure** Fahrräder hingestellt?
*Where did you put your bikes?*

In dieser Stadt gibt es **viele** Hochhäuser.
*In this city there are many high-rise buildings.*

Sie wohnen seit **mehreren** Jahren in Österreich.
*They have lived in Austria for several years.*

## II

Im Rheinland **befinden sich** viele Burgen.
*In the Rhineland there are many castles.*

Ich **erinnere mich** sehr gut **an** diesen Film.
*I remember this film very well.*

Fritz, geh und **wasch dir** die Hände!
*Fritz, go wash your hands.*

**Haben** Sie **sich von** Ihrer Krankheit **erholt?**
*Have you recovered from your illness?*

Ich **hole mir** schnell eine Zeitung.
*I'm going to get (me) a newspaper fast.*

## III

Antworten Sie **mir** doch!
*Answer me, please.*

Ich danke **Ihnen** sehr.
*I thank you very much.*

**Es** ist **mir** nicht **gelungen,** ihn zu überreden.
*I did not succeed in persuading him.*

## GRAMMAR EXPLANATIONS

### I. DER and EIN words

These are two groups of noun modifiers. The first group is declined like the definite article **der, die, das;** the second, like the indefinite article **ein, eine, ein.**

#### A. DER words

The most common **der** words are:

> **dieser**[1] *this, that*
> **jeder** *each, every* (used only in the singular)
> **mancher** *many a;* pl.: *several, some*
> **welcher** *which*

[1] For **that** one may still hear the obsolescent **jener,** especially in highly formal language where **dieser** often stands for *the latter* and **jener** for *the former.*

| | | | |
|---|---|---|---|
| **Dieser** Film ist sehr interessant. | *This (that) film is very interesting.* | | |
| Heinz ging **jede²** Woche ins Kino. | *Heinz went to the movies every week.* | | |
| **Mancher** Student schreibt nicht gern. | *Many a student doesn't like to write.* | | |
| **Manche** Leute gehen jede Woche ins Theater. | *Many people go to the theater every week.* | | |
| **Welches** Theaterstück möchtest du sehen? | *Which play would you like to see?* | | |

To determine the form of a **der** word, take the stem—for instance **dies**—and add the appropriate case ending of the definite article.

*Declension of* **der** *words:* **dieser**

| | | SINGULAR | | PLURAL |
|---|---|---|---|---|
| | MASCULINE | FEMININE | NEUTER | ALL GENDERS |
| *nom.* | dies**er** | dies**e** | dies**es** | dies**e** |
| *acc.* | dies**en** | dies**e** | dies**es** | dies**e** |
| *dat.* | dies**em** | dies**er** | dies**em** | dies**en** |
| *gen.* | dies**es** | dies**er** | dies**es** | dies**er** |

## Check your comprehension

*Fill in the appropriate form of the* **der** *words indicated in parentheses.*

1. In _____ Richtung müssen wir fahren? (*welcher*)
2. In _____ Städten gibt es Fußgängerwege. (*mancher*)
3. Kennen Sie _____ Schauspieler? (*dieser*)
4. Was bedeutet _____ Wort? (*dieser*)
5. Wir arbeiten _____ Tag im Büro. (*jeder*)
6. _____ Fernsehfilm drückt etwas über _____ Problem aus. (*mancher, dieser*)
7. _____ Vorstellung _____ Theaterstückes habt ihr gesehen? (*welcher, dieser*)

## B. EIN *words*

The **ein** words include the *possessive adjectives.*

| POSSESSOR | | | | |
|---|---|---|---|---|
| ich | **mein** | *my* | Dort ist **mein** Vater. | *My father is there.* |
| du | **dein** | *your* | Suchst du **deinen** Anzug? | *Are you looking for your suit?* |

² The accusative case is used with expressions of *definite time:* **jede Woche** (*every week*); **nächsten Montag** (*next Monday*); **letzten Monat** (*last month*); etc. This usage occurs throughout the chapter.

| | | | | |
|---|---|---|---|---|
| er | **sein** | *his* | Kennst du **seine** Tochter? | *Do you know his daughter?* |
| sie | **ihr** | *her* | Wo ist **ihr** Regenschirm? | *Where is her umbrella?* |
| es | **sein** | *its* | Sind **seine** Eltern hier? (For instance: die Eltern **des Kindes**.) | *Are his parents here?* |
| wir | **unser** | *our,* | Wir werden in **unserem** Garten arbeiten. | *We will work in our garden.* |
| ihr | **euer** | *your* | Wann werdet ihr **euren** Urlaub haben? | *When will you have your vacation?* |
| sie | **ihr** | *their* | Ist das **ihr** Klavier? | *Is that their piano?* |
| Sie | **Ihr** | *your* | Wo sind **Ihre** Freunde? | *Where are your friends?* |

The negative **kein** is another **ein** word, as are **solch ein** (*such a*), **was für ein** (*what a, what kind of a*), and **welch ein** (*what a*).

**Solch einen** Film muß man gesehen haben!    *One has to see such a film!*

**Was für** ein Vergnügen wir haben werden!    *What fun we'll have!*

**Was für** ein Buch hat er geschrieben?    *What kind of a book did he write?*

**Welch eine** Vorstellung!    *What a performance!*

Notice that **was für ein** can be used in either exclamations or questions.

To determine the form of an **ein** word, take the stem—for instance, **mein**—and add the appropriate case ending of the indefinite article in the singular and of **kein** in the plural (since the indefinite article does not have a plural form).

| | | SINGULAR | | PLURAL |
|---|---|---|---|---|
| | MASCULINE | FEMININE | NEUTER | ALL GENDERS |
| *nom.* | mein | mein**e** | mein | mein**e** |
| *acc.* | mein**en** | mein**e** | mein | mein**e** |
| *dat.* | mein**em** | mein**er** | mein**em** | mein**en** |
| *gen.* | mein**es** | mein**er** | mein**es** | mein**er** |

*Declension of **ein** words:* **mein**

Notice that the **ein** words differ from the **der** words only in the nominative masculine singular and the nominative and accusative neuter singular (as is to be expected from the declension of **der** and **ein**).

When **euer** takes a declensional ending, it drops **-e-** in front of **-r.** For instance:

| euere > **eure** | Wo sind **eure** Fahrräder? | *Where are your bikes?* |
| euerern > **euren** | Wo habt ihr **euren** Koffer hingestellt? | *Where did you put your suitcase?* |

The **ein** words, especially the possessives, may replace a noun and so become pronouns. In that case the nominative masculine singular adds **-er** and the nominative and accusative neuter singular add **-s** or **-es.** The other cases remain the same.

| Sein Wagen ist auf der Straße. **Meiner** steht vor dem Hotel. | *His car is on the street. Mine is in front of the hotel.* |
| Hast du mein Buch? Nein, ich habe **seins.** | *Do you have my book? No, I have his.* |
| Ist das sein Auto? Nein, es ist **unseres.** | *Is that his car? No, it's ours.* |

In connection with the **der** and **ein** words, you should learn a number of words, most of them called *indefinite numerical adjectives,* that occur in the plural. They take the endings of the **der** or **ein** words (which are the same in the plural, as you can tell from the charts above).

| **alle**[1] *all* **andere**[2] *other* **beide** *both* **einige** *some* | **mehrere** *several* **solche** *such* (plural of **solch ein**) **viele**[3] *many* **wenige**[3] *(a) few* |

| **Alle** Einwohner sind gegen diesen Plan. | *All inhabitants are against this plan.* |
| Es gibt **andere** Möglichkeiten. | *There are other possibilities.* |
| Ich kenne **beide** Teile von Goethes „Faust". | *I know both parts of Goethe's Faust.* |
| Herr Härtling ist schon seit **einigen** Tagen krank. | *Mr. Härtling has been sick for some days.* |
| Sie hatten **mehrere** Wochen Urlaub. | *They had several weeks of vacation.* |
| **Solche** Leute sind gefährlich. | *Such people are dangerous.* |
| Auf **vielen** Bergen stehen Burgen. | *There are castles on many mountains.* |

[1] There is also an undeclined singular form: **alles,** which does not refer to specific items, but rather to a general idea. **Was bedeutet das alles?** *What does all that mean?*

[2] **Andere** is also used in the singular and plural with an article as an attributive adjective: **Der andere Wagen ist besser.** *The other car is better.* For attributive adjectives, see Chapter 11.

[3] **Viele** and **wenige** may also occur in the singular, but then they remain undeclined. **Viel Vergnügen!** *Have fun!* **Er hat wenig Zeit.** *He has little time.*

In **wenigen** Tagen wird unser Sohn zurückfahren.

*In a few days our son will drive back.*

---

## Check your comprehension

**A.** *Fill in the appropriate form of the* **ein** *word or numerical adjective indicated in parentheses.*

1. Wohin ging _____ Tochter in die Ferien? (*euer*)
2. _____ Mitglieder _____ Clubs haben einen Unfall gehabt. (*mehrere, unser*)
3. Die Interpretation _____ Theaterstückes läßt _____ Möglichkeiten offen. (*sein, viele*)

4. Was für _____ Wagen hat _____ Bruder gekauft? (*ein, dein*)
5. In _____ Orten sah man _____ Touristen. (*solche, wenige*)
6. Das ist _____ Tisch, nicht _____. (*ihr, mein*)
7. Seit _____ Tagen sucht die Polizei _____ Sohn. (*einige, ihr*)

**B.** *Fill in the appropriate form of the* **der** *or* **ein** *word or numerical adjective indicated in English.*

1. _____ Anzug ziehst du an? (*which*)
2. Wo habt ihr _____ Regenschirme hingestellt? (*your, fam.*)
3. _____ Woche geht Franz einmal ins Kino. (*every*)
4. _____ Gärtner hat _____ Glück mit _____ Garten. (*Many a, no, his*)
5. _____ Freund ist das!? (*What a*)
6. Das ist nicht _____ Auto, es ist _____. (*their, ours*)
7. _____ Eltern leben seit _____ Jahren in _____ Schweiz. (*My, several, the*)
8. Ich spiele nicht gern auf _____ Klavier. (*his*)
9. Wir haben in _____ Garten _____ Blumen gepflanzt. (*our, many*)
10. _____ Töchter werden in _____ Tagen aus _____ Ferien zurückkommen. (*her, a few, their*)

---

## II. Reflexive pronouns and verbs

Reflexive pronouns refer the action of the verb back to its subject.

| SUBJECT | VERB | REFLEXIVE PRONOUN | |
|---------|------|-------------------|---|
| Er | fragte | sich | = *he asked himself* (not somebody else) |

In German, a number of verbs occur only as reflexives.

| | |
|---|---|
| Er hat **sich** von seiner Krankheit **erholt.** | *He has recovered from his illness.* |
| Im Rheinland **befinden sich** viele Burgen. | *There are many castles in the Rhineland.* |
| Sie **kümmern sich** kaum um ihre Eltern. | *They hardly take care of their parents.* |

Most verbs can be made reflexive without change of basic meaning.

| | |
|---|---|
| Ich frage **dich,** was das bedeutet. | *I'm asking you what that means.* |
| Ich frage **mich,** was das bedeutet. | *I'm asking myself what that means.* |

Some verbs have a different (though related) meaning in the reflexive form.

| | |
|---|---|
| Ich **erinnerte mich** gut an das Gespräch. | *I remembered the conversation well.* |
| *But:* Ich **erinnerte ihn** an das Gespräch. | *I reminded him of the conversation.* |

Notice that in some of the above sentences the reflexive verb is followed by a preposition such as **von, um, an.**[1]

---

[1] Some reflexive verbs must always be used with a preposition, such as **sich kümmern um** + acc.; these verbs are listed in vocabularies with the preposition not in parentheses. Other verbs may or may not be used with a prepositional object such, as **sich erholen** (**von** + dat.); these verbs are listed with the preposition in parentheses.

Usually the reflexive pronoun is in the accusative. However, if the verb already has an accusative object, the reflexive is in the dative case. This happens especially with reference to parts of the body. In that case one uses the reflexive pronoun in the dative and the definite article of the accusative object, rather than the possessive adjective.

| | |
|---|---|
| Ich wasche mir die Hände. | *I wash my hands.* |

Or one may use this structure to emphasize the significance of an action to its performer:

| | |
|---|---|
| Ich kaufe **mir** ein Auto. | *I'm buying myself a car.* |
| Ich hole **mir** eine Zeitung. | *I'm going to get (me) a paper.* |

Notice the position of the reflexive pronoun.

| | |
|---|---|
| NORMAL: | { Ich kaufe **mir** einen Anzug.<br>{ Ich habe **mir** einen Anzug gekauft. |
| INVERTED: | Morgen kaufe ich **mir** einen Anzug. |
| DEPENDENT: | Ich glaube, daß ich **mir** bald einen Anzug kaufen muß. |

In the first and second persons, the reflexive pronouns are identical with the dative and accusative object pronouns. In the third person and formal address, the reflexive has a special form: **sich.**

*Reflexive pronouns*

| | SINGULAR | | PLURAL |
|---|---|---|---|
| | ACCUSATIVE | DATIVE | ACCUSATIVE AND DATIVE |
| *1st* | mich | mir | uns |
| *2nd fam.* | dich | dir | euch |
| *3rd* | **sich** | **sich** | **sich** |
| *2nd formal* | **sich** | **sich** | **sich** |

## Check your comprehension

**A.** *Supply the appropriate form of the reflexive pronoun.*

1. Kurt, wasch _____ die Hände!
2. Herr Graf, haben Sie _____ von der Reise erholt?
3. Ihr müßt _____ mehr um eure Eltern kümmern.
4. Wann hat Albert _____ Zigaretten geholt?
5. Endlich kann ich _____ ein Fahrrad kaufen!
6. In welchem Land befinden _____ viele Burgen?
7. Wir fragen _____, wann die Kinder zurückkommen werden.

**B.** *Translate into German.*

1. I remember her very well.
2. We reminded him of our appointment.
3. He washed his hands.
4. He washed his car.

## III. Verbs requiring the dative

A number of important German verbs cannot have an accusative object and are most often followed by an object in the dative.

| | |
|---|---|
| **antworten** *to answer* | Sie antwortete **ihm** nicht.<br>*She didn't answer him.* |
| **danken** *to thank* | Ich danke **Ihnen** sehr.<br>*I thank you very much.* |
| **folgen (ist gefolgt)** *to follow* | Ich konnte **seinem** Argument nicht folgen.<br>*I couldn't follow his argument.* |
| **gefallen** *to please* | Das Theaterstück gefiel **mir** nicht.<br>*The play didn't please me. (I didn't like the play.)* |
| **gehören** *to belong* | Dieses Fahrrad gehört **der Tochter** meines Freundes.<br>*This bike belongs to my friend's daughter.* |
| **helfen** *to help* | Hilf **ihr** doch ein wenig!<br>*Please help her a little.* |
| **zu·hören** *to listen* | Leider hören diese Kinder **ihren** Eltern nicht zu.<br>*Unfortunately, these children don't listen to their parents.* |

The verb **glauben** takes the dative with a person, but the accusative with a fact or at times a thing.

|  | Wir glauben **ihr** nicht. | *We don't believe her.* |
|---|---|---|
| *But:* | Ich glaube **das** nicht. | *I don't believe that.* |
|  | Er glaubt die Geschichte nicht. | *He doesn't believe the story.* |

Some verbs can be used only with the impersonal subject **es** (or **das**); the person concerned is in the dative.

| | |
|---|---|
| **gelingen (ist gelungen)** *to succeed* | **Es** ist **ihnen** nicht gelungen, ihn zu überreden.<br>*They did not succeed in convincing him.* |
| **genügen** *to be enough, be sufficient* | **Das** genügt **uns**.<br>*That is sufficient for us.* |

## Check your comprehension

*Fill in the appropriate form of the indicated words.*

1. Ich kann _____ leider mit _____ Arbeit nicht helfen. (*du, diese*)
2. Es ist _____ Bergsteiger nicht gelungen, das Matterhorn zu besteigen. (*der*)
3. Gefiel _____ der Film? (*Sie*)
4. _____ gehört diese Zeitung? (*wer*)
5. Wir danken _____ für _____ Bericht. (*ihr, 2nd fam.; dieser*)
6. Ich kann _____ nicht glauben. (*er*)
7. Ich habe _____ noch nicht geantwortet. (*sie, 3rd sing.*)
8. Danke sehr, das genügt _____. (*ich*)

**USEFUL PHRASES**

| | |
|---|---|
| **im Vergleich mit** | *in comparison with* |
| **Meine Güte!** | *{ Good Lord!* <br> *{ My goodness!* |
| **ganze (fünf) Mark!** | *a whole (five) Marks!* |

**CONVERSATION**

## Der Umrechnungskurs°

*rate of exchange*

*Herr und Frau Kohler, Deutschamerikaner, befinden sich auf einer Ferienreise durch ihre alte Heimat.° Sie sind vor zwei Tagen im Flugzeug aus Chicago in Frankfurt angekommen und haben sich inzwischen von ihrer Reise erholt. Nun kommen sie ins Frühstückszimmer ihres Hotels und setzen sich an einen Tisch. Sie haben gerade ihr Frühstück bestellt und fangen an sich zu unterhalten.*

*homeland*

FRAU K. Du, da hat einer[1] seine Zeitung vergessen.
HERR K. Das glaube ich nicht. Sie gehört sicher dem Hotel. Siehst du

---

[1] Often **einer** (the **ein** word as a noun) is used for **jemand** (*someone*).

# SüddeutscheZeitung

Ausgabe M • Preis 80 Pf

MÜNCHNER NEUESTE NACHRICHTEN AUS POLITIK · KULTUR · WIRTSCHAFT · SPORT

| 24. Jahrgang | München, Freitag, 18. August | B 7979 A | Nummer 188 / 33. W. |

# Franksurter Allgemeine

ZEITUNG FÜR DEUTSCHLAND

D 2954 A

Dienstag, 29. August   Nr. 187 D-Ausgabe   Herausgegeben von Bruno Dechamps, Jürgen Eick, Fritz Ullrich Fack, Joachim Fest, Johann Georg Reißmüller, Erich Welter   1 DM

die Zeitungen auf dem Tisch da drüben? Die sind alle für die Gäste da.

FRAU K. Ach ja, ich muß mich wieder an die Gebräuche hier gewöhnen.

HERR K. Moment bitte, ich hole mir schnell die „Frankfurter Allgemeine"[2]!. Was für eine Zeitung möchtest du dir ansehen?

FRAU K. Ach ja, ich muß mich wieder an die Gebräuche hier gewöhdem Umrechnungskurs des Dollars erkundigen.

*Herr Kohler geht zu dem Tisch und kommt mit beiden Zeitungen zurück.*

HERR K. Hoffentlich ist der Kurs° nicht noch weiter gefallen. Für Amerikaner hat das Wirtschaftswunder[3] leider auch seine Schattenseiten°.

*rate*

*dark side(s)*

[2] A well-known daily in the Federal Republic of Germany.

[3] **Wirtschaftswunder** (*economic miracle*) is the term commonly used to describe the amazing economic recovery of Germany from the Second World War, and its continued prosperity. In its initial stages the recovery was greatly stimulated by Marshall Plan aid from the United States.

FRAU K. Fantastisch! Hier steht°: „Dollar erholt sich an der Frankfurter Börse."°    *it says* / *money and stock exchange*

HERR K. Gut, dann gehen wir zur Bank, sobald wir gegessen haben, und wechseln noch einige Reiseschecks.

*Eine Stunde später vor der Bank.*

FRAU K. Wieviel Mark auf zweihundert Dollar haben wir nun gewonnen im Vergleich mit dem Kurs von gestern?

HERR K. Wart mal! Ich rechne es schnell aus.°—Meine Güte! Ganze fünf Mark. Das genügt vielleicht gerade für das Taxi ins Hotel zurück.    *I'm computing*

## Questions

1. Was haben Herr und Frau Kohler getan, seitdem sie in Frankfurt angekommen sind?
2. Was machen Herr und Frau Kohler, nachdem sie ins Frühstückszimmer gekommen sind?
3. Wem gehören die Zeitungen im Hotel?
4. Was hofft Herr Kohler?
5. Warum sagt Frau Kohler „Fantastisch!"?
6. Was wollen die beiden nach dem Frühstück tun?
7. Ist es ihnen gelungen, etwas Geld zu gewinnen? Wieviel?

8. Liest du oft eine Zeitung, nachdem du dich an den Tisch gesetzt hast?
9. Welche Zeitungen liest du?
10. Wenn du in die Ferien gehst, nimmst du dann immer Reiseschecks mit?
11. Wo kann man auf einer Reise seine Reiseschecks wechseln?

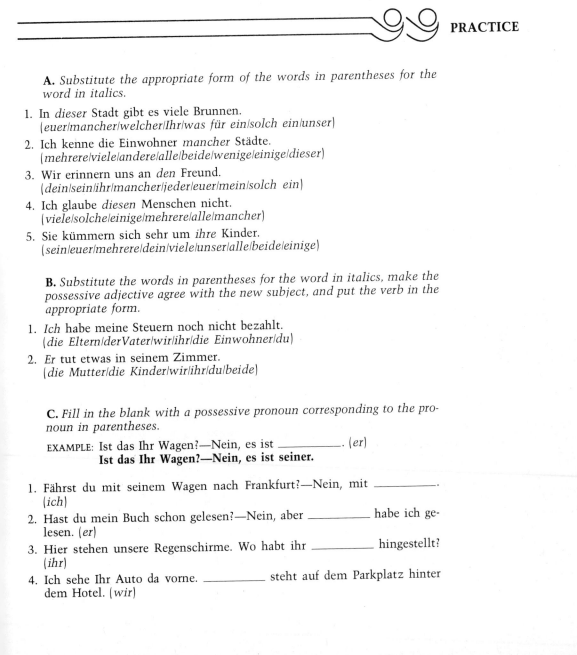

**PRACTICE**

**A.** *Substitute the appropriate form of the words in parentheses for the word in italics.*

1. In *dieser* Stadt gibt es viele Brunnen.
   (*euer/mancher/welcher/Ihr/was für ein/solch ein/unser*)
2. Ich kenne die Einwohner *mancher* Städte.
   (*mehrere/viele/andere/alle/beide/wenige/einige/dieser*)
3. Wir erinnern uns an *den* Freund.
   (*dein/sein/ihr/mancher/jeder/euer/mein/solch ein*)
4. Ich glaube *diesen* Menschen nicht.
   (*viele/solche/einige/mehrere/alle/mancher*)
5. Sie kümmern sich sehr um *ihre* Kinder.
   (*sein/euer/mehrere/dein/viele/unser/alle/beide/einige*)

**B.** *Substitute the words in parentheses for the word in italics, make the possessive adjective agree with the new subject, and put the verb in the appropriate form.*

1. *Ich* habe meine Steuern noch nicht bezahlt.
   (*die Eltern/der Vater/wir/ihr/die Einwohner/du*)
2. *Er* tut etwas in seinem Zimmer.
   (*die Mutter/die Kinder/wir/ihr/du/beide*)

**C.** *Fill in the blank with a possessive pronoun corresponding to the pronoun in parentheses.*

EXAMPLE: Ist das Ihr Wagen?—Nein, es ist _____. (*er*)
   **Ist das Ihr Wagen?—Nein, es ist seiner.**

1. Fährst du mit seinem Wagen nach Frankfurt?—Nein, mit _____.
   (*ich*)
2. Hast du mein Buch schon gelesen?—Nein, aber _____ habe ich gelesen. (*er*)
3. Hier stehen unsere Regenschirme. Wo habt ihr _____ hingestellt?
   (*ihr*)
4. Ich sehe Ihr Auto da vorne. _____ steht auf dem Parkplatz hinter dem Hotel. (*wir*)

**D.** *Insert the appropriate form of the verb in parentheses, putting it in the indicated form. Watch the word order.*

EXAMPLE: Maria/gut mit unseren Eltern. (*sich unterhalten, pres. perf.*)
**Maria hat sich gut mit unseren Eltern unterhalten.**

1. Bitte, Frau Kohler,/an diesen Tisch! (*sich setzen, imperative*)
2. Gestern/wir/nach dem Umrechnungskurs. (*sich erkundigen, past*)
3. Ich/schnell/die Reiseschecks. (*sich holen, future*)
4. Wir/nicht mehr an Sie. (*sich erinnern, past*)
5. Wir wissen, daß er/nie/um seine Eltern. (*sich kümmern, pres. perf.*)
6. Hans, wie schmutzig du bist! Geh und/das Gesicht und die Hände! (*sich waschen, imperative*)
7. Wart mal, ich/schnell eine Tasse Kaffee. (*sich holen, pres.*)
8. Ich/gut von meiner Krankheit. (*sich erholen, pres. perf.*)
9. Vor vielen Jahren/hier ein Theater. (*sich befinden, past*)
10. Helga,/die Haare! (*sich waschen, imperative*)

**E.** *Fill in the appropriate form of the indicated words.*

1. Der Film gefällt _____ nicht. (*wir*)
2. Ich danke _____ für _____ Bericht. (*Sie, der*)
3. Dieser Schlüssel gehört nicht _____ sondern _____. (*er; sie, sing.*)
4. Folgst du _____ Wagen auf die Einbahnstraße? (*dieser*)
5. _____ hört der Junge zu? (*wer*)
6. Ich glaube _____ einfach nicht. (*du*)
7. Es gelingt _____ Autofahrer nicht, _____ Polizisten zu überreden. (*der, der*)

**F.** *Put each of the above sentences into the past and the present perfect.*

**G.** *Give the English equivalent.*

1. Erika und Hans, geht und wascht euch die Hände!
2. Setz dich an den Tisch und fang an zu essen!
3. Warum hast du mich nicht an die Vorstellung erinnert?
4. Ich kann mich nicht an dieses Theaterstück erinnern.
5. Was für ein Fernsehprogramm möchten Sie sich ansehen?
6. Du, da hat einer seine Badehose vergessen.
7. Ich muß mich zuerst an dieses Klavier gewöhnen.
8. Wir können ihm einfach nicht glauben.
9. Während des Essens haben sie sich sehr gut unterhalten.
10. Fährt Ihr Freund in Ihrem Auto?—Nein, in seinem.

Pretend that you and several classmates are American tourists who have just met in a hotel in Germany. Ask one another if you came to Germany by plane, and when. Ask one another if you have recovered from the trip, and if you are having a good time. Ask if the dollar has recovered, or if it has fallen again. Ask one another if you are getting used to the money, the customs, the language, the people, etc.

## Von Burgen und Hochburgen°

*strongholds*

Seit dem Ende des Zweiten° Weltkrieges ist Frankfurt a.M.[1] das
Finanzzentrum° Deutschlands geworden. In dieser Stadt erheben sich
jetzt neben einigen Gebäuden aus dem Mittelalter viele Hochhäuser
gegen den Horizont. Da ist zum Beispiel das Rathaus, wo einmal die
Kaiser Deutschlands ihre Bankette hielten°; aber es ist nun überschat-
tet° von einem Bankgebäude und anderen Hochhäusern. Sogar der
Dom scheint klein im Vergleich mit diesen Riesen.° Und neben vielen
Brunnen aus dem Mittelalter befinden sich große Parkplätze. Hier
erlebt man gleichzeitig die Vergangenheit und die Gegenwart.

*second*
*financial center*



*held their banquets*
*overshadowed*
*giants*

Man gewinnt diesen Eindruck° auch, wenn man mit dem Zug
durch das Rheintal ins Ruhrgebiet[2] fährt. Nachdem der Zug die Bahnhofshalle verlassen hat, fängt man an zu lesen, zu rauchen oder aus
dem Fenster zu schauen. Bald öffnet sich dem Auge eine Traumland-
schaft.° Der Rhein windet sich gegen Norden durch Hügel und Wein-
berge, um Felsen und an vielen Dörfern mit hübschen Häusern und
Kirchen vorbei. Auf vielen Felsen und Hügeln stehen Burgen wie
Wächter.° Aber das Leben auf dem Rhein scheint sich kaum um sie
zu kümmern. Viele Frachter,° mit Kohle° und anderen Industriepro-
dukten voll beladen,° fahren langsam den Rhein hinauf oder hinab;

*impression*




*dreamland*



*guards*

*freighters / coal*
*loaded*

[1] **a.M.** is the abbreviation for **am Main**; the river Main flows into the Rhine.

[2] The Ruhr district is one of the world's most important industrial areas; its financial
and banking center is Düsseldorf.

*der Rhein*

*Frankfurt*

der Rhein ist für die Wirtschaft Deutschlands und Europas sehr wichtig. Im Zug studieren Geschäftsleute Dokumente, schreiben Berichte oder unterhalten sich über Wirtschaftsprobleme. Sie haben keine Zeit, sich über die schöne Landschaft zu freuen. Da sagt einer: „Sobald wir mehrere Kernkraftwerke° haben, werden wir nicht mehr soviel Kohle brauchen." Eine Kollegin° antwortet ihm: „Ha, das wird noch lange dauern,° wenn es überhaupt möglich ist."

    Für einen Moment scheinen Vergangenheit, Gegenwart und Zukunft zusammenzufließen—die Burgen auf den Felsen, die Kohle auf den Frachtern und die Kernkraftwerke im Gespräch der Geschäftsleute. Und wenn man aus dem Fenster zu den Burgen aufschaut,° hat man fast das Gefühl, daß diese Wächter der Vergangenheit sich fragen: was soll das alles bedeuten?

    Nicht weit hinter Köln fängt das Ruhrgebiet an. Anstatt der Burgen, Kirchen und Dome des Rheinlandes **sieht** man die Kamine° vieler

nuclear power plants
colleague
take a long time

looks up

chimneys

*Düsseldorf*

Fabriken, aber in Städten wie Düsseldorf stehen wieder viele Hochhäuser neben mehreren Gebäuden aus dem Mittelalter. Besonders in Düsseldorf ist es den Einwohnern gelungen, das Alte mit dem Neuen zu verbinden. Da ist die „Königsallee",[3] wo sich viele moderne Geschäfte und Banken befinden. Ganz in der Nähe der „Kö", wie die Düsseldorfer die Königsallee nennen, ist die „Altstadt". Da gibt es viele Gebäude aus dem Mittelalter und anderen Zeiten, die° man restauriert hat. In diesen Gebäuden befinden sich viele Restaurants und Diskotheken, wo man gut essen und sich unterhalten kann. Am Ende der Königsallee liegt ein Park mit vielen Brunnen, und durch die Allee fließt ein Kanal mit Brücken. Man erinnert sich daß Napoleon Düsseldorf „mein kleines Paris" nannte.

    Man darf wohl sagen, daß man während einer Reise von wenigen Stunden die Dynamik° mancher Jahrhunderte° erlebt hat—von den Burgen des Mittelalters zu den Hochburgen der Finanz und Industrie unserer Zeit.

°which

°dynamics / centuries

[3] This literally means the *King's Promenade.*

## Questions

1. Was ist Frankfurt a.M. seit dem Ende des Zweiten Weltkrieges geworden?
2. Was sieht man in dieser Stadt?
3. Durch was für eine Landschaft fließt der Rhein?
4. Wo befinden sich die Burgen?

5. Was sieht man auf dem Fluß? Womit (*with what*) sind sie beladen?

6. Was tun die Geschäftsleute im Zug?

7. Was scheint zusammenzufließen?

8. Was für ein Gefühl hat man, wenn man aus dem Fenster zu den Burgen aufschaut?

9. Was sieht man überall im Ruhrgebiet statt der Burgen des Rheinlandes?

10. Was ist den Einwohnern in Düsseldorf gelungen?

11. Was befindet sich auf der Königsallee? in der Altstadt?

12. Hast du einmal Gebäude aus dem Mittelalter oder Hochhäuser gesehen? Wenn ja, wo?

13. In welcher Stadt wohnst du? Ist diese Stadt alt oder neu? Ist es den Einwohnern gelungen, das Alte mit dem Neuen zu verbinden?

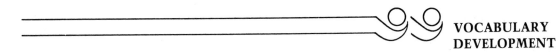

**VOCABULARY DEVELOPMENT**

## A. Hans, setz dich an den Tisch und sitz still!

**Sich setzen** denotes the action of sitting down, while **sitzen (saß, gesessen)** denotes the position of sitting or being seated. The first is a motion *toward*, the second a position *in*. Therefore, what cases will they take?

ACCUSATIVE:    Ich setze mich an **den** Tisch.    *I sit down at the table.*

DATIVE:    Ich sitze **am** Tisch.    *I'm sitting at the table.*

Now ask a classmate if he or she is standing or sitting, and get an answer. Then ask someone else if they sat down at a table in the dining room (**das Eßzimmer**) today.

The same distinction has to be made between **legen** and **liegen (lag, gelegen)**, namely between *to lay* in the sense of *to put*, and *to lie* in the sense of *to recline*. Translate:

Sie legte ihren Schlüssel auf **den** Tisch.
Ihr Schlüssel lag auf **dem** Tisch.

Use the same pair of sentences with other nouns that you know.

## B. Getting a rise out of a verb: HEBEN, HOB, GEHOBEN

In its basic form this verb means *to lift:*

Sie hob das Kind auf den Stuhl.    *She lifted the child onto the chair.*

But separable prefixes can do much to extend the basic meaning of a verb. Among other things, **auf·heben** can mean *to lift* or *pick up*, or *to preserve, keep.*

| | |
|---|---|
| Bitte, heb das Geld auf! | *Please pick up the money.* |
| Ich werde dein Bild für immer aufheben. | *I will keep your picture forever.* |

But **sich erheben** means *to rise.* A popular song starts with the line: **Wo Berge sich erheben, da ist mein Heimatland** (*Where mountains rise, there is my homeland*).

Many other verbs lend themselves to the same manipulation with prefixes. In the Reading of this chapter you encountered **aus dem Fenster schauen** and **zu den Burgen auf·schauen.** Can you see through the following phrase?

Er hat dich **durch**schaut?

## C. The time of your life: DIE VERGANGENHEIT, DIE GEGENWART, DIE ZUKUNFT

When one ends and the next begins is an old and insoluble philosophic question. Cut the Gordian knot by simply memorizing the words for the three portions of your life.

Speaking of time, you already know **gestern** (*yesterday*) and **morgen** (*tomorrow*). What then do **vorgestern** and **übermorgen** mean? Use each in a sentence.

---

**REVIEW**

**A.** *Form sentences with the given cues. Put nouns and pronouns into the appropriate form and use the tense indicated in parentheses.*

1. stehen/mehrere/Hochhäuser/neben/Gebäude/aus/das Mittelalter. (*pres.*)
2. hinstellen/du/wo/dein Regenschirm? (*pres. perf.*)
3. sich erinnern/können/er (*subject*)/an/ich. (*past*)
4. sich kümmern/seine Eltern (*subject*)/nie/um/er. (*past*)
5. sich befinden/Restaurants/in/manche Gebäude. (*pres.*)
6. stellen/ich (*subject*)/jeder Student/eine Frage. (*future*)
7. sehen/wir/während/eine Reise/von/wenige Stunden/viel. (*pres. perf.*)
8. sich ziehen/ein Kanal/durch/der Wald. (*pres.*)
9. sich erholen/du/von/deine Krankheit? (*pres. perf.*)
10. abreisen/sie (*pl.*)/schon/vor/einige Tage. (*pres. perf.*)

11. sich kaufen/ihr/ein Auto/oder/andere Fahrräder? (*future*)
12. sich fragen/ich (*subject*)/ob/können/folgen/ihr/das Argument. (*past*)

**B.** *Answer the following questions with complete sentences.*

EXAMPLE: Gehört dieser Regenschirm dir?
   **Ja, er gehört mir.**

1. Erinnern Sie sich an Ihren Großvater?
2. Hast du mir wirklich zugehört?
3. Ist es euch gelungen, ihn zu überreden?
4. Habt ihr ihm bei seiner Arbeit geholfen?
5. Was gefällt Ihnen besser: eine Stadt mit Gärten und Brunnen, oder eine mit Hochhäusern und Diskotheken?

**C.** *Express in German.*

1. We came back from Switzerland several weeks ago.
2. May I remind you (*Sie*) of your appointment with your students?
3. We did not succeed in persuading them.
4. Please get yourself a newspaper, sit down on this chair, and don't say a word!
5. The Rhine winds toward the north through hills and vineyards.
6. Peter, go and wash your hands!
7. I can't get used to such buildings.
8. We would like to converse (**sich unterhalten**) with you about the economy of our country!
9. We must inform ourselves about the rate of exchange of the dollar.
10. Don't give me any more vegetables; this is enough for me!

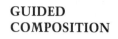

**GUIDED COMPOSITION**

Describe certain features of your city where old and new have been combined successfully. Have old buildings been restored? Are there new buildings nearby? Do they give you the feeling that you are experiencing the past and present simultaneously? Has an old section of the town been rebuilt to house shops, restaurants, movie houses, discothèques, etc.? Are there pedestrian malls, gardens, or parks outside or inside the city? State whether you like to go there or not, and what your favorite pastime is when going there: shopping, talking with friends, having a drink and seeing the world go by, etc. If you do not wish to describe your own town or city, look at the two pictures of Frankfurt a.M. and Düsseldorf below and describe some striking features in the scenery of these cities.

*Frankfurt*

*Düsseldorf*

**VOCABULARY**

## Easily recognized words

| | | |
|---|---|---|
| die | **Bank,** -en | *bank* |
| die | **Diskothek,** -en | *discothèque* |
| | **fallen (fällt), fiel (ist) gefallen** | *to fall* |
| das | **Haar,** -e | *hair* |
| die | **Hand,** ⸚e | *hand* |
| | **waschen (wäscht), wusch, gewaschen** | *to wash* |
| sich | **winden** | *to wind* |
| | | |
| die | **Brücke,** -n | *bridge* |
| die | **Burg,** -en | *castle* |
| das | **Dorf,** ⸚er | *village* |
| die | **Fabrik,** -en | *factory* |
| der | **Felsen,** - | *rock, cliff* |
| das | **Flugzeug,** -e | *airplane* |
| der | **Gast,** ⸚e | *guest* |
| das | **Gebäude,** - | *building* |
| das | **Gebiet,** -e | *region* |
| der | **Gebrauch,** ⸚e | *custom* |
| die | **Gegenwart** | *present* |
| das | **Geschäft,** -e | *business, firm* |
| das | **Gesicht,** -er | *face* |
| das | **Hochhaus,** ⸚er | *high-rise building* |
| der | **Hügel,** - | *hill* |
| die | **Landschaft,** -en | *countryside, landscape* |
| das | **Mittelalter** | *Middle Ages* |
| die | **Nähe** | *proximity;* **in der Nähe** *in the neighborhood, nearby* |
| das | **Rathaus,** ⸚er | *city hall* |
| der | **Reisescheck,** -s | *traveler's check* |
| das | **Tal,** ⸚er | *valley* |
| die | **Vergangenheit** | *past* |
| der | **Vergleich,** -e | *comparison,* **im Vergleich mit** *in comparison with* |

| | | |
|---|---|---|
| der | **Weinberg,** -e | *vineyard* |
| die | **Wirtschaft** | *economy* |
| | | |
| | **an·fangen (fängt), fing, angefangen** | *to start, begin* |
| sich | **befinden, befand, befunden** | *to be (located)* |
| | **danken** (+ *dat.*) | *to thank* |
| sich | **erheben, erhob, erhoben** | *to rise* |
| sich | **erholen (von** + *dat.*) | *to recover (from)* |
| | **erinnern (an** + *acc.*) | *to remind (of)* |
| sich | **erinnern (an** + *acc.*) | *to remember* |
| sich | **erkundigen (nach** + *dat.*) | *to make inquiries about* |
| | **erleben** | *to experience* |
| | **fließen, floß, (ist) geflossen** | *to flow* |
| | **folgen (ist gefolgt)** | *to follow* |
| sich | **freuen (über** + *acc.*) | *to be glad, be happy (about)* |
| | **gefallen (gefällt), gefiel, gefallen** (+ *dat.*) | *to please, appreciate* |
| | **gehören** (+ *dat.*) | *to belong to* |
| | **gelingen, gelang, (ist) gelungen** (*impers.* + *dat.*) | *to succeed* |
| | **genügen** (*impers.* + *dat.*) | *to suffice* |
| | **gewinnen, gewann, gewonnen** | *to win, gain* |
| sich | **gewöhnen an** (+ *acc.*) | *to get used to, become accustomed to* |
| | **helfen (hilft), half, geholfen** (+ *dat.*) | *to help* |
| sich | **kümmern um** (+ *acc.*) | *to take care of, worry about* |
| | **legen** | *to lay, put* |
| | **nennen, nannte, genannt** | *to name, call* |
| | **restaurieren** | *to restore* |

| | | | | |
|---|---|---|---|---|
| | **schauen** | *to look* | **zu·hören** (+ *dat.*) | *to listen (to)* |
| sich | **setzen** | *to sit down* | | |
| sich | **unterhalten (unterhält), unterhielt, unterhalten** | *to converse, to have a good time* | **inzwischen** | *meanwhile* |
| | | | **nun** | *now* |
| | **wechseln** | *to change (exchange)* | | |

See also the noun modifiers on pp. 188-189.

## I

Der neue Bahnhof ist sehr groß.
*The new railway station is very big.*

Trotz des schlechten Wetters ist unser Onkel in die Ferien gereist.
*Despite the bad weather our uncle left on his vacation.*

Schade, daß du dieses schöne Gebiet nicht kennst.
*Too bad you don't know this beautiful region.*

Von welchen großen Fabriken sprichst du?
*Which big factories are you talking about?*

## II

Hast du mein schönes, neues Auto schon gesehen?
*Have you already seen my beautiful new car?*

Hinter dem Hügel befindet sich ein tiefer See.
*Behind the hill there is a deep lake.*

Wir kennen Ihre hübsch**e** Tochter.
*We know your pretty daughter.*

Wo habt ihr unsere alt**en** Fahrräder hingestellt?
*Where did you put our old bikes?*

## III

Ich trinke gern dunk**les** Bier.
*I like to drink dark beer.*

In diesem Café erhält man gut**en** Kuchen.
*In this café you get good cake.*

Haben Sie gut**e** oder schlecht**e** Nachrichten von Ihren Eltern erhalten?
*Have you received good or bad news from your parents?*

Er ist der Sohn reich**er** Eltern.
*He is the son of rich parents.*

**GRAMMAR
EXPLANATION**

## I. Declension of adjectives preceded by a DER word

An adjective in the *predicate* position is not declined.

Dieses Problem ist **wichtig.**     *This problem is important.*

In most cases the predicate adjective is separated from the noun it modifies by the verb **sein.**[1]

But an *attributive* adjective—one that immediately precedes the noun—is declined.

Wir dürfen dieses **wichtige** Prob-     *We mustn't forget this important*
lem nicht vergessen.     *problem.*

If the adjective itself is preceded by a **der** word, it takes the ending **-e** or **-en** according to the following chart:

---

[1] Remember that German differs from English in not having distinguishable forms for the predicate adjective and the adverb.

ADJECTIVE:  Meine Freundin ist immer sehr     *My girlfriend is always very careful.*
**vorsichtig.**

ADVERB:  Meine Freundin fährt immer     *My girlfriend always drives very carefully.*
sehr **vorsichtig.**

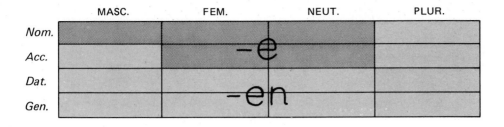

| | MASC. | FEM. | NEUT. | PLUR. |
|---|---|---|---|---|
| *Nom.* | | | | |
| *Acc.* | | −e | | |
| *Dat.* | | | | |
| *Gen.* | | −en | | |

That is to say, the adjective ending is **-e** in the masculine, feminine, and neuter nominative singular, and the feminine and neuter accusative singular. It is **-en** in all other instances.

Here then is what is sometimes called the "weak" declension of adjectives:

|  | SINGULAR | | | | | | | | |
|---|---|---|---|---|---|---|---|---|---|
|  | MASC. | | | FEM. | | | NEUT. | | |
| *nom.* | der | neue | Bahnhof | diese | schöne | Farbe | welches | große | Dorf |
| *acc.* | den | neuen | Bahnhof | diese | schöne | Farbe | welches | große | Dorf |
| *dat.* | dem | neuen | Bahnhof | dieser | schönen | Farbe | welchem | großen | Dorf |
| *gen.* | des | neuen | Bahnhofs | dieser | schönen | Farbe | welches | großen | Dorf |

|  | PLURAL | | |
|---|---|---|---|
| *nom.* | manche | hübschen | Häuser |
| *acc.* | manche | hübschen | Häuser |
| *dat.* | manchen | hübschen | Häusern |
| *gen.* | mancher | hübschen | Häuser |

Adjectives ending in **-el** or **-er** drop **-e-** in front of a declensional ending: **teuer** > **der teure Wagen** (*the expensive car*); **dunkel** > **das dunkle Bier** (*the dark beer*).

## Check your comprehension

*Fill in the blanks with the appropriate adjective endings.*

1. Ich will nicht über diese alt _____ Brücke fahren.
2. Hast du dir den neu_____ Anzug schon einmal angezogen?
3. Diese schmutzig_____ Hosen gehören nicht mir.
4. Trotz des schlecht_____ Wetters ist sie abgefahren.

5. Ich erinnere mich an dieses klein_____ Dorf.
6. Welches groß_____ Haus habt ihr gemietet?
7. Von welchem teuer_____ Restaurant sprichst du?
8. Manche schön_____ Wagen sind zu teuer.
9. Wer hat dieses alt_____ Rathaus so gut restauriert?
10. Wir konnten die Fragen dieser jung_____ Leute nicht verstehen.

## II. Declension of adjectives preceded by an EIN word

As you know, **ein** words have the same form in the masculine nominative singular and the neuter nominative and accusative singular.

> **Ein** Mann ist gekommen.
> **Ein** Kind ist gekommen.
> Ich habe **ein** Kind gesehen.

When an attributive adjective is inserted in these instances, it takes the endings of the **der** word, so as to show the gender of the noun it modifies.

> Ein groß**er** Mann ist gekommen.
> Ein hübsch**es** Kind ist gekommen.
> Ich habe ein hübsch**es** Kind gesehen.

The endings in all other cases are the same as for adjectives preceded by a **der** word.

| | MASC. | FEM. | NEUT. | PLUR. |
|---|---|---|---|---|
| *Nom.* | -er | -e | -es | |
| *Acc.* | | -e | -es | |
| *Dat.* | | -en | | |
| *Gen.* | | -en | | |

This so-called "mixed" declension of adjectives is as follows:

| | SINGULAR | | | | | |
|---|---|---|---|---|---|---|
| | MASC. | | FEM. | | NEUTER | |
| *nom.* | ein tiefer See | | seine hübsche Tochter | | ihr krankes Kind | |
| *acc.* | einen tiefen See | | seine hübsche Tochter | | ihr krankes Kind | |
| *dat.* | einem tiefen See | | seiner hübschen Tochter | | ihrem kranken Kind | |
| *gen.* | eines tiefen Sees | | seiner hübschen Tochter | | ihres kranken Kindes | |

| | PLURAL |
|---|---|
| *nom.* | deine lieben Eltern |
| *acc.* | deine lieben Eltern |
| *dat.* | deinen lieben Eltern |
| *gen.* | deiner lieben Eltern |

## Check your comprehension

*Fill in the blanks with the appropriate endings of the* **der** *words,* **ein** *words, and adjectives.*

1. Auf dies_____ groß_____ Hügel steht ein_____ schön_____ Burg.
2. Neben d_____ Rathaus befindet sich ein_____ alt_____ Brunnen.
3. In dies_____ Gebäude gibt es ein elegant_____ Geschäft.
4. Monika hat ein_____ hübsch_____ und interessant_____ Gesicht.
5. Ich habe mir ein_____ neu_____ Pullover gekauft.
6. Sie machten ein_____ lang_____ Reise durch mehrere wichtig_____ Gebiete.
7. Ich möchte in ein_____ klein_____ Dorf in der Nähe ein_____ groß_____ Stadt wohnen.
8. Ein vorsichtig_____ Autofahrer hat kein_____ Unfälle.
9. In dies_____ tief_____ Tal gibt es einig_____ schön_____ Dörfer.

## III. Declension of adjectives not preceded by a DER or EIN word

In some sentence constructions no **der** or **ein** word is required in front of the attributive adjective. In that case the adjective takes the endings of the **der** words, so as to show the gender and case of the noun it modifies.

Diese reichen Leute kümmern sich nicht um arme Leute.
[(**der** word) **-en**]          [(no **der** word) **-e** like **die**]
*These rich people don't worry about poor people.*

An exception is the masculine and neuter genitive singular, where **-en** is used instead of **-es.**[1]

Here finally is the so-called "strong" declension of adjectives.

| | MASC. | FEM. | NEUT. |
|---|---|---|---|
| | SINGULAR | | |
| *nom.* | gut**er** Kuchen | schwierig**e** Arbeit | frisch**es** Wasser |
| *acc.* | gut**en** Kuchen | schwierig**e** Arbeit | frisch**es** Wasser |
| *dat.* | gut**em** Kuchen | schwierig**er** Arbeit | frisch**em** Wasser |
| *gen.* | gut**en** Kuchens | schwierig**er** Arbeit | frisch**en** Wassers |
| | PLURAL | | |
| *nom.* | krank**e** Leute | | |
| *acc.* | krank**e** Leute | | |
| *dat.* | krank**en** Leuten | | |
| *gen.* | krank**er** Leute | | |

## Check your comprehension

*Fill in the blanks with the appropriate endings of the* **der** *words,* **ein** *words, and adjectives.*

1. In dies_____ Restaurant erhält man heiß_____ Suppe und kalt_____ Bier.
2. Fritz, setz dich nicht mit schmutzig_____ Händen an d_____ Tisch!
3. Geh und wasch dir auch dein_____ schmutzig_____ Gesicht.
4. Im Ruhrgebiet gibt es groß_____ Fabriken.
5. Wir haben schlecht_____ Nachrichten von unser_____ Eltern erhalten.
6. Heute muß unser lieb_____ Freund abfahren.
7. Wir müssen frisch_____ Brot kaufen.
8. In deutsch_____ Städten sieht man alt_____ Rathäuser neben neu_____ Gebäuden.

---

[1] Nowadays the construction with a noun in the genitive modified by an adjective is becoming rare; instead, for instance, of **das Einatmen dichten Rauches ist gefährlich** (*the inhaling of dense smoke is dangerous*), one hears **das Einatmen von dichtem Rauch ist gefährlich.**

**USEFUL PHRASES**

| | |
|---|---|
| **auf jeden Fall** | *by all means; in any event* |
| **Wie seh' ich aus?** | *How do I look?* |
| **einigermaßen akzeptabel** | *fairly acceptable* |
| **Wo denkst du hin?** | *{ What do you mean?* <br> *{ Are you out of your mind?* |
| **sich die Haare schneiden lassen** | *to get a haircut* |
| **bei kaltem Wetter** | *in cold weather* |

**CONVERSATION**

## *Die langen Haare*

*Frau Eichendorff ist eine werktätige° Mutter. Ihr Sohn Jürgen, 16 Jahre*     working
*alt, ist Schüler an einem städtischen Gymnasium.[1] Er zieht sich gerade*
*um,° um zu einer kleinen Geburtstagsfeier° seines guten Freundes Paul,*     is changing clothes / birthday
*Sohn reicher Leute, zu gehen.*     party

JÜRGEN (*ruft vom oberen° Stock herunter*): Du, Mutti, was soll ich     upper
    denn anziehen?
MUTTER Auf jeden Fall ein frisches Hemd und die neue Krawatte.
JÜRGEN Welche neue Krawatte? Ach so, die langweilige Krawatte, die°     that
    mir Onkel Emil geschenkt hat! Aber was für einen Anzug ziehe
    ich an?
MUTTER Den dunkelblauen° natürlich. Warum fragst du denn? Vergiß     dark blue
    auch nicht, frische passende° Socken anzuziehen.     matching

*Nach kurzer Zeit kommt Jürgen die Treppe herab.°*     down

JÜRGEN So, wie seh' ich aus?
MUTTER Einigermaßen akzeptabel. Aber zieh den warmen Mantel an
    und setz dir eine Mütze auf! Bei diesem kalten Wetter!

---

[1] The **Gymnasium** corresponds roughly to an American high school, but if offers a nine-year program. Essentially it is a preparatory school for the university.

JÜRGEN Aber nein! Ich friere doch nicht. Und übrigens will ich nicht wie ein ambulanter Kleiderhaken° herumlaufen. *mobile clothes hanger*

MUTTER Aber wart mal! Sagtest du nicht, du wolltest dir deine[2] langen Haare schneiden lassen?

JÜRGEN Wo denkst du hin? Bei kaltem Wetter halten° mich die langen Haare schön warm. Tschüß! *keep*

---

[2] When an adjective modifies the noun denoting a part of the body, the possessive adjective is most often used: **deine langen Haare,** rather than **die langen Haare.**

## Questions

1. An welchem Gymnasium ist Jürgen Schüler?
2. Warum zieht sich Jürgen gerade um?
3. Wessen (*whose*) Sohn ist Paul?
4. Gefällt Jürgen die Krawatte, die ihm der Onkel geschenkt hat?
5. Was für einen Anzug zieht Jürgen an?
6. Was fragt Jürgen, als er die Treppe herunterkommt?
7. Was antwortet ihm seine Mutter?
8. Warum will er den warmen Mantel nicht anziehen?
9. Warum ließ Jürgen sich seine langen Haare nicht schneiden?
10. Was tragen Sie, wenn Sie eine sehr elegante Party besuchen?
11. Was tragen Sie bei kaltem Wetter? bei warmem Wetter?
12. Tragen Sie oft eine Mütze? Warum oder warum nicht?
13. Haben Sie lange oder kurze Haare? Lassen Sie sich oft die Haare schneiden? Sogar bei kaltem Wetter?

**PRACTICE**

**A.** *Substitute the items in parentheses for the noun in italics, and make the necessary changes in the adjective endings.*

1. Wo ist der neue *Wagen*?
   (Geschäft/Fabrik/Anzug/Büro/Brunnen)
2. Vor vielen Jahren stand hier eine alte *Brücke*.
   (Haus/Brunnen/Kirche/Baum/Burg)
3. Jürgen, zieh doch deinen warmen *Mantel* an.
   (Jacke/Hemd/Anzug/Socken/Pullover)

**B.** *Put sentences 1 and 2 of exercise A into the plural.*

**C.** *Replace the* **der** *word by the word in parentheses and change the adjective ending where necessary.*

1. Da ist *das* schöne Haus. (unser)
2. Hast du *den* neuen Mantel gekauft? (ein)
3. Wo befindet sich *dieser* große Parkplatz? (ein)
4. Kennt er *das* städtische Gymnasium? (euer)
5. Sie hat sich endlich von *der* gefährlichen Krankheit erholt. (ein)

**D.** *Eliminate the* **der** *or* **ein** *word in italics and adjust the ending of the adjective.*

1. Hast du *dieses* kalte Bier getrunken?
2. Wir haben *die* schlechten Nachrichten erhalten.

3. Er hat sich *die* warmen Socken angezogen.

4. Sie ist die Tochter *dieser* reichen Leute.

5. Habt ihr *den* guten Kaffee gekauft?

**E.** *Fill in the blanks with the appropriate form of the word in parentheses.*

EXAMPLE: Hier ist _____ Zimmer. Hier ist _____ schönes Zimmer. Hier ist _____. (*unser*)
   **Hier ist unser Zimmer. Hier ist unser schönes Zimmer. Hier ist unseres.**

1. Ich sehe _____ Haus. Ich sehe _____ hübsches Haus. Ich sehe _____. (*euer*)

2. Suchst du _____ Fahrrad? Suchst du _____ neues Fahrrad? Suchst du _____? (*dein*)

3. Wo ist _____ Wagen? Wo ist _____ alter Wagen? Wo ist _____? (*unser*)

4. _____ Garten ist hinter dem Haus. _____ großer Garten ist hinter dem Haus. _____ ist hinter dem Haus. (*mein*)

5. Zeige mir _____ Auto! Zeige mir _____ teures Auto! Zeige mir _____! (*sein*)

**F.** *Fill in the blanks with the appropriate endings of the* **der** *words,* **ein** *words, and adjectives. Use contractions where possible.*

1. In dies_____ Stadt befindet sich ein_____ schön_____ Rathaus.

2. In d_____ Rheintal gibt es viel_____ Dörfer mit hübsch_____ Häusern und Kirchen.

3. Felix rief von d_____ ober_____ Stock herunter: „Gibt es heute ein_____ interessant_____ Film in d_____ Fernsehen?"

4. Von welch_____ groß_____ Gebäude redet ihr?

5. Du sollst dir ein_____ warm_____ Mantel anziehen.

6. Wo habt ihr unser_____ neu_____ Regenschirme hingestellt? Hier sind euer_____.

7. In d_____ Sommer trinke ich gern kalt_____ Wein von d_____ Weinbergen d_____ Rheintals.

8. Oskar, wasch dir doch dein_____ schmutzig_____ Gesicht und zieh dies_____ frisch_____ Hemd an!

9. Dies_____ Sportclub hat viel_____ Mitglieder; aber manch_____ sind kein_____ gut_____ Athleten.

10. Zu lang_____ Ferien können langweilig werden und sind nicht immer gut für unser_____ Gesundheit.

11. Wir sind durch dunkel_____ Wälder und tief_____ Täler gegangen.

12. Ich konnte d_____ langweilig_____ Gespräch mein_____ Gäste nicht mehr zuhören.

**G.** *Give the English equivalent.*

1. Vor einigen Tagen habe ich mir einen neuen Anzug gekauft; er gefällt meiner Freundin sehr gut.

2. Seit mehreren Wochen trinkt sie nur noch warmen Tee, aber keinen Kaffee mehr.

3. Wem gehörten diese dunkelblaue Jacke und die rote (*red*) Mütze?

4. Wann willst du dir die Haare schneiden lassen?

5. Ach, Albert, wie siehst du denn aus? Wasch dir schnell dein schmutziges Gesicht und die Hände und zieh dir ein anderes Hemd an!

6. Bei diesem kalten Wetter wirst du doch nicht ohne Mantel in die Stadt gehen! Wo denkst du denn hin?

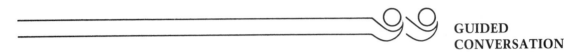

**GUIDED
CONVERSATION**

An old adage says **Kleider machen Leute**[1] (*Clothes make the man*). Do you believe that? Look at the pictures below and describe what the people in them are wearing (the words listed in the Vocabulary Development of Chapter 9 (p. 183-184) will be of help), and what impression they make on you. What do you yourself prefer to wear when you go downtown, shopping, to a movie, a play, a concert, a party, a football game, etc.? Maybe you also wish to describe the clothes of an acquaintance of yours which you consider to be somewhat eccentric. (But don't be too satiric.)

[1] This is also the title of a novella by the noted Swiss-German writer, Gottfried Keller (1819–90).

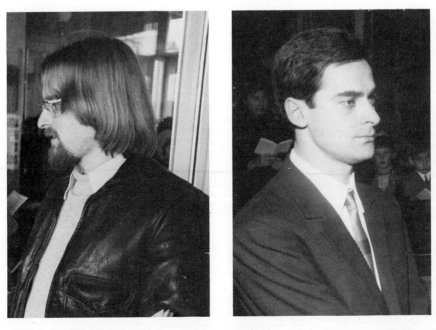

## Die verkehrte Welt

Ich stehe auf der Terrasse des Bundeshauses[1] in Bern und schaue auf das farbige° Häusermeer der Stadt hinab°. In den letzten zwanzig Jahren haben sich viele Dinge verändert. Der Schweizerfranken° ist teuer geworden. Und schaut Euch mal den dichten Stadtverkehr an— zu viele Autos in den engen Straßen! Dann die Kleidung der Jugend— die engen Hosen, die offenen, bequemen Hemden. Und unter den jungen Männern tragen manche einen langen oder kurzen Bart oder auch einen Schnurrbart. Als ich noch ein junger Mann war, denke ich, da trugen unsere Professoren und Väter die Bärte. Heutzutage ist alles verkehrt: die jungen Leute tragen jetzt die Bärte. Ich gehöre zu einer bartlosen° Zwischengeneration. Aber alles wiederholt sich in der Geschichte, sagt man. Und für einen kurzen Moment denke ich an die Idee der „ewigen Wiederkehr" von Nietzsche[2] und muß lachen.

Aber viele Dinge sind gleich geblieben: das gemütliche „Schwy-

*colorful / down*
*Swiss frank*

*beardless*

[1] The Federal Building in Berne, where the Swiss Parliament meets.
[2] Friedrich Nietzsche (1844–1900), the great poet-philosopher and classical scholar, was born in Germany, but lived most of his life in Switzerland. The culmination of his thought is a complicated idea of the "eternal return" of all things, which of course is trivialized here, hence the laugh.

zerdüütsch"[3] der Berner°; die Altstadt mit ihren Lauben,[4] Riegelhäu-
sern[5] und Brunnen. Die Aare[6] windet sich immer noch durch die Altstadt. Und am Horizont erheben sich immer noch die Alpen.

   „Sali Roobi"?[7] höre ich plötzlich hinter mir. Mein alter Schul-
kamerad ist gerade angekommen und grüßt mich in seinem breiten
Baseldeutsch. „Wir müssen uns beeilen", sagt er, „um halb neun Uhr
erwarten uns viele Freunde im Restaurant ‚Zum Rüden' in Zürich".
—„Wann, wo? Das geht doch nicht, da müssen wir ja fliegen!" —Mach
dir keine Sorgen, mit dieser Maschine werden wir schnell da sein",
sagt er und zeigt auf° seinen Mercedes-Sportwagen.

    Bald winden wir uns durch den Stadtverkehr und erreichen die
Autobahn. Und nun geht's los:° 100, 120, 160, einmal sogar 180 km
pro° Stunde. So schnell bin ich noch nie gefahren! „Hat dein Wagen
einen Flugzeugmotor? Was ist seine Abhebegeschwindigkeit?"° frage
ich. —„Ha, ha, in den USA fahrt ihr wohl nicht so schnell." —„Nein,
nicht ganz, so 55 bis 60 Meilen pro Stunde." —„Schneckentempo!"°

*the Bernese*

*points to*

*and now the fun begins*
*per*
*lift-off speed*

*snail's pace*

---

[3] Swiss-German differs considerably in structure, vocabulary, and pronunciation from
standard German. Moreover, there are many distinct dialects, which make the stand-
ardization of the spelling nearly impossible. But **Schwyzerdüütsch** for **Schweizerdeutsch**
is a fairly accurate rendering of the pronunciation.

[4] Berne is known for its **Lauben,** Swiss for arcades or covered sidewalks.

[5] A Swiss expression denoting a type of half-timbered house.

[6] A tributary of the Rhine, winding through the city.

[7] Basle dialect for **Salü, Robi** (*hi, Bob*).

„Siehst du da in der Mitte der Autobahn die langen Barrieren? Im Kriegsfall° kann man diese Barrieren entfernen° und—presto—die Autobahn wird zum Flugplatz".—„Wo denkst du hin? Im Kriegsfall?" sage ich, „wer will denn die Schweiz heutzutage schon angreifen?"° —„Ja, hör mal, man kann nie wissen." —„Ja, vielleicht wenn einmal ein anderes Land euer Bankgeheimnis° erschließen° will!" sage ich mit einem kurzen Lachen. Mein Freund macht ein unfreundliches Gesicht und sagt nichts. Er ist Präsident einer großen Bank. Lange hört man nur das böse Brummen° des Motors.

    In Zürich im Restaurant „Zum Rüden" gibt es viel Händedrücken°, Erzählen und ein gutes Essen mit Weißwein und Rotwein. Während des Gesprächs kommen wir auch auf den Verkehr zu sprechen. „Wir leben in einer verkehrten Welt", sagt ein alter Kamerad, „jetzt haben wir die schnellen Wagen, aber wegen des dichten Autoverkehrs braucht man eine Ewigkeit,° in die Stadtmitte zu fahren". —„Fahrt doch mit dem Velo[8]", sage ich, „dann werdet ihr auch nicht so viel Abgase° einatmen müssen." —„Was! Du meinst, daß wir unsere Velos vom Estrich[9] herunterholen sollen? Wo denkst du hin? Erstens ist mein Drahtesel[10] verrostet°, zweitens will ich nicht

*in case of war / remove*

*attack*

*banking secret / unlock*

*angry roar*

*handshaking*

*eternity*

*exhaust fumes*

*rusted*

[8] Swiss for **Fahrrad**.

[9] Swiss for **Dachboden** (*attic*).

[10] A colloquial expression used in Switzerland, Austria, and Germany for **Velo**, literally meaning *wire-donkey*.

in den Tramschienen[11] hinfallen und drittens ist im Spital[12] nicht genug Platz für Velounfälle!"

„Na", denke ich, „vielleicht sind nicht die Welt und der Verkehr verkehrt, sondern die Menschen."

[11] **Tramschienen** is southern German for **Straßenbahnschienen** (*streetcar tracks*).
[12] Swiss for **Krankenhaus** (*hospital*).

## Questions

*Although the above Reading is written in the first person, in the questions we will refer to the* **Ich** *narrator as* **er** *or* **der Erzähler** (the narrator).

1. Wo steht der Erzähler und wohin schaut er?
2. Was hat sich verändert?
3. Wer trug einen Bart, als er noch ein junger Mann war? Und heutzutage?
4. Welche Dinge sind gleich geblieben?
5. Wer ist gerade angekommen?
6. Warum müssen sie sich beeilen?
7. Warum fragt der Erzähler seinen Freund, ob sein Wagen einen Flugzeugmotor hat?
8. Wovon (*about what*) sprechen die beiden?
9. Was für ein Gesicht macht der Freund? Warum?
10. Warum sagt ein alter Kamerad, daß wir in einer verkehrten Welt leben?
11. Was sagt der Erzähler, sollen seine Freunde tun?
12. Warum will der Kamerad es nicht tun?
13. Was denkt dann der Erzähler?

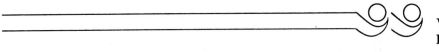

**VOCABULARY DEVELOPMENT**

**A.** *Why not add a little color to your German?*

It's time to learn the German words for a few colors. Many of them can easily be recognized, since they are close to their English equivalents. Here then are **die Farben** (*the colors*):

| | | | |
|---|---|---|---|
| blau | *blue* | grün | *green* |
| braun | *brown* | rot | *red* |
| gelb | *yellow* | schwarz | *black* |
| grau | *gray* | weiß | *white* |

Ask a classmate **welche Farbe hat Milch?** and get an answer. Now ask someone the color of several of the following:

| | |
|---|---|
| der Himmel (*sky*) | die Bäume im Frühling |
| sein Regenschirm | die Bäume im Herbst |
| frischer Schnee | das Meer |
| schmutziger Schnee | das Blut |
| Feuer | ein altes Gebäude |
| Kohle | die Sonne |
| eine Zitrone (*lemon*) | seine Schuhe |
| Eier | |

One can shade the colors (linguistically, at least) by adding either **hell** (*light, pale*) or **dunkel** (*dark*): **hellblau, dunkelgrün,** etc.

**Hell** and **dunkel** may of course be used independently, as in **helles Bier** or **dunkles Bier.** Ask a classmate which he or she likes, and get an answer. Now ask another classmate if he or she likes **Rotwein** or **Weißwein.**

Colors occur quite often in idioms like these:

| | |
|---|---|
| vor Neid grün werden | *to be green with envy* |
| sich schwarz ärgern } | |
| rot vor Wut sein    } | *to be beside oneself with anger* |

Now ask someone if they are any of these things, and see what kind of an answer you get!

**B.** *An unfriendly friend*

The adjective derived from **der Freund** is **freundlich** (*friendly*). A number of adjectives (though not all) form their opposites with the prefix **un-: unfreundlich.** Give the opposites of the following adjectives, all of which have occurred so far in this book:

möglich                        nötig
aufmerksam                     sicher
gefährlich                     vorsichtig
natürlich                      wichtig
wahrscheinlich

Now use each one in a sentence.

**C.** *The eternal return*

Some basic forms of words—especially verbs—return again and again in various combinations. In the Reading of this chapter, for instance, you noticed **die Wiederkehr,** which comes from **wieder·kehren** (*to return again and again*).

The noun **der Verkehr** is derived from the verb **verkehren** (*to come and go frequently*). Translate: **Unsere Freunde verkehren sehr viel in diesem Restaurant!**

But a verb may turn chameleon: **verkehren** can also mean *turn topsy-turvy, to turn around the wrong way.* Thus something that is **verkehrt** is *all turned around* in the sense of *mixed-up.*

 **REVIEW**

**A.** *Answer the questions with the cues given in parentheses. Use the appropriate endings, and the same tense as in the question.*

EXAMPLE: Wen erwartet ihr heute abend?
    (*erwarten/wir/Freund/unser/alt*)
    **Wir erwarten unseren alten Freund.**

1. Wo wohnt Ihr Freund jetzt?
   (*wohnen/er/seit/mehrere/Jahre/in/ein/groß/Hotel*)

2. Wohin werden Sie in die Ferien gehen?
   (*machen/ich/eine Reise/lang/durch/das Rheintal/schön/und/der Norden/ Deutschland*)

3. Wo seid ihr gestern abend gewesen?
   (*gehen/wir/in/das Kino/und/sich ansehen/ein Film/sehr interessant*)

4. Was für ein Gesicht macht deine Freundin?
   (machen/sie/auf/jeder Fall/kein/Gesicht/freundlich)
5. Wann trugen die alten Herren Bärte?
   (sein/ich/als/noch/ein Mann/jung,/tragen/Herren/viel/Bärte/lang)

**B.** *Answer the following questions with an attributive adjective.*

EXAMPLES: Was für eine Mütze trägt Peter?
**Er trägt eine graue Mütze.**

Welchen Koffer soll ich mitnehmen?
**Nimm den kleinen Koffer mit!**

1. Welcher Wagen gehört dir?
2. Welchen Pullover soll ich mir anziehen?
3. Welcher Mantel gefällt Ihnen?
4. Was für Geschichten hat er erzählt?
5. Was für eine Krawatte hat dir dein Onkel geschenkt?

**C.** *Fill in the appropriate form of the* **der** *and* **ein** *words, adjectives, nouns, and pronouns suggested.*

1. _____ gehören _____ _____ Socken? (Wer, dies, grün)
2. Was tragen _____ _____ Männer? (manch, jung)
3. In _____ _____ Straßen stehen _____ Autos. (die, eng, viel)
4. Für _____ _____ Moment dachte ich an _____ _____ Tochter. (ein, kurz, sein, hübsch)
5. Das war _____ _____ Vergnügen, sich mit _____ Freunden zu unterhalten. (ein, groß, gut)
6. Zieht _____ doch _____ _____ Pulli an! (ihr, fam., ein, warm)
7. Wo sind _____ _____ Hemden? (das, frisch)
8. Gefällt _____ _____ _____ Jacke? (er, dies, neu)

**D.** *Fill in the appropriate form of the words given in English.*

1. Seit _____ Jahren lebt er allein in _____ Haus. (long, his)
2. In den _____ Monaten haben sich _____ Dinge verändert. (last, many)
3. Unter den _____ Männern tragen _____ _____ Bart. (old, many, a)
4. Hier ißt man _____ Fleisch. (good)
5. Während der _____ Vorstellung schlief ich ein. (boring)
6. Die _____ Kleidung der _____ Leute gefällt mir. (modern, young)
7. Wir erinnern uns sehr gut an _____ _____ Eltern. (his, dear)
8. _____ _____ _____ Film muß man gesehen haben. (Such, an, interesting)

**E.** *Express in German.*

1. The city traffic has become too dense, and too many people park their cars in the narrow streets.
2. When I was a young man, the old men wore long or short beards or mustaches.
3. All things repeat themselves in the long history of mankind (men).
4. Albert, why don't you put on a warm overcoat or at least the new jacket?
5. Be careful. Even on this new freeway you mustn't drive so fast.
6. In any event please get a haircut.
7. My friend made a frightful face.
8. What do you mean? In this cold weather I won't walk around with short hair.

## GUIDED COMPOSITION

Describe some part of a city that you particularly like. Give one or two impressions of the people you see, what they look like, how they are dressed; what the traffic is like; whether there are many policemen around; whether the people drive carefully or not. What is the traffic like on the nearby freeways? How fast do people drive? How fast *should* they drive?

## VOCABULARY

### Easily recognized words

|     |                    |                 |     |                  |                                                                          |
| --- | ------------------ | --------------- | --- | ---------------- | ------------------------------------------------------------------------ |
|     | **elegant**        | *elegant*       | das | **Meer,** -e     | *sea*                                                                    |
| die | **Idee,** -n       | *idea*          | die | **Mitte**        | *middle*                                                                 |
| der | **Kamerad,** -en   | *comrade*       | die | **Mütze,** -n    | *cap*                                                                    |
|     | **lernen**         | *to learn*      | der | **Schnurrbart,** ¨e | *mustache*                                                            |
|     |                    |                 | der | **Schüler,** -   | *pupil*                                                                  |
|     |                    |                 | die | **Sorge,** -n    | *worry, care;* **sich Sorgen machen** (um + *acc.*) *to worry (about)*   |
| die | **Autobahn,** -en  | *freeway*       |     |                  |                                                                          |
| der | **Bart,** ¨e       | *beard*         |     |                  |                                                                          |
| die | **Farbe,** -n      | *color*         | der | **Stock,** ¨e    | *floor, story (of a building)*                                          |
| die | **Geschichte,** -n | *history, story* |     |                  |                                                                          |
| die | **Jugend**         | *youth*         | der | **Verkehr**      | *traffic*                                                                |
| die | **Kleidung**       | *clothing*      | die | **Wiederkehr**   | *return*                                                                 |

sich **beeilen** — *to hurry*

**erwarten** — *to await, expect*

**fliegen, flog, (ist) geflogen** — *to fly*

**frieren, fror, gefroren** — *to be cold*

**lachen** — *to laugh*

**rufen, rief, gerufen** — *to call*

**schenken** — *to give (a gift)*

**schneiden, schnitt, geschnitten** — *to cut*

**verändern** — *to change (something);* **sich verändern** *to change (be changed)*

**arm** — *poor*

**bequem** — *comfortable*

**breit** — *broad, wide*

**dicht** — *dense*

**drittens** — *in the third place*

**dunkel** — *dark*

**einigermaßen** — *somewhat, to some extent, fairly*

**eng** — *narrow*

**erstens** — *in the first place*

**frisch** — *fresh*

**gemütlich** — *jolly, good-natured*

**hell** — *light, pale (of color)*

**klein** — *little, small*

**kurz** — *short*

**langweilig** — *boring, dull*

**letzt-** — *last*

**reich** — *rich*

**rot** — *red*

**städtisch** — *municipal*

**tief** — *deep*

**unfreundlich** — *unfriendly*

**verkehrt** — *topsy-turvy*

**weiß** — *white*

**zweitens** — *in the second place*

See also the colors on p. 225.

# 12

## I

Im Rheinland befinden sich **viele** bekannte Burgen.
*In the Rhineland there are many well-known castles.*

Diese Band spielt **mehrere** gute Schlager.
*This band plays several good hit songs.*

**Alle** neuen Studenten treffen sich heute abend in einer Diskothek.
*All new students will meet tonight in a discothèque.*

## II

Endlich erhielten wir die **bestellten** Bücher.
*Finally we received the books that we had ordered.*

Die neue Band heißt „Die **singenden** Vampire".
*The new band is called "The Singing Vampires."*

Wir kaufen kein **gefrorenes** Obst.
*We do not buy frozen fruit.*

**III**

**Der Alte** erinnert sich an viele Länder.
*The old man remembers many countries.*

Er ist **ein Bekannter** von mir.
*He is an acquaintance of mine.*

Wir wünschen Euch **alles Gute.**
*We wish you all the best (everything good).*

Möchtest du **etwas Erfrischendes?**
*Would you like something refreshing?*

Bei den Müllers gibt's **nichts Neues.**
*There's nothing new at the Müllers'.*

**GRAMMAR
EXPLANATIONS**

## I. Attributive adjectives with numerical words

**A. Andere** (*other*), **einige** (*some*),[1] **mehrere** (*several*), **viele** (*many*), and **wenige** (*few*) are numerical words that may function as attributive adjectives. But quite often they are followed by a descriptive attributive adjective. In that case, the descriptive adjective takes the strong endings.

| | |
|---|---|
| Natürlich haben **andere** große Städte auch Universitäten. | *Naturally other large cities also have universities.* |
| Kennst du **einige** junge Amerikanerinnen? | *Do you know some young American women?* |
| An diesem Stadttheater sind **mehrere** bekannte Schauspieler. | *In this municipal theater there are several well-known actors.* |
| Gibt es in Köln **viele** große Fabriken? | *Are there many big factories in Cologne?* |
| Nur **wenige** alte Leute gehen in Diskotheken. | *Only a few old people go to discothèques.* |

**B.** With **alle, beide,** and **solche,** however, a descriptive attributive adjective that follows takes the weak endings.

| | |
|---|---|
| **Alle** neuen amerikanischen Studenten treffen sich heute abend im Deutsch-Institut. | *All new American students will meet tonight at the German Institute.* |

[1] *Einige* may occur in the singular, quite often in the sense of *considerable:* **Dieses Buch ist von einigem soziologischen Interesse.**

## Check your comprehension

*Supply the appropriate attributive adjective endings.*

1. Die Studentinnen kennen ander_____ englisch_____ Zeitungen nicht.
2. In der Stadtmitte befinden sich nur wenig_____ grün_____ Gärten.
3. Im Vergleich mit einig_____ alt_____ Gebäuden scheint das Rathaus neu.
4. Neben viel_____ schön_____ Brunnen sind große Parkplätze.
5. In der Einbahnstraße da drüben gibt es mehrer_____ interessant_____ Geschäfte.
6. Nicht all_____ neu_____ Hosen sind bequem.
7. Hast du tatsächlich mit solch_____ wichtig_____ Leuten gesprochen?
8. Er will beid_____ deutsch_____ Städte besuchen.

## II. Participles used as adjectives

In English and German there are two types of participles: the past participle and the present participle. Both may be used as adjectives.

### A. *Past participle*

The formation of the past participle in German was discussed in Chapter 5. If used as an attributive adjective, it takes the usual adjectival endings already discussed.

| | |
|---|---|
| Wir kaufen kein **gefrorenes** Gemüse. (frieren > gefroren) | *We don't buy frozen vegetables.* |
| Habt ihr das **verlorene** Buch wiedergefunden? (verlieren > verloren) | *Have you found the lost book again?* |

The past participle may also function as a predicate adjective.

| | |
|---|---|
| Dieses Gemüse ist nicht **gefroren.** | *These vegetables aren't frozen.* |

### B. *Present participle*

In German the present participle is formed by adding **-end** to the verb stem. The ending **-end** corresponds to the English *-ing*.[1]

fahrend = *moving* (a train, etc.)
fließend = *flowing*

---

[1] In English the present participle occurs most often in the progressive form of the verb: They were laughing as I entered. As explained in Chapter 1, this formation is not possible in German.

If used as an attributive adjective, it also takes the usual adjectival endings.

> Er ist auf den **fahrenden** Zug ge-    *He jumped on the moving train.*
> sprungen.
>
> Dieses Zimmer hat **fließendes** Was-    *This room has running water.*
> ser.

Quite often the German present participle must be translated into English as a relative clause.

> Das **lachende** Mädchen ist meine    *The girl who's laughing is my sis-*
> Schwester.    *ter.*

At times, a present participle may also function as a predicate adjective.

> Diese Limonade ist **erfrischend.**    *This lemonade is refreshing.*

## Check your comprehension

**A.** *Fill in the past participle of the verb in parentheses.*

1. Sie essen kein _____ Gemüse. (*frieren*)
2. Ich habe die _____ Hemden erhalten. (*bestellen*)
3. In diesem _____ Auto hatten wir einen Unfall. (*mieten*)
4. Ich kann mich an diese _____ Gebäude nicht gewöhnen. (*restaurieren*)
5. Hast du den _____ Brief erhalten? (*erwarten*)

**B.** *Form the present participle of the verb in parentheses and use it as an adjective.*

1. Die Studentin sprang auf den _____ Bus. (*fahren*)
2. Der _____ Herr da ist der Vater seiner Freundin. (*rauchen*)
3. Wo sind die _____ jungen Leute hingegangen? (*singen*)
4. Kennst du das _____ Mädchen da drüben? (*lachen*)
5. Wir mieteten ein Zimmer mit _____ Wasser. (*fließen*)
6. Diese _____ Kinder brauchen warme Mäntel. (*frieren*)

## III. Adjectives used as nouns

In German, adjectives may be used as nouns. If an adjective functions as a noun it is capitalized, but it retains the appropriate ending of the attributive adjective. Its gender and number are those of the noun that it has absorbed.

| | |
|---|---|
| Der alte Mann ist krank. | *The old man is sick.* |
| Der **Alte** ist krank. | *The old one is sick.* |
| Die neue Schauspielerin ist elegant. | *The new actress is elegant.* |
| Die **Neue** ist elegant. | *The new one is elegant.* |

Adjectival nouns in the neuter refer most often to something abstract or general.

| | |
|---|---|
| Das ist **das Gute** an diesem Fahrrad. | *That is the good thing about this bicycle.* |

Neuter adjectival nouns occur frequently after **etwas, nichts, viel,** and **wenig.** After these words, adjectival nouns take the strong endings.

| | |
|---|---|
| Er hat mir **etwas** Unglaubliches geschrieben. | *He wrote me something unbelievable.* |
| Es gibt **nichts** Neu**es.** | *There is nothing new.* |
| Sie hat uns **viel** Interessant**es** erzählt. | *She told us a lot of interesting things.* |
| Ihr habt sehr **wenig** Gut**es** über uns gesagt. | *You said very little good about us.* |

When an adjectival noun follows **alles,** however, it takes the weak endings.

| | |
|---|---|
| Ich wünsche euch **alles** Gute. | *I wish you all the best (everything good).* |

Present and past participles may also function as adjectival nouns.

| | |
|---|---|
| Ich möchte **etwas Erfrischendes** trinken. | *I would like to drink something refreshing.* |
| Sie ißt **nichts Gefrorenes.** | *She eats nothing frozen.* |

## Check your comprehension

**A.** *Substitute the adjectival noun for the words in italics.*

EXAMPLE: In dieser Stadt gibt es viele *arme Leute.*
     **In dieser Stadt gibt es viele Arme.**

1. So wie es *die alten Leute* machten, so machen es *die jungen Leute.*
2. Der *kleine Junge* lief über die Straße.
3. *Die reichen Leute* machen sich keine Sorgen um *die armen Leute.*
4. Der *kranke Mann* lag im Bett.

**B.** *Fill in the blanks with the adjectival nouns corresponding to the words in parentheses.*

EXAMPLE: Ich weiß nichts _____. *(new)*
 **Ich weiß nichts Neues.**

1. Er hat viel _____ getan. *(good)*
2. Das ist das _____ an meiner Arbeit. *(nice)*
3. Hier, trink etwas _____! *(refreshing)*
4. Es gibt wenig _____ zu erzählen. *(important)*
5. Sie wünschte uns alles _____ zum neuen Jahr. *(good)*
6. Ich will nichts _____ tun. *(unhealthy)*
7. Viktor möchte alles _____ lesen. *(written)*

## USEFUL PHRASES

| | |
|---|---|
| **befreundet sein** | *to be friends* |
| **Was gibt's Neues?** | *What's new?* |
| **das Übliche** | *the usual* |
| **Unglaublich!** | *You don't say! Unbelievable!* |
| **Du mußt es ja wissen.** | *You should know.* |
| **Zum Kuckuck!** | *Ah, forget it!* |

## CONVERSATION

## Die Diskothek

*Jutta Jünger (22) ist Chemiestudentin in Köln. Hansjörg Braun (23) studiert Soziologie. Sie sind befreundet und treffen sich zufällig in der Stadt.*

JUTTA Hansjörg! Hansjörg! Hallo Hansjörg! Hörst du mich denn nicht? Hansjörg!!!

HANSJÖRG Was? Wie bitte? Ach Jutta, du bist es! Guten Tag!

JUTTA Wie geht es dir? Was gibt's Neues?

HANSJÖRG Nichts Neues. Das Übliche. Ich studiere und schreibe und bin wieder einmal mit einer Seminararbeit° verspätet.° Du kennst mich ja.  *seminar paper | late*

JUTTA Aber wo kommst du denn jetzt her?

HANSJÖRG Wie bitte?

JUTTA *(schreit)* Wo du jetzt herkommst?[1] Aus der Uni-Bibliothek?

---

[1] In repeating a question, an introduction such as **ich fragte** or **ich sagte** is most often omitted. But the repeated question or statement is in the subordinate word order. In English: *(I asked) where you are coming from!*

HANSJÖRG  He? Ja, da aus der „Jimmy"-Diskothek. Da spielt jetzt eine
 ganz tolle Band—„Die singenden Vampire".

JUTTA  Warum heißen sie nicht die „brüllenden° Vampire"? Du hörst
 ja fast nichts mehr.

*howling*

HANSJÖRG  Auch gut. So höre ich nicht jeden Lärm. Übrigens singen
 die Vampire mehrere gute Schlager von einigem soziologischen
 und politischen Interesse.

JUTTA  Unglaublich, aber warum laden die Leute nicht einmal den Bier-
 mann² ein?

HANSJÖRG  Wie bitte? Du willst mich zum Bier einladen?

JUTTA  Ach, zum Kuckuck! Na, gut! Komm! Wir trinken da drüben
 schnell etwas Erfrischendes. Das Schlucken° wird deinem Gehör
 gut tun.

*swallowing*

HANSJÖRG  Was sagst du?

² Wolf Biermann, born in 1936, is a poet and balladeer from East Germany. Having
become embroiled with the regime, he was expelled from there in 1977. He now lives
in West Germany, where his songs and poems satirizing both East and West have earned
him a large following.

*Wolf Biermann*

## Questions

1. Wo treffen sich Jutta und Hansjörg zufällig?
2. Sind Jutta und Hansjörg Bekannte oder Freunde?
3. Gibt es etwas Neues bei Hansjörg? Was hat er kürzlich getan?
4. Woher kommt er?
5. Wie heißt die ganz fantastische Band?
6. Wie nennt Jutta die Band?
7. Warum kann Hansjörg nicht alles verstehen?
8. Warum findet Hansjörg einige Schlager dieser Band gut?
9. Was wird Hansjörgs Gehör gut tun?
10. Gibt es in Ihrer Stadt eine Diskothek? Gehen Sie gern hin?
11. Was hast du gern, laute oder leise Musik?
12. Hört man in amerikanischen Diskotheken Schlager von einigem soziologischen oder politischen Interesse? Welche, zum Beispiel?

 **PRACTICE**

**A.** *Substitute the adjectival noun for the word in italics.*

1. Die *neue Professorin* ist wirklich populär.
2. Der Vater spielte mit der *kleinen Tochter.*
3. Da drüben ist ein *alter Mann.*
4. Die Geschichte habe ich von der *alten Frau* da drüben gehört.

5. Die *kranke Mutter* muß zu Hause bleiben.
6. In dieser Stadt wohnen nicht viele *reiche Leute.*

**B.** *Supply the appropriate form of the past participle of the verb in parentheses.*

1. Da drüben sind die _____ Kleider. (*bestellen*)
2. Der Professor zeigte mir den _____ Dom. (*restaurieren*)
3. Das _____ Programm ist hier. (*verändern*)
4. Eßt ihr _____ Gemüse gern? (*frieren*)
5. Wir haben die _____ Schecks wieder gefunden. (*verlieren*)

**C.** *Add the appropriate ending to the adjectival noun.*

1. Während des Gesprächs erzählte sie uns nichts Interessant_____.
2. Die Nachricht ist den Studenten nichts Neu_____.
3. In der Zeitung lasen wir wenig Wichtig_____.
4. Bier ist sicher etwas Erfrischend_____.
5. Ich wünsche dir alles Gut_____.
6. Von ihm hört man nie etwas Schlecht_____.

**D.** *Supply the inflected present participle of the verb in parentheses.*

1. Sie geben dem _____ Sohn ein Fahrrad. (*spielen*)
2. Der Student sprang aus dem _____ Auto. (*fahren*)
3. Die _____ Studentin da drüben heißt Lotte. (*diskutieren*)
4. Der _____ Student da drüben ist mein Freund. (*lachen*)
5. Wer ist der _____ Herr? (*reden*)
6. Die _____ Freundin geht schnell nach Hause. (*frieren*)
7. Der _____ Journalist da ist sehr bekannt. (*lesen*)

**E.** *Substitute the items in parentheses for the words in italics and make any necessary changes.*

1. Wo gibt es *mehrere* alte Brunnen?
   (*andere/einige/wenige/viele*)
2. Alle *städtischen* Parkplätze sind voll.
   (*billig/bekannt/offen/frei/neu*)

**F.** *Fill in the blanks with the appropriate adjective endings.*

1. In mehrer_____ deutsch_____ Städten gibt es alte Brücken.
2. Einig_____ klein_____ Häuser sind noch nicht vermietet.
3. Natürlich haben viele groß_____ Geschäfte auch Hochhäuser in Berlin.
4. Hast du all_____ neu_____ Filme von Fellini gesehen, Peter?
5. Ander_____ städtisch_____ Diskotheken haben eine Band.
6. Zuviel_____ erfrischend_____ Biere können gefährlich werden.
7. Er kennt wenig_____ intelligent_____ Studenten im Deutsch-Institut.

**G.** *Substitute each word as it is introduced into the previous sentence and make any necessary changes.*

Natürlich haben andere deutsche Städte auch einen Flugplatz.

_____ alle _____ .

_____ Länder _____ .

_____ mehrere _____ .

_____ Universität.

_____ viele _____ .

---

**GUIDED CONVERSATION**

Begin a conversation with two or three classmates. Pretend you just came from a discothèque. Discuss your favorite songs, whether you like to dance, what songs you like to dance to, what bands you like especially, whether you like loud or soft music. Suggestions:

Wo ist die Diskothek?

Wieviel kostet ein Bier oder ein Glas Wein?

Tanzt du gern?

Zu welchen Hits tanzt du besonders gern?

READING

## Popmusik[1]

Seit der Erfindung des Phonographen° durch Thomas Edison hat     phonograph
sich die Produktion von Schallplatten zu einem gigantischen internationalen Geschäft entwickelt. Die Bundesrepublik produziert jährlich fast zweihundert Millionen Platten. Nur die USA und Japan produzieren noch mehr Platten als Deutschland. Oft nimmt der Verkauf
von Platten in Deutschland von einem Jahr zum andern um fast
fünfzehn Prozent zu. Viele andere Industrien können von solchen Ge-
schäftsentwicklungen nur träumen. Und wer ist für diese Entwicklung verantwortlich? Die Antwort ist einfach: die Jugendlichen[2] mit
ihrer Popmusik.

"Popmusik" nennt man in den deutschsprechenden Ländern viele

---

[1] **Popmusik, Hit** and other linguistic imports denoting musical style such as Beat and
Rock'n'Roll have become commonplace in Germany, even in the DDR.

[2] **Die Jugendlichen** is used in the general sense of *young people*, whereas **die Jungen**
means *the young* as opposed to **die Alten** (*the old*). **Die Jugend** means *youth*. **Der Junge**,
of course, denotes *boy*; its plural is **die Jungens.**

verschiedene Stile: Vom Heimatlied[3] über den Jazz bis zum Punkrock. Für die Jugend ist die Popmusik zum Ausdruck ihrer Weltanschauung° geworden. In Deutschland kaufen Jugendliche unter 25 Jahren fast neunzig Prozent aller neuen Platten. So kommt es, daß neunzig Prozent der verkauften Platten Popmusik und nur zehn Prozent klassische° Musik bieten.°

    Die deutsche Jugend von heute will aber nicht nur deutsche Popmusik hören. Sie möchte auch zu allen internationalen Schlagern tanzen, besonders am Wochenende in den Diskotheken. Und die deutsche Schallplattenindustrie hat ein sehr gutes Musikgehör: sie hört auf° die musikalischen Interessen der Jugend und produziert viele international bekannte Hits. Die Lizenzgebühren° sind klein im Vergleich mit dem Gewinn. Das Risiko ist nicht groß.

    Das Interesse der deutschen Jugend an internationalen Hits begann bald nach dem Zweiten Weltkrieg. Vielleicht hat sie während des Krieges zu viele Marschlieder° gehört! Auch konnte man bald nach dem Krieg wieder in andere europäische Länder reisen. Und man lernte Englisch! Schließlich kam die Invasion des Rock'n'Roll, der vielen großen Hits von Elvis Presley und mehrerer bekannter Gruppen, wie zum Beispiel der Beatles.

    "Beat", wie man die amerikanische Rockmusik in Deutschland nennt, wurde zu einem eigentlichen Lebensstil. Er beeinflußte° die Haartracht° der Jungen, ihre Kleidung, ihre Freizeit. Und die Popsänger wurden zu Idolen.

    Inzwischen haben die Eltern mit diesem Lebensstil und der Ideologie der Jungen einige Kompromisse gemacht. Was sie aber kaum verstehen können, ist die Vorliebe° der Jugend für ohrenbetäubende° Musik. Das ist etwas anderes. Man kann die Ohren an neue Musik und einen neuen Rhythmus gewöhnen, aber warum soll man dabei schwerhörig° werden?

    Die Alten fragen sich, warum die Jungen so laute Musik lieben und nicht leise Musik vorziehen. Will die Jugend vielleicht die Leere° der modernen Zivilisation mit der lauten Musik ausfüllen°? Oder wollen die Jungen den Lärm der modernen Zivilisation—des Stadt- und Flugverkehrs und der Industrie—durch die laute Musik vergessen? Wer weiß? Niemand scheint die Antwort zu haben. Auf jeden Fall darf man sagen, daß das alte Sprichwort° "Wie die Alten sungen, so zwitschern° die Jungen"[4] auf dem Gebiet° des musikalischen Geschmacks nicht mehr so ganz wahr ist.

| | |
|---|---|
| perception of the world | |
| classical / offer | |
| listens to | |
| license fees | |
| marching songs | |
| influenced | |
| hairdo | |
| preference/deafening | |
| hard of hearing | |
| emptiness | |
| fill | |
| proverb | |
| chirp/in the area | |

---

[3] A song expressing (an often maudlin) sentiment about one's native land or region.

[4] Literally: *As the old ones sang, so do the young,* that is, like father like son. (**Sungen** is used instead of **sangen** for the sake of rhyme.)

## QUESTIONS

1. Was war die Erfindung von Thomas Edison?
2. Was hat sich zu einem gigantischen Geschäft entwickelt?
3. Wieviele Schallplatten produziert die Bundescrepublik jährlich?
4. Wer ist für die Entwicklung in der Schallplattenindustrie verantwortlich?
5. Was nennt man in den deutschsprechenden Ländern "Popmusik"?
6. Wer kauft in Deutschland fast alle neuen Platten?
7. Was tut die deutsche Jugend am Wochenende?
8. Warum produziert die deutsche Schallplattenindustrie auch viele internationale Hits?
9. Wann begann das Interesse der deutschen Jugend an internationalen Hits?
10. Was beeinflußte die "Beatmusik"?
11. Warum liebt die Jugend die laute Musik und zieht nicht leise Musik vor?
12. Warum ist das alte Sprichwort nicht mehr so ganz wahr?

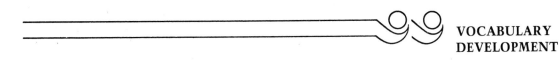

**VOCABULARY
DEVELOPMENT**

### A. Freunde, befreundet, *or* Bekannte?

**Der Freund, -e, die Freundin, -nen,** denote good friends who would in most cases use the **du** form in addressing each other.

The adjective **befreundet** suggests being more than just chance acquaintances, without being intimate friends. People who are **befreundet** may use the **du** or **Sie** form among themselves, depending on their respective ages, their relationship, their agreed-upon preferences, etc.

**Der (die) Bekannte, -n** (from **kennen**) are mere acquaintances, often of a distant or superficial sort, who will always use the formal **Sie** in addressing each other. You may say:

| | |
|---|---|
| Er ist ein Bekannter von mir. | *He is an acquaintance of mine.* |
| Sie ist eine Bekannte von mir. | *She is an acquaintance of mine.* |
| *Or:* Ich bin mit ihm (ihr) bekannt. | *I'm acquainted with him (her).* |

Now tell your fellow students with whom you are friends, on friendly terms, or merely acquainted.

**B.** *How good is your hearing?*

**das Gehör** is obviously derived from **hören.** It denotes both the hearing mechanism and the sense of hearing.

**das Gefühl** is from **fühlen** (*to feel*), and denotes many related things: the sense of touch; feeling; sentiment; emotion; etc.

The other nouns referring to the senses are:

**der Geruch** from **riechen** (*to smell*), denoting the sense of smell or a smell.

**der Geschmack** from **schmecken** (*to taste*), denoting the sense of taste, but also the taste of something, and to have (good) taste: **Sie hat sehr guten Geschmack.** The verb **schmecken** is often heard at the table:

**Wie schmeckt es?**     *How does it taste?*
**Es schmeckt sehr gut.**  *It tastes very good.*

The sense of sight, however, is **das Sehvermögen** (the ability to see). **Das Gesicht,** also derived from **sehen,** of course denotes *the face.*

At this point, you might wish to learn and practice some words referring to parts of the human body. Easily recognized words are:

der Arm, -e                der Mund, ⸚er
die Hand, ⸚e               der Fuß, ⸚e
der Finger, -              das Haar, -e
die Nase, -n

Others:

der Körper, - *body*        das Ohr, -en *ear*
der Kopf, ⸚e *head*         der Bauch, ⸚e *stomach*
das Bein, -e *leg*          die Brust, ⸚e *chest, breast*
das Auge, -n *eye*          der Zahn, ⸚e *tooth*

Describe briefly a few facial or bodily features of yourself or someone else. Use the common descriptive adjectives (long, short, big, little, etc.), the colors, and even **fantastisch** if it seems appropriate. A comment on **der Intellekt** might also be included.

**REVIEW EXERCISES**

**A.** *Supply the appropriate adjectival form of the past participle.*

1. Monika fand die _____ Mütze wieder. (*verlieren*)
2. Die Journalisten aßen die _____ Brötchen. (*mitbringen*)

3. Ich erkannte die _____ Gäste nicht. (*einladen*)

4. Endlich erhielten wir das _____ Klavier. (*bestellen*)

5. Die _____ Briefe waren alle für ihn. (*ankommen*)

6. Das _____ Buch war teuer. (*illustrieren*)

7. Die _____ Reise hörte wegen schlechten Wetters auf. (*anfangen*)

**B.** *Fill in the appropriate form of the present participle.*

1. Der Tourist sprang aus dem _____ Zug. (*fahren*)

2. Peter kam _____ nach Hause zurück. (*frieren*)

3. Sehen Sie das _____ Kind dort? (*lachen*)

4. Im Stadtpark sieht man viele _____ Menschen. (*lesen*)

5. Jetzt können Sie die _____ Straßenbahn schon hören. (*herankommen*)

6. Kennen Sie den _____ Studenten? (*sprechen*)

7. Die _____ Studenten werden sehr durstig. (*diskutieren*)

**C.** *Answer the questions with the cues provided.*

EXAMPLE: Was wünschen Sie einem guten Freund? (*alles/gut*) (—/best-)
**Ich wünsche ihm alles Gute.**
**Ich wünsche ihm das Beste.**

1. Was gibt's heute bei Ihnen? (*nichts/neu*) (*wenig/interessant*)

2. Was sagt man über ihn? (*viel/schlecht*) (*nichts/gut*)

3. Was hat er Ihnen erzählt? (*wenig/unterhaltend*) (*viel/langweilig*)

4. Was kommt jetzt? (—/interessantest-) (—/unterhaltend)

**D.** *Translate into German.*

1. The old man (old one) doesn't like that crazy band.
2. Many well-known books are not here.
3. When can we drink something refreshing?
4. Many young people of the Federal Republic of Germany like to listen to Western hits.
5. I know several popular professors.
6. From one year to the next, the production of records in the Federal Republic has increased by fifteen percent.
7. The arriving train was full.
8. The polluted water of the river is dangerous for our health.
9. The old people (old ones) do not know why the young prefer to listen to loud music.
10. Some American songs express something sociological.

**GUIDED COMPOSITION**

Describe your favorite discothèque, restaurant, or bar (**die Bar, -s**). State whether you go there very often and why you choose that particular place. Do you prefer going there with a friend or alone? Also talk about your favorite pastime, e.g., talking to people, listening to music, meeting new people, enjoying good food, dancing, having a cup of coffee, or the like.

**VOCABULARY**

### Easily recognized words

| | | | | | |
|---|---|---|---|---|---|
| | amerikanisch | *American* | der | **Kompromiß, -sse** | *compromise* |
| die | **Band, -s** | *band* | die | **Musik** | *music* |
| | beginnen, begann, begonnen | *to begin* | | musikalisch | *musical* |
| | gigantisch | *gigantic* | | politisch | *political* |
| der | **Hit, -s** | *hit* | die | **Produktion** | *production* |
| die | **Ideologie, -n** | *ideology* | | produzieren | *to produce* |
| das | **Idol, -e** | *idol* | | soziologisch | *sociological* |
| das | **Interesse, -n** | *interest* | | | |
| | international | *international* | der | **Bekannte, -n (ein Bekannter)** | *acquaintance* |
| die | **Invasion, -en** | *invasion* | die | **Chemie** | *chemistry* |

| | | | |
|---|---|---|---|
| die | **Entwicklung, -en** | *development* | |
| die | **Erfindung, -en** | *invention* | |
| das | **Gehör** | *sense of hearing* | |
| der | **Geschmack** | *taste, sense of taste; good taste* | |
| der | **Gewinn, -e** | *gain* | |
| die | **Gruppe, -n** | *group* | |
| der | **Jugendliche, -n (ein Jugendlicher)** | *the youth* | |
| das | **Prozent, -e** | *per cent, percentage* | |
| das | **Risiko, -s** | *risk* | |
| der | **Sänger, -** | *singer, entertainer* | |
| der | **Schlager, -** | *hit, popular song* | |
| der | **Stil -e** | *style* | |
| das | **Wochenende, -n** | *weekend* | |

See also the parts of the body on p. 244.

**ein·laden (lädt), lud, eingeladen** — *to invite*

sich **entwickeln** — *to develop*

sich **erfrischen** — *to refresh*
**lieben** — *to love*
**singen, sang, gesungen** — *to sing*
**tanzen** — *to dance*
**träumen** — *to dream*
**vor·ziehen, zog, vorgezogen** — *to prefer*
**zu·nehmen (nimmt), nahm, zugenommen** — *to increase*
**wünschen** — *to wish*

**dabei** — *in so doing*
**erst** — *only*
**gern: etwas gern haben** — *to like something*
**laut** — *loud*
**leise** — *silent, quiet*
**niemand** — *nobody*
**toll** — *fabulous (slang), mad, crazy*
**üblich** — *usual*
**verantwortlich** — *responsible*
**zufällig** — *by coincidence, by chance*

## I

Paul spricht Deutsch nicht **so gut wie** ich.
*Paul doesn't speak German as well as I.*

Brötchen sind **billiger als** Kuchen.
*Rolls are cheaper than cake.*

Klara ist die **älteste** Studentin.
*Klara is the oldest student.*

Wenn er Polizei sieht, fährt er **am vorsichtigsten.**
*When he sees police, he drives most carefully.*

## II

Wir **waren** gerade am Bahnhof **angekommen,** als der Zug abfuhr.
*We had just arrived at the railroad station, when the train left.*

Wir **hatten abgemacht,** uns um elf Uhr zu treffen.
*We had agreed to meet at eleven o'clock.*

## III

Was geschah am Sonntag, dem **20. November 1977?**[1]
*What happened on Sunday, November 20, 1977?*

**Um 20 Uhr** beginnt der Film.
*The movie starts at 8:00 p.m.*

**Um viertel vor zwölf** gehe ich zu Bett.
*At a quarter to twelve I go to bed.*

**GRAMMAR EXPLANATION**

### I. Comparison of adjectives and adverbs

In German as in English, there are three degrees of comparison: the *positive,* the *comparative,* and the *superlative.* When used as attributive adjectives, all three degrees add adjective endings, as discussed in Chapter 11.

**A.** *The positive*

The positive represents the basic form of an adjective, as listed in the dictionary.

To indicate equality between two persons or items, the positive form of the predicate adjective or adverb is used with the particles **so . . . wie** *(as . . . as).*

Das Auto ist **so alt wie** das Fahrrad.    *The car is as old as the bicycle.*
Jutta schwimmt **so gut wie** Brigitte.    *Jutta swims just as well as Brigitte.*

**B.** *The comparative*

The comparative is formed by adding the suffix **-er** to the adjective stem; it denotes a comparison between two unequal objects.

ATTRIBUTIVE: Jutta ist die **schönere** Frau.    *Jutta is the more beautiful woman.*

The word **als** *(than)* is used with predicative adjectives and adverbs in the comparative form.

PREDICATE ADJECTIVE/ADVERB:
Peter ist **kleiner als** Jutta.    *Peter is shorter than Jutta.*
Unser Auto fährt **schneller als** eures.    *Our car goes faster than yours.*

---

[1] Read: **dem zwanzigsten November neunzehnhundertsiebenundsiebzig.**

In conjunction with the comparative, the word **immer** (*always*) suggests a progressive increase. Note the equivalent in English.

| | |
|---|---|
| Die Filme werden **immer schlechter.** | *The movies are getting worse and worse.* |
| Ich werde **immer vorsichtiger.** | *I'm becoming more and more careful.* |

## C. *The superlative*

The superlative is formed by adding the suffix **-st: das kleinste Haus.** However, **-est** is added after **-d, -t, -s, -ß, -sch, -x,** and **-z: der unterhaltendeste Film, die frischeste Milch.**

ATTRIBUTIVE: Jörg hat das **kleinste** Stück Brot.    *Jörg has the smallest piece of bread.*

When used as a predicate adjective or as an adverb, the superlative form occurs as the phrase **am . . . -sten.**

PREDICATE ADJECTIVE/ADVERB:

| | |
|---|---|
| Hier ist der Fluß **am tiefsten.** | *Here the river is deepest.* |
| Er spricht **am lautesten.** | *He speaks the loudest.* |

There are some deviations from the above rule in order to facilitate pronunciation:

(a) Adjectives with stems ending in **-e** merely add an **-r** in the comparative: **leise** (*quiet*) > **leiser.**

Hans sprach **leiser** als ich.    *Hans spoke more quietly than I.*

(b) Adjectives with stems ending in **-el** or **-er** drop the **-e-** in the comparative: **dunkel > dunkler; teuer > teurer.**

Unser Auto ist **teurer** als der Volkswagen.    *Our car is more expensive than the VW.*

In addition, some monosyllabic adjectives with the stem vowels **a, o,** or **u** form the comparative and superlative by adding an umlaut to the vowel. The following adjectives which you have studied follow this pattern:

| | | |
|---|---|---|
| alt | älter | am ältesten |
| arm | ärmer | am ärmsten |
| groß | größer | am größten[1] |
| jung | jünger | am jüngsten |
| kalt | kälter | am kältesten |

[1] Note that this is a special superlative form.

| | | |
|---|---|---|
| klug | klüger | am klügsten |
| krank | kränker | am kränksten |
| kurz | kürzer | am kürzesten |
| lang | länger | am längsten |
| schwach | schwächer | am schwächsten |
| stark | stärker | am stärksten |
| warm | wärmer | am wärmsten |

| | |
|---|---|
| Fred liest das längere Buch. | *Fred is reading the longer book.* |
| Hilde ist die Jüngste von uns. | *Hilde is the youngest of us.* |

There are a number of common adjectives and adverbs that form irregular comparatives and superlatives.

| POSITIVE | COMPARATIVE | SUPERLATIVE |
|---|---|---|
| gut | **besser** | am **besten** |
| hoch/hoh- (*high*) | **höher** | am **höchsten** |
| nahe (*near*) | **näher** | am **nächsten** |
| oft | **öfter** | am **meisten** (*most often*) |
| viel | **mehr** | am **meisten** (*the most*) |

Note that **hoch** is the predicate adjective and the adverb, while **hoh-** is the attributive adjective.

| | |
|---|---|
| Der Berg ist **hoch.** | *The mountain is high.* |
| Das ist **hoch** interessant. | *That's extremely (highly) interesting.* |
| *But:* Der **hohe** Berg heißt das Matterhorn. | *The high mountain is called the Matterhorn.* |

The irregular adverb **gern** adds the meaning *to like to* to the verb; the comparative **lieber** adds the meaning *to prefer to;* the superlative **am liebsten** adds the meaning *to prefer to . . . most of all* or *to like to . . . best of all.*

| | |
|---|---|
| Sie schreibt **gern** Briefe. | *She likes to write letters.* |
| Er trinkt **lieber** Bier. | *He prefers to drink beer.* |
| Wir essen **am liebsten** Obst. | *We like to eat fruit best of all.* |

## Check your comprehension

*Supply the appropriate adjective or adverb in parentheses.*

1. Ich verstehe Deutsch _____ Englisch. (*as well as*)
2. Ich werde leider immer _____. (*weaker*)
3. Er nahm natürlich das _____ Zimmer. (*more expensive*)

4. Wenn die Tage _____ werden, kommt bald der Winter. (*shorter*)
5. Der Bahnhof ist _____ als der Flugplatz. (*nearer*)
6. Hier sind die Zigaretten _____. (*cheapest*)
7. Das _____ Auto ist der Mercedes 600. (*biggest*)
8. Ihr seid heute _____ gekommen. (*late*)

## II. Past perfect tense

The past perfect tense is formed with the past tense of the auxiliaries **haben** or **sein,** and the past participle of the principal verb.

*Past perfect tense*

| *With* **haben** | *With* **sein** |
|---|---|
| SINGULAR | |
| ich **hatte** gesagt | ich **war** abgefahren |
| du **hattest** gesagt | du **warst** abgefahren |
| er | er |
| sie } **hatte** gesagt | sie } **war** abgefahren |
| es | es |
| PLURAL | |
| wir **hatten** gesagt | wir **waren** abgefahren |
| ihr **hattet** gesagt | ihr **wart** abgefahren |
| sie **hatten** gesagt | sie **waren** abgefahren |
| SINGULAR/PLURAL | |
| Sie **hatten** gesagt | Sie **waren** abgefahren |

This tense is used to indicate that one event or action (A) had already occurred when another event (B) took place in the past. If the other event is stated, it uses the past tense.

             (EVENT B)              (EVENT A)

(1) Als Hans **ankam, hatten** wir den Kaffee schon **getrunken.**
    *When Hans arrived, we had already drunk the coffee.*

             (EVENT A)              (EVENT B)

(2) Nachdem wir **gegessen hatten, fuhren** wir nach Hause.
    *After we had eaten, we drove home.*

In example 1, the drinking of the coffee had already been completed when Hans arrived. The entire occurrence—both the drinking of the coffee and the arrival of Hans—lies in the past. In example 2, the eating precedes the driving home.

---

## Check your comprehension

*Supply the correct form of the past perfect tense, using the verbs in parentheses.*

1. Bevor es zu regnen begann, _____ die Sonne _____. (*scheinen*)
2. Als ich ankam, _____ die Polizei schon _____. (*abfahren*)
3. Sie _____ drei Jahre Deutsch _____, bevor sie nach Deutschland kam. (*studieren*)
4. Wir gaben das Geld sofort aus, nachdem wir es vom Vater _____ _____. (*bekommen*)
5. Wir _____ _____, daß das Wetter besser wird. (*hoffen*)

---

## III. Numbers, dates , and expressions of time

**A.** *Numbers*

There are two major groups of numbers: the cardinal and the ordinal numbers. *Cardinal numbers* were discussed in the introductory chapter. When cardinal numbers are used as nouns, they are always feminine.

Für mich ist **die Dreizehn** eine Glückszahl.   *For me, thirteen is a lucky number.*

*Ordinal numbers* refer to a specific number in a series and are declined like adjectives. They rarely occur without a preceding **der** or **ein** word.

| | |
|---|---|
| Er trinkt schon die **dritte** Tasse Kaffee. | *He's already drinking his third cup of coffee.* |
| Ihr **zweiter** Mann heißt Eugen. | *Her second husband's name is Eugen.* |

When written in figures, ordinal numbers are followed by a period.

| | |
|---|---|
| Lincolns Geburtstag ist am **12.** Februar. | *Lincoln's birthday is on February twelfth.* |

Ordinal numbers are formed by adding **-t** to the cardinal numbers one to nineteen, and **-st** to twenty and above, plus the adjective ending. Note the slight irregularities in **erste, dritte, siebte,** and **achte,** and the formation of **hunderterste** (*hundred and first*).

*Ordinal numbers*

| | |
|---|---|
| 1. der/die/das } **erste** | 19. der/die/das } neunzehnte |
| 2. zweite | 20. zwanzigste |
| 3. **dritte** | 21. einundzwanzigste |
| 4. vierte | 30. dreißigste |
| 5. fünfte | 40. vierzigste |
| 6. sechste | 50. fünfzigste |
| 7. **siebte** | 60. sechzigste |
| 8. **achte** | 70. siebzigste |
| 9. neunte | 80. achtzigste |
| 10. zehnte | 90. neunzigste |
| 11. elfte | 100. (ein)hundertste |
| 12. zwölfte | 101. (ein)hundert**erste** |
| 13. dreizehnte | 200. zweihundertste |
| 14. vierzehnte | 1000. (ein)tausendste |
| 15. fünfzehnte | 2000. zweitausendste |
| 16. sechzehnte | 1000000. millionste |
| 17. siebzehnte | 2000000. zweimillionste |
| 18. achtzehnte | |

Ordinal numbers can be used as nouns, in which case they follow the same rules as adjectives used as nouns (see Chapter 12) and are capitalized.

| | |
|---|---|
| Heinrich der Achte hatte sechs Frauen. | *Henry the Eighth had six wives.* |

---

## Check your comprehension

*Write out the number in parentheses.*

1. Das ist meine _____ Tasse Kaffee. (1.)
2. _____ dieser beiden Fahrräder ist meins. (1)
3. Die _____ ist meine Glückszahl. (7)
4. Meine Tante raucht jetzt schon die _____ Zigarette. (3.)
5. Ihren _____ Mann kenne ich nicht. (2.)
6. Unser Studium hört nicht nach dem _____ Jahr auf. (6.)
7. Zwischen dem _____ und dem _____ Schlager hat sie etwas Unbekanntes gespielt. (4., 5.)

---

**B.** *Additional times of the day*

In Chapter 8 (p. 154) you learned certain common expressions with **an: am Morgen** (*in the morning*), **am Nachmittag** (*in the afternoon*), **am Abend** (*in the evening*), **am Montag** (*on Monday*). Here now are some additional times of day:

| | | |
|---|---|---|
| **am** Vormittag | *about ten to twelve a.m.* | der Vormittag, -e |
| **zu** Mittag | *at noon* | der Mittag, -e |
| **in der** Nacht | *during the night* | die Nacht, ⸗e |
| **um** Mitternacht | *at midnight* | die Mitternacht, ⸗e |

Habitual or repetitious actions are expressed by the corresponding adverbs which end in **-s.** Remember that adverbs are not capitalized.

Elsa geht **vormittags** ins Büro, und **nachmittags** macht sie Einkäufe.  *In the morning Elsa goes to the office, and in the afternoon she goes shopping.*

In the same way adverbs can be formed with the days of the week:

Er fährt **dienstags** immer nach Köln.  *On Tuesdays, he always goes to Cologne.*

---

## Check your comprehension

**A.** *Answer each question with a sentence that includes a prepositional phrase expressing a time of day.*

EXAMPLE: Wann tanzen Sie gern?
**Ich tanze gern am Abend.**

1. Wann studieren Sie am liebsten?
2. Wann schlafen Sie am besten?
3. Wann machen Sie Einkäufe?

4. Wann hören Sie auf zu arbeiten?

5. Wann beginnt diese Klasse?

6. Wann trinken Sie morgens die erste Tasse Kaffee?

    **B.** *Replace the prepositional time phrases by their corresponding adverbs.*

1. Am Vormittag gehe ich immer zur Universität.

2. Zu Mittag esse ich meistens nicht viel.

3. Am Abend sehe ich oft einen Film im Kino oder im Fernsehen.

4. In der Nacht arbeiten viele Leute.

5. Am Sonntag gehe ich oft zur Kirche.

## C. *Telling time*

Telling time is based on a twenty-four hour clock in German; a.m. and p.m. are not used. The twenty-four hour clock is particularly used in official announcements like the news, and in programs, timetables, etc.

| | |
|---|---|
| Es ist jetzt **18.55 Uhr.** | *It is now 6:55 p.m.* |
| (*Read:* Es ist jetzt achtzehn Uhr fünfundfünfzig.) | |
| Der Film beginnt **um 20 Uhr.** | *The movie starts at 8:00 p.m.* |
| Der Bus fährt **um 15.38 Uhr** ab. | *The bus leaves at 3:38 p.m.* |

As in English, however, the twelve-hour clock is generally used in conversation to indicate both morning and afternoon. Sometimes an adverb of time is used to indicate a.m. and p.m.

| Er fährt um neun Uhr **morgens** ab. | *He's leaving at nine o'clock in the morning.* |

German is similar to English in its use of **nach** and **vor** to indicate minutes past or before the hour.

| Es ist zwanzig Minuten **nach** neun. | *It's twenty minutes after nine.* |
| Es ist zehn Minuten **vor** acht. | *It's ten minutes before eight.* |

Fractions are more commonly used—for the twelve-hour clock only—to express the English *a quarter after, half past,* and *a quarter to.*

| Es ist viertel nach zwei. | *It's a quarter after two.* |
| Es ist viertel vor eins. | *It's a quarter to one.* |
| Es ist dreiviertel vier. | *It's 3:45 (lit., three-quarters of the way to four).* |
| Es ist halb acht. | *It's 7:30 (lit., half way to eight).* |

Thus 7:45 p.m. can be expressed in all of the following ways.

Es ist fünfzehn Minuten vor acht.
Es ist sieben Uhr fünfundvierzig.
Es ist viertel vor acht.
Es ist dreiviertel acht.
Es ist neunzehn Uhr fünfundvierzig.

## Check your comprehension

**A.** *Read the following times as a.m. and p.m. times in German, using (a) the colloquial and (b) the official way, wherever possible.*

1. Es ist fünf Uhr zwanzig.
2. Es ist 3 Uhr 38.
3. Mein Bus fährt um 9.29 Uhr.
4. Ich trinke meinen Kaffee immer um viertel vor sechs.
5. Um halb acht höre ich meistens Nachrichten.
6. Es ist gerade viertel nach eins.

**B.** *Read the following times as many ways as you can, in both the colloquial and the official ways.*

1. 5:20 a.m.
2. 3:38 p.m.
3. 8:45 p.m.
4. 10:15 a.m.

### D. *Dates*

Dates are always written in the order: day, month, year.

| | |
|---|---|
| Konrad Adenauer wurde **am 5. Januar 1876** geboren. | *Konrad Adenauer was born on January 5, 1876.* |
| **Am 22. 3. 1832** starb Goethe in Weimar. | *On March 22, 1832, Goethe died in Weimar.* |

It is not possible to say *in 1832* in German; say either **1832** or **im Jahre 1832.**

Goethe starb 1832.
Goethe starb im Jahre 1832.

When you ask for the date, you may say it in either of two ways:

**Welches Datum** haben wir heute? ⎫
**Der wievielte** ist heute? ⎭ *What's the date today?*

### E. *Definite and indefinite time expressions*

Certain time expressions are used without any preposition to specify when something happened or will happen. Expressions that refer to *definite time* are in the *accusative* case.

| Er ist **jeden Winter** in die Alpen gefahren. | *He went to the Alps every winter.* |
| Wir fahren **nächsten Montag** in Urlaub. | *We are going on vacation next Monday.* |

The expressions **heute morgen** and **heute früh** (*this morning*), **gestern abend** (*last night*), **morgen nachmittag** (*tomorrow afternoon*), etc., are considered adverbs of time and so are not capitalized.

Other expressions refer to *indefinite time* and take the *genitive* case.

| **Eines Tages** wird er zurückkommen. | *He'll come back someday.* |
| **Eines Abends** ging ich sehr früh zu Bett. | *One evening I went to bed quite early.* |

## Check your comprehension

**A.** *Supply the dates.*

1. Mein Geburtstag ist am _____.
2. Vor drei Wochen war der _____.
3. George Washingtons Geburtstag ist am _____.
4. Welches Datum haben wir heute?

**B.** *Fill in the definite or indefinite time expressions as indicated in parentheses.*

1. Wir fahren _____ in die Berge. (*every summer*)
2. Sie geht fast _____ in ein Café. (*every afternoon*)
3. Ich reise _____ in die Schweiz. (*next Tuesday*)
4. _____ wird er ein bekannter Mann sein. (*someday*)
5. Ich habe _____ einige Gäste eingeladen. (*last week*)
6. _____ stand er sehr früh auf. (*one morning*)

## USEFUL PHRASES

| **außer Atem** | *out of breath* |
| **Zu dumm!** | *Too bad! How dumb (of me)!* |
| **Allerdings!** | *Indeed! I should say so!* |
| **Abgemacht!** | *Agreed! It's a deal!* |
| **Ehrlich?** | *Really? Honestly?* |

**CONVERSATION**

## Nach der Vorlesung

*Werner ist Physikstudent an einer deutschen Universität und seine Freundin Helga ist im vierten Semester Medizin. Beide sind 23 Jahre alt. Helga kommt ganz außer Atem in die Mensa.[1] Dort findet sie ihren Freund. Er sitzt halb träumend vor seinem Essen.*

HELGA Werner, ach, da bist du ja!

WERNER Ja, natürlich. Wo sonst? Es ist doch schon . . . *(schaut auf seine Uhr)* . . . zwanzig nach zwölf und höchste Zeit zum Essen.

HELGA Aber wir hatten doch abgemacht, uns um viertel vor zwölf vor dem Labor°-Gebäude zu treffen und in der Stadt zu essen.     *lab(oratory)*

WERNER Aber hatten wir das nicht für morgen abgemacht?

HELGA Nein, für heute.

WERNER Du, da habe ich mich tatsächlich geirrt. Zu dumm!

HELGA Allerdings!

WERNER Bitte, sei mir nicht böse. Setz dich doch hin. Ich habe schon für uns beide das Essen geholt.

HELGA Na gut, aber dann essen wir morgen in der Stadt. Unsere Seminare fangen doch erst um halb fünf nachmittags an.

WERNER Abgemacht! Aber weißt du, die Vorlesung von Frau Professor Schürmann heute morgen war fantastisch; klar und unterhaltend.

HELGA Ehrlich? Eine unterhaltende Mathematik-Vorlesung ist wirklich etwas Ungewöhnliches.

WERNER Aber Professor Schürmann hat tatsächlich guten Humor.

HELGA Dann komme ich morgen am besten mit zur Vorlesung.

WERNER Warum denn?

HELGA Sonst vergißt du unsere Verabredung wieder.

[1] **Die Mensa** is the student cafeteria at the university. The word is of Latin origin.

## Questions

1. Wer sind Werner und Helga. Was studieren sie?
2. Wo findet Helga ihren Freund Werner? Was tut er?
3. Wieviel Uhr ist es gerade?
4. Wo und wann wollten sich Werner und Helga treffen?
5. Wer hat sich geirrt?
6. Wo will Helga morgen essen?
7. Welche Vorlesung findet Werner klar und unterhaltend?
8. Warum will Helga morgen mit zur Vorlesung kommen?
9. Irren Sie sich oft? Geben Sie ein Beispiel.
10. Wenn ein Freund (oder eine Freundin) für eine Verabredung spät kommt, sind Sie ihm (oder ihr) böse?
11. Wie finden Sie die Vorlesungen Ihrer Professoren? Sind sie meistens klar und unterhaltend, oder . . . ?
12. Haben Ihre Professoren guten Humor? Glauben Sie, daß das wichtig ist? Warum oder warum nicht?

**PRACTICE**

**A.** *Fill in the appropriate comparative form of the adjectives or adverbs in parentheses.*

1. Sind die Studenten an dieser Universität ＿＿＿＿ oder ＿＿＿＿ bei uns. (*older/younger than*)
2. Finden Sie diese Vorlesung ＿＿＿＿ und ＿＿＿＿ die erste? (*clearer/ more interesting than*)

3. Immer _____ Menschen sagen, daß die Luft immer _____ wird. (*more/dirtier*)

4. Ein _____ Land ist _____ ein _____ Land. (*smaller/weaker than/larger*)

5. Die _____ Bands sind _____ aber _____ die _____ Bands. (*louder/crazier/more entertaining than/quieter*)

6. Fahren die Europäer im Stadtverkehr _____ oder _____ die Amerikaner? (*faster/slower than*)

**B.** *Fill in the appropriate superlative form of the adjectives or adverbs in parentheses.*

1. Wer am _____ studiert, verdient später am _____ Geld. (*lang/viel*)

2. Der Urlaub ist für uns die _____ aber auch die _____ Zeit des Jahres. (*schön/teuer*)

3. Am _____ fahre ich ins Rheintal. (*gern*)

4. Der _____ Berg in Deutschland ist die Zugspitze. (*hoch*)

5. Amerika ist eines der _____, _____ und _____ Länder der Welt. (*groß/stark/reich*)

6. Im Dezember sind die Tage am _____. (*kurz*)

**C.** *Transform the following sentences into the past perfect tense.*

1. Der Kaffee sah gestern dunkler aus.

2. 1978 gab es in Deutschland viele Touristen.

3. Die Berge hatten viel mehr Regen als ich dachte.

4. Bis zu seinem Unfall machte ihm das Skilaufen viel Spaß.

5. Sie wohnten drei Jahre in Marburg, bevor sie nach Basel kamen.

6. Der Bus fuhr einfach weiter, ohne auf mich zu warten.

7. Als er im Hotel ankam, war sein Gepäck schon da.

8. Weil das Wetter schön war, ging ich ohne Regenschirm in die Stadt.

9. Der Rhein war sehr schmutzig.

**D.** *Give the English equivalent.*

1. Können Sie mir bitte einen Scheck über DM 526,72 schreiben?

2. Sind Sie älter oder jünger als 18 Jahre?

3. Geben Sie mehr als $125.00 für Ihre Wohnung aus?

4. Das Benzin ist schon wieder um 16% teurer geworden. Wieviel bezahlen Sie jetzt für Benzin?

5. Welcher Präsident der Vereinigten Staaten wurde am 22.2.1732 geboren?

6. Ich bin 1,72 m groß. (m = Meter)

**E.** *Write down and read aloud the exact time as shown on the* **Weltzeituhr,** *assuming that the clock shows the a.m. time.*

EXAMPLE: In Berlin ist es jetzt genau neun Uhr drei. (*official*)
    *Or:* In Berlin ist es jetzt genau drei Minuten nach neun. (*colloquial*)

1. London
2. New York
3. Johannisburg
4. Moskau
5. Schanghai
6. Sidney

*Then announce the official time, assuming that the clock shows the p.m. time.*

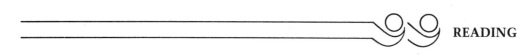

Ask your neighbor what he usually does in the morning, at noon, in the afternoon, in the evening, at night, and at midnight. Then tell him what you generally do at these times.

Ask one of your classmates where his or her parents live, how far that is from here, and how to get there.

Ask your neighbor his or her weight, or how tall or old he or she is.

**READING**

## *Ehe oder Partnerschaft?°*                                                      partnership

In den letzten zehn Jahren ist in der Bundesrepublik wie auch in der DDR die Zahl der Ehescheidungen bemerkenswert gestiegen. In den fünfziger Jahren° gab es in Deutschland als Resultat des Krieges    in the fifties sehr hohe Ehescheidungsraten. Diese hohen Zahlen sind inzwischen wieder erreicht. Innerhalb von zwölf Jahren ist die Zahl der Ehescheidungen um fast 100 Prozent gestiegen. So gab es im Jahr 1975 in der Bundesrepublik allein 106 829 Ehescheidungen.

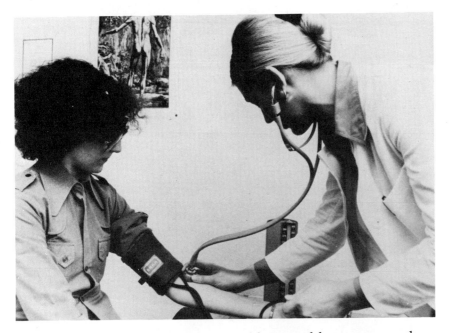

Aber die Gründe für diese Entwicklung sind heute ganz anderer Art als nach dem Krieg, das heißt vor zwanzig oder fünfundzwanzig Jahren. In Industriestaaten wie Deutschland ist die Frau heutzutage häufiger in einem Beruf tätig als früher. Viele Frauen sind durch ihren Beruf unabhängiger geworden. Und je unabhängiger die Frauen, desto höher die Ehescheidungsrate. Die Ehescheidungsgesetze sind dadurch° for this reason liberaler geworden und es ist kein sozialer Makel° mehr, geschieden stigma zu sein. Es ist bemerkenswert, daß Ehescheidungen in den Industriestaaten Osteuropas so häufig sind wie im Westen. In der DDR ist die Ehescheidungsrate sogar noch etwas höher als in der Bundesrepublik.[1] Kapitalismus und Sozialismus teilen das gleiche Problem.

Aber hinter den Statistiken steht ein sehr menschliches Problem. Während die Männer für die Familie das Geld verdienen, müssen viele Frauen die besten Jahre ihres Lebens für die Erziehung der Kinder und den Haushalt hergeben. Ihre Chancen, wieder in ihren Beruf zurückzukehren, nachdem die Kinder älter geworden sind, sind gering. Und doch brauchen viele Frauen die soziale Anerkennung° im Beruf. Was recognition ist die Lösung? Soll der Mann mehr im Haushalt mithelfen, so daß die Frau auch in ihrem Beruf tätig sein kann? Ist diese Arbeitsteilung° division of labor die beste Lösung für die Erziehung der Kinder? Man kann da geteilter Meinung sein.

---

[1] For instance, in 1974 there were 30 divorces per 100 marriages in the DDR as compared to 23 in the BRD. In the Eastern Bloc the churches obviously have little influence, and the marriage and divorce laws are practically as liberal as in the industrial nations of the West. However, in the DDR—unlike in the BRD—specific reasons for a divorce must always be given.

Oder ist eine Zweierbeziehung°—ein modernes Wort für Partner-
schaft ohne Trauschein°—die Lösung? Die Gesellschaft ist offener geworden und scheint eine solche Beziehung zu akzeptieren. Wenigstens
können die Partner in einer solchen Beziehung herausfinden, ob sie
zueinander passen, ohne sich zu früh zu binden, sagt man. Aber in
einer solchen Beziehung ist die Frage der Arbeitsteilung oder Kinder-
erziehung nicht unbedingt gelöst. Interessant ist immerhin°, daß
nach einer Umfrage° im Juli 1977, 73 Prozent der Männer, aber nur
61 Prozent der Frauen, in der Bundesrepublik für eine konventionelle
Ehe gestimmt° hatten. 21 Prozent waren für eine Ehe ohne Trauschein.

In einer anderen Umfrage unter jungen Leuten von 15–19 Jahren
sagten die meisten, daß sie mit 24–26 Jahren eine konventionelle Ehe
eingehen° möchten. Aber über die schwierige Frage der Arbeitsteilung

a relationship of two
marriage license

nevertheless
poll

voted

enter upon

in der Ehe hatten die meisten jungen Leute noch nicht nachgedacht°. reflected
Sie glaubten zuversichtlich°, dieses wichtige Problem im gegebenen confidently
Moment schon lösen zu können. In diesen Fall möchte man sagen:
„Wie die Alten sungen, so zwitschern die Jungen."

## Questions

1. Wo sind in den letzten zehn Jahren die Zahl der Ehescheidungen bemerkenswert gestiegen?
2. Warum gab es in Deutschland in den fünfziger Jahren sehr hohe Ehescheidungsraten?
3. Um wieviel Prozent ist die Zahl der Ehescheidungen innerhalb von zwölf Jahren gestiegen?
4. Warum sind Frauen in Deutschland heutzutage unabhängiger als früher?
5. Welche Probleme teilen Kapitalismus und Sozialismus?
6. Wofür (*for what*) müssen viele Frauen die besten Jahre ihres Lebens hergeben?
7. Welche schwierige Frage muß man in einer konventionellen oder unkonventionellen Ehe lösen?
8. Wofür sollen die Frauen, Ihrer Meinung nach (*in your opinion*), die besten Jahre ihres Lebens hergeben: für die Kinder und den Haushalt oder für einen Beruf?
9. Soll der Mann mehr im Haushalt mithelfen, so daß die Frau einen Beruf haben kann?
   a. Für die Männer: Werden Sie eines Tages eine solche Arbeitsteilung akzeptieren?
   b. Für die Frauen: Gefällt Ihnen eine solche Arbeitsteilung?
10. Scheint die Gesellschaft in Amerika die Ehe ohne Trauschein zu akzeptieren? Akzeptieren Sie eine solche Ehe? Warum oder warum nicht?

**VOCABULARY
DEVELOPMENT**

**A.** *Sind Sie ledig, verheiratet oder geschieden?*

There are a number of words relating to marriage or getting married that you should learn.

**heiraten** or **sich verheiraten mit** = *to marry*

Er wird meine Kusine heiraten.
Er wird sich mit meiner Kusine verheiraten. } *He will marry my cousin.*

**Die Trauung** denotes the wedding—more specifically the civil and/or church ceremony. (From **trauen**, *to trust*, and related to **anvertrauen**, *to entrust*.)

**Die Hochzeit** (literally, *high time!*) denotes all the celebrations and festivities connected with a wedding.

> Wann werden die beiden Hochzeit feiern?     *When will the two of them celebrate their wedding?*

The opposite of **verheiratet** (*married*) could be **unverheiratet**, but **ledig**, used for both men and women, is more common.
**Die Heirat** denotes generally the process of entering upon matrimony, including all preliminaries and legal and social aspects.
**Die Ehe** denotes matrimony—the state of being married.
Marriage is a complicated business, even linguistically, isn't it?
**scheiden, schied, geschieden** means *to divorce* or *separate*.
**sich scheiden lassen** means *to get a divorce*
**geschieden** = *divorced.*
State who among your friends is unmarried, married, or divorced.

**B.** *Are you right or wrong?*

In Chapter 7 you encountered the expression **recht haben** (*to be right*). The opposite would be **unrecht haben** (*to be wrong*). The verb **sich irren** means *to make a mistake, to be mistaken.*

> Ich habe mich im Weg geirrt.     *I went the wrong way.*
> Da irren Sie sich.     *There you are mistaken.*

**Der Irrtum, ⁼er** means *mistake, error.*

> Er hat den gleichen Irrtum begangen.     *He made the same error.*

But if you make a more trivial mistake, such as an error in spelling, the expression **einen Fehler machen** should be used:

> Hier hast du einen kleinen Fehler gemacht.     *Here you made a small mistake.*

**REVIEW**

*A. Supply the appropriate comparative form by using the adjective or adverb in parentheses.*

1. Mein Freund hatte das _____ Haus eigentlich nie gesehen. (*schön*)
2. Je _____ Obst ich esse, desto _____ werde ich sein. (*viel, gesund*)

3. Studenten sind viel _____, als man denkt. (*aufmerksam*)

4. Vater ist _____ als wir wußten. (*krank*)

5. Ich finde den Kuchen viel _____ als den Kaffee. (*gut*)

6. Die _____ Kirche steht in der Stadtmitte. (*alt*)

7. Thomas nimmt immer den _____ Zug. (*spät*)

8. Es gibt immer _____ Parkplätze in dieser Stadt. (*viel*)

**B.** *Supply the appropriate superlative form by using the adjective or adverb in parentheses.*

1. Der Dom in Köln ist nicht der _____ und auch nicht der _____ in Deutschland. (*hoch/alt*)

2. Nach dem Abendessen gehe ich _____ ins Kino. (*gern*)

3. Nächsten Samstag gehen wir zum Abendessen in das _____ Restaurant der Stadt. Leider ist es aber auch das _____. (*gut/teuer*)

4. Die _____ Leute haben keine Ahnung, wie schön Skilaufen sein kann. (*viele*)

5. Seine dritte Frau ist _____. (*klug*)

6. Wir haben jetzt seit 12 Jahren die _____ Ehescheidungsrate. (*hoch*)

7. Zum Glück war das _____ Buch _____. (*lang/interessant*)

**C.** *Tell someone the following story in the past perfect tense. Those verb forms which have to be changed are in italics.*

**Der Unfall**

Eines Tages—es *war* genau am 27. Februar dieses Jahres—*fuhr* ich mit meiner Freundin am späten Nachmittag auf der Autobahn in Richtung Regensburg. Es *schneite* den ganzen Tag. Das Autofahren war höchst gefährlich. Um etwa 17.30 Uhr *hielten* wir auf einem Parkplatz *an*, um zu Abend zu essen. Die frische Luft *machte* uns hungrig.

Plötzlich *hörten* wir einen furchtbaren Lärm. Es war ein Unfall: Ein Mercedes *ist* auf einen langsam fahrenden Bus *gefahren*. Der Mercedes-Fahrer versuchte wahrscheinlich den Bus zu überholen, aber das *war* in dem hohen Schnee nicht möglich. Der Autofahrer war schwer verletzt (*badly injured*).

Wir *liefen* sofort zum nächsten Telefon und *riefen* die Polizei *an*. Zum Glück gibt es auf den deutschen Autobahnen alle 1000 Meter ein Autobahn-Telefon. Einige Minuten später *kam* ein Polizeiwagen zu der Unfallstelle und *brachte* den schwer verletzten Fahrer zu dem nächsten Arzt (*doctor*). Wir waren sehr müde, als wir endlich in Regensburg *ankamen*.

**D.** *Express in German.*

1. Fortunately, traveling from New York to London is becoming cheaper and cheaper.

2. In my opinion, the fastest bicyclists are in France.

3. The air is best in the highest mountains.

4. German is her fifth language.
5. The most beautiful castles are in the oldest regions of France and Germany.
6. At eight o'clock in the morning he listens to the news.
7. This is not the most expensive car. There are even more expensive cars than this one.
8. Do you know George Orwell's book *1984*?
9. The number of divorces had climbed remarkably.
10. Often the worst problem has the simplest solution.
11. It had been her fourth accident this year.
12. Do you prefer to drink your coffee with or without sugar?
13. Someday the last shall be the first.

## GUIDED COMPOSITION

What are your plans for this week (month, summer, year, etc.)? Look at your calendar and write down in German when you plan to do what. For example, you might want to see a movie this week, or study for a class or pay the rent for your apartment.

Write down in German your activities on any given day, indicating the appropriate time. You may also wish to state how you intend to organize your daily work differently from now on.

## VOCABULARY

### Easily recognized words

| | | |
|---|---|---|
| | **akzeptieren** | *to accept* |
| die | **Chance,** -n | *chance* |
| der | **Humor** | *humor, sense of humor* |
| der | **Kapitalismus** | *capitalism* |
| | **konventionell** | *conventional* |
| | **liberal** | *liberal* |
| die | **Rate,** -n | *rate* |
| | **sozial** | *social* |
| der | **Sozialismus** | *socialism* |
| der | **Westen** | *west* |
| | | |
| die | **Art,** -en | *kind, sort* |
| der | **Atem** | *breadth* |

| | | |
|---|---|---|
| der | **Beruf,** -e | *profession* |
| die | **Beziehung,** -en | *relationship* |
| die | **Ehe,** -n | *marriage* |
| die | **Ehescheidung,** -en | *divorce* |
| die | **Frage,** -n | *question* |
| der | **Geburtstag,** -e | *birthday* |
| die | **Gesellschaft,** -en | *society* |
| das | **Gesetz,** -e | *law* |
| der | **Grund,** ⸚e | *reason (for something)* |
| der | **Haushalt,** -e | *household* |
| die | **Lösung,** -en | *solution* |
| die | **Meinung,** -en | *opinion;* **meiner Meinung nach** *in my opinion* |

der **Osten** — *east*

die **Uhr, -en** — *clock, watch;* **Wieviel Uhr ist es?** *What time is it?*

die **Vorlesung, -en** — *lecture*

die **Zahl, -en** — *number*

**ab·machen** — *to arrange, agree upon*

sich **irren** — *to be mistaken, make a mistake*

**lösen** — *to solve*

**passen: zueinander passen** — *to be compatible, suit each other*

**steigen, stieg, (ist) gestiegen** — *to climb, rise*

**teilen** — *to share, divide*

**zurück·kehren, (ist) zurückgekehrt** — *to return*

**bemerkenswert** — *remarkable, noteworthy*

**böse** (+ *dat.*) — *angry (with)*

**dumm** — *stupid, dumb*

**ehrlich** — *honest*

**gering** — *insignificant, slight*

**geschieden** — *divorced*

**gleich** — *same*

**häufig** — *frequent*

**hoch, hoh·** — *high*

**je ... desto** — *the (more) ... the (more)*

**klar** — *clear*

**menschlich** — *human*

**nahe** — *near*

**sonst** — *otherwise, else*

**tätig** — *employed, occupied, active*

**unabhängig** — *independent*

**ungewöhnlich** — *unusual*

See also the ordinal numbers and expressions of time on pp. 254–257.

### I

Dies ist der psychologische Test, **den** wir gestern besprochen haben.
*This is the psychological test that we discussed yesterday.*

Das alte Haus, in **dem** wir wohnen, gehört nicht uns.
*The old house in which we live doesn't belong to us.*

Der Psychologe, **dessen** Theorien ich nicht verstehe, ist sehr bekannt.
*The psychologist whose theories I don't understand is very well known.*

Die Kaiser Österreichs, **die** wir gestern im Seminar besprachen, waren sehr populär.
*The emperors of Austria, whom we discussed yesterday in the seminar, were very popular.*

### II

**Wer** viel Zeit hat, hat meistens kein Geld.
*He who has lots of time usually has no money.*

Das Erste, **was** die Wiener wieder aufbauten, war die Staatsoper.
*The first thing that the Viennese rebuilt was the Opera House.*

Ich weiß nicht, mit **wem** sie tanzt.
*I don't know whom she's dancing with (with whom she's dancing).*

Er weiß, **wann** sie kommen wird.
*He knows when she'll arrive.*

Peter erklärte, **warum** er gestern nicht hier war.
*Peter explained why he wasn't here yesterday.*

**GRAMMAR EXPLANATIONS**

## I. Relative pronouns

A relative pronoun introduces a dependent clause, which relates to and further characterizes an element in the main clause.

The singer **whom I heard** is famous.

In this sentence the dependent clause *whom I heard*, introduced by the relative pronoun *whom*, relates to *the singer* and tells us something about him: he is not just any singer, but that particular singer whom I heard.
The forms of relative pronouns in German are quite similar to those of the definite article **der, die, das.**

*Relative pronoun forms*

|  | SINGULAR | | | PLURAL |
|---|---|---|---|---|
|  | MASCULINE | FEMININE | NEUTER | ALL GENDERS |
| *nom.* | der | die | das | die |
| *acc.* | den | die | das | die |
| *dat.* | dem | der | dem | **denen** |
| *gen.* | **dessen** | **deren** | **dessen** | **deren** |

In the table above, note that certain forms differ from those of the definite article: the genitive in all four instances, and the dative plural.
In German the relative clause is set off by commas. Since it is a dependent clause, the inflected verb stands at the end of the clause.

Wie heißt der Schlager, **den** man jetzt überall hört?   *What's the name of the song one hears everywhere these days?*

The *gender* and *number* of the relative pronoun are determined by the noun to which the relative pronoun is related. The *case* of the relative pronoun depends on how it is used in the clause. In the above example, the relative pronoun **den** functions as a direct object of the verb **hören** and is therefore in the accusative.

In English the relative pronoun may sometimes be omitted, as in the above example. This omission is not possible in German.

**Der Sänger, der** kürzlich am Fernsehen sang, ist sehr bekannt.

masc. sing.   subj.=nominative

*The singer who sang on television recently is very famous.*

Hier ist das Bild **des Politikers, den** ich kürzlich getroffen habe.

masc. sing.   dir. obj.=accusative

*Here's the picture of the politician whom I met recently.*

**Die Frau,** mit **der** er tanzt, ist seine Freundin.

fem. sing.   obj. of **mit**=dative

*The woman he's dancing with (with whom he's dancing) is his friend.*

Hier ist **das Bild, dessen** Bedeutung ich nicht interpretieren kann.

neuter sing.   genitive

*Here's the picture whose meaning I can't interpret.*

## Check your comprehension

*Fill in the appropriate form of the relative pronoun.*

1. Das ist das neue Haus, _____ ich letzte Woche gekauft habe.
2. Das ist übrigens der Professor, bei _____ ich studiere.
3. Nicht alle Studenten, _____ dieses Buch gelesen haben, konnten es verstehen.
4. Die Band, _____ Musik ich gehört habe, ist aus Berlin.
5. Die Professorin, von _____ ich viel gehört, aber von _____ ich noch nichts gelesen habe, ist in Amerika sehr bekannt.
6. Der Mercedes gehört zu den teuersten Wagen, _____ es gibt.
7. Das Kind, _____ wir geholfen hatten, war ganz außer Atem.
8. Es gibt viele Probleme, _____ Lösung nicht einfach ist.

## II. Question words functioning as conjunctions

Question words like **wann, warum, was, wer, wie, wieviel, wo, woher, wohin,** etc., often introduce a dependent clause, in which case they function as conjunctions.

| Ich weiß nicht, **wann** er ankommt. | *I don't know when he's arriving.* |
|---|---|
| Ich weiß, **wo** er ist. | *I know where he is.* |
| Wer weiß, **wieviel** das Buch kostet. | *Who knows how much the book costs.* |
| Sie wußten nicht, **woher** er kam. | *They didn't know where he was coming from.* |

When used as a conjunction, **wer** must be declined in the usual fashion.

| Ich weiß nicht, **wer** dich angerufen hat. | *I don't know who called you.* |
|---|---|
| Sag mir, **wen** ich anrufen soll. | *Tell me whom I should call.* |
| Er wollte uns nicht sagen, mit **wem** er getanzt hat. | *He wouldn't tell us whom he danced with.* |
| Sag mir, **wessen**[1] Freund du bist, und ich sage dir, **wer** du bist. | *Tell me whose friend you are, and I'll tell you who you are.* |

Especially in proverbs, **wer** and **was** at times occur as relative pronouns that refer to no specific, identifiable noun. In this case they have the sense of *he who* or *whoever*, and *that which* or *whatever*.

| **Wer** zuletzt lacht, lacht am besten. | *He who laughs last, laughs best.* |
|---|---|
| **Was** ich nicht weiß, macht mich nicht heiß. | *What I don't know doesn't bother me.* |

**Was** must also be used as a relative pronoun to refer back to:

(a) a neuter superlative adjective (including expressions like **das Erste, das Letzte**)

| **Das Beste, was** er jetzt tun kann, ist nichts zu sagen. | *The best he can do now is to say nothing.* |
|---|---|
| **Das Erste, was** ich jetzt brauche, ist etwas zu essen. | *The first thing I need now is something to eat.* |

(b) indefinite pronouns like **alles, etwas, nichts, viel, wenig**, etc.

| Es gibt **nichts, was** er nicht weiß. | *There's nothing he doesn't know.* |
|---|---|

## *Check your comprehension*

**A.** *Begin the following sentences with* **Ich weiß nicht,** *and make the appropriate changes.*

1. Wieviel Uhr ist es?
2. Warum ist er noch nicht hier?

[1] **Wessen** is the genitive form. It can also be used to ask a question, but in the spoken language it is not heard very often. **Wessen Buch ist das?** *Whose book is this?* Preferable: **Wem gehört dieses Buch?** *To whom does this book belong?*

3. Wem gehört das Bild?

4. Wann ist Helga zurückgekehrt ?

5. Wer hat sich geirrt?

**B.** *Fill in the appropriate form of the indefinite relative pronoun* **wer** *or* **was.**

1. Es gibt nichts, _____ Franz nicht kann.

2. _____ soviel Geld hat wie er, braucht nicht mehr.

3. _____ ich nicht verstehen kann, ist der Schmutz in diesem Haus.

4. Das Letzte, _____ ich jetzt brauche, ist mehr Arbeit.

5. _____ dir das sagte, ist dumm.

6. Es gibt etwas, _____ ich noch nicht weiß.

7. _____ nicht für uns ist, ist gegen uns.

8. Das ist das Schönste, _____ ich je gesehen habe.

## USEFUL PHRASES

| | |
|---|---|
| **Schon wieder?** | *Again!* |
| **Das hört sich fürchterlich an.** | *That sounds horrible.* |
| **Wer weiß?** | *Who knows!* |
| **Stell Dir mal vor!** | *Imagine!* |

## CONVERSATION

## Der Psychologe

*Franz und Ferdi[1] sind Studenten an der Universität Wien°. Franz ist im*    Vienna
*zweiten Semester Psychologie und Ferdi im ersten Semester Germani-*
*stik°. Sie wohnen zusammen in einer kleinen gemieteten Wohnung und*    Germanics
*sind auf dem Weg nach Hause von der Universität.*

FRANZ Wir müssen uns beeilen, um schnell nach Hause zu kommen.

FERDI Aber warum denn so schnell? Ich möchte zuerst im Café da
drüben etwas Süßes essen.

FRANZ Schon wieder! Aber ich will dir doch den psychologischen Test
geben, den wir gestern im Seminar besprochen haben.

FERDI Ach, ich soll wieder Versuchskaninchen° spielen? Wie heißt    guinea pig
denn der Test, von dem du dieses Mal so begeistert bist.

---

[1] **Ferdi** is the nickname for **Ferdinand**. For many other first names the nickname used
in Austria ends in **-l**, from **-lein**, as in **Franz > Franzl**. But nowadays this form is heard
more often in the countryside than in the city.

*Universität Wien*

FRANZ (*aufgeregt*) Es ist ein „Thematischer Apperzeptionstest."[2]
FERDI Was? Das hört sich ja fürchterlich an. Was ist denn das, was ihr
 Psychologen euch wieder mal ausgedacht habt?
FRANZ Sehr einfach. Wir zeigen dir ein Bild, dessen Bedeutung du in-
 terpretieren mußt. Dabei drückt sich deine Persönlichkeit aus.
FERDI Du kennst ja, wie du sagst, meine „Persönlichkeit"!
FRANZ Wer weiß? Vielleicht ist sie viel tiefer als ich glaube.
FERDI Oh ja? Das kann ja interessant werden.

[2] In a Thematic Apperception Test the subject is usually given a series of pictures
showing human beings in various situations or predicaments. From the problems that
the subject reads into the picture the psychologist may draw some interesting, if not
wholly accurate, conclusions about the subject's personality.

FRANZ Stell Dir mal vor: auf einer Test-Karte siehst du einen Mann, der träumend vor einem Bild steht. Was ist auf dem Bild, und was denkt der Mann?

FERDI Hm, sehr einfach. Das Bild ist ein Stilleben°: ein großes Stück    *still life*
Sachertorte,[3] und der Mann denkt: „ich bin aber wirklich hungrig."

[3] A kind of chocolate cake served with whipped cream. It is a well-known Viennese specialty.

## Questions

1. Wo und was studieren Franz und Ferdi?
2. Wieviele Semester haben Franz und Ferdi schon studiert?
3. Was will Ferdi noch tun, bevor er nach Hause geht?
4. Was will Franz Ferdi zu Hause geben?
5. Wie heißt der Test, von dem Franz so begeistert ist?
6. Wie hört sich dieser Test Ferdis Meinung nach an?
7. Was soll Ferdi mit dem Bild des Tests machen?
8. Was ist auf der Test-Karte, die Franz beschreibt (*describes*)?
9. Was ist auf dem Bild, und was denkt der Mann, der träumend vor dem Bild steht?
10. Kannst du Ferdis Interpretation interpretieren? Warum sagt er das?
11. Wie hört sich dieser Test an? Scheint er dir interessant oder langweilig?
12. Hast du je träumend vor einem Bild gestanden? War für ein Bild war das?

---

**PRACTICE**

**A.** *Fill in the indicated forms.*

1. Ist Inge das Mädchen, _____ Heinz gearbeitet hat? (*with whom*)
2. Kennen Sie schon das neue Buch, _____ jeder gelesen haben soll? (*which*)
3. Dies ist mein Freund, _____ Vater in Hamburg wohnt. (*whose*)
4. Der Zug, _____ ich nach Hamburg fuhr, kam 33 Minuten zu spät an. (*by which*)
5. Gehören Sie zu den Männern, _____ Frauen nicht an die Emanzipation glauben? (*whose*)
6. Der Bekannte, _____ wir nach Rom gereist sind, wohnt jetzt in Düsseldorf. (*with whom*)
7. Dies ist der Professor, _____ ich am meisten gelernt habe. (*from whom*)
8. Der Tisch, _____ ich arbeite, ist aus dem 18. Jahrhundert. (*at which*)
9. Um wieviel Uhr fährt der Bus ab, _____ du immer in die Stadt fährst? (*by which*)
10. Wie heißt die Universität, _____ Sie studieren? (*at which*)

**B.** *Fill in the appropriate form of* **wer** *or* **was**.

1. _____ das sagt, weiß nicht, _____ er sagt.
2. _____ nicht weiß, _____ er tun soll, soll mich fragen.
3. _____ Deutsch gelernt hat, kann auch andere Sprachen lernen.
4. Mit _____ bist du nach Zürich gereist? Mit deinem Freund?
5. Ich weiß nicht, _____ er das Auto gegeben hat.
6. _____ hast du mitgebracht? Deine Freundin oder Kollegin?
7. _____ hast du mitgebracht? Bier oder Wein?
8. Von _____ hast du diese gute Nachricht gehört?
9. Bei _____ wohnen diese zwei Studenten?
10. Tun Sie das Beste, _____ Sie können.
11. Wissen Sie nicht, _____ Sie geholfen haben?
12. Er hatte nichts gesagt, _____ ich glauben konnte.

**C.** *Combine each pair of sentences by using the appropriate relative pronoun.*

EXAMPLE: Was denkt der Mann? Er steht träumend vor einem Bild.
**Was denkt der Mann, der träumend vor einem Bild steht?**

1. Zeigen Sie mir den Anzug. Sie haben den Anzug gestern gekauft.
2. Endlich traf ich den Mann. Helga ist mit dem Mann verheiratet.
3. Das ist eine Studentin. Sie bekommt immer nur A's.
4. Ich kenne die Leute. Du hast so oft von den Leuten gesprochen.
5. Wieviel kosteten die Blumen? Sie standen auf dem Tisch.

*Arkadenhof der
Wiener Universität*

6. Schon fuhr der Zug ab. Ihr wart mit dem Zug angekommen.
7. Ich kenne die Frau nicht. Dieser Student wohnt bei der Frau.
8. Das ist ein großes Problem. Man kann das Problem nicht leicht lösen.
9. Wiederhole bitte das Wort. Du versteht die Bedeutung dieses Wortes nicht.
10. Die Schlager sind aus dem Westen. Die Jungen hören den Schlagern am liebsten zu.

**D.** *Express in German.*

1. There is nothing he doesn't know.
2. All you said is correct.
3. That which I like most is too expensive for me.
4. Whom are you talking about? (of whom?)
5. Tell me what he said about your friend.

**E.** *Give the English equivalent.*

1. Ich glaube nicht, was Willi uns erzählt hat.
2. Wer zur Universität geht, hat nicht viel Zeit.
3. Willst du wissen, wem dieser Wagen gehört?
4. Was du studiert hast, wirst du nie vergessen!
5. Ist das der Zug, mit dem Sie aus Heidelberg kamen?
6. Das Letzte, was er braucht, ist mehr Geld.

**GUIDED CONVERSATION**

**A.** Have you ever taken a psychological test? If so, was it a written test or an interview (**das Interview**)? What questions did the psychologist ask you? If a written test, did you have to interpret pictures or ink blots (**Tintenkleckse**)? Would you be willing to reveal one or two of your answers? Do you think that, through these tests, you expressed your deepest personality?

**B.** Describe the picture below. Where are the couple and what are they doing?

**READING**

## *Wienerblut*[1]

Wer den Namen „Wien" hört, denkt wohl gleich an die Walzer von Johann Strauss[2], wie zum Beispiel „An der schönen blauen Donau"° oder „Wienerblut". Tatsächlich ist die Musik ein Teil der Kultur Wiens, den man nicht vergißt und der weit in die Geschichte

Danube

---

[1] Literally, *Viennese Blood.* It means the temper or disposition of the Viennese.

[2] Johann Strauss the Younger (1825–99), probably the most famous waltz composer of all time.

*Die Wiener Staatsoper*

der Stadt zurückgeht. Die größten Namen der deutschen Musik sind mit ihrer Geschichte eng verbunden. Haydn[3] war lange in Wien tätig und starb, als Napoleon im Jahre 1809 zum zweiten Mal mit seiner Armee die Stadt besetzte. Mozart[4] komponierte° in Wien einige seiner größten Werke und dirigierte° die Erstaufführung° seiner Oper „Die Zauberflöte“° in einem Theater, das heute noch steht. Auch Beethoven[5] lebte lange in Wien. Drei seiner Symphonien erlebten da ihre Erstaufführung. Das Titelblatt° der bekannten dritten Symphonie, der *Eroica*, enthielt eine Zueignung° Beethovens an Napoleon, die Beethoven allerdings später zerriß, nachdem er seine Begeisterung für den Kaiser verloren hatte.[6] Ungefähr zur gleichen Zeit war auch der junge Schubert[7] in Wien tätig, in dessen Musik sich die Seele Wiens und Österreichs vielleicht am besten ausdrückt. Auch am Anfang dieses Jahrhunderts war Wien wieder eine der führenden Städte Europas auf den meisten Gebieten der Musik.

Am Ende des Krieges, im Jahr 1945, als ein großer Teil der Stadt

*composed*

*conducted / premiere*
*The Magic Flute*

*title page*
*dedication*

---

[3] Franz Josep Haydn (1732–1809), noted for his symphonies, quartets, sonatas, etc.

[4] Wolfgang Amadeus Mozart (1756–91) composed in all musical forms; especially famous are his quartets, concertos, symphonies, and operas.

[5] Ludwig van Beethoven (1770–1827) is known for his symphonies, sonatas, concertos, and quartets.

[6] A number of German writers and artists, such as Goethe and Beethoven, at first admired Napoleon for his military and political genius, and his imposition of greater political unity on Germany; but their enthusiasm soon began to fade.

[7] Franz Schubert (1797–1828), the noted Austrian composer of quartets, symphonies, and songs.

zerstört dalag, waren die Staatsoper[8] und das Burgtheater[9] das Erste, was die Wiener wieder aufbauten. Und schlecht angezogene Wiener wanderten oft hungrig durch die halbdunklen Straßen, um sich ein Konzert oder eine Oper anzuhören° oder um ein Theaterstück zu se- listen to hen.

Auch im tiefsten Unglück verliert der Wiener seinen Lebensmut nicht. Er hat diesen Mut in der Vergangenheit oft gezeigt. Im 16. und 17. Jahrhundert belagerten° die Türken° zweimal die Stadt; am Anfang  besieged / the Turks des 19. Jahrhunderts besetzte sie Napoleon, und während des Zweiten

[8] The famous Opera House in Vienna. Built and rebuilt in complex early French Renaissance style, it somehow achieves a noble architectural harmony.

[9] The National Theater, originally built in the nineteenth century in a kind of Neo-Renaissance style.

*Wiener Opernball*

*Innenansicht des
Stephansdomes*

Weltkrieges war es Hitlers Armee, die über die Stadt und das ganze
Land herrschte.° Aber diese Katastrophen verstärkten nur den Lebens- ruled
mut der Wiener. Nach der Belagerung° durch die Türken im Jahr 1683 siege
schmolzen° die Wiener die Kanonen der Feinde in eine Glocke[10] um, recast
die auch heute noch im bekannten Stephansdom[11] hängt und deren
Klang an vergangenes° Unglück erinnert, aber gleichzeitig auch zu past
neuem Leben aufruft.° inspires

    Und das neue Leben zeigt sich überall. Neue Gebäude und Hoch-
häuser stehen neben alten Palästen, die man gleich nach dem Krieg
wieder aufgebaut hatte, und bald wird eine Untergrundbahn fertig sein,
die sich unter der ganzen Stadt hindurchwindet.

    Auch im Bewußtsein° der Wiener sind Altes und Neues eng ver- consciousness
bunden. Viele denken noch gern und oft an die schöne Zeit von Franz
Joseph I[12] zurück, als Österreich im Zenith seiner Macht stand. Und
viele moderne Restaurants, Bars und Tanzlokale° sind in alten, im- dance halls

[10] The bell is called the **Pummering.** For the Viennese it has perhaps the same significance as the Liberty Bell for the Americans. It was severely damaged during the Second
World War, but was recast largely with the original material.

[11] St. Stephen's Cathedral, a much-loved Viennese landmark begun in the twelfth century, rebuilt after a disastrous fire in the fourteenth, and expanded several times there-
after. It is an interesting blend of Romanesque, Gothic, and Renaissance architecture.

[12] Emperor of Austria from 1848 until his death in 1916, he enjoyed one of the longest
reigns of any monarch in European history and became a symbol of Austrian unity.

*Stephansdom*

*Wien nach dem Krieg*

posanten Gebäuden untergebracht°. Fast möchte man sagen, daß der °installed
Wiener von heute seine Unterhaltung im Schatten der Vergangenheit
sucht. Und wie in der Vergangenheit hören die Theatervorstellungen
und Konzerte um 22 Uhr auf. Ein Humorist sagte einmal, daß die
Wiener genug Zeit zum Träumen haben wollen und daß Sigmund
Freud[13], dessen Theorie der Traumanalyse in der ganzen Welt bekannt
ist, ein Wiener sein mußte. Auf jeden Fall ist der alte Schlager, in
dem es heißt: „Wien, Wien, nur du allein, sollst stets° die Stadt mei- °forever
ner Träume sein", mehr als nur in einem Sinne° wahr. °sense

[13] Sigmund Freud (1856–1939), the Austrian psychiatrist whose theories of psycho-
analysis have had a vast influence on psychology, anthropology, education, literature,
and art.

## Questions

1. An welche Walzer denkt man, wenn man den Namen Wien hört?
2. Welche Namen der Musik sind mit der Geschichte Wiens eng verbunden?
3. Wann besetzte Napoleon Wien zum zweiten Mal?
4. Die Erstaufführung welcher Oper dirigierte Mozart in Wien?
5. Welche Symphonie enthielt eine Zueignung von Beethoven an Napoleon?
6. Warum zerriß Beethoven diese Zueignung später?
7. In wessen Musik drückt sich die Seele Wiens am besten aus?

8. Was bauten die Wiener nach dem Zweiten Weltkrieg sofort wieder auf?

9. Wer belagerte Wien im 16. und 17. Jahrhundert zweimal?

10. Woraus (*out of what*) hat man die Glocke im Stephansdom gemacht?

11. Wann stand Österreich im Zenith seiner Macht?

12. Wie heißt der Wiener, dessen Theorie der Traumanalyse in der ganzen Welt bekannt ist?

## VOCABULARY DEVELOPMENT

**A.** *What is your profession?*

Many names of professions are derived from the words denoting academic and other fields of endeavor; a suffix will do the trick. Note these corresponding suffixes:

| THE OCCUPATION | THE PERSON |
|---|---|
| **-(log)ie** | **-e** |
| **-ik** | **-er** |
| **-t** | **-ler** |
| die Psycholog**ie** | der Psycholog**e** *psychologist* |
| die Mus**ik** | der Musik**er** *musician* |
| der Spor**t** | der Sport**ler** *athlete* |

The corresponding feminine forms (as you expected!) end in **-in:**

die Psycholog**in**

die Musiker**in**

die Sportler**in**

Now derive the names of the professions from the following disciplines and occupations:

| | |
|---|---|
| die Kunst (*hint: add an umlaut*) | die Politik |
| die Biologie | die Metereologie |
| die Archäologie | die Mathematik |
| die Geologie | die Physik |

Of course not all names of professions are formed this way. For instance, there is **der Geschäftsmann** (*businessman*), whose plural you have already encountered—what is it? And if **der Arzt, ∹e** and **die Ärztin, -nen** mean *doctor*, what does **der Zahnarzt** mean?

Now state which of these professionals you yourself would most like to be or become (**Ich möchte am liebsten . . . sein** or **werden**). Remember that in German you do not need the indefinite article to state your profession: **Ich bin Physikerin.**

### B. Stell dir das mal vor! (*Just imagine that!*)

The verb **vor·stellen** has multiple uses. Its literal meaning is *to put in front of (oneself), to place before,* or *to put forward.*

> Wenn man mit dem Flugzeug reist, muß man seine Uhr oft **vorstellen.** (*Opposite: nach*stellen.)

In a figurative sense it means *to introduce* one person to another—literally, *to place one before the other.*

> Darf ich Ihnen meine Freundin **vorstellen**? Fräulein Kleinert, Herr Staiger.

After that the two persons introduced usually shake hands and say **sehr angenehm, sehr erfreut,** or **freut mich sehr.** Now introduce two of your classmates to each other and go through the brief ceremony of introduction.

*Wieder aufgebautes Foyer der Wiener Staatsoper*

When used as a reflexive, **sich vorstellen** means *to imagine*, with **sich** in the dative case.

> Stell **dir** das mal vor!
> Ich kann **mir** das nicht gut vorstellen.

The noun **die Vorstellung** is most often used in the sense of a *stage performance*:

> Morgen gehen wir zu einer Theatervorstellung.

A synonym is **die Theateraufführung,** and a *premiere* must always be expressed as **eine Erstaufführung.** (Linguistically, **vorstellen** was apparently too much involved in its own metamorphoses to make it to the premiere!)

**REVIEW**

**A.** *Complete the following sentences with a relative pronoun and another word or phrase, so as to make a personal statement.*

EXAMPLE: _____ ist ein Staat, _____ ich gut kenne.
 **California ist ein Staat, den ich gut kenne.**

1. _____ ist eine Stadt, _____ mir gefällt.
2. _____ ist ein Gebiet, _____ ich eines Tages besuchen will.
3. _____ ist ein Fluß, _____ ich nie gesehen habe.
4. Das Letzte, _____ ich von ihm erhielt, war _____.
5. _____ ist ein Mensch, _____ Persönlichkeit mir nicht gefällt.
6. _____ ist ein bekannter Mann, _____ sich sehr oft irrt.
7. _____ ist ein Land, _____ Sprache ich ein wenig verstehe.
8. _____ ist eine Schwäche, _____ ich nie gehabt habe.
9. _____ ist ein Beruf, _____ mir unwichtig scheint.
10. _____ sind Menschen, _____ ich nicht oft glaube.
11. _____ ist ein Sport, _____ sich gefährlich anhört.
12. Das Erste, _____ ich morgens tue, ist _____.

**B.** *Fill in the appropriate conjunction or relative pronouns.*

1. Ich fragte ihn, _____ ich ihm am besten helfen kann. (*how*)
2. Das Fahrrad, _____ ich gekommen bin, ist furchtbar schmutzig. (*with which*)
3. Das ist der Bus, _____ Sie am schnellsten zur Universität kommen. (*by which*)

4. Es gibt niemand, _____ immer sagt, _____ er denkt. (*who/what*)

5. Alles, _____ ich über Hans weiß, ist, daß er wirklich nett ist. (*that*)

6. Sag mir, _____ du dein Geld verdienst? (*where*)

7. Das Buch, _____ wir hier im ersten Jahr arbeiten, ist nicht sehr schwierig. (*with which*)

8. _____ das sagt, hat eigentlich recht. (*he who*)

9. Aber _____ Sprachen lernen will, muß das, _____ er gelernt hat, immer wiederholen, und das ist natürlich das, _____ wir hier tun. (*he who/which/what*)

10. Sag mir, was für ein Fahrrad das ist, _____ du immer zur Klasse kommst. (*with which*)

11. Sie möchte gern wissen, _____ du das gehört hast? (*from whom*)

12. Welche Bücher habt ihr gelesen, _____ über die Burgen in der DDR informieren? (*which*)

13. Wissen Sie, _____ Einwohner das kleine Land Österreich hat? (*how many*)

**C.** *Express in German.*

1. Vienna is a lovely city whose soul Schubert expresses best.
2. The movie that didn't sound very interesting was really very good.
3. The first thing they did was to rebuild the theater.
4. Napoleon, who occupied Vienna twice, was Emperor of France.
5. What I know, I learned at home.
6. They never lose the courage that they have often shown in the past.
7. I don't know whom I should believe.
8. Can you tell me why you were so enthusiastic?
9. The book I know best is *Who's Who in America.*
10. Ask him when the new subway will be ready.

---

**GUIDED COMPOSITION**

Try to describe in a few sentences what you consider to be the prominent traits in the life style of the citizens of your hometown or place of residence. How do they spend their free time? Do they go to movies? Is there a theater or concert hall in town? Are concerts and plays well attended? Are there many bars and discothèques? Or are the citizens more oriented toward the outdoors? Do they go hiking, jogging, swimming, skiing, etc.? Is there one cultural or recreational activity in your town that you consider to be outstanding?

You may also wish to state what your own preferences for cultural activities are. What is your favorite music? Who is your favorite composer?

**VOCABULARY**

## Easily recognized words

| | | |
|---|---|---|
| die | **Analyse, -n** | *analysis* |
| die | **Armee, -n** | *army* |
| der | **Humorist, -en** | *humorist* |
| | **interpretieren** | *to interprete* |
| die | **Kanone, -n** | *canon* |
| die | **Katastrophe, -n** | *catastrophe* |
| das | **Konzert, -e** | *concert* |
| der | **Psychologe, -n** | *psychologist* |
| die | **Psychologie** | *psychology* |
| | **psychologisch** | *psychological* |
| die | **Symphonie, -n** | *symphony* |
| der | **Test, -s** | *test (psychological)* |
| die | **Theorie, -n** | *theory* |
| | **wandern** | *to wander* |
| das | **Werk, -e** | *work (of an author, composer, etc.)* |

| | | |
|---|---|---|
| die | **Seele, -n** | *soul* |
| der | **Traum, ⸚e** | *dream* |
| das | **Unglück, -e** | *misfortune, accident* |
| die | **Untergrundbahn, -en** | *subway* |
| die | **Unterhaltung, -en** | *entertainment, talk* |
| der | **Walzer, -** | *waltz* |
| der | **Weg, -e** | *way;* **auf dem Weg** *on the way* |
| die | **Wohnung, -en** | *apartment* |

See also the names of professions on pp. 287.

| | | |
|---|---|---|
| | **auf·bauen** | *to rebuild* |
| sich | **aus·denken, dachte, ausgedacht** | *to think up* |
| | **besetzen** | *to occupy* |
| | **besprechen (bespricht), besprach, besprochen** | *to talk over, discuss* |
| | **führen** | *to lead* |
| | **sterben (stirbt), starb, (ist) gestorben** | *to die* |
| | **verstärken** | *to strengthen* |
| | **vor·stellen:** see pp. 288–289. | |
| | **zerreißen, zerriß, zerrissen** | *to tear up* |
| | **zerstören** | *to destroy* |

| | | |
|---|---|---|
| die | **Aufführung, -en** | *performance* |
| die | **Bedeutung, -en** | *meaning* |
| die | **Begeisterung** | *enthusiasm* |
| das | **Bild, -er** | *picture* |
| der | **Fall, ⸚e** | *case;* **auf jeden Fall** *in any case* |
| der | **Feind, -e** | *enemy* |
| die | **Glocke, -n** | *bell* |
| das | **Jahrhundert, -e** | *century* |
| die | **Macht, ⸚e** | *power* |
| das | **Mal, -e** | *occasion, time;* **zum ersten Mal** *for the first time* |
| der | **Mut** | *courage* |
| die | **Persönlichkeit, -en** | *personality* |
| der | **Schatten, -** | *shadow, shade* |

| | | |
|---|---|---|
| | **allerdings** | *to be sure, indeed* |
| | **aufgeregt** | *excited* |
| | **begeistert (von** + *dat.***)** | *enthusiastic (about)* |
| | **fertig** | *finished, ready* |
| | **fürchterlich** | *terrible, horrible* |
| | **imposant** | *imposing* |
| | **süß** | *sweet* |

### I

Ich **wünschte,** er **käme** schon zu Weihnachten.
*I wish he would come for Christmas.*

Wenn sie nur nicht so konservativ **wären!**
*If only they weren't so conservative!*

Wir **wünschten,** ihr **könntet** besser Deutsch **sprechen.**
*We wish you could speak better German.*

Wenn sie nur schon da **gewesen wären!**
*If only they had already been there!*

**Hätte** ich nur etwas mehr Geld **gehabt!**
*If only I had had some more money!*

### II

Wenn Paula doch nur **schreiben würde!**
*If Paula would only write.*

**Würden** Sie mir bitte das Buch **geben.**
*Would you please give me the book.*

Wir **würden** lieber hier **bleiben.**
*We would rather stay here.*

### III

Ich **würde** mich **erkundigen,** wenn ich interessiert **wäre.**
*I would find out, if I were interested.*

Wenn ich nicht so beschäftigt **wäre, hätte** ich wahrscheinlich Heimweh.
*If I weren't so busy, I'd probably be homesick.*

Wenn ich ihn gekannt **hätte, wäre** ich zu ihm **gegangen.**
*If I had known him, I would have gone to him.*

**GRAMMAR
EXPLANATION**

## I. Subjunctive

The subjunctive is a mood or mode of the verb. Generally speaking, "mood" signifies the manner in which a statement is made. In both German and English, the indicative mood is used to state facts and ask direct questions, while the imperative mood is used for commands. The subjunctive mood, however, has other uses: for instance, to express wishes, requests, and hypothetical situations.

**A.** *Present subjunctive: formation*

The present subjunctive is formed by adding the subjunctive personal endings to the second principal part of the verb (the past indicative stem).[1] If the verb is irregular, the stem vowel is umlauted wherever possible.
The personal endings of the subjunctive are:

|  | SINGULAR | PLURAL |  | SINGULAR | PLURAL |
|---|---|---|---|---|---|
| *1st* | -e | -en | *3rd* | **-e** | -en |
| *2nd fam.* | -est | -et | *2nd formal* | -en | -en |

*Subjunctive endings*

[1] Traditionally this subjunctive is referred to as subjunctive II, because it is based on the *second* principal part of the verb. The "special" subjunctive discussed in Chapter 18 is referred to as subjunctive I, because it is based on the *first* principal part of the verb.

Strong verbs, irregular weak verbs (like **bringen, denken, wissen**), and the four modals **dürfen, können, mögen,** and **müssen** add the personal endings to the past indicative stem to form the present subjunctive.

| | PAST INDICATIVE | PRESENT SUBJUNCTIVE |
|---|---|---|
| *strong verbs* | er fuhr | er **führe** |
| | du liefst | du **liefest** |
| *irreg. weak verbs* | ich brachte | ich **brächte** |
| | ihr wußtet | ihr **wüßtet** |
| *modals* | sie durfte | sie **dürfte** |
| | es konnte | es **könnte** |
| | ich mochte | ich **möchte** |
| | wir mußten | wir **müßten** |

Notice the stem vowels with umlauts.

The auxiliary verbs **haben** and **sein** are very often used in the subjunctive mood.

**haben**

| ich hätte | wir hätten |
|---|---|
| du hättest | ihr hättet |
| er hätte | sie hätten |
| Sie hätten | |

**sein**

| ich wäre | wir wären |
|---|---|
| du wärest | ihr wäret |
| er wäre | sie wären |
| Sie wären | |

*Present subjunctive:*
**haben** *and* **sein**

The present subjunctive of weak verbs and of the modals **sollen** and **wollen** is identical in form with the past indicative, and is therefore not commonly used.

| | PAST INDICATIVE | PRESENT SUBJUNCTIVE |
|---|---|---|
| *weak verbs* | ich lachte | ich lachte |
| *modals with o-stem* | du solltest<br>ihr wolltet | du solltest<br>ihr wolltet |

*Check your comprehension*

*Restate in the present subjunctive.*

1. sie fährt
2. er ist
3. ihr hattet
4. er kommt
5. ich kann
6. Sie bringen
7. ihr schreibt
8. du liest

**B.** *Present subjunctive: usage*

The subjunctive in English is not as commonly used as in German. Most frequently it occurs in certain idioms and in formal resolutions and recommendations.

I move that the motion **be** passed.
We ask that he **act** in the interest of the community.
**Be** that as it may, . . .
**Had** we only known then what we know now!

However, there exists in English an equivalent of the subjunctive formed with *would* + infinitive, which occurs frequently to express wishful thinking and polite requests.

I wish **you would stay** a little longer.
**I would prefer** to come home.
**Would you be** so kind as to give me another piece of cake?
**I'd like** another cup of coffee.
**Would you** please **answer** the question?

The subjunctive is used in German more frequently than in English. Its principal uses are the following:

## 1. Wishful thinking

Wishful thinking is frequently expressed by an introductory clause with a subjunctive form of **wünschen.**

| | |
|---|---|
| Ich **wünschte,** er **käme** sofort. | *I wish he would come at once.* |
| Wir **wünschten,** sie **wäre** schon hier. | *We wish she were already here.* |

Wishful thinking can also be expressed by a clause with **wenn** (*if*).

| | |
|---|---|
| Wenn ich nur mehr Geld **hätte!** | *If only I had more money!* |
| Wenn er doch nur **anriefe!** | *If only he would call!* |

## 2. Polite requests

The subjunctive is used to make a request more polite.

| | |
|---|---|
| **Hätten** Sie einen Moment Zeit? | *Would you have a moment?* |
| **Könntest** du mir bitte **sagen,** wo das Restaurant ist. | *Could you please tell me where the restaurant is.* |

Many wishes and polite requests contain the adverbs **gern, lieber, am liebsten.**

| | |
|---|---|
| Ich **hätte gern** das Stück Kuchen. | *I would like that piece of cake.* |
| **Möchten** Sie **lieber** etwas Obst essen? | *Would you rather eat some fruit?* |
| Ich **hätte am liebsten** Bier. | *I'd like beer best of all.* |

## 3. Contrary-to-fact statements

Contrary-to-fact statements are expressed in the subjunctive to underline the hypothetical nature of the idea expressed.

| | |
|---|---|
| Wenn das Wetter schön **wäre, führen** wir mit dem Fahrrad. | *If the weather were nice, we'd go bike riding.* |
| Es **täte** mir leid, wenn er nicht **käme.** | *I'd be sorry if he didn't come.* |
| Wenn ich genug Geld **hätte, ginge** ich nach Wien. | *If I had enough money, I would go to Vienna.* |

## Check your comprehension

*Fill in the appropriate subjunctive forms, using the cues given in parentheses.*

1. Wenn er doch zu Hause _____! (*bleiben*)
2. Ich _____, Karl _____ öfter. (*wünschen, schreiben*)

3. Wir _____, wir _____ mehr Zeit für dich. (*wünschen/haben*)
4. Wenn er das Bild nur _____! (*bringen*)
5. Verzeihung, _____ ich Sie bitten, Ihre Zigarre nicht hier zu rauchen. (*dürfen*)
6. _____ Sie mir bitte sagen, wie spät es ist? (*können*)
7. Wenn ich Zeit _____, _____ ich ins Kino. (*haben, gehen*)
8. Wenn es keine Taxis _____, _____ ich einen Bus. (*geben, neh-men*)

## C. *Past subjunctive*

The *past subjunctive* in German is similar to English in usage; it generally indicates an unreal or hypothetical action that could have occurred in the past but did not.

| | |
|---|---|
| Wir **hätten** gern **angerufen**. | *We would have liked to call.* |
| Er **wäre** lieber mit uns **gekommen**. | *He would have preferred to come with us.* |

As one might expect, the past subjunctive in German consists of the subjunctive form of the auxiliary **haben** or **sein** and the past participle of the principal verb.

### Check your comprehension

*Change the following sentences into the past.*

1. Wenn er doch anriefe!
2. Sie käme lieber später.
3. Hätten Sie Lust, mit uns nach Nürnberg zu fahren?
4. Wer bliebe lieber in Österreich?
5. Wenn Sie nur nicht nach Rom führen!

## II. Würden plus infinitive construction

The subjunctive of **werden** plus the infinitive is often used to express the subjunctive idea, similar to *would* + infinitive in English.

| SUBJUNCTIVE OF THE MAIN VERB | **würde** + INFINITIVE OF THE MAIN VERB |
|---|---|
| Ich wünschte, er **käme** sofort. | Ich wünschte, er **würde** sofort **kommen**. |
| | *I wish he'd come at once.* |
| Wenn er doch nur **anriefe**! | Wenn er doch nur **anrufen würde**! |
| | *If only he would call.* |

The present subjunctive of **werden** is as follows:

**werden**

| | |
|---|---|
| ich würde | wir würden |
| du würdest | ihr würdet |
| er würde | sie würden |
| | Sie würden |

Since weak verbs have identical forms in the past indicative and present subjunctive (see p. 295), this substitute subjunctive construction must be used with them to avoid ambiguity.

| | |
|---|---|
| Wenn er doch nicht so viel **kaufen würde!** (*Not:* Wenn er doch nicht so viel kaufte.) | *If only he wouldn't buy so much!* |
| Ich wünschte, sie **würden** mich am Bahnhof **abholen.** (*Not:* Ich wünschte, sie holten mich am Bahnhof ab.) | *I wish they would pick me up at the railroad station.* |

The **würde** construction must also be used in polite requests with all verbs except **haben, sein,** and the modals.

| | |
|---|---|
| **Würden** Sie bitte etwas langsamer **sprechen.** | *Would you please speak more slowly.* |
| **Würden** Sie mir bitte **helfen.** | *Would you please help me.* |
| **Würdest** du ihm das bitte **erklären.** | *Would you please explain that to him.* |

As a matter of fact, the **würde** construction has become the prevailing form in most instances, especially in conversation, while the subjunctive form proper has taken on a more literary flavor. With **haben, sein,** and the modals, however—whether in polite requests or otherwise—the **würde** construction *cannot* be used.

| | |
|---|---|
| **Könnten** Sie mir bitte **helfen?** | *Could you please help me?* |
| Wenn er doch hier **wäre!** | *If only he were here!* |
| Ich **hätte** lieber eine Tasse Kaffee. | *I would rather have a cup of coffee.* |

In the past subjunctive the **würde** construction is not used.

| | |
|---|---|
| Ich **hätte** ihn **angerufen.** (*Not:* Ich würde ihn angerufen haben.) | *I would have called him.* |
| Er **wäre** wahrscheinlich **gekommen.** (*Not:* Er würde wahrscheinlich gekommen sein.) | *He probably would have come.* |

*Check your comprehension*

*Express the following statements by using the* **würde** + *infinitive construction.*

EXAMPLE: Sprechen Sie bitte langsamer!
**Würden Sie bitte langsamer sprechen.**

1. Fahren Sie bitte nicht so schnell!
2. Ich lese das Buch nicht.
3. Helfen Sie dem Herrn da drüben bitte!
4. Bringen Sie mir noch ein Glas Bier!
5. Das tue ich nicht gern.
6. Wenn sie doch nur käme!

## III. Contrary-to-fact statements

A conditional sentence consists of a clause containing a *condition* and a clause containing a *conclusion*. Since the condition is generally expressed with *if*, it is called the *if*-clause in English and the **wenn**-clause in German.

Some conditions are contrary to fact, while others are not.

| | CONDITION | CONCLUSION |
|---|---|---|
| *not contrary to fact* | If I have the book (and maybe I do or will), | I'll read it. |
| *contrary to fact* | If I had the book (but I don't), | I would read it. |

In German, if a condition is *not* contrary to fact, it is expressed with the indicative.

Wenn ich das Buch habe,    lese ich es.
*If I have the book,*    *I'll read it.*

However, if a statement is contrary to fact, it is expressed with the subjunctive in German.

| CONDITION | CONCLUSION |
|---|---|
| Wenn ich das Buch **hätte**, <br> *If I had the book,* | { **läse** ich es. <br> { **würde** ich es lesen. <br> *I would read it.* |
| Wenn sie **gekommen wäre**, <br> *If she had come,* | **hätte** ich mich gefreut. <br> *I would have been happy.* |

Note that the **würde** construction can be used only in the conclusion, and then only in the present tense. However, it is possible—especially in writing or formal speech—to use the subjunctive in the conclusion.

Remember that the **würde** construction is not used with **haben, sein,** and the modals.

The tenses in the condition and the conclusion of a sentence are not necessarily the same. The whole sentence may be in the present or in the past, or it may consist of a condition in the past and a conclusion in the present.

| | CONDITION | CONCLUSION | |
|---|---|---|---|
| *present* | Wenn er mich **anriefe,** | **ginge** ich jetzt.<br>**würde** ich jetzt gehen. | *present* |
| | *If he called me,* | *I would go now.* | |
| *past* | Wenn er mich **angerufen hätte,** | **wäre** ich gegangen. | *past* |
| | *If he had called me,* | *I would have gone.* | |
| *past* | Wenn er mich **angerufen hätte,** | **ginge** ich jetzt.<br>**würde** ich jetzt gehen. | *present* |
| | *If he had called me,* | *I would go now.* | |

Either clause may be in first position in the sentence. Since **wenn** is a subordinating conjunction, *dependent* word order is required; that is, the finite verb comes last in the clause.

| CONCLUSION | CONDITION |
|---|---|
| Ich ginge jetzt, | **wenn** er mich anriefe. |
| *I would go now,* | *if he called me.* |

When the conclusion follows the conditional clause, *inverted* word order is used.

Wenn du willst, **kannst** du jetzt gehen.
*If you want, you may go now.*

The conjunction **wenn** may be omitted, in which case the finite verb comes at the beginning of the condition. The conclusion often starts with **so** or **dann.**

| | |
|---|---|
| Hätte ich mehr Zeit, (so) würde ich mehr Bücher lesen. | *If I had more time, I'd read more books.* |
| Wäre sie hier, (dann) würden wir sofort einkaufen gehen. | *If she were here, we would go shopping right away.* |

## Check your comprehension

**A.** *Change the following sentences into contrary-to-fact statements. Remember to use the* **würde** + *infinitive construction wherever necessary to avoid ambiguity.*

1. Wenn du das tust, gebe ich dir zwanzig Mark.
2. Wenn sie keine Zeit haben, kommen sie bestimmt nicht.
3. Ich kaufe mir das Auto, wenn ich das Geld habe.
4. Wenn er mehr Zeit hat, macht er eine Reise.
5. Ihr kommt früher an, wenn ihr mit dem Zug fahrt.
6. Sind wir wirklich hungrig, dann essen wir etwas.
7. Wenn er diese Nachricht hört, freut er sich ganz sicher.
8. Wir kommen nicht zu spät, wenn wir uns beeilen.

**B.** *Now change the sentences above into contrary-to-fact statements of the past.*

## USEFUL PHRASES

| | |
|---|---|
| **Mir schwirrt der Kopf.** | *My head is swimming.* |
| **Fabelhaft!** | *Fantastic!* |
| **Stell dich doch nicht so an!** | *Don't make a fuss!* |
| **Hör dir das mal an!** | *Listen to that!* |
| **Daß ich nicht lache!** | *Don't make me laugh!* |
| **Was ist (denn schon wieder) los?** | { *What's the matter (again)?* <br> *What's this all about (again)?* |

## CONVERSATION

## Das Abitur[1]

*Anita, Anton und Wolfgang sind drei Oberprimaner[2], die vor dem Abitur stehen°. Seit fast drei Monaten studieren sie dreimal in der Woche zusammen, um sich auf die Prüfung vorzubereiten. Eines Abends unterhalten sie sich während einer kurzen Pause.*

° *are about to take*

[1] The Abitur is a stiff general examination that lasts several days and covers all core subjects (mathematics, science, languages, German literature, etc.) taught in the Gymnasium over nine years. It is a prerequisite for admission to a university. Because of overcrowded facilities, only students with high passing grades have a chance to be accepted at a university. The so-called *Numerus Clausus* (Latin for "closed number") sets an upper limit to the number of admissions authorized in many academic disciplines.

[2] **Oberprimaner** are students in the last year of the Gymnasium.

ANTON Hört mal! Mir schwirrt der Kopf. Das ist ein ganz gemeines°    *mean*
   mathematisches Problem, das wir da gelöst haben.

WOLFGANG Du solltest sagen: „das Anita für uns gelöst hat."

ANTON Allerdings. Wenn wir nur das Abitur zusammen als eine
   Gruppe machen dürften, dann würden wir ganz großartig ab-
   schneiden!°    *pass*

ANITA Fabelhafte Idee! Dann würde ich die Mathematik übernehmen°    *take on*
   und Anton könnte für uns den englischen Aufsatz schreiben.

WOLFGANG Und ich?

ANTON Stell dich doch nicht so an! Du kennst doch die deutsche Literatur vorwärts und rückwärts.

WOLFGANG Ja, ja. Aber ich möchte lieber mein eigenes Gedicht schreiben, als ein abgedroschenes Zitat° aus einem Schiller[3]-Gedicht    *hackneyed quote*
   kommentieren.

ANTON Ha, ha! Sein eigenes Gedicht! Hör dir das mal an, Anita! Die

---

[3] Though recognized as the greatest classical dramatist in German literature, Friedrich
Schiller (1759–1805) also wrote historic treatises, philosophic essays, and poems, often
of a didactic nature.

Lehrer würden ihm sicher für sein Gedicht den Nobel-Preis verleihen°.  *to confer*

WOLFGANG Anita, siehst du, jetzt verhöhnt er mich schon wieder. Anton, du hast leider keine Phantasie.

ANTON „Phantasie"! Daß ich nicht lache!

WOLFGANG Und wenn die Lehrer etwas mehr poetischen Sinn hätten, dann würden sie unserem eigenen Denken und Fühlen etwas mehr Raum lassen.

ANITA Was ist denn schon wieder los? Streitet euch doch nicht. Wir können alle den Stress⁴ fast nicht mehr aushalten. Warum gehen wir nachher nicht in unsere Diskothek?

WOLFGANG Na, gut! Aber versprich mir, auf dem Heimweg keine Vorlesung über die Physik des Schalls° zu halten!  *sound*

⁴ The English word *stress* is now commonly used in German. An approximation in German would be **der Druck** (*pressure*).

## Questions

1. Warum studieren die drei Oberprimaner seit drei Monaten dreimal in der Woche zusammen?

2. Warum schwirrt Anton der Kopf?

3. Wer hat das mathematische Problem gelöst?

4. Wer von den drei Oberprimanern kann einen englischen Aufsatz am besten schreiben?

5. Was möchte Wolfgang am liebsten tun?

6. Warum streiten sich Wolfgang und Anton?

7. Wohin will Anita gehen, wenn sie fertig sind mit dem Studieren?

8. Wer scheint gern Vorlesungen zu halten?

9. Schwirrt Ihnen manchmal der Kopf, wenn Sie studieren? Warum?

10. Wenn Sie das Abitur machen müßten, welche Prüfung hätten Sie am liebsten—Mathematik, Literatur oder Physik? Warum?

11. Möchten Sie Ihr eigenes Denken und Fühlen in einer Prüfung ausdrücken? Ist es Ihnen jemals gelungen, das zu tun? Was für eine Note (*grade*) haben Sie bekommen?

12. Gibt es etwas, was Sie vorwärts und rückwärts kennen? Was? Gibt es etwas anderes, was Sie gern vorwärts und rückwärts kennen möchten?

13. Schreiben Sie gern Ihre eigenen Gedichte, oder kommentieren Sie lieber ein Gedicht?

 **PRACTICE**

**A.** *Put the sentences into the subjunctive, or into the substitute construction* (**würde** + *infinitive*), *by using the phrase* **Ich wünschte,** ...

1. Meine Freundin löst dieses mathematische Problem für mich.

2. Der Busfahrer fährt jetzt etwas schneller.

3. Sie bringen mir bessere Nachrichten.
4. Er spricht etwas lauter.
5. Ihr streitet euch nicht jeden Tag.
6. Du hast mehr Glück.
7. Wir gehen auf dem Heimweg in unser Café.
8. Mein Freund mietet das Zimmer in unserem Haus.
9. Du kommst nicht immer zu spät.
10. Die Studenten halten den Stress besser aus.

**B.** *Put the sentences in Exercise A into the past subjunctive by using the phrase* **Ich wünschte, . . .**

**C.** *Using the substitute construction for the subjunctive, express the request more politely.*

1. Geben Sie mir bitte die Zeitung!
2. Setzen Sie sich bitte da drüben an den Tisch!
3. Fahren Sie bitte weiter!
4. Bringen Sie mir bitte noch ein Glas Wein!
5. Mach bitte das Fenster zu!
6. Kommt bitte sofort nach Hause!
7. Geht bitte einen Moment hinaus!

**D.** *Change the following statements into contrary-to-fact statements.*

1. Wenn das wahr ist, haben wir keine Chance.
2. Wenn Klaus das Gedicht kennt, kommentiert er es.
3. Wenn Sie genug Zeit haben, studieren Sie auch Deutsch.
4. Wenn er das tut, weiß ich es auch.
5. Wenn das Buch zu teuer ist, kaufen wir es bestimmt nicht.
6. Ist er durstig, dann trinkt er ein Glas Wasser.
7. Wenn es möglich ist, gehe ich gern im Herbst nach Deutschland.
8. Wenn wir ein Haus kaufen, haben wir mehr Platz als jetzt.

**E.** *Now change the sentences in exercise D into contrary-to-fact statements of the past.*

**F.** *Give the English equivalent.*

1. Ich würde lieber zu Hause bleiben.
2. Könnten Sie mir bitte das Buch da drüben geben.
3. Wenn er nicht bald kommt, gehe ich nach Hause.
4. Wenn er doch nur nicht so schnell spräche.
5. Ich wünschte, ich kennte die deutsche Literatur vorwärts und rückwärts.
6. Wenn er mehr Zeit gehabt hätte, wäre er sicher gekommen.
7. Wenn doch meine Seminararbeit endlich fertig wäre.
8. Wenn Brigitte nicht hier gewesen wäre, hätten wir sie vielleicht vergessen.

**GUIDED CONVERSATION**

**A.** Ask someone in your class whether he or she would like to
   drink a cup of coffee
   smoke a cigarette
   study in Vienna
   go shopping
   play the guitar
Now tell him or her what you yourself would prefer to do.

**B.** Do you often study for an exam with a friend or friends? Which subjects do you study? What kinds of tests would you prefer? Would you rather write an essay or composition (**der Aufsatz**) at home or answer questions in class? Would you rather have a long exam at the end of a term (**das Semester, das Quartal**), or a series of short tests during the term? What assignments would you give, if you were the instructor? Perhaps you have some ideas about improving education in general. What would you do? Express two or three ideas: **Wenn ich Professor wäre, würde ich . . .** Then describe your habitual place of study; if you don't particularly like it, describe in what kind of environment you would most like to study. You may also describe the picture below, and say what you would rather do and where you would rather study.

## Studentenprobleme

*Sabine und Stefan sind gute Freunde, die wegen des Numerus Clausus an verschiedenen Universitäten studieren müssen.[1] Sie schreiben sich ziemlich oft.*

München, den 5. November

Lieber Stefan:

   Nun sind es schon drei Wochen, seitdem ich hier in München mein Winter-Semester begonnen habe. Wenn ich nicht schon so sehr mit meinem Medizinstudium beschäftigt wäre, hätte ich sehr wahrscheinlich Heimweh. Denn so gute Freunde wie Dich, Hanspeter und Liselotte werde ich wohl hier nicht so schnell finden. Ich wünschte, es wäre schon Weihnachten, dann könnten wir alle zusammen wieder Skilaufen gehen. Du hast doch unsere Verabredung nicht vergessen, oder? Der Winter ist ja dieses Jahr vielversprechend. Kürzlich habe ich in der Zeitung gelesen, daß in den Bayrischen Alpen° schon tiefer       Bavarian Alps
Schnee liegt.

   Du hast wohl auch gehört, daß die meisten Studenten hier wieder einmal streiken. Es hat bei den Germanisten und Juristen[2] begonnen,

[1] In Dortmund there is a central clearing house for student admissions; under the **Numerus Clausus** provisions, students are assigned to universities and have little choice in the matter.

[2] Germanists and jurists—here, students of Germanic languages, literatures, and linguistics, and law students.

denn die leiden an einer ganz großen Berufsangst[3] und sagen, daß sie
für die Arbeitslosigkeit studieren. Es ist auch verständlich. Die beiden
Fachbereiche° sind einfach übervölkert°. Man müßte entweder we-
niger Studenten zulassen oder mehr Stellen schaffen. Aber wie?

disciplines / over-enrolled

Dann sind die meisten Studenten auch mit der Bafög[4]-Erhöhung°
nicht zufrieden. Wenn sie anständig° leben wollten, hätten sie 690

increase
properly

[3] Fear of not finding a job. In the BRD as elsewhere, the job prospects in many academic
professions are not very rosy these days. Many prospective students have therefore opted
for a practical trade. But even apprenticeship positions are difficult to find, since there
are so many applicants.

[4] Abbreviation for **Bundesausbildungsförderungsgesetz** (ouch!)—the federal law for
higher education. Students whose parents' income is below a certain level are eligible
for a monthly stipend of almost 600 Marks ($300–$350) even during the long summer
recess. Almost half of all students in institutions of higher learning in the BRD receive
such aid.

Mark im Monat nötig und nicht nur 580, sagen sie. Fast hätten auch die Medizinstudenten mitgemacht, wenn sie nicht so konservativ wären, heißt es in der Studentenzeitung. Das stimmt aber nicht ganz. Erstens erhalten nur ein Drittel der Medizinstudenten Bafög, und zweitens, wenn wir zu häufig abwesend sind, erhalten wir keine Zulassung° mehr zu weiteren Pflichtvorlesungen°. Und dann ist es praktisch mit dem Medizinstudium aus!° Wer ist da konservativ, die Studenten oder die Fakultät?

    Jetzt muß ich wieder zu einer Anatomievorlesung rennen. Mehr später. Ich freue mich schon auf die Skiferien. Gruß, Kuß und Tschüß. In Eile

Deine Sabine.

Marburg, den 11. November

Liebe Sabine:

    Natürlich habe ich unsere Pläne für die Skiferien nicht vergessen. Wenn sie nur schon da wären! Der Gedanke an unsere Ferien macht mir das Wintersemester etwas erträglicher.° Ob Liselotte und Hanspeter mitkommen wollen, ist noch nicht ganz sicher. (In letzter Zeit streiten sie sich sehr oft!) Wenn nicht, müßten wir eben allein gehen. Umso besser!

    Auch hier wird der Studentenstreik wohl bald anfangen. Und ich werde mitmachen müssen. Du weißt doch, daß ich einer der armen Jura°-Studenten bin, die für die Arbeitslosigkeit studieren und Bafög erhalten, weil sie keine wohlhabenden° Eltern haben. Du scheinst das

admission / required lectures
it is finished with

more bearable

law
well-to-do

vergessen zu haben. Oder glaubst du, daß ich einer der Glücklichen sein werde, die nach dem Studium eine Stelle finden? Hoffen wir das Beste! Vielleicht könntest Du nach Deinem Studium mit der finanziellen Hilfe Deines Vaters eine Klinik eröffnen, und ich würde Dein juristischer Berater° werden. Dann würden wir beide reich! Aber ich will nicht zynisch° werden und verspreche Dir, während der Ferien von meinen Berufsaussichten° nicht zu sprechen. Es ist ohnehin noch zu früh.

    Aber es wäre großartig, wenn Du hier in Marburg studieren könntest. Dann würden wir manchmal über unsere Zukunft offen reden, nicht wahr? Hast du übrigens gehört, daß Studenten anfangen, für Geld Studienplätze° zu wechseln?[5] Ich könnte hier vielleicht jemand finden, der mit Dir den Platz wechseln möchte. Ich weiß nicht, ob solch ein Wechsel° legal ist. Ich würde mich aber natürlich sofort erkundigen°, wenn Du interessiert wärest. Du wärst dann mein erster „Rechtsfall".°

    Bis bald. Die Skiferien werden toll werden, das verspreche ich Dir.

*Dein Stefan*

*legal counsel*

*cynical*

*job prospects*

*openings for study*

*exchange*

*inquire*

*legal case*

---

[5] For personal or academic reasons, students have recently begun trading places; money is sometimes involved. Thus medical student A in Munich may pay medical student B in Marburg to take A's place in Munich, while B goes to study in Marburg.

## Questions

1. Wann hat Sabines Winter-Semester in München begonnen?
2. Hat sie Heimweh? Warum oder warum nicht?
3. Was für eine Verabredung haben Sabine und Stefan für die Weihnachtsferien?
4. Warum streiken die Studenten an Sabines Universität?
5. Haben die Medizinstudenten während des Studentenstreiks mitgemacht? Warum oder warum nicht?
6. Warum werden Liselotte und Hanspeter vielleicht nicht zum Skilaufen mitkommen?
7. Was studiert Stefan, und was sind seine Berufsaussichten?
8. Was wäre nach Stefans Meinung großartig?
9. Für welchen Beruf studierst du? Leidest du an einer großen Berufsangst, oder sind deine Berufsaussichten gut?
10. Kennst du Studenten, die sagen, daß sie für die Arbeitslosigkeit studieren? Für welche Berufe studieren sie?
11. Gibt es Studentenstreiks in Amerika? Warum oder warum nicht?
12. Was hältst du von Studenten, die streiken?

**VOCABULARY DEVELOPMENT**

**A. Was ist los?** *(What's going on? What's the matter?)*

The particle **los** is a kind of "free agent" in German grammar. Or call it a chameleon, since it adapts easily to its "free" grammatical environment. Its basic meaning is something like *loose, free, -less* (meaning *without*, as in *senseless*).

As an *adverb* it occurs in some frequently used colloquial expressions:

| | |
|---|---|
| Was ist los? | *What's the matter?* |
| Nur los! | *Fire away! Go on!* |
| Der Teufel ist los! | *Hell is let loose.* |
| Es muß etwas los sein! | *Something must be afoot.* |

It also occurs as a *separable prefix* with several verbs:

| | |
|---|---|
| los·fahren *to depart* | Fahrt mal los! *Get going!* |
| los·gehen *to begin, get under way* | Es geht bald los. *Things will soon get under way.* |
| | Nun geht's los! *Now things are getting under way!* |
| los·lassen *to let loose, let go* | Laß doch deinen Hund mal los! *Unleash your dog, will you!* |
| los·machen *to loosen, disengage, get away from* | Ich kann mich von ihm nicht losmachen. *I can't get away from him.* |

As a *suffix* it combines with many nouns to form adjectives:

| | | |
|---|---|---|
| die Arbeit | arbeitslos | *out of work* |
| der Atem | atemlos | *out of breath* |
| das Ende | endlos | *endless* |
| das Herz | herzlos | *heartless* |
| das Kind, die Kinder | kinderlos | *childless* |
| die Ruhe | ruhelos | *restless* |
| der Staat | staatenlos | *stateless* |

What then are the adjectives ending in **-los** based on the nouns **der Boden, die Farbe, die Frage, die Freude?** Use each one in a sentence.

There is really nothing wrong with **los**, except that grammatically it is a little **sorglos** *(carefree)*!

**B.** *Be careful when you make a promise (***das Versprechen***)*

**Versprechen** (from **sprechen**) means *to promise:*

Sie hat mir versprochen, ihm zu helfen.        *She promised me to help him.*

But the reflexive **sich versprechen** means *to make a slip of the tongue, to say something wrong.* Therefore: **Wenn Sie etwas versprechen, versprechen Sie sich nicht!**

 **REVIEW**

**A.** *Answer the following questions with the appropriate* **würde** *construction where applicable.*

**Was würden Sie tun, wenn ...**

1. Ihre Freundin oder Ihr Freund Sie um Geld bäte?
2. es so stark schneite, daß Sie das Haus nicht verlassen könnten?
3. Sie einen Autounfall gehabt hätten und der andere Autofahrer den Unfallort verlassen hätte?
4. Sie plötzlich $20,000 gewännen?
5. Sie drei Wochen Urlaub machen dürften ohne bezahlen zu müssen? Flögen Sie dann am liebsten nach Jamaika, Hawaii, Japan, Deutschland, Österreich oder in die Schweiz?
6. Sie wohnen könnten, wo Sie wollten? Wohnten Sie dann am liebsten in Los Angeles, New York, New Orleans, San Francisco, Boston oder in Vancouver, B.C.?
7. Sie mit einem Freund ausgehen könnten? Gingen Sie am liebsten ins Kino, ins Theater, in die Oper, in den Stadtpark oder in ein französisches Restaurant?

**B.** *Put the following sentences in the present tense.*

1. Wenn ich so lange in andern Ländern gewohnt hätte wie du, hätte ich oft Heimweh gehabt.
2. Wenn das Wetter besser gewesen wäre, wären wir vielleicht schwimmen gegangen.
3. Wenn er nicht so konservativ gewesen wäre, hätte er vielleicht mitgemacht.
4. Hätte der Bus hier angehalten, dann wäre ich hier ausgestiegen.
5. Wäret Ihr später gekommen, so hättet Ihr kaum eine Chance gehabt.
6. Wenn er mehr Zeit gehabt hätte, hätte er vielleicht den Stress besser ausgehalten.

7. Hättest du auf mich gehört, so hättest du eine Stelle gefunden.

8. Wenn ihr euch nicht so oft gestritten hättet, hättet ihr das Problem schneller gelöst.

9. Ich hätte dich öfter angerufen, wenn ich nicht so sehr mit meinen Kursen beschäftigt gewesen wäre.

10. Hättest du ihm mehr Geld gegeben, so wäre er doch nicht zufrieden gewesen.

11. Wenn du Jurist gewesen wärest, hättest du auch an einer großen Berufsangst gelitten.

**C.** *Express the following requests more politely by using the* **würde** + *infinitive construction.*

1. Bezahlen Sie bitte das Bier.

2. Raucht bitte nicht im Schlafzimmer.

3. Ruf mich bitte nicht immer so spät an.

4. Trinken Sie bitte Ihren Kaffee.

5. Fahren Sie bitte nicht, wenn Sie Alkohol getrunken haben.

6. Öffne bitte der Frau die Tür.

**D.** *Express in German.*

1. Would you call me tomorrow, please.

2. If I couldn't drive, I would have to walk (go on foot).

3. If I were Peter, I would definitely buy the car.

4. Would you please speak a little louder.

5. I wish we could live in Munich.

6. If only it weren't so terribly expensive!

7. If I had money, I would give you some.

8. If only I had more time!

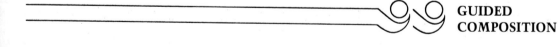

**GUIDED COMPOSITION**

Tell what you would do if some of the students at your college or university proposed a student strike. Would you be conservative or radical (**radikal**)? Explain under what circumstances you would go along with the strike, and under what circumstances you would be against it. Mention also the conditions you would like to change. Use the subjunctive and the **würde** construction throughout where appropriate.

## VOCABULARY

### Easily recognized words

| | | |
|---|---|---|
| die | **Fakultät,** -en | *faculty* |
| | **konservativ** | *conservative* |
| | **legal** | *legal* |
| die | **Medizin** | *medicine* |
| | **poetisch** | *poetic* |
| | **radikal** | *radical* |
| das | **Semester,** - | *semester* |
| der | **Stress** | *stress* |

| | | |
|---|---|---|
| das | **Abitur** | *Abitur: the final general examination covering all secondary-school studies* |
| die | **Angst,** ⸚e | *fear* |

| | | |
|---|---|---|
| die | **Arbeitslosigkeit** | *unemployment* |
| der | **Aufsatz,** ⸚e | *written composition* |
| das | **Drittel,** - | *third* |
| der | **Gedanke,** -n | *thought* |
| das | **Gedicht,** -e | *poem* |
| der | **Heimweg,** -e | *way (or return) home;* **auf dem Heimweg** *on the way home* |
| das | **Heimweh** | *homesickness;* **Heimweh haben** *to be homesick* |
| der | **Kuß,** ⸚sse | *kiss* |
| der | **Lehrer,** - | *teacher* |
| die | **Phantasie** | *imagination* |
| die | **Prüfung,** -en | *examination* |
| die | **Stelle,** -n | *position, job* |
| der | **Streik,** -s | *strike* |
| das | **Studium,** die **Studien** | *study* |
| das | **Weihnachten,** - | *Christmas* |

**aus·halten (hält), hielt, ausgehalten** — *to endure, bear, stand*

**kommentieren** — *to comment on*

**leiden, litt, gelitten** — *to suffer*

**mit·machen** — *to go along (with something)*

**schaffen** — *to create*

**streiken** — *to strike*

sich **streiten, stritt, gestritten** — *to quarrel*

**verhöhnen** — *to mock, deride*

**versprechen (verspricht), versprach, versprochen** (+ *dat.*) — *to promise*

**vor·bereiten (auf +** acc.) — *to prepare (for)*

**zu·lassen (läßt), ließ, zugelassen** — *to admit*

**abwesend** — *absent*

**beschäftigt** — *busy*

**eigen** — *own*

**entweder . . . oder** — *either . . . or*

**fabelhaft** — *fabulous*

**finanziell** — *financial*

**glücklich** — *happy, lucky*

**großartig** — *magnificent*

**nachher** — *later*

**nötig** — *necessary;* **etwas nötig haben** *to need something*

**ohnehin** — *anyway*

**praktisch** — *practical*

**rückwärts** — *backward*

**umso besser!** — *so much the better!*

**verschieden** — *different*

**verständlich** — *understandable*

**vielversprechend** — *very promising*

**vorwärts** — *forward*

**zufrieden (mit +** *dat.*) — *satisfied (with)*

**I**

**Darauf** war ich nicht vorbereitet.
*I was not prepared for that.*

Ich bat sie **darum,** doch mitzukommen.
*I asked her to come along.*

**Wofür** hielt mich der Mann wohl?
*Who did the man think I was?*

**Woran** erinnert dich das?
*What does that remind you of?*

Wie heißt der Stadtteil, **worin** wir uns befinden?
*What's the name of the part of town we're in?*

## II

Er **wird** wohl **gedacht haben,** daß ich ein Spion bin.
*He probably thought that I was a spy.*

Was **werden** die Leute wohl **gedacht haben?**
*What must the people have thought?*

Darüber **werden** die meisten Autofahrer sicher **gelacht haben.**
*Most of the drivers probably laughed about it.*

**GRAMMAR
EXPLANATION**

### I. DA and WO compounds

In German, pronouns or question words following a preposition may refer to persons.

| | |
|---|---|
| Ich käme gern **mit ihr.** | *I would like to go with her.* |
| Wissen Sie, **von wem** er den Brief erhalten hat? | *Do you know from whom he received the letter?* |

But the pronoun or the question word may also refer to an *inanimate object* or an *idea.* In that case, the pronoun or question word is replaced by a compound.

### A. Da *compounds*

In a statement, the pronoun which would normally follow a preposition is replaced by a **da** compound: **da** + preposition, or if the preposition begins with a vowel, **dar** + preposition.

| | |
|---|---|
| Wir experimentieren **mit dem Motor.** | *We're experimenting with the motor.* |
| Wir experimentieren **damit.** | *We're experimenting with it.* |
| Peter spricht **über ein mathematisches Problem.** | *Peter is talking about a mathematical problem.* |
| Peter spricht **darüber.** | *Peter is talking about it.* |

Prepositions governing the genitive, and the prepositions **außer** and **seit,** do not form **da** compounds.

The **da** compounds also anticipate infinitives which function as the object of a preposition.

| | |
|---|---|
| Er denkt nicht **daran,** das Buch zu lesen. | *He doesn't consider reading the book.* |

**B. Wo** *compounds*

In a question the question word **was,** when following a preposition, is replaced by a **wo** compound: **wo** + preposition, or if the preposition begins with a vowel, **wor** + preposition.

| | |
|---|---|
| Heidi erzählt **von der Reise.** | *Heidi is telling about the trip.* |
| **Wovon** erzählt Heidi? | *What is Heidi telling about?* |
| Karl sitzt **auf dem Stuhl.** | *Karl is sitting on the chair.* |
| **Worauf** sitzt Karl? | *What is Karl sitting on?* |

The **wo** compound may also be used as a relative pronoun.

| | |
|---|---|
| Hier ist das Zimmer, **worin** (= in dem) er gestorben ist. | *Here is the room in which he died.* |
| Ich lese das Buch, **wovon** (= von dem) sie gesprochen hat. | *I am reading the book she talked about.* |

Here the use of the **wo** compound is optional.

If the preceding idea is not identified, the **wo** compound must be used:

| | |
|---|---|
| Ich weiß nicht, **wovon** (*not* von was) sie sprechen. | *I don't know what they are talking about.* |

Note that with verbs of motion—especially **fahren, gehen,** and **kommen**—the directional compounds **dahin, dorthin, daher, dorther, wohin,** and **woher** are used, rather than **da** and **wo** compounds.

| | |
|---|---|
| Woher kommst du? | *Where are you coming from?* |
| Ich komme daher. | *I'm coming from there.* |
| Wohin gehst du? | *Where are you going?* |
| Ich gehe dorthin. | *I'm going there.* |

## Check your comprehension

**A.** *Substitute a* **da** *compound for the prepositional phrase in the sentence.*

EXAMPLE: Wir sprechen über den Unfall.
       **Wir sprechen darüber.**

1. Er denkt an die Geburtstagsfeier.
2. Birgit versteht etwas von Soziologie.
3. Wir antworten nicht auf die Frage.
4. Sie helfen ihr bei der Arbeit.
5. Gleich gehen wir zum Bahnhof.
6. Wir sind durch den Garten gelaufen.

**B.** *Using a* **wo** *compound, ask questions to which the following statements are answers.*

EXAMPLE: Ich denke an die Reise.
       **Woran denkst du?**

1. Sie weiß nichts über den Unfall.
2. Morgen kommen wir nach Hamburg.
3. Peter spricht von dem Film.
4. Herr und Frau Müller sitzen im Auto.
5. Ich fahre mit Ingeborgs Wagen.
6. Er hat sie an ihre Verabredung erinnert.

**C.** *Replace the relative pronoun by a* **wo** *compound.*

1. Hast du das Buch schon gelesen, über das der Professor gestern sprach?
2. Ich kenne den Ort nicht, von dem er so begeistert ist.
3. Hier ist das Auto, mit dem wir einen Unfall hatten.
4. Zeigen Sie mir das Haus, in dem Sie wohnten.

## II. Future perfect tense

The future perfect tense is formed with the present tense of **werden,** the past participle of the principal verb, plus **haben** or **sein.** In its literal sense, it expresses the conclusion of an action in the future.

| | |
|---|---|
| Bis nächsten Montag **wird** sie das Buch **gelesen haben.** | *By next Monday she will have read the book.* |
| Ich hoffe, daß sie bis morgen **abgefahren sein werden.** | *I hope they will have left by tomorrow.* |

But this tense is more often used with words like **wohl** and **sicher** to express past or future probability. In English this probability is most often expressed with *must, probably,* or *I guess.*

| | |
|---|---|
| Bis morgen **werden** wir **wohl** den Brief **geschrieben haben.** | *By tomorrow we will probably have written the letter.* |
| Sie **wird sicher** hungrig **gewesen sein.** | *She must have been hungry.* |

### Check your comprehension

*Put each sentence into the future perfect tense, then translate into English.*

1. Er hat wohl nicht daran gedacht.
2. Bis morgen hat er sicher den Brief geschrieben.
3. In zwei Jahren macht sie ihr Abitur.

4. Bis zum 1. April erhält er von mir eine Antwort.
5. Das ist wohl richtig.
6. Sie hat wohl Heimweh gehabt.

## USEFUL PHRASES

| | |
|---|---|
| **Ach, ich Esel!** | *How stupid of me!* / *Oh, what a dummy I am!* |
| **Es trifft sich gut.** | *That's fortunate.* |
| **Prima!** | *Great!* |
| **Zum Glück (nicht)!** | *Luckily (not)!* / *Fortunately (not)!* |
| **Sachte, sachte!** | *Easy now!* |

**CONVERSATION**

## Der Autostop

*Ray ist ein amerikanischer Student deutscher Abstammung,° der an der*     *descent*
*Freien Universität in Berlin studiert. Er steht am Stadtrand° West-Ber-*     *city limits*
*lins in der Nähe der Berliner Mauer an einem Ausgangspunkt° in die*     *exit*
*DDR. Er hält einen Pappdeckel° in den Händen, worauf er „Nach Ham-*     *piece of cardboard*
*burg" geschrieben hat. Monika und Freddy nähern sich in einem Opel*
*und halten vor ihm an.*

MONIKA *(aus dem Wagen)* Hallo, worauf warten Sie?

RAY Worauf ich warte? Auf eine freundliche Seele, die mich nach
    Hamburg mitnimmt.

MONIKA Nach Hamburg? Aber was steht denn da auf ihrem Pappdeckel?

RAY Was darauf steht? „Nach Hamburg", natürlich.

FREDDY Aber sehen Sie sich den Deckel doch mal von vorne an!

RAY *(lacht)* Ach, ich Esel. Ich hatte den Deckel auf den Kopf gestellt.
    Darüber werden die meisten Autofahrer wohl so gelacht haben,
    als sie mich sahen. Aber keiner wollte anhalten.

FREDDY Einige werden wohl gedacht haben, Sie sprechen eine exo-
    tische Sprache. Aber steigen Sie doch ein!

MONIKA Ja, bitte. Es trifft sich gut. Wir fahren nämlich° nach Ham-     *as it happens*
    burg.

RAY *(steigt ein)* Prima! Vielen Dank!

    *Etwas später im Wagen:*

MONIKA Warum haben Sie sich dazu entschieden, nach Hamburg zu
    fahren?

RAY Wir haben Semesterferien! Ich habe einfach einen Pfeil° auf eine     *dart*
    Landkarte von Deutschland geworfen, und wo der Pfeil traf, dahin
    fahre ich jetzt.

MONIKA Hatten Sie die Landkarte auch auf den Kopf gestellt?

RAY Nein, zum Glück nicht, sonst hätte ich eine so nette Person wie
    Sie wahrscheinlich nicht getroffen.

FREDDY Sachte, sachte! Keine Cupido-Pfeile!°     *no Cupid's arrows!*

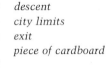

## Questions

1. Welcher Abstammung ist Ray?
2. Wo befindet sich Ray gerade?
3. Was hält Ray in der Hand?
4. Was für einen Wagen fahren Monika und Freddy?
5. Wohin will Ray?
6. Warum konnte man Rays Pappdeckel nicht lesen?
7. Wie hat sich Ray dazu entschieden, nach Hamburg zu reisen?
8. Wo auf der Landkarte der Bundesrepublik befindet sich Hamburg?
9. Sind Sie jemals per Autostop gereist? In welchem Land? Und wohin? Hatten Sie Glück oder mußten Sie oft lange warten?
10. Was für einen Wagen fahren Sie? Sind Sie zufrieden damit, oder würden Sie einen anderen kaufen, wenn Sie genug Geld hätten? Warum?
11. Wenn Sie einen Anhälter (*hitchhiker*) sähen, würden Sie ihn in Ihrem Wagen mitnehmen? Warum oder warum nicht?

 **PRACTICE**

**A.** *Substitute a* **da** *compound for the prepositional phrase.*

1. Ursula schreibt Frau Schmidt über ihr Problem.
2. Ihre Antwort auf dieses Problem ist fabelhaft.
3. Das Mädchen denkt nur an ihre Arbeit.
4. Wir warten schon eine halbe Stunde auf eine Auskunft.
5. Ich spreche nicht gern über Politik.
6. Wir hören uns die Nachrichten über den Unfall an.
7. Morgen beginnen die Studenten mit der Prüfung.
8. Er will wieder eine Vorlesung über Physik halten.
9. Helga bittet um eine zweite Tasse Kaffee.
10. Die Europäer erinnern sich noch sehr gut an den letzten Weltkrieg.

**B.** *Using a* **wo** *compound, ask questions to which the following statements are answers.*

EXAMPLE: Ich spreche von meinem Studium.
           **Wovon sprichst du?**

1. Ich weiß nichts über die Industrie in Amerika.
2. Die Touristen reden alle über die hohen Preise.
3. Frau Hagen kommt mit dem Zug.
4. Meine Freundin fährt gern mit meinem Auto.
5. Gisela liest viel über Theater und Oper.
6. Ich trinke auf seine Gesundheit.

7. Wir halten nichts von dieser Diskothek.
8. Sie versuchen alles mit Geld zu erreichen.
9. Helmut interessiert sich gar nicht für Geschichte.
10. Klaus kümmert sich um die Reise.

**C.** *Fill in the appropriate relative pronoun, then substitute a* **wo** *compound if possible.*

1. Ist dies das Gedicht, über _____ du ein Examen schreiben mußtest?
2. Wer ist die Frau, von _____ er so oft spricht?
3. Hier ist das neue Haus, in _____ unsere Eltern jetzt wohnen.
4. Was ist das für eine Krankheit, an _____ ihr Vater gestorben ist?
5. Wie heißt der Herr, mit _____ ihr eine Verabredung habt?

**D.** *Substitute a directional compound (***dahin** *or* **dorthin, daher** *or* **dorther***) for the prepositional phrase, then rephrase as a question.*

EXAMPLE: Morgen fahre ich nach Berlin.
　　　　**Ich fahre dorthin. Wohin fahre ich?**

1. Ursula geht jeden Tag ins Kino.
2. Das Taxi kommt gerade vom Flugplatz.
3. Du fährst zum Bahnhof.
4. Wir gehen zu Fuß in die Stadt.
5. Ich komme gerade aus dem Theater.
6. Peter kommt jeden Tag um zwei Uhr von der Universität.
7. Sie gehen zum Abendessen ins Restaurant „Gold".
8. Der Zug kommt aus Hamburg.
9. Sie geht mit mir nach Hause.

**E.** *Adding the expression of probability in parentheses, put each sentence into the future perfect tense, then translate.*

EXAMPLE: Sie ist durstig. (*wohl*)
　　　　**Sie wird wohl durstig gewesen sein.**
　　　　*She must have been thirsty.*

1. Er hat nicht daran gedacht. (*sicher*)
2. Sie ist krank. (*wohl*)
3. Ihr freut euch auf die Geburtstagsfeier. (*sicher*)
4. Sie fahren gleich in die Stadt. (*wohl*)
5. Das ist richtig. (*sicher*)
6. Er hat sehr viel zu tun gehabt. (*wahrscheinlich*)
7. Du hast das Buch endlich gefunden. (*wohl*)
8. Der Zug ist schon abgefahren. (*sicher*)
9. Du hast von meinem Unfall gehört. (*sicher*)
10. Ihr habt euch keine Sorgen gemacht. (*hoffentlich*)

**F.** *Give the English equivalent.*

1. Darüber weiß ich nicht viel.
2. Woher kommt ihr gerade?
3. Sie sagt, darüber spricht sie nicht.
4. Er wird wohl nicht sehr gesund gewesen sein.
5. Worüber hat euch Erna erzählt?
6. Damit kann ich nichts machen.
7. Sie wird den Brief wohl schon unterschrieben haben.
8. Um acht Uhr werden wir sicher hier gewesen sein.

**GUIDED CONVERSATION**

Pretend to meet your neighbor(s) in town. Ask them what they are waiting for, where they are coming from, where they are going. Ask them also if they have heard of the recent marriage or divorce of a mutual friend, and whether they will go to the wedding reception given by a mutual friend. Say also that you had forgotten to go to a party given by another mutual friend, and you ask yourself what they thought about your lapse of memory (use the future perfect). Perhaps you may also wish to invite them for a cup of coffee after you have finished your errands; tell them where you wish to meet (**sich treffen**).

**READING**

## Ein Besuch in Ost-Berlin: Ein Monolog

„Haben Sie Zeitungen oder Bücher bei sich", fragt mich ein Vopo[1] am Checkpoint Charlie.[2] „Nein." Komische Frage! Darauf war ich nicht vorbereitet. Ich gehe doch nicht nach Ost-Berlin, um Zeitungen zu lesen. Jetzt öffnet der Mann noch einmal alle Autotüren und schaut sogar unter den Wagen. Endlich läßt er mich weiterfahren.

Wofür hielt der Mann mich wohl? Er wird wohl gedacht haben, daß ich ein Spion° bin. Natürlich, ich, mit meiner langen Nase und der dunklen Sonnenbrille°! Nun, wohin? Ach, da vorne ist eine Verkehrspolizistin. Das erkennt man an ihren weißen Hemdärmeln°.

spy
sunglasses
shirtsleeves

[1] Abbreviation for **Volkspolizist,** a member of the **Volkspolizei,** the East German state police force.

[2] The point of entry to East Berlin for non-German nationals.

*Checkpoint Charlie*

„In welcher Richtung ist der Hitler Bunker?"[3] „Da, nach links, aber schnell. Sie halten ja den Verkehr auf!" Verkehr? Ich sehe ja fast keinen. Die Straßen scheinen mir ziemlich leer.

Ach, hier ist ein Grashügel. Darunter soll der Bunker liegen, worin Hitler Selbstmord beging?° Stimmt. Bittere Ironie der Geschichte! Das ganze Dritte Reich[4] auf einen Grashügel zusammengeschrumpft!°    committed / shrunk

Aber weiter! Da vorne komme ich zur berühmten Allee „Unter den Linden."° Hier werde ich den Wagen mal parken und zu Fuß gehen. Das ist aber eine wirklich schöne Allee mit ihren zwei Reihen von Bäumen in der Mitte; dazwischen, im Schatten der Bäume, der Fußgängerweg und daneben, auf beiden Seiten, die Straße und der Bürgersteig. Das ist also der Ort, an dem sich ein großer Teil des kulturellen und politischen Lebens besonders des Zweiten und Dritten Reiches abspielte!° Und einige Monumente dieser Epochen in der Geschichte Deutschlands sind immer noch da: das alte Museum, die    took place

under the Linden Trees

---

[3] Now a mere grassy knoll, the bunker in which Hitler died is very close to the Berlin Wall.

[4] The "Third Empire," the Nazis' dramatic name for their state (1933–45), was in fact taken from the title of a book published in 1923 by Arthur Moeller van den Bruck (1876–1925), a cultural critic whom the Nazis denied as a precursor. The First Reich was the Holy Roman Empire (of the German Nation), which Napoleon ended by force in 1806; the Second Reich (1871–1918) was the new empire created by the policies of Bismarck.

Staatsbibliothek, die Humboldt-Universität,[5] etwas weiter unten der
Berliner Dom.[6]

    Wohin rennen denn die Leute? Ach, die Wachablösung!° Schwarz     changing of the guard
uniformierte Soldaten, Stechschritt.° Woran erinnert mich das? Kann     goose step
man hier ein Echo des Dritten Reiches hören?

    Ich glaube, ich gehe lieber in die andere Richtung. Da ist der weite
Platz, in dessen Mitte das imposante „Brandenburger Tor" steht. Unter dem Tor geht ein braun-rot uniformierter russischer Soldat auf und
ab. Woran muß ich nun wieder denken? Ach ja, der Stadtteil, worin
ich mich befinde, heißt „Mitte". Nannte nicht Thomas Mann einmal

[5] Originally the University of Berlin, founded in 1810; later renamed by the East German
regime for the university's founder, Alexander von Humboldt.

[6] Severely damaged during the war, the Berlin Cathedral has not been rebuilt. It is a
blackened mass of stone.

*Kaiser-Wilhelm-Gedächtniskirche*

Deutschland „das Reich der Mitte"?[7] Ja, ja, wenn es nur noch in der Mitte wäre! Der Osten ist bis in die Mitte vorgedrungen.° penetrated

Aber jetzt zurück zum Auto und schnell noch zum Alexanderplatz. Hier sind lange Reihen von großen Geschäfts- und Wohnhäusern in etwas einförmigem° Stil. Pastellfarbige Rechtecke° sollen wohl die Monotonie des Baustils etwas auflockern.° uniform / pastel-colored  squares relieve

Da drüben ist das moderne Wahrzeichen von Ost-Berlin, der Fernsehturm,[8] worauf sich ein großes Restaurant befindet, das sich langsam dreht. Wenn ich daran denke, dreht sich mir der Magen. Wenn ich esse, bin ich lieber auf festem° Boden. Ich gehe mal in das Restaurant, das sich da auf der anderen Seite des unglaublich weiten Platzes befindet. Das Gehen wird mich noch hungriger und durstiger machen. solid

[7] In a famous defense of the Weimar Republic (1919–33), Thomas Mann used the term **Mitte** in the sense of a mean between extremist tendencies.

[8] The Television Tower was the East German regime's first great prestige project—357 meters (1170 feet) high. It dominates the Berlin landscape and has a revolving restaurant 800 feet above the ground. Since it had to be erected on Berlin's sandy soil, the tower represents a great engineering feat and is seen by East Germans as a symbol of their capital.

*Brandenburger Tor*

*Karl-Marx-Allee*

Die Studenten, mit denen ich da im Restaurant gesprochen habe, waren wirklich sehr nett. Volkswirtschaft° studieren sie. Aber warum mußte ich Ihnen auch so eine dumme Frage stellen, worauf sie nicht antworteten. Was für Theorien sie studieren müssen? Marxistische° Theorien natürlich, ich Esel. Was werden sich diese jungen Leute wohl gedacht haben? Jetzt aber zurück in die Volkswirtschaft des Westens.

political science

Marxist

Gut, daß der Checkpoint Charlie wieder hinter mir ist! Da vorne ist der Kudamm. Was für eine Menschenmasse und was für ein Verkehr! Auf der anderen Seite war es wenigstens ruhiger! Und die vielen Lichter machen mich fast blind. Fast scheint es mir, daß der ausgebrannte° Turm der Gedächtniskirche[9] gedankenvoll° auf die Stadt heruntersieht.

burnt-out / thoughtfully

[9] The **Kaiser-Wilhelm-Gedächtniskirche,** whose blackened main tower has been left as a war memorial. It and the modern church now built beside it are known simply as the Memorial Church (**Gedächtniskirche**)—a symbol of Berlin's indomitable will to live even in the midst of rubble, as it had to do for a long time after the war.

## Questions

1. Wonach fragt der Vopo den Besucher?
2. Warum schaut der Vopo in und unter den Wagen?
3. Woran erkennt man die Verkehrspolizistin?
4. Wonach sucht der Besucher in Ost-Berlin?
5. Wo parkt unser Besucher seinen Wagen?
6. Was sieht man nur noch von Hitlers Bunker?
7. Was sind einige Monumente, die aus der Vergangenheit Deutschlands erzählen?
8. Wo steht das Brandenburger Tor?
9. Wer geht darunter auf und ab?
10. Was ist das Wahrzeichen von Ost-Berlin?
11. Welche dumme Frage hat der Besucher den Studenten gestellt? Warum ist diese Frage dumm?
12. Wo möchten Sie lieber einen Besuch machen, in Ost-Berlin oder in West-Berlin? Warum?

**A.** *Meet—but don't hit—each other! The verb* **(sich) treffen.**

**Treffen** means *to hit or strike a target,* as with an arrow.

> Er hat einen Stein auf den Hund geworfen und ihn getroffen.
>
> *He threw a rock at the dog and hit him.*

What would this sentence mean: **Ich habe daneben getroffen.**

The participle **treffend** means *well-aimed, to the point:* **ein treffendes Wort** (*a pertinent word*).

**Treffen** can also mean to meet someone: **Wir haben ihn gestern in der Stadt getroffen.** In this sense, the verb may also occur in the reflexive form: **Sie trafen sich spät am Abend.**

As a reflexive, it may also be used in the idiom **Das (es) trifft sich gut** (*that's lucky, fortunate*).

**B. Wirt, Wirtschaft, Volkswirtschaft**

**Der Wirt (die Wirtin)** is an *innkeeper* or *host.*

> Ich werde den Wirt machen.
>
> *I'll do the honors.*

**Die Wirtschaft** is *an inn,* but can also mean *management of affairs* or, pejoratively, *a mess.*

> Was ist das für eine Wirtschaft!
>
> *What a mess!*

**Die Volkswirtschaft** means *public economy* or *political science*—not a "mess," though it often seems so! What then is **ein Volkswirt?**

**A.** *Replace the* **da** *compound by a prepositional phrase that includes the words in parentheses.*

1. Wir wohnen direkt daneben. (*factory*)
2. Du wirst hoffentlich bald darüber erzählen. (*your examination*)
3. Hat er wirklich nichts davon gegessen? (*meat*)
4. Die Eltern hatten schon darüber gehört. (*wedding*)
5. In einem Moment werden wir auch darüber sprechen. (*accident*)
6. Damit kann er kein Geld verdienen. (*his humor*)

7. Vor Jahrhunderten wußte man davon noch nicht viel. (*wedding*)
8. Leider fängt er schon wieder an, davon zu reden. (*his illness*)
9. Mir hat wenig daran gefallen. (*her interpretation*)
10. Darüber sollten Sie nicht lachen. (*my poems*)
11. Davon versteht Ursula mehr als ich. (*mountain climbing*)

**B.** *Answer the questions by using the words in parentheses.*

1. Wovon hat er dir etwas gezeigt? (*of the museums and monuments*)
2. Womit sollen wir jetzt weiterfahren? (*by train*)
3. Wozu habt ihr keine Zeit? (*to talk with visitors*)
4. Wodurch wurde diese schöne, alte Stadt berühmt? (*through its cathedral*)
5. Wovon spricht der Politiker gerade? (*about the catastrophe*)
6. Womit fuhr der Kerl gegen einen Baum? (*with his car*)
7. Wovon redet er? (*about Hitler's suicide*)
8. Womit kocht man Kaffee? (*with water*)
9. Worüber stellt er Fragen? (*about the architectural style of this building*)
10. Wozu braucht man einen Koffer? (*in order to travel*)

**C.** *Express in German. In cases of probability, use the future perfect.*

1. We cannot talk about it now.
2. I will probably have paid for it by (*bis*) June.
3. With what were the children playing?
4. What he's writing about doesn't interest me.
5. You were probably sitting in front of the television set when we called.
6. She must have been very hungry.
7. He knows much more about that than about German literature.
8. Surely she has been a member of this club for a long time.
9. I guess Wilfried's parents weren't very delighted about his plans.
10. Inge told him something that perhaps he didn't know yet.

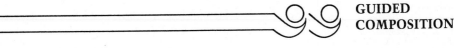

**GUIDED COMPOSITION**

Write a short monologue on the thoughts and impressions that you had when driving into a new city or country. Describe some of the architectural features or public monuments that impressed you most. You may also report some of the conversations you had with strangers or friends. Use **da** and **wo** compounds whenever possible, and one or two sentences in the future perfect.

**VOCABULARY**

## Easily recognized words

| | | | | | | |
|---|---|---|---|---|---|---|
| | **bitter** | *bitter* | der | **Selbstmord, -e** | *suicide* | |
| | **blind** | *blind* | der | **Soldat, -en** | *soldier* | |
| die | **Epoche, -n** | *epoch* | das | **Tor, -e** | *gate* | |
| | **exotisch** | *exotic* | der | **Turm, ⸚e** | *tower* | |
| das | **Monument, -e** | *monument* | das | **Wahrzeichen, -** | *landmark* | |
| das | **Museum, die Museen** | *museum* | das | **Wohnhaus, ⸚er** | *apartment building* | |

| | | | | | |
|---|---|---|---|---|---|
| die | **Allee, -n** | *avenue* | | **auf·halten (hält), hielt, aufgehalten** | *to stop, hinder* |
| der | **Autostop** | *hitchhiking;* **per Autostop reisen** *to hitchhike* | sich | **drehen** | *to turn* |
| der | **Baustil, -e** | *architectural style* | sich | **entscheiden, entschied, entschieden** | *to decide* |
| der | **Besucher, -** | *visitor* | | **halten für** (+ *acc.*) **(hält), hielt, gehalten** | *to take for, consider* |
| der | **Deckel, -** | *top, lid* | sich | **nähern** | *to approach* |
| der | **Esel, -** | *jackass* | | **werfen (wirft), warf, geworfen** | *to throw* |
| das | **Geschäftshaus, ⸚er** | *business building* | | | |
| das | **Gras, ⸚er** | *grass* | | | |
| die | **Landkarte, -n** | *map* | | **berühmt** | *famous* |
| das | **Licht, -er** | *light* | | **komisch** | *funny* |
| der | **Magen, -** | *stomach* | | **kulturell** | *cultural* |
| die | **Masse, -n** | *mass, crowd* | | **prima!** | *great! (slang)* |
| die | **Mauer, -n** | *wall* | | **ruhig** | *quiet* |
| das | **Reich, -e** | *empire* | | **russisch** (*adj.*) | *Russian* |
| die | **Reihe, -n** | *row* | | **uniformiert** | *in uniform* |
| die | **Seite, -n** | *side* | | | |

# 17

## MODEL SENTENCES

München **wird** manchmal „die geheime Hauptstadt der Bundesrepublik" **genannt.**
*Munich is sometimes called the secret capital of the Federal Republic.*

Ich **wurde** von weinenden Kindern **geweckt.**
*I was awakened by crying children.*

Die gute Luft **ist** von der Industrie **verschmutzt worden.**
*The good air has been polluted by industry.*

Die berühmte Bierstube in München **kann** heute noch **besichtigt werden.**
*The famous beer hall in Munich can be visited to this day.*

Du **mußt** in eine bessere Laune **versetzt werden.**
*You need to be cheered up.*

Hier **wird** nicht **getanzt!**
*No dancing here!*

Es **wurde** viel **erzählt** und **gelacht.**
*There was much talk and laughter.*

## Passive voice

**A.** *Formation*

The passive in English is formed from the auxiliary *to be* and the past participle of the principal verb.

The "Oktoberfest" *is celebrated* every year in the early fall.
The letter *was (being) written* by Karl.

In German the passive voice is formed by using the conjugated form of the auxiliary **werden** and the past participle of the principal verb. The passive voice can be formed in all six tenses merely by conjugating the auxiliary **werden.**

| | | |
|---|---|---|
| PRES.: | Der Brief **wird** von Karl **ge-schrieben.** | *The letter is (being) written by Karl.* |
| PRES. PERF.: | Der Brief **ist** von Karl **geschrieben worden.** | *The letter has been written by Karl.* |
| PAST: | Der Brief **wurde** von Karl **geschrieben.** | *The letter was (being) written by Karl.* |
| PAST PERF.: | Der Brief **war** von Karl **geschrieben worden.** | *The letter had been written by Karl.* |
| FUTURE: | Der Brief **wird** von Karl **geschrieben werden.** | *The letter will be written by Karl.* |
| FUT. PERF.: | Der Brief **wird** von Karl **geschrieben worden sein.** | *The letter will have been written by Karl.* |

In the perfect tenses, note that the past participle of the auxiliary **werden** drops the **ge-: worden;** this form occurs only in the passive and only in these tenses. Also notice that the auxiliary of **werden** is **sein.**

## Check your comprehension

*Put the following verbs into the passive voice, using the indicated subject and tense.*

EXAMPLE: Ich / aufhalten (*present perfect*)
**Ich bin aufgehalten worden.**

1. Sie (*3rd sing.*) / erkennen (*past*)
2. Die Frage / entscheiden (*future*)
3. Das Problem / lösen (*present perfect*)

4. Das Theater / aufbauen (*present*)

5. Die Städte / besetzen (*past perfect*)

6. Die Dörfer / zerstören (*future perfect*)

7. Diese Mauer / verstärken (*present perfect*)

8. Ein Walzer / spielen (*past*)

**B.** *Usage*

The passive voice is used when the subject does *not* perform the action, but is *acted upon.*

Die Stadt München wird jedes Jahr
von vielen Touristen besucht.   *The city of Munich is visited by
many tourists every year.*

Since the focus of a sentence is usually on the subject, the passive voice allows the speaker to emphasize the receiver, rather than the performer, of the action. Compare the above sentence with its equivalent in the active voice:

Viele Touristen besuchen jedes Jahr
die Stadt München.   *Many tourists visit the city of
Munich every year.*

Here the emphasis is on **viele Touristen.**

  In the passive voice the performer of the action (or "agent") may thus be omitted:

Sie wird jeden Tag am Bahnhof
(von ihrem Mann) abgeholt.   *Every day she is picked up at the
railway station (by her husband).*

In passive constructions, the performer of the action is used in conjunction with a preposition, in German usually with **von.** Remember that **von** always governs the dative case.

Sie wird jeden Tag **von ihm** abgeholt.   *She is picked up by him every day.*

Notice the structural changes as a sentence is converted from the active into the passive voice.

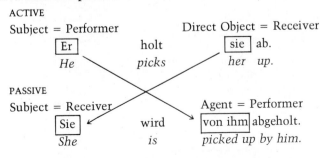

## Check your comprehension

*A. Form the passive voice in the tense indicated in parentheses.*

1. Er _____ lange _____. (*aufhalten, present perfect*)
2. Der Schauspieler _____ sofort vom Publikum _____. (*erkennen, past*)
3. Wir _____ am Bahnhof _____. (*abholen, future*)
4. Dieser junge Professor _____ für einen Studenten _____. (*halten, present*)
5. Das Problem _____ endlich _____. (*lösen, present perfect*)
6. Von wem _____ diese Theorie _____? (*ausdenken, present perfect*)
7. Ein Teil der Kirche _____ während des Krieges _____. (*zerstören, past perfect*)
8. Nach dem Krieg _____ sie wieder _____. (*aufbauen, past*)

*B. Change the following sentences from the active to the passive voice.*

1. Sie hat dieses Gedicht sehr gut interpretiert.
2. Er ruft sie jeden Tag an.
3. Die Professoren haben das Problem sehr lange besprochen.
4. Sie hatte ihn gleich erkannt.

**C.** *Passive voice with modal auxiliaries*

A sentence in the passive voice may of course contain a modal auxiliary, especially in the present and the simple past. In that case the word order is: conjugated form of the modal + past participle of the principal verb + infinitive of **werden.**

> Hilde **will** vom Bahnhof **abgeholt werden.**     *Hilde wants to be picked up at the railroad station.*

## Check your comprehension

*Form a sentence in the passive voice with the modal indicated in parentheses.*

EXAMPLE: Er zeigte dieses Bild nicht. (*dürfen*)
**Dieses Bild durfte von ihm nicht gezeigt werden.**

1. Mit der finanziellen Hilfe seines Vaters eröffnete er eine Klinik. (*können*)
2. Ingeborg interpretiert ein bekanntes Gedicht von Schiller. (*sollen*)
3. Was für Theorien studiert ihr bei Professor Weimann? (*müssen*)
4. Wir besprechen dieses Problem jetzt nicht. (*können*)
5. Seine Freunde verhöhnten ihn nicht. (*wollen*)

**D.** *Special problems with the passive in German*

In English the indirect object in the active voice can be made into the subject of the passive voice.

| INDIRECT OBJECT | SUBJECT |
|---|---|
| They told *him* the truth. | *He* was told the truth. |

In German this is not possible. The direct object of the active voice is always used as the subject in the passive voice. The indirect object remains in the dative case.

| | |
|---|---|
| Man sagte **ihm** die Wahrheit. | *They told him the truth.* |
| Die Wahrheit wurde **ihm** gesagt. | *He was told the truth.*<br>*(The truth was told to him.)* |

For the sake of emphasis, the indirect object may move to first position in the sentence.

| | |
|---|---|
| **Ihm** wurde die Wahrheit gesagt. | *They told him the truth.* |

This leads to certain constructions seemingly without a subject, often called *impersonal* sentences, which occur primarily with verbs that govern the dative case (**mir wurde gedankt**) or in situations where the direct object is a subordinate clause (**mir wurde gesagt, daß . . .**). Thus it is *not* possible to say „Ich wurde gesagt, daß . . .“ (*I was told that . . .*) because, in this instance, the verb **sagen** governs the dative case. The construction **mir wurde gesagt, daß . . .** is used instead.

In such clauses, the rather meaningless "filler" **es** can at times be used as a subject.

| | |
|---|---|
| **Es** wurde **mir** gesagt, daß . . . | *I was told that . . .* |

But if some other expression is in first position in the sentence, such as an adverb of time or the indirect object, the **es** is not required. Note that **es,** however, is always the *implied subject,* therefore the verb is always in the third-person singular.

| | |
|---|---|
| Gestern abend wurde ihm gesagt, daß . . . | *Last night he was told that . . .* |
| Ihnen wurde gesagt, daß . . . | *They were told that . . .* |

Notice that in the active voice the indefinite **man** would be used.

| | |
|---|---|
| **Man** sagte ihm gestern abend, daß . . . | *Last night they told him that . . .* |
| **Man** sagte ihnen, daß . . . | *They told them that . . .* |

*Hofbräuhaus*

The passive voice of some verbs, such as **arbeiten** and **lachen,** which do not normally govern an accusative object, may express *an activity as such.* This leads to a characteristically German construction that can hardly be translated.

| | |
|---|---|
| Hier wird gearbeitet. ⎱ <br> Es wird hier gearbeitet. ⎰ | *There is work going on here.* <br> *(Lit.: Here is being worked.)* |
| Es wurde viel gelacht. | *There was much laughing.* <br> *(Lit.: It was being laughed a lot.)* |

Frequently such impersonal passive constructions are used as commands.

| | |
|---|---|
| Hier wird nicht geraucht! | ⎰ *There will be no smoking here.* <br> ⎱ *No smoking here!* |
| Es wird nicht geredet! | ⎰ *There will be no talking.* <br> ⎱ *No talking!* |

## Check your comprehension

**A.** *Put the following sentences into the passive voice, first without* **es** *and then with it.*

1. Man machte ihm klar, daß . . .
2. Man versprach uns nichts.
3. Man wird Ihnen nicht danken.

**B.** *Translate the following sentences into English.*

1. Es wurde getrunken.
2. Was wird hier vorbereitet?
3. Hier wird nicht getanzt.

## USEFUL PHRASES

| | |
|---|---|
| **Dem kann eben nicht abgeholfen werden.** | *Too bad, but that can't be helped.* |
| **Stimmt.** | { *Agreed.*<br>{ *True.* |
| **So schlimm ist es wiederum nicht.** | *It's not as bad as all that.* |
| **In eine bessere Laune versetzen** | *to cheer up (someone)* |
| **Zum Teufel nochmal!** | *To hell with it!* |

## CONVERSATION

## *Die¹ Maß Bier*

*Josef, der in New York bei einer deutschen Firma arbeitet, befindet sich in seiner Heimatstadt München auf einer Geschäftsreise und kommt mit seinem alten Freund Franz in einer Bierstube° zusammen.*

beer hall

FRANZ Und hast du einen angenehmen Flug über den Atlantik gehabt?
JOSEF Das Übliche. Es wurde viel gegessen und getrunken und, wie immer, wurde irgendein alter Film gezeigt.

¹ In Munich and most parts of Bavaria **die Maß,** denoting a tankard or stein, is used in the feminine. **Das Maß,** however, means *measure, size, dimension,* etc.

FRANZ Konntest du dich auch etwas ausruhen?

JOSEF Ach was! Ich wurde immer wieder von weinenden Kindern oder herumspazierenden Passagieren geweckt.

FRANZ Ja, ja, dem kann eben nicht abgeholfen werden.

JOSEF Stimmt, es ist wie im Krankenhaus. Man schläft ein, um gleich wieder aufgeweckt zu werden.

FRANZ Na, so schlimm ist es wiederum nicht. Du mußt in eine bessere Laune versetzt werden. (*Zur Kellnerin:*) Zwei Maß, bitte!

*Die Kellnerin bringt zwei enorme Krüge Bier.*

FRANZ Zum Teufel nochmal! Sieh dir mal diese Maß an!

JOSEF Was ist denn los?

FRANZ Zwei oder drei Zentimeter Schaum°. Der große Betrug° im    *foam / fraud*
Krug! Die Maß sollte um zwei Zentimeter verlängert werden! Mehr Raum für Bier und Schaum![2]

JOSEF Na, so schlimm ist es wiederum nicht. Trink doch! Du mußt in eine bessere Laune versetzt werden!

[2] A large number of beer-drinking enthusiasts in Munich have formed an association, the **Verein gegen betrügerisches Einschenken** (*Association against Fraudulent Drafting*) to reduce the amount of foam served in a stein of beer!

## Questions

1. Bei was für einer Firma arbeitet Josef in New York?
2. Warum ist Josef in München?
3. Wie war Josefs Flug über den Atlantik?

4. Wurde auf dem Flug ein Film gezeigt?

5. Warum konnte Josef sich nicht ausruhen?

6. Woran erinnert Josef sein Flug über den Atlantik?

7. Womit will Franz seinen Freund Josef in eine bessere Laune versetzen?

8. Fliegen Sie gern? Warum?

9. Sind Sie schon einmal über den Atlantik geflogen? Wohin?

10. Kann man in einer amerikanischen Bierstube eine Maß bestellen?

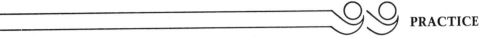 **PRACTICE**

**A.** *Change the following sentences from the active to the passive voice. Watch the change in the subject (the performer of the action), and be careful of the verb tense.*

EXAMPLE: Die Passagiere haben Josef geweckt.
**Josef ist von den Passagieren geweckt worden.**

1. Der Feind hat einen großen Teil der Stadt zerstört.

2. Die Studenten kaufen hier ihre Bücher.

3. Die Kellnerin hat uns zwei enorme Maß Bier gebracht.

4. Sie hat uns an den Stadtrand geführt.

5. Auf dem Flug aß man wenig und trank viel.

6. Mein Bruder weckt mich jeden Morgen um sechs Uhr.

7. Hier darf man nicht rauchen.

8. Man öffnet das Museum schon sehr früh.

9. Man hat einen berühmten Walzer gespielt.

10. Er hat den Brief zerrissen.

11. Ich habe gestern Herrn und Frau Kunz zum Konzert eingeladen.

12. Er wird die Musik zu Weihnachten spielen.

13. Mein Vater hat mir einen weißen Volkswagen versprochen.

14. Frauen rauchen Zigarren und Pfeife nicht oft.

15. Klara brachte nur wenig Gepäck mit.

**B.** *Using the impersonal construction, change each sentence into the passive voice.*

EXAMPLES: Man sagte uns, daß wir hier bleiben können.
**Uns wurde gesagt, daß wir hier bleiben können.**

Man arbeitet hier viel.
**Hier wird viel gearbeitet.**

1. Man sagte mir, heute ist Sonntag.

2. Man antwortete ihm auf seine Frage.

3. Man tanzte den ganzen Abend.

4. Man erzählt uns von dem Museum.
5. Man redete viel.

**C.** *Put the following sentences into the active voice.*

1. Mir werden die Haare geschnitten.
2. Uns wird die Landkarte geschickt.
3. Uns wird Wein gebracht.
4. Ein Taxi wird für sie gerufen.
5. Du wirst mit dem Büro verbunden.

**D.** *Put the sentences in exercise C into the present perfect.*

**E.** *Give the English equivalent.*

1. Dieses Auto ist gestern nicht gefahren worden.
2. Dieses Buch wurde von den Studenten nicht gut verstanden.
3. Diese Platte ist von ihr nicht gespielt worden.
4. Darüber wird sehr viel kommentiert.
5. Darüber wird wohl sehr oft gestritten.
6. Ihm wird von seinen Freunden sehr geholfen.
7. Dieser Brief soll von uns unterschrieben werden.
8. Die Maß muß um ein paar Zentimeter verlängert werden.
9. Auf dem Flug wurde viel gegessen und wenig geschlafen.
10. Diesem Problem muß abgeholfen werden.

Ask your neighbor what people do during a flight (perhaps an overseas flight). In some of your sentences practice the impersonal passive form: **Es wird . . . (gegessen, geredet,** etc.). As an opening you may use one of several grammatical versions of what is fundamentally the same question:

> Was tut man während eines Fluges?
> Was tun die Passagiere während eines Fluges?
> Was tust du (tun Sie) während eines Fluges?

The picture above may give you some ideas.

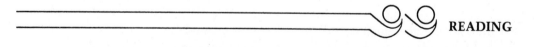

**READING**

## *München und das Oktoberfest*

München wird manchmal „die geheime Hauptstadt der Bundesrepublik" genannt, denn sie hat jene Eigenschaften, die oft mit einer Hauptstadt verbunden werden. Sie hat ein reges kulturelles Leben— viele Theater, Museen, Bibliotheken, Orchester und heutzutage auch Filmproduktionsgesellschaften°—und viele schöne Paläste und Kirchen, in denen die großen Baustile der Vergangenheit, zum Beispiel der Barock, das Rokoko oder der Neo-Klassizismus,[1] großartig verwirk-

film production companies

---

[1] *Baroque, rococo, neoclassicism:* important architectural styles.

licht° worden sind. Sie hat aber auch schöne Parks und viel „saubere"   realized
Industrie, durch die die gute Luft, die von den Alpen herunterweht°,   blows down
nicht zu sehr verschmutzt wird. Die Alpen liegen nur ungefähr 45
Kilometer außerhalb der Stadt und können an schönen Tagen von den
Türmen der bekannten Frauenkirche[2] gesehen werden.

Im Jahr 1972 wurden in München die Olympischen Spiele ausgetragen, wofür ein großer Teil der Stadt restauriert wurde. Auch
wurde ein großes, modernes Stadion gebaut und eine Untergrundbahn, durch die der Straßenverkehr sehr erleichtert worden ist. Nach
Berlin und Hamburg ist jetzt München die drittgrößte Stadt in der

[2] A cathedral built in the fifteenth century, whose massive cupola-capped towers are
conspicuous landmarks of Munich.

Bundesrepublik und wird jedes Jahr von mehr Touristen als die meisten anderen Städte Deutschlands besucht.

Wie die meisten Städte Deutschlands hat München eine Geschichte, die bis ins Mittelalter zurückgeht. In der neuesten Geschichte wird die Stadt oft auch als Ausgangspunkt° der Nazi-Bewegung genannt, denn im Jahre 1923 fand da der Hitler-Putsch[3] in einer Bierstube statt, die heute noch besichtigt werden kann. Aber trotz dieses schwarzen Blattes° in ihrer Geschichte hat die Stadt nach dem Krieg ihre frühere „Gemütlichkeit" wiedergefunden. Bezeichnend für diese Gemütlichkeit ist das Oktoberfest, wofür München in der ganzen Welt bekannt geworden ist.

Das Oktoberfest beginnt Mitte September und hört Anfang Oktober auf. Es wurde zum ersten Mal im Jahr 1810 gefeiert. Es ist eine Art Jahrmarkt, an dem sich das ganze Volk über zwei Wochen lang großartig unterhält. Es gibt Umzüge durch die ganze Stadt, zu denen die meisten Gegenden Deutschlands und viele andere Länder Europas, zum Beispiel Österreich, die Schweiz oder Italien, ihre folkloristischen Gruppen senden.

Von manchen dieser Gruppen werden auch Vorstellungen gege-

starting point

leaf, page

[3] A revolt staged on November 8, 1923, by Hitler and his Nazi followers, which failed. But within ten years the Nazis came to power in Germany.

ben. Volkstänze werden von den vielen „Dirndln und Buam"⁴ aufge-
führt, und natürlich werden auch viele Volkslieder gesungen. Und auf
der „Wies'n"⁵ gibt es Schaubuden° und Verkaufsstände°. Es wird viel
getanzt und noch viel mehr getrunken. Münchner Bier, natürlich,
denn das Oktoberfest wird besonders von den weltbekannten Braue-
reien Münchens organisiert und unterstützt. Das Fest wird in einer
großen Halle vom Oberbürgermeister° der Stadt eröffnet. Er zapft ein
großes Faß° Bier an und erklärt „o'zapft is!"⁶ Und dann geht es los!

    Wer einmal erfahren will, was die Worte des alten Volksliedes
„Trink, trink, Brüderlein° trink, lasse die Sorgen zu Haus" bedeuten,
der muß einmal nach München zum Oktoberfest gehen. Man kann
da tatsächlich für kurze Zeit seine Sorgen vergessen. Es kann aber
auch sein, daß man am Tag nach dem Fest mit einem großen Kater
aufwacht.

booths for games / vending
  stands

Lord Mayor
barrel

little brother

⁴ **Dirndln** (also **Dirndls**) is a dialect term, used especially in Bavaria and Austria, for *girl*
or *young woman*. **Buam** is an approximation of the Bavarian pronunciation of **Buben**,
here meaning *young men*.

⁵ Bavarian for **Wiese**, a big open space (i.e., meadow) where the fair is held.

⁶ Bavarian for **Es ist angezapft!** *It (the barrel) has been tapped!*

## Questions

1. Warum wird München manchmal „die geheime Hauptstadt der Bundesrepublik" genannt?
2. Was hat München an kulturellen Dingen zu bieten?
3. Warum ist die Luft in München so gut?
4. Wie weit entfernt sind die Alpen von München?
5. Welches sind die zwei größten Städte der Bundesrepublik?
6. Wie weit geht die Geschichte Münchens zurück?
7. Wann beginnt das Oktoberfest und wann hört es auf?
8. Wer organisiert und unterstützt das Oktoberfest?
9. Wie weit geht die Geschichte Ihrer Stadt zurück?
10. Was für Feste werden in Ihrer Stadt gefeiert?

## VOCABULARY DEVELOPMENT

**A. Maß halten ist gut!** *(To know one's bounds is good.)*

**Das Maß** has many uses and meanings. Fundamentally it means measure, measurement, size, dimension, gauge; also proportion and moderation. (As you see, in its range of meaning it is not that moderate!) Some examples:

| | |
|---|---|
| in hohem Maße | *to a high degree* |
| in großem Maße | *to a large extent* |
| in gewissem Maße | *to a certain extent* |
| in vollem Maße | *amply, completely* |

(Notice that in these set expressions the old dative ending **-e** is retained.) Tell your neighbor what kind of activities (talking, smoking, swimming, etc.) you enjoy, and to what extent.

You will also find **das Maß** in some idioms such as:

| | |
|---|---|
| Das Maß ist voll. | *My patience is exhausted.* |
| Das geht über alle Maßen. | *That exceeds all bounds.* |
| Das Maß vollmachen. | *Fill the cup to the brim.* |

What then is **ein Anzug nach Maß**? And what is the meaning of: **Halte Maß in allen Dingen!** Do you agree? The adjective derived from **Maß** is **mäßig**, its antonym **unmäßig**. State whether you do certain things (sleeping, eating, drinking, dancing, etc.) **mäßig** or **unmäßig**.

**B.** *What do you prefer,* **aufwachen** *or* **(auf)wecken?**

The verb **auf·wachen** means *to awaken, wake up (oneself).* The verb **auf·wecken,** however, means *to wake somebody else up.* Now answer the following questions:

> Um wieviel Uhr wachst du auf?
>
> Wachen Sie immer selber auf oder müssen Sie (auf)geweckt werden?
>
> Haben Sie einen Wecker *(alarm clock)*?

What would be **ein aufgewecktes Mädchen?**

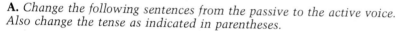

**REVIEW**

**A.** *Change the following sentences from the passive to the active voice. Also change the tense as indicated in parentheses.*

1. Auf seiner Reise ist er von vielen Autofahrern mitgenommen worden. *(past)*
2. Von den Studenten wurden verschiedene Theorien zur Psychologie diskutiert. *(present perfect)*
3. Das Medizinstudium ist von Renate im Herbst begonnen worden. *(present)*
4. Die finanzielle Hilfe für das Studium wird vom Staat organisiert. *(past perfect)*
5. Dieses Buch ist sicher nicht von ihm geschrieben worden. *(past)*
6. Diese Vorlesung muß von uns natürlich besprochen werden. *(past)*
7. Die größten Namen der Musik werden oft mit der Geschichte Wiens verbunden. *(present perfect)*
8. Während des Krieges wurde ein großer Teil dieser Stadt von Napoleon zerstört. *(past perfect)*
9. Mir ist gestern von meinem Arzt ein psychologischer Test gegeben worden. *(past)*
10. Die Sachertorte ist von uns sofort gegessen worden. *(present)*
11. Diese Ehe mußte als ein großes Risiko betrachtet werden. *(present)*
12. Von den Männern muß im Haushalt mehr getan werden. *(past)*

**B.** *Complete the following passive sentences with the cue in parentheses.*

1. Im Kriegsfall _____ die Barrieren auf der Autobahn _____. *(can be removed)*
2. In den USA _____ langsamer als in Europa _____. *(one drives)*
3. München _____ als die geheime Hauptstadt der Bundesrepublik _____ _____. *(can be considered)*

> *Mit freundlichen Grüßen*
> *With kind regards*
> *Avec nos compliments*
>
> Landeshauptstadt München, Fremdenverkehrsamt
> Munich Tourist Office
> Office du Tourisme de Munich
>
> Rindermarkt 5, D-8000 München 2
> Tel. (089) 2 39 11, Telex 05-24 801 frast d

4. Das Rathaus _____ vor vielen Jahren _____ _____. (*was destroyed*)

5. Hitlers Bierstube _____ heute noch _____ _____. (*can be seen*)

6. Die Vergangenheit _____ manchmal durch die Augen der Gegenwart _____ _____. (*has to be understood*)

7. Das Theater _____ vom Film und Fernsehen _____ _____. (*has been replaced*)

8. Es _____ _____ _____, daß England auf eine lange Tradition zurückschauen kann. (*has to be recognized*)

9. Auf diesem Fest _____ viele Volkslieder _____. (*were sung*)

10. Während der Pause _____ Sekt _____ und Kuchen _____. (*is being drunk, eaten*)

**C.** *Express in German.*

1. The air in Munich is not being polluted by industry.
2. The Alps can be seen from the church.
3. In the year 1936 the Olympic Games were held in Berlin.
4. During the war many famous theaters, museums, and libraries were destroyed.
5. This city is being visited by many tourists every year.
6. The city of Munich has become famous for its "Oktoberfest."
7. Performances were given by many groups.
8. The Olympic Games are being organized and supported by almost all countries.
9. I don't want to be awakened by crying children.
10. She had to be cheered up by me.

## GUIDED COMPOSITION

Describe what people in your town or region do at a local festival, such as a county or state fair. Are there parades? Who participates (**teilnehmen an** + *dat.*)? Is there a lot of dancing, drinking, eating? Are there special performances given by certain groups? The picture above may give you some suggestions.

## VOCABULARY

### Easily recognized words

| | | | | |
|---|---|---|---|---|
| der | **Atlantik** | *Atlantic* | **organisieren** | *to organize* |
| der | **Diskjockey,** -s | *disk-jockey (in a discothèque)* | das **Stadion,** die **Stadien** | *stadium* |
| das | **Fest,** -e | *festival* | der **Volkstanz,** ⸚e | *folk dance* |
| | **folkloristisch** | *folkloric* | | |
| das | **Orchester,** - | *orchestra* | die **Bewegung,** -en | *movement* |

| | | |
|---|---|---|
| die | **Eigenschaft, -en** | *characteristic, attribute* |
| der | **Flug, ⸚e** | *flight* |
| die | **Gegend, -en** | *region, area* |
| die | **Gemütlichkeit** | *coziness* |
| die | **Geschäftsreise, -n** | *business trip* |
| die | **Hauptstadt, ⸚e** | *capital* |
| der | **Jahrmarkt, ⸚e** | *annual fair* |
| der | **Kater, -** | *hangover (slang)* |
| die | **Kellnerin, -nen** | *waitress* |
| das | **Krankenhaus, ⸚er** | *hospital* |
| der | **Krug, ⸚e** | *pitcher* |
| die | **Laune, -n** | *mood* |
| die | **Maß, -e** | *stein* |
| der | **Passagier, -e** | *passenger* |
| das | **Spiel, -e** | *game* |
| der | **Umzug, ⸚e** | *parade* |

| | |
|---|---|
| **ab·helfen (hilft), half, abgeholfen (+ *dat.*)** | *to remedy* |
| **auf·führen** | *to stage* |
| **auf·wachen** | *to wake up (oneself)* |

| | |
|---|---|
| **auf·wecken** | *to wake up (someone)* |
| sich **ausruhen** | *to rest up* |
| **aus·tragen (trägt), trug, ausgetragen** | *to carry out, hold (games)* |
| **besichtigen** | *to visit (a place), to tour* |
| **erfahren (erfährt), erfuhr, erfahren** | *to experience* |
| **erleichtern** | *to make easier, relieve* |
| **feiern** | *to celebrate* |
| **statt·finden, fand, stattgefunden** | *to take place, occur* |
| **verlängern** | *to prolong, lengthen* |
| **wecken** | *to awaken (someone)* |
| **weinen** | *to cry* |
| **zapfen** | *to tap* |

| | |
|---|---|
| **angenehm** | *pleasant* |
| **bezeichnend** | *significant, typical* |
| **geheim** | *secret* |
| **irgendein** | *some, any* |
| **rege** | *busy, lively* |
| **sauber** | *clean* |

# 18

**MODEL SENTENCES**

Peter sagte, daß er nichts von Rockkonzerten **halte/hielte.**
*Peter said that he didn't think much of rock concerts.*

Anita sagt, daß sie morgen zu Hause **sei/wäre.**
*Anita says that she'll be home tomorrow.*

Sie erzählte uns, daß sie in einem teuren Restaurant gegessen **habe/hätte.**
*She told us that she had eaten in an expensive restaurant.*

Sie versprach, sie **werde/würde** später kommen.
*She promised she would come later.*

Heinz sagte, daß er sich nicht an das Wetter gewöhnen **könne/könnte.**
*Heinz said that he couldn't get used to the weather.*

Sag deinem Bruder, er **solle/sollte** einmal mit uns ausgehen.
*Tell your brother he should go out with us sometime.*

Hilde fragte, wo der Bahnhof **sei/wäre.**
*Hilde asked where the railroad station was.*

Er erkundigte sich, ob ich etwas gelernt **habe/hätte.**
*He inquired whether I had learned anything.*

**GRAMMAR
EXPLANATION**

## I. The special subjunctive used for indirect discourse

**A.** *Formation*

The special subjunctive[1] is formed by adding to the first principal part of the verb (the infinitive stem) the same set of endings that are added to the subjunctive:

| | SINGULAR | PLURAL | | SINGULAR | PLURAL |
|---|---|---|---|---|---|
| *1st* | -e | -en | *3rd* | -e | -en |
| *2nd fam.* | -est | -et | *2nd formal* | -en | -en |

*Special subjunctive endings*

Study the forms of the special subjunctive, as compared to the present indicative.

| | **kommen** | | **laufen** | |
|---|---|---|---|---|
| | SUBJUNCTIVE | INDICATIVE | SUBJUNCTIVE | INDICATIVE |
| *ich* | komme | (komme) | laufe | (laufe) |
| *du* | kommest | (kommst) | laufest | (läufst) |
| *er* | | | | |
| *sie* | komme | (kommt) | laufe | (läuft) |
| *es* | | | | |
| *wir* | kommen | (kommen) | laufen | (laufen) |
| *ihr* | kommet | (kommt) | laufet | (lauft) |
| *sie* | kommen | (kommen) | laufen | (laufen) |
| *Sie* | kommen | (kommen) | laufen | (laufen) |

*Special subjunctive:* **kommen** *and* **laufen**

[1] Some grammarians call this "Subjunctive I," because it is based on the first principal part of the verb.

| lesen | | haben | |
|-------|-------|--------|--------|
| SUBJUNCTIVE | INDICATIVE | SUBJUNCTIVE | INDICATIVE |
| lese | (lese) | habe | (habe) |
| lesest | (liest) | habest | (hast) |
| lese | (liest) | habe | (hat) |
| lesen | (lesen) | haben | (haben) |
| leset | (lest) | habet | (habt) |
| lesen | (lesen) | haben | (haben) |
| lesen | (lesen) | haben | (haben) |

*Special subjunctive:*
**lesen** *and* **haben**

Learn also the special subjunctive of **sein.**

| | |
|---|---|
| ich sei | wir seien |
| du seist | ihr seiet |
| er sei | sie seien |
| | Sie seien |

*Special subjunctive:*
**sein**

**B.** *Usage*

In grammar, a distinction is made between direct discourse and indirect discourse. The special subjunctive is used to express indirect discourse.

Direct discourse is used when you quote someone's words directly.

Er sagte: „Ich verstehe nichts von Psychologie."  *He said, "I don't know anything about psychology."*

But since it is cumbersome, repetitive, and somewhat primitive to speak or write in direct discourse—except, of course, for dramatic or imitative purposes—direct discourse is seldom used. In most cases, indirect quotation is preferred, giving a second-hand report of someone else's words.

Er sagte, er verstehe nichts von Psychologie.  *He said he knew nothing about psychology.*

In indirect discourse quite often a shift from the first to the third person occurs, because the speaker is telling someone what a third person said.

| DIRECT DISCOURSE | INDIRECT DISCOURSE |
|---|---|
| "I am healthy." | He said he was healthy. |
| "We are healthy." | They said they were healthy. |

English also requires a change of tense, if the opening verb is in the past (*said* or *told,* for example). The present tense in the words to be reported becomes the simple past tense, and both the simple past and present perfect tenses are changed to the past perfect. A verb already in the past perfect, however, does not change.

*Tense Shift: Direct to Indirect Discourse*

| | DIRECT DISCOURSE | OPENING VERB | INDIRECT DISCOURSE |
|---|---|---|---|
| *Present* | "I am healthy." | He said | he was healthy. |
| | "I was healthy." | | |
| *Any past* | "I have been healthy." | He said | he had been healthy. |
| | "I had been healthy." | | |

In German, the shift from first to third person, as dictated by the situation, also occurs. But instead of a change in indicative tenses,

German has a change in mood. To report a statement to someone else, the special subjunctive is used in the dependent clause. By using the subjunctive, the speaker suggests that he does not know whether what he is quoting is fact; he refuses to take responsibility for the statement, neither agreeing nor disagreeing with it. In the sentence "I am very sick," for instance, the person himself says he is sick, but we do not definitely know that he is.

Which tense of the subjunctive to use depends not on the tense of the opening verb, but on the time of the reported action in relation to the speaker's time. If the times are simultaneous, use the present tense in the indirect statement. If the action reported is prior to the speaker's time, use the past tense. If the action reported is subsequent to the speaker's time, use the future tense. The opening verb may be any tense in all situations. Schematically, this system can be presented as follows:

| TIME | DIRECT DISCOURSE | OPENING VERB (ANY TENSE) | INDIRECT DISCOURSE | |
|---|---|---|---|---|
| *Simultaneous* | ,,Ich **bin** krank." | | er **sei** krank. | *Tenses of subjunctive in indirect discourse* |
| | ,,Ich **habe** genug Geld." | | er **habe** genug Geld. | |
| *Prior* | ,,Ich **war** krank." | Er sagt, Er sagte, Er hat gesagt, Er hatte gesagt, Er wird sagen, | er **sei** krank **gewesen.** | |
| | ,,Ich **hatte** genug Geld." | | er **habe** genug Geld **gehabt.** | |
| *Subsequent* | ,,Ich **werde** krank sein." | | er **werde** krank **sein.** | |
| | ,,Ich **werde** genug Geld haben." | | er **werde** genug Geld **haben.** | |

Although there are three ways of stating past time in the indicative (simple past, present perfect, and past perfect), there is only one past tense in the special subjunctive. Any one of these three tenses is reported as past of the special subjunctive in the indirect statement.

,,Ich **hatte** genug Geld."
,,Ich **habe** genug Geld **gehabt.**"　　Er sagt, er **habe** genug Geld **gehabt.**
,,Ich **hatte** genug Geld **gehabt.**"

## Check your comprehension

**A.** *Form the special subjunctive.*

1. Gerd sagt, sie _____ morgen nicht zu Hause. (*sein*)
2. Er sagte, er _____ sofort. (*kommen*)
3. Fritz hat geschrieben, er _____ letzte Woche krank geworden. (*sein*)
4. Karin erzählte uns, daß du ihn gut _____ . (*kennen*)

**B.** *Put each sentence into indirect discourse by using the opening phrase,* **Sie sagt, . . .**

1. „Karl bleibt hier."
2. „Monika ist nach Frankfurt gefahren."
3. „Willi hat das Buch noch nicht gelesen."
4. „Das Wetter ist heute furchtbar."

## II. Special problems with the special subjunctive

### A. *Special or regular subjunctive?*

Notice that the forms of the special subjunctive do not differ from the corresponding indicative forms in the first-person singular and plural, and the third-person plural and the formal address.

|          |     | INDICATIVE | SPECIAL SUBJUNCTIVE |
|----------|-----|------------|---------------------|
| *1st sing.* | ich | komme | komme |
| *1st pl.* | wir | kommen | kommen |
| *3rd pl.* | sie | kommen | kommen |
| *Formal* | Sie | kommen | kommen |

If one wishes to make sure that the form is understood as a subjunctive, it is possible to substitute the regular subjunctive forms:

> Wir schrieben ihnen, daß wir um vier Uhr **ankämen.** (instead of **ankommen**)
>
> *We wrote them that we would arrive at four.*

Many people use the regular subjunctive even in the other persons.

> Er schrieb uns, daß sie um fünf Uhr **ankäme.** (instead of **ankomme**)
>
> *He wrote us that she would arrive at five.*

Nowadays, in *conversational style* there is an increasing tendency to do away with the subjunctive in indirect discourse altogether.

> Er sagte, daß sie um sechs Uhr an-**kommt.**    *He said she'd arrive at five.*

In this area of grammar, the German language is very much in flux. But in a written, more formal style, the subjunctive in indirect discourse is maintained.

Notice also that the indirect discourse in the subordinate clause is often introduced with **daß,** which requires dependent word order.

> Er sagt, **daß** er krank **sei.**    *He says (that) he's sick.*

When **daß** is omitted, the clause returns to regular word order, with the verb in the second position.

> Er sagt, er **sei** krank.    *He says (that) he's sick.*

## Check your comprehension

*In the following sentences, use the subjunctive form that does not coincide with the form of the indicative.*

1. Er sagt, sie (*pl.*) _____ bald zurück. (*kommen*)
2. Klara erzählt uns, daß ihre Eltern noch eine Woche hier _____. (*bleiben*)
3. Fritz sagt, sie (*pl.*) _____ uns heute _____. (*anrufen*)
4. Er sagt, ihr _____ euch noch diesen Monat. (*entscheiden*)

5. Seine Eltern schrieben, sie _____ es bei uns nicht länger _____. (*aushalten*)
6. Er erzählte, daß sie alle sehr gelitten _____. (*haben*)

## B. *The modals and* WISSEN

Except in the first and third-person plural and the second-person formal, the modals and **wissen** have distinctive forms for the special subjunctive.

| | dürfen | können | mögen | müssen | sollen | wollen | wissen | |
|---|---|---|---|---|---|---|---|---|
| *ich* | dürfe | könne | möge | müsse | solle | wolle | wisse | *Special subjunctive of* |
| *du* | dürfest | könnest | mögest | müssest | sollest | wollest | wissest | *modals and* **wissen** |
| *er* *sie* *es* | dürfe | könne | möge | müsse | solle | wolle | wisse | |
| *wir* | dürfen | können | mögen | müssen | sollen | wollen | wissen | |
| *ihr* | dürfet | könnet | möget | müsset | sollet | wollet | wisset | |
| *sie* | dürfen | können | mögen | müssen | sollen | wollen | wissen | |
| *Sie* | dürfen | können | mögen | müssen | sollen | wollen | wissen | |

With these verbs, the special subjunctive is used most often in the singular, while the regular subjunctive is used in the plural.

Er sagte, du **dürfest** mit uns aus-gehen.    *He said you could go out with us.*

Er sagte, wir **dürften** mit euch aus-gehen.    *He said we could go out with you.*

## Check your comprehension

*Supply the appropriate subjunctive form.*

1. Franz sagte, er _____ lieber hier bleiben. (*wollen*)
2. Fräulein Müller sagt, daß sie mich nicht verstehen _____. (*können*)
3. Meine Eltern sagten, daß sie mir einen Brief schreiben _____. (*wollen*)
4. Er erzählte uns, daß er darüber nichts _____. (*wissen*)
5. Wir glaubten, daß sie (*pl.*) heute nicht arbeiten _____. (*müssen*)
6. Wir sagten, wir _____ alles. (*wissen*)

## C. *Imperatives and questions in indirect discourse*

If the direct discourse contains an *imperative*, it is converted into indirect discourse with the aid of the modals **sollen** or **müssen**.

| DIRECT DISCOURSE | INDIRECT DISCOURSE |
|---|---|
| „Geh nach Hause!" | Sie sagte, ich **solle/müsse** nach Hause gehen. |
| *"Go home!"* | *She said that I ought/had to go home.* |

*Questions* without a question word are rendered into indirect discourse with the help of the conjunction **ob** (*if, whether*). If there is a question word, it introduces the indirect clause.

| DIRECT DISCOURSE | | INDIRECT DISCOURSE | |
|---|---|---|---|
| „Kommt dein Vater?" | *"Is your father coming?"* | Er fragte mich, **ob** mein Vater käme. | *He asked me if my father was coming.* |
| „Wann kommt dein Vater?" | *"When is your father coming?"* | Er fragte mich, **wann** mein Vater käme. | *He asked me when my father was coming.* |

Notice that **ob** and **wann** are subordinating conjunctions, therefore dependent word order, or verb-last position, is required.

---

### Check your comprehension

*Change the sentences into indirect discourse.*

1. Hans sagt: „Komm sofort hierher!"
2. Sie sagte: „Hört auf zu reden!"
3. Sie fragt: „Wieviel Uhr ist es?"
4. Wir fragten sie: „Kommt ihr morgen zu uns?"

---

## D. **Werden** *or* **würden?**

As illustrated in the table on p. 356, a direct discourse statement in the future tense will be rendered in indirect discourse with the subjunctive forms of **werden.**

| DIRECT DISCOURSE | INDIRECT DISCOURSE |
|---|---|
| „Ich werde nicht zu spät kommen." | Er versprach, daß er nicht zu spät kommen **werde.** |
| *"I won't come too late."* | *He promised he wouldn't come too late.* |

The regular subjunctive form **würde** may be substituted.

| | |
|---|---|
| Er versprach, daß er nicht zu spät kommen **würde**. | *He promised that he wouldn't come too late.* |

Often the **würde** form is used, even if the direct discourse statement is in the present (by analogy with the **würde** substitute for the regular subjunctive):

| DIRECT DISCOURSE | INDIRECT DISCOURSE |
|---|---|
| „Er schreibt nicht gern." | Sie behauptet, er **würde** nicht gern schreiben. |
| *"He doesn't like to write."* | *She claims that he doesn't like to write.* |

But with **sein** and the modals, the **würde** construction may not be used in indirect discourse.

| | |
|---|---|
| „Er ist krank." | Sie schrieben, er **sei/wäre** krank. |
| *"He is sick."* | *They wrote that he was sick.* |
| „Er kann noch nicht arbeiten." | Sie schrieben, daß er noch nicht. arbeiten **könne/könnte**. |
| *"He still can't work."* | *They wrote that he still couldn't work.* |

## Check your comprehension

*Put each sentence into indirect discourse with the* **würde** *form by using the opening phrase,* **Wir sagten, ...**

1. „Wir werden mitkommen."
2. „Er wird wohl zu Hause bleiben."
3. „Sie liest gern."
4. „Wir geben ihnen den Schlüssel."
5. „Ihr findet das Hotel schon."

**USEFUL PHRASES**

| | |
|---|---|
| **Blödsinn!** | *Nonsense!* |
| **Das hätte ich von ihm (ihr, etc.) nicht erwartet.** | *I wouldn't have expected that of him (her, etc.)* |
| **Gib doch nicht so an!** | *Don't be so conceited!* |

## Der Kriminal-Schriftsteller°

*mystery writer*

*Eine Gruppe junger Leute geht zu einem Rockkonzert. Aber Gerds Bruder Franz will nicht mitgehen.*

ANITA Gerd, wo ist denn dein Bruder? Kommt er nicht mit?

GERD Er sagt, er wolle zu Hause bleiben, da er von Rockkonzerten nicht viel halte.

HILDEGARD Er wird wohl wieder einen langen Roman lesen. Er ist doch so ein literarischer Kopf.°

*has a bent for literature*

GERD Blödsinn! Er will sich einen Krimi im Fernsehen ansehen.

BERTHOLD Was, dein Bruder? Das hätte ich von ihm nicht erwartet.

GERD Oh ja! Er behauptet, daß man dabei etwas vom wirklichen Leben lerne.

HILDEGARD Ha, Anita, hast du das gehört? Gerd, sag doch deinem Bruder, er solle mal mit uns ausgehen, dann würde er etwas vom wirklichen Leben lernen!

BERTHOLD Ach, Hilde, gib doch nicht so an!

GERD Übrigens sagt Franz, er wolle selber Kriminal-Schriftsteller werden. Man könne dabei sehr viel Geld verdienen.

ANITA Jetzt denkt er schon wieder ans Geld. Was macht er übrigens mit seiner Eintrittskarte?

GERD Er hat sie mir gegeben und gesagt, ich solle sie am Eingang zum doppelten Preis verkaufen.

BERTHOLD Siehst du, Hilde, Franz versteht doch etwas vom wirklichen Leben!

## Questions

1. Wohin will die Gruppe junger Leute gehen?
2. Warum will Franz nicht mitgehen?
3. Warum sagt Gerd, Franz würde zu Hause bleiben?
4. Was glaubt Hildegard, was Franz tun wird?
5. Warum hat Berthold nicht erwartet, daß Franz sich einen Krimi im Fernsehen ansehen würde?
6. Was behauptet Franz von Krimis im Fernsehen?
7. Warum sagt Hildegard, Franz solle mal mit ihnen kommen?
8. Was sagt Franz, was er einmal werden wolle?
9. Was hat Franz mit seiner Eintrittskarte getan?
10. Glauben Sie, daß Franz recht hat, wenn er sagt, daß man von Krimis etwas über das wirkliche Leben lernen kann?
11. Gehst du lieber zu einem Rockkonzert, oder siehst du dir lieber zu Hause ein Fernsehprogramm an? Warum?
12. Sagen deine Freunde, daß du ein literarischer Kopf seist? Wenn nicht, glaubst du, daß du ein wissenschaftlicher (*scientific*), künstlerischer oder politischer Kopf bist?

**PRACTICE**

**A.** *Put the sentences into direct discourse.*

EXAMPLE: Sie sagte, sie sei immer zu Hause.
**„Ich bin immer zu Hause."**

1. Sie hatte gesagt, die Polizei sei da gewesen.
2. Er sagte, er sei sehr müde.
3. Sie sagte, sie habe ein neues Klavier gekauft.
4. Sie sagten, sie hätten nichts gehört.
5. Ihr sagtet, wir kämen zu spät.
6. Du sagtest, du werdest morgen abfahren.
7. Er hat gesagt, Sie seien sehr krank.
8. Sie wird sagen, das habe sie schon gewußt.
9. Ich sagte, das Wetter sei nicht sehr schön.
10. Wir sagten, daß er ein neues Auto habe.

**B.** *Put the sentences into indirect discourse by using the opening phrase,*
**Er sagte, . . .**

1. „Franz will nicht mitgehen."
2. „Franz will zu Hause bleiben, da er von Rockkonzerten nichts hält."
3. „Franz wird wieder einen langen Roman lesen."

4. „Franz ist wirklich ein literarischer Kopf."

5. „Wir sehen uns keinen Film im Fernsehen an."

6. „Das habe ich nicht von euch erwartet."

7. „Franz muß kein Schriftsteller werden."

8. „Denkt nicht schon wieder ans Geld!"

9. „Sie haben uns die Eintrittskarte gegeben."

10. „Franz versteht etwas vom wirklichen Leben."

**C.** *Put the regular subjunctive form into the special subjunctive.*

1. Er sagte, er käme später.

2. Sie sagte, sie gäbe mir keine Eintrittskarte.

3. Sie hat gesagt, sie schriebe mir einen Brief.

4. Er sagt, er wäre glücklich mit mir.

5. Er hatte gesagt, ich telefonierte zu lange.

6. Sie sagt, sie würde das Geld nicht bringen.

7. Er sagte, er ginge nach Hause.

8. Sie sagte, sie hätte die Musik gehört.

9. Ich sagte, er wäre immer sehr intelligent gewesen.

10. Man sagt, Deutsch wäre nicht so schwierig.

**D.** *Put the questions into indirect discourse by using the opening phrase,*
**Er fragte, . . .**

EXAMPLES: „Gehen Sie zu einem Rockkonzert?"
**Er fragte mich, ob ich zu einem Rockkonzert ginge.**

„Warum sind sie müde?"
**Er fragte uns, warum sie müde seien.**

1. „Hast du einen Moment Zeit?"

2. „Haben Sie eine Zigarette für mich?"

3. „Bist du gleich fertig?"

4. „Kann man hier die Medizin bekommen?"

5. „Was ist denn los?"

6. „Was tun die Passagiere?"

7. „Warum ist alles so teuer?"

8. „Lesen Sie gern?"

9. „Von wem wissen Sie das?"

10. „Willst du auch die Haupstadt besichtigen?"

11. „Geht es Ihnen gut?"

12. „Wird hier getanzt?"

13. „Um wieviel Uhr wachen Sie meistens auf?"

14. „Hat dein Freund schon geschrieben?"

15. „Wie spät ist es?"

16. „Wo wohnen Sie?"

17. „Wann findet das Konzert statt?"
18. „Wozu studieren Sie Deutsch?"
19. „Warum weint das Kind?"
20. „Darf ich Sie zu einer Tasse Kaffee einladen?"

**E.** *Put the command into indirect discourse by using the opening phrase,* **Sie sagt,** . . . *and the correct form of either* **sollen** *or* **müssen.** *Do not use the conjunction* **daß.**

EXAMPLE: „Wecke mich früh auf!"
      **Sie sagt, ich solle/müsse sie früh aufwecken.**

1. „Komm doch mit zum Konzert!"
2. „Geh sofort nach Hause!"
3. „Setzen Sie sich!"
4. „Sprecht etwas langsamer!"
5. „Warten Sie einen Moment!"
6. „Kauf ein paar Brötchen!"
7. „Streitet euch nicht!"
8. „Schreib mir mal!"
9. „Fahrt doch in Urlaub!"
10. „Stell dich nicht so an!"

**F.** *Give the German equivalent.*

1. Gerd asks where his brother is.
2. Franz said he didn't want to come along.
3. Anita asked what time it was.
4. They said he was reading a novel.
5. We asked where they lived.
6. Ray wanted to know what was going on.
7. She said that Ingrid knew German literature backwards and forwards.
8. Peter said that he would rather write his own poem than interpret one by Schiller.
9. He asked me what I was waiting for.
10. She asked me where I was now.

**GUIDED CONVERSATION**

Form a group of three or four persons and talk about someone who is absent. Pretend that you want to go to a movie or a concert, and state why the other person doesn't wish to join the group. Repeat in indirect discourse the reasons that person gave for not coming with you.

## Das Publikum spielt James Bond

Man hört oft, daß das Fernsehen das Publikum in einen passiven Zustand des Sehens und Nicht-Denkens versetze. Es wird auch gesagt, daß viel, was im Fernsehen gezeigt wird, das Publikum nur aufrege und nicht belehre. Oder es wird darauf aufmerksam gemacht, daß den Kindern und Schülern im Fernsehen ein schlechtes Beispiel des menschlichen Lebens gegeben werde und daß sie durch das viele Fernsehen von ihren Studien abgehalten° würden. Einige Pessimisten sagen sogar voraus, daß zukünftige Generationen große Augen wie Nachteulen° und ganz kleine Ohren haben würden, weil ihnen durch die laute Musik, der sie täglich zuhören, das Gehör beeinträchtigt° werde. Es kann natürlich nicht verneint werden, daß in solchen Behauptungen ein Kern° von Wahrheit enthalten° ist.

*kept away from*

*night owls*
*impaired*

*grain / contained*

Aber auf der anderen Seite muß doch auch gesagt werden, daß viele Kritiker das Problem des Fernsehens übertreiben. Das deutsche Fernsehen bietet auch viel Interessantes, zum Beispiel Sendungen über fremde Länder, über Politik, Medizin, die neuesten Entdeckungen in den Wissenschaften oder auch Gespräche über wichtige Tagesprobleme. Außerdem muß hervorgehoben werden, daß das Fernsehen in Deutschland mit seinen drei Programmen[1] vom Staat Subventionen

[1] **Programme** here means *channels*. There are only three channels, all public, for the whole of the Bundesrepublik. Channels I and II are the most popular. Channel III corresponds in some ways to the Educational TV stations in America. The Federal Government subsidizes all three channels, and the owners of TV sets must pay a small monthly fee.

## Aktenzeichen: XY...ungelöst
**Die Kriminalpolizei bittet um Mithilfe der Zuschauer**

**20.15**

Wieder einmal sollen die Fernsehzuschauer der Kripo helfen, in bislang ungeklärten Kriminalfällen ein Stück weiterzukommen. – Im ersten Fall, Mord, schien das abgebrochene Blatt einer Topfpflanze zur wichtigsten Spur zu werden. Doch dann stieß die Kripo auf eine Vorgeschichte, die alle bisherigen Erkenntnisse in neuem Licht erscheinen ließ. Auch im zweiten Fall ist die Mordkommission zuständig. Vieles spricht dafür, daß der Täter mehrere Opfer auf dem Gewissen hat und wieder töten könnte. – Beim dritten Fall geht es um Bankraub, einen nicht alltäglichen. Schließlich: aktuelle Fahndungen. Telefonnummern der Aufnahmestudios: München: 089/95 01 95 Wien: 82 36 21 Zürich: 2 41 47 47

**Plötzlich findet eine Spaziergängerin eine Leiche**

erhält, so daß die Werbung auf ein Minimum reduziert worden ist und die Sendungen nicht immer unterbrochen werden. Die Werbung ist auf° eine halbe Stunde abends von 7.30 bis 8 Uhr beschränkt.° So ist es nicht erstaunlich, daß viele Besucher, die aus Deutschland nach den USA kommen, sagen, sie könnten sich nie an die vielen Unterbrechungen der Sendungen im amerikanischen Fernsehen gewöhnen.

to / restricted

Natürlich gibt es im deutschen Fernsehen auch viele Unterhaltungssendungen mit Shows, Quizzes und Krimis, die bei der großen Masse beliebt sind, weil man eben nach anstrengender° Arbeit die Probleme des Tages vergessen will. Viele Krimis kommen aus den USA, zum Beispiel die Serie „Die Straßen von San Franzisko". Neben den typischen Fernsehfilmen gibt es im Fernsehen aber auch eigentliche Spielfilme[2], wie sie in den Kinos gezeigt werden. Das sind oft gute Filme, die einen oder mehrere Oscars erhalten haben. Sehr populär sind natürlich auch die Sportsendungen im Fernsehen, besonders Fußball[3]. Nie sind die Straßen im ganzen Land so leer wie bei großen Fußballspielen, weil dann fast jeder vor dem Fernsehapparat sitzt. Ein

strenuous

[2] One usually distinguishes between films made specially for TV (**Fernsehfilme**) and movies broadcast on TV (**Spielfilme**).

[3] **Fußball:** *soccer.* American "football" is not known in Europe.

Journalist aus den USA hat einmal bemerkt, er hätte während eines
Fußballspiels, das im Fernsehen gezeigt wurde, den Eindruck gehabt,
die ganze Bevölkerung° sei an einem Virus erkrankt° und läge zu     population / fallen ill
Hause im Bett.

    Eine Serie, die schon seit zehn Jahren läuft, ist besonders beliebt.
Sie heißt „Aktenzeichen XY—ungelöst".[4] In dieser Sendung werden
Szenen aus Kriminalfällen gespielt, die bis zur Stunde noch nicht auf-
geklärt worden sind. Nur authentische Fälle werden gezeigt. Und die
Kripo[5] gibt Erklärungen. In einem Fall zum Beispiel wurde hervorge-
hoben, daß ein abgebrochenes Blatt° einer Hauspflanze° ein wichtiger     broken off leaf / house plant
Beweis für einen Mord sei. In einem anderen Fall wurden Bilder von
einem Bankraub° gezeigt und das Publikum gewarnt, daß die Täter     bank robbery
Waffen trügen und gefährlich seien. Die Zuschauer können während
der Sendung die Fernsehstudios über Verdächte° telefonisch informie-     suspicions
ren, worauf die Kripo sofort solchen Tips nachgeht. Auf diese Weise
wurden in den letzten Jahren viele schwierige Kriminalfälle aufgeklärt.
Die Serie ist besonders wirkungsvoll°, weil fast alle deutschsprachi-     effective
gen Länder—die Bundesrepublik, Österreich und die Schweiz— daran
teilnehmen. Ein Zyniker° schrieb darüber in einer bekannten Tages-     cynic
zeitung, daß die Zuschauer des deutschsprachigen Fernsehens alle gern
James Bond spielen möchten. Aber warum denn nicht, wenn dadurch
der Justiz geholfen werden kann?

---

[4] *Criminal Dossier XY—Unsolved.*
[5] **Kripo:** abbreviation for **Kriminalpolizei** (*detective squad*).

Auf jeden Fall darf man sagen, daß das deutsche Fernsehen viel bietet. Seine Direktoren scheinen sich an einige Zeilen aus dem Vorspiel[6] zu Goethes *Faust I* zu erinnern, worin über das Theater die folgende Bemerkung° gemacht wird: remark

> Die Masse könnt ihr nur durch Masse zwingen,
> Ein jeder sucht sich endlich selbst was aus.
> Wer vieles bringt, wird manchem etwas bringen;
> Und jeder geht zufrieden aus dem Haus.[7] adapt

Nur müßte man vielleicht die letzte Zeile dem Fernsehen anpassen° und sagen: Und jeder bleibt vergnügt zu Haus.

[6] **Vorspiel:** *Prelude.* In the Prelude the Poet, Actor, and Director argue over the most important feature of a drama, the Poet defining its literary merits, the Actor its suitability for acting, and the Director its appeal to the masses.

[7] In Walter Kaufmann's translation (Doubleday Anchor, 1961, p. 63):
> The mass is overwhelmed only by masses,
> Each likes some part of what has been presented.
> He that gives much, gives something to all classes,
> And everybody will go home contented.

## Questions

1. Was hört man oft über das Fernsehen?
2. Warum kann man im deutschen Fernsehen die Werbung auf ein Minimum reduzieren?
3. Was für Unterhaltungssendungen gibt es im deutschen Fernsehen?
4. Was für Filme werden im Fernsehen gezeigt?
5. Wann sind in der BRD und anderen Ländern die Straßen fast leer?
6. Welche Kriminalserie ist in der BRD besonders beliebt?
7. In welchen anderen Ländern wird diese Serie auch gezeigt?
8. Warum ist diese Serie nicht nur interessant sondern auch wichtig?
9. Finden Sie, daß es im amerikanischen Fernsehen zuviel Werbung gibt? Würden Sie lieber sehen, daß das amerikanische Fernsehen auch vom Staat Subventionen erhielte?
10. Welche amerikanische Fernsehserie finden Sie besonders gut?

## VOCABULARY DEVELOPMENT

### A. Geht ihr miteinander aus und kommt ihr miteinander aus?

The expression **aus·gehen mit (jemand)** means *to go out with (somebody).*

Ich gehe heute abend mit Hildegard aus.     *Tonight I'll go out with Hildegard.*

But **aus·kommen mit** means *to get along with somebody.*

> Kommen sie gut miteinander aus?     *Are they getting along well together?*

Ask your neighbor whether he/she is going out with a friend and whether they are getting along well together.

## B. Versetzen

**Versetzen** can mean *to put into* (a certain condition).

> Das hat sie in eine gute Laune versetzt.     *That put her in a good mood.*
>
> Das Fernsehen versetzt viele Menschen in einen Zustand des Nicht-Denkens.     *Television puts many people in a state of nonthinking.*

It can also mean *to transfer, to remove to another place.*

> Hans-Peter wurde von seiner Firma nach Berlin versetzt.     *Hans-Peter was transferred by his firm to Berlin.*
>
> Hilde wurde ins vierte Schuljahr versetzt.     *Hilde was promoted to fourth grade.*

## C. Bejahen und verneinen

**Ja** and **nein** may occur in verbs. **Bejahen** means *to answer in the affirmative* or *to assent to.*

> Ich wollte seine Frage nicht bejahen.     *I didn't want to answer yes to his question.*
>
> Wer schweigt, bejaht.     *Silence signifies assent. (Lit., He who is silent, assents.)*

**Verneinen** means *to give a negative answer, to deny, to disavow.*

> Sie gab uns eine verneinende Antwort.     *She gave us a negative answer.*
>
> Es kann nicht verneint werden, daß . . .     *It cannot be denied that . . .*

# REVIEW

**A.** *Put the sentences into indirect discourse by using an appropriate opening phrase such as* **sie fragt, er behauptete, sie fragten,** *etc.*

1. „Das Fernsehen bietet viel Interessantes."

2. „Geh doch einmal mit mir aus! Wir werden gut miteinander auskommen."

3. „Diese Frage kann nicht bejaht werden."

4. „Das Fernsehen gibt den Kindern keine guten Beispiele des menschlichen Lebens."

5. „Viele Kritiker haben das Problem des Fernsehens übertrieben."

6. „Ich konnte mich nicht an die vielen Unterbrechungen der Sendungen gewöhnen."

7. „Nie sind die Straßen so leer wie bei großen Fußballspielen."

8. „Werden nur authentische Kriminalfälle gezeigt?"

9. „Ist das ein wichtiger Beweis für diesen Mord?"

10. „Habt ihr an dieser Sendung von ‚Aktenzeichen XY' teilgenommen?"

**B.** *Put each passage into indirect discourse.*

1. Ärger° mit der Hauswirtin°

Heute morgen sagte meine Hauswirtin zu mir: „Herr Fischer, Sie hatten gestern abend Damenbesuch.° Das wünsche ich nicht. Das wissen Sie doch." Ich antwortete „Frau Neubauer, es tut mir leid, aber das ist wirklich meine Sache.° Ich bezahle meine Miete,° sogar eine sehr hohe Miete, für mein Studentenzimmer, und da kann ich einladen, wen ich will." Meine Hauswirtin war ärgerlich° über diese Antwort und sagte: „Sie, junger Mann, hören Sie mal. Vielleicht verstehen Sie etwas von Musik oder was Sie studieren, aber von einer Hausordnung° verstehen Sie offensichtlich° nichts! Ich erwarte, daß Sie auf Ihrem Zimmer keinen Damenbesuch empfangen. Basta!"° Ich war wütend° und sagte: „Das ist Diskriminierung! Das ist unsozial! Ich habe mit jener Studentin nur für das Examen gelernt, und das ist ja wohl nicht verboten!" „So, fürs Examen gelernt haben Sie", sagte sie. „Kein Student lernt am Samstagabend mit einer Dame für ein Examen!" Ich sagte: „Dann müssen Sie Ihre Vorstellungen° über die Studenten von heute revidieren!"°

|  | dispute / landlady |
|---|---|
|  | a visit from a lady |
|  | concern / rent |
|  | angry |
|  | house rules / obviously |
|  | Enough! |
|  | furious |
|  | ideas / revise |

2. Die Verfolgung°

Fräulein Bäuziger sieht sich immer die Fernsehsendung „Aktenzeichen XY—ungelöst" an. Eines Tages glaubt sie, einen Verbrecher, dessen Bild im Fernsehen gezeigt wurde, zu sehen, gerade als er in eine Limousine einsteigt. Später erzählt sie einer Freundin, was geschah.

Ich sprang in ein Taxi und sagte zum Taxifahrer: „Bitte, folgen Sie der schwarzen Limousine da drüben!" Der Taxifahrer wollte wissen: „Warum soll ich dem Auto folgen? Sind Sie denn von der Kriminalpolizei?" Ich antwortete: „Fragen Sie nicht soviel! Fahren Sie lieber etwas schneller, sonst verlieren wir den Wagen aus den Augen." Er sagte: „Furchtbares Wetter haben wir heute. Der Regen will überhaupt nicht aufhören." Ich sagte: „Passen Sie auf, Mann! Der schwarze Wagen ist gerade links abgebogen.° Fahren Sie schneller!" Er sagte: „Es tut mir leid, mein Fräulein, aber ich muß die Straßenbahn zuerst vorbeifahren lassen." Ich sagte ärgerlich: „Der Gangster ist uns entkommen.° Fahren Sie mich nach Hause!"

pursuit

turned

escaped

3. Der Augenzeuge°

Herr Beckmann, Co-Pilot einer DC-10, war Augenzeuge einer Flugzeugentführung.° Er mußte die Kriminalpolizei genau darüber informieren, was geschehen war. Er erzählte:

eye witness

airplane hijacking

Plötzlich stand ein Mann im Cockpit mit einer Handgranate in der Hand und sagte: „Tun Sie, was ich sage. Dann passiert nichts. Fliegen Sie sofort nach Havanna!" Der Chefpilot sagte: „Das ist unmöglich! Soviel Benzin haben wir nicht." Daraufhin sagte der Luftpirat: „Ich habe gesagt, fliegen Sie nach Kuba! Sonst wird dieses kleine runde Ding explodieren." Der Chefpilot sagte: „Sehen Sie doch selbst! Wir haben nur noch 800 Liter Benzin. Damit kommen wir bestenfalls noch bis Atlanta." Der Luftpirat fluchte° wie verrückt° und   swore / crazy
sagte schließlich: „Okay. Landen Sie in Atlanta und tanken Sie voll! Sagen Sie dem Tower, daß ich die Maschine in die Luft jage,° wenn die Polizei auf   blow up
uns schießt."° Ich zeigte dem Luftpiraten die Flugkarte und sagte: „Sehen   shoots
Sie, wir sind jetzt hier. In einer halben Stunde . . ." In diesem Moment schlug°   felled
unsere Stewardess den Mann mit einem Karate-Schlag° nieder.   chop

## GUIDED COMPOSITION

Give a short description of the TV programs that you like best. Also state what some of your family or friends think and say about these programs. In so doing, use indirect discourse.

## VOCABULARY

### Easily recognized words

|  | authentisch | authentic |
|---|---|---|
| die | Justiz | justice, law |
| der | Kritiker, - | critic |
|  | literarisch | literary |
| das | Minimum | minimum |
|  | passiv | passive |
| die | Serie, -n | series, serial |

|  | | |
|---|---|---|
| die | Behauptung, -en | claim |
| der | Beweis, -e | proof, evidence |
| der | Blödsinn | nonsense |
| der | Eindruck, ⸚e | impression |
| der | Eingang, ⸚e | entrance |
| die | Eintrittskarte, -n | (admission) ticket |
| die | Entdeckung, -en | discovery |

| der | Krimi (short for der Kriminalroman), -s | thriller |
|---|---|---|
| der | Kriminalfall, ⸚e | criminal case |
| der | Mord, -e | murder |
| der | Roman, -e | novel |
| der | Schriftsteller, - | writer |
| die | Sendung, -en | broadcast |
| die | Subvention, -en | subsidy |
| der | Täter, - | culprit |
| die | Waffe, -n | weapon |
| die | Weise, -n | way, method; **auf diese Weise** in this way |
| die | Werbung, -en | advertising |
| die | Wissenschaft, -en | science |
| die | Zeile, -n | line (of text) |
| der | Zuschauer, - | viewer, audience |

der **Zustand,** ⸚e — *condition, state*

**auf·klären** — *to clear up, solve (a mystery)*

**auf·regen** — *to excite*

**behaupten** — *to claim, assert*

**bejahen** — *to affirm; see p. 370*

**belehren** — *to instruct*

**bemerken** — *to notice, observe*

**hervor·heben, hob, hervorgehoben** — *to point out*

**reduzieren** — *to reduce*

**übertreiben, übertrieb, übertrieben** — *to reduce*

**unterbrechen (unterbricht), unterbrach, unterbrochen** — *to interrupt*

**verneinen** — *to deny; see p. 370*

**versetzen** — *to put; see p. 370*

**voraus·sagen** — *to predict*

**beliebt** — *popular, well-liked*

**deutschsprachig** — *German language (adj.)*

**doppelt** — *double*

**erstaunlich** — *surprising*

**telefonisch** — *by telephone*

**ungelöst** — *unsolved*

**vergnügt** — *happy, glad*

**zukünftig** — *future (adj., adv.)*

# APPENDIX

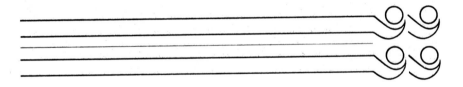

Since the standards of pronunciation for English and German differ widely, it is essential that you develop proper speaking habits from the very beginning. This can best be accomplished by carefully listening to and closely imitating your instructor and the voices on the tapes of the Lab program. The following nevertheless gives some practical phonetic guidelines for speaking German.

As a rule, in the German language sounds are much more concise and forceful than the gliding sound patterns characteristic of the English spoken in the United States, and in pronunciation the tongue and lips are slightly more forward.

## The German vowel system

In German, there are long and short single vowel sounds (including umlauted vowels, or umlauts)—also known as monophthongs—and diphthongs, sounds that contract two different vowels. In contrast to English, German vowels are predominantly of a single vowel quality: they do not glide, as so frequently is the case in English, but rather hold their pitch.

The following table roughly represents German vowel sounds, and wherever possible attempts to give an English sound that resembles its German counterpart. Keep in mind, however, that the English sounds are only approximations of the German, and are similar in sound only and not in length.

| VOWEL SOUND | LONG ENGLISH | GERMAN | SHORT ENGLISH | GEPMAN |
|---|---|---|---|---|
| a | father | Name | blunt | genannt |
| e | Santa Fe | Tee | met | wenn |
| -e(-) | — | — | ago | bitte |
| -er | — | — | mother | Arbeiter |
| i | me | Vieh | it | bitte |
| o | slogan | Lohn | cloth | kommen |
| u | soon | tun | book | und |
| ä | fair | Fähre | men | Männer |
| ö | — | König | — | können |
| ü | — | fühlen | — | füllen |
| au | now | Frau | — | — |
| ei, ai | mine | mein | — | — |
| eu, äu | joy | heulen | — | — |

A vowel is always *long* if it

1. stands at the end of a syllable: ge-ben
2. is followed by an **h**: sah
3. is followed by an **ß** plus an **e**: Grüße
4. is doubled (only possible with **a, e,** and **o**): Tee
5. is an **i** followed by an **e**: sie

A vowel is always *short* if it is followed by a double consonant: kom-men. A vowel is usually short if it is followed by two or more different consonants, not including **h**: Stadt. However, neither long nor short vowels are always predictable by the spelling of a word.

The following English vowel phonemes do not occur in German:

1. the short *a* as in "mat"
2. the long gliding *a* as in "male," "fail"
3. the long gliding *o* as in "go," "bloat," "globe," and "snow"

*The* **a**

The German **a** resembles the English *a* as in "father" (long) or *u* as in "bl**u**nt" (short).

| LONG | | SHORT | |
|------|------|------|------|
| Kahn | Samen | kann | sammeln |
| Name | Haar | genannt | lang |
| Schal | | Schall | |

*The* **e**

The German **e** slightly resembles pronunciation of the *e* in "Santa Fe" (long) or the English *e* as in "met" (short).

| LONG | | SHORT | |
|------|------|------|------|
| wen | Tee | wenn | Tennis |
| wer | sehen | Herr | setzen |
| stehen | | Student | |

*The unstressed* **e** *and* **er**

The unstressed **e** usually occurs at the end of a word or syllable, as in **-en** or **-te,** and in the prefixes **be-** and **ge-.** It resembles the English *a* as in "ago." The unstressed **er** occurs at the end of many words. It vaguely resembles the British *er* as in "mother." Many Americans find it difficult to distinguish between these two sounds, but the difference can be critical. Therefore it is particularly important that you listen closely to your instructor and the tapes of the Lab program.

| | | | |
|------|------|------|------|
| diese | Begriff | dieser | leider |
| fahren | rauchte | Fahrer | Raucher |
| bitte | | bitter | |

*The* **i**

The German **i** resembles the English *e* as in "me" (long) or *i* as in "it" (short).

| LONG | | SHORT | |
|------|------|------|------|
| bieten | Miene | bitten | Minne |
| Schiefer | Sieb | Schiff | Sippe |
| ihren | | irren | |

## The o

The German **o** slightly resembles the English *o* as in "slogan" (long) or "cloth" (short).

| LONG | | SHORT | |
|------|------|------|------|
| Kohle | Ton | kommen | Tonne |
| Sohn | Lohn | Sonne | von |
| Boot | | Bock | |

## The u

The German **u** resembles the English *oo* as in "soon" (long) or "book" (short).

| LONG | | SHORT | |
|------|------|------|------|
| Mut | Buch | Mutter | Bucht |
| tun | Luke | und | Lust |
| Schuh | | Schutz | |

## The ä

The umlaut **ä** quite frequently resembles the German *e* and slightly approximates the English *ai* as in "fair" (long) or *e* as in "men" (short). For practice, say an open "a" as in "father," hold the lips in that position, and lift the tongue to say "e."

| LONG | | SHORT | |
|------|------|------|------|
| Gespräch | Fähre | Schwäche | ändern |
| Mädchen | Gerät | Männer | hätte |
| nämlich | | Klänge | |

Note the difference between **a** and **ä**.

| LONG | | SHORT | |
|------|------|------|------|
| Name | nämlich | Mann | Männer |
| Sprache | spräche | lang | Länge |

## The ö

The umlaut **ö** is a sound that cannot be compared to any English sound. Listen closely to your instructor and the tapes of the Lab program.

| LONG | | SHORT | |
|------|------|------|------|
| König | schön | können | nördlich |
| Höhle | rötlich | Hölle | rösten |
| Öl | | öffnen | |

Note the difference between **o** and **ö**.

| LONG | | SHORT | |
|------|------|-------|------|
| schon | schön | kommen | können |
| hohe | Höhe | offen | öffnen |

### *The* **ü**

The umlaut **ü** is a sound that cannot be compared to any English sound. Listen closely to your instructor and the tapes.

| LONG | | SHORT | |
|------|------|-------|------|
| fühlen | Mühle | füllen | Müller |
| grüßen | glühen | küssen | Glück |
| für | | füttern | |

Note the difference between **i**, **u**, and **ü**.

| LONG | | SHORT | SHORT |
|------|------|-------|-------|
| vier | Kultur | Mitte | Kuß |
| fuhren | führen | Mutter | Mütter |
| Tier | Tür | Kissen | küssen |

Generally, the English vowels are evenly balanced in the mouth. If the tongue is forward and high, the lips are pulled back: "pl*ea*se." When the tongue is pulled back, the lips are pushed forward: "b*oa*t." This is not the case with the German **ö** and **ü**. The German **ö** is produced with the tongue in position for an *e* as in the English "bed," and the lips forward for an *o* as in "hope." Similarly for the **ü**: the tongue is forward for an *ee* as in "meet," and the lips are also forward for an *oo* as in "soon." With the lips and tongue both forward, one can enunciate the German **ö** and **ü**. There is a slight difference other than the length between short **ö** and **ü** and long **ö** and **ü**: for the short vowels, the tongue is not quite so far forward.

### *The* **au**

The German diphthong **au** resembles the English *ow* as in "now," but the shift from one vowel to the other is done rapidly in German.

| | |
|------|------|
| Fr**au** | gl**au**ben |
| **Au**fschrift | **au**ch |
| R**au**m | |

*The* **ei** *and* **ai**

The German diphthong **ei** or **ai** resembles the English *i* as in "mine."

mein
nein
Mai
arbeiten
gleich

Note the difference between the diphthong **ei** as in English "high" and the combination **ie** as in English "he."

| | |
|---|---|
| Wein | Wien |
| arbeiten | bieten |
| heiraten | hier |
| Bein | Bier |
| sein | sieben |

*The* **eu** *and* **äu**

The German diphthong **eu** or **äu** resembles the English *oi* as in "joy."

| | |
|---|---|
| heulen | Fräulein |
| Deutschland | Häuser |
| Freund | |

## The glottal stop

In German words or syllables that begin with a vowel, the flow of air is halted instantaneously just prior to articulation, and then released suddenly. This phenomenon is called the "glottal stop." Thus you would say **im Áugenblick** and not **imaugenblick.** Compare

| | |
|---|---|
| veréisen | verreisen |
| veréngen | verrenken |
| eréignen | erreichen |

*Study the following statements.*

1. Ein altes Auto ist oft unsicher.     *An old car is often unsafe.*
2. Er ist ungeheuer beeindruckt.     *He is tremendously impressed.*
3. Dein englischer Plattenspieler ist ausgezeichnet.     *Your English record player is excellent.*

## The German consonant system

Many German consonants differ from English only in their more precise and forceful pronunciation. Only those consonants that require particular attention because of basic differences are discussed here.

The following English consonant phonemes do not occur in German:

1. the soft *g* or *j* as in "gentle," "rage," "ledger," and "jot"
2. the *l* as in "loan," "ball," and "tailor"
3. the *r* as in "riot," "berry," "clear," and "harm"
4. the *th* as in "the," "leather," and "bath"
5. the *w* as in "wood" and "where"

*The* **ch**

For Americans, the back and the front **ch** sounds are quite difficult to master, therefore listen closely to your instructor and the tapes of the Lab program. The back **ch**, so called because it is produced in the back of the mouth, is preceded by an **a, o, u,** or **au**; the front **ch**, produced in the front, is preceded by any letter other than **a, o, u, au,** or **s**. The front **ch** (**ich**) is quite like the English *h* in "huge," "Hughes," or a whispered "he."

| BACK | FRONT |
|------|-------|
| na**ch** | ni**ch**t |
| no**ch** | schle**ch**t |
| Ko**ch** | Kö**ch**e |
| schwa**ch** | Schwä**ch**e |
| au**ch** | Ar**ch**itekt |

When the **ch** is part of the **-chen** suffix, it is pronounced like the front **ch**.

Mäd**ch**en
Häus**ch**en

Be careful not to use a **k** sound for the **ch**. Compare:

| | |
|------|------|
| A**ck**er | a**ch**t |
| Fla**ck** | fla**ch** |
| La**ck** | la**ch**en |
| Fle**ck** | Flä**ch**e |
| fli**ck**en | Pfli**ch**t |

If a **ch** is followed by an **s** it is pronounced like the English *x*.

| | |
|---|---|
| se**chs** | Sa**chs**en |
| La**chs** | we**chs**eln |
| wa**chs**en | |

## The **l** *and* **r**

For Americans, the German **l** and **r** are quite difficult to pronounce. Listen closely to your instructor and the tapes.

The German **l** is produced by pushing the tip of the flat tongue against the back of the upper teeth and the front part of the palate. There are two ways to pronounce the **r** in German, the commonly used uvular **r**, which is a gargling sound produced in the back of the throat, and the regional trilled **r**, produced in the front of the mouth.

| **l** | | **r** | |
|---|---|---|---|
| ENGLISH | GERMAN | ENGLISH | GERMAN |
| *l*and | **L**and | *r*ight | **r**ichtig |
| *l*iterature | **L**iteratur | *r*ule | **R**egel |
| ba*ll* | Ba**ll** | co*rr*ect | ko**rr**ekt |
| tunne*l* | Tunne**l** | a*rr*ogant | a**rr**ogant |
| a*l*so | a**l**so | pai*r* | Paa**r** |

Final **r** is pronounced like the unstressed **er** discussed earlier.

| | |
|---|---|
| wi**r** | Roh**r** |
| de**r** | Ba**r** |
| pu**r** | |

## The **s, ß, ss, sch, sp,** *and* **st**

If a single **s** is followed by a vowel, it is voiced—that is, it is pronounced like the English *z* as in "zoo." If, however, the **s** stands at the end of a word or if it is doubled, it is voiceless—that is, it is pronounced like the English *s* as in "son."

| VOICED | VOICELESS |
|---|---|
| **s**agen | bi**s** |
| **s**ein | be**ss**er |
| ge**s**und | Gla**s** |
| Phy**s**ik | wi**ss**en |
| be**s**itzen | verla**ss**en |

The double **s** is expressed by the voiceless letter **ß** if

1. the preceding vowel is long: Gruß, grüßen
2. it appears at the end of a word: Kuß
3. it is followed by a **t**: vergißt

The German **sch** is pronounced like the English *sh* as in "shall."

| | |
|---|---|
| **sch**wimmen | Ent**sch**luß |
| **sch**icken | Bu**sch** |
| be**sch**ädigen | |

The German **sp** and **st,** if they appear at the beginning of a word or an independent component of a word, are pronounced like the English *sh* plus *t* or *p* respectively. Otherwise they are pronounced as in the English "spoon" or "stood."

| **sh + p/t** | **sp/st** |
|---|---|
| **sp**rechen | We**sp**e |
| Bei**sp**iel | A**sp**ekt |
| **St**udium | Fen**st**er |
| **St**and | fa**st** |
| be**st**ellen | ge**st**ern |

### The **z** and **tz**

The German **z** and **tz** are both pronounced like the English *ts* as in "nuts."

| | |
|---|---|
| **Z**ucker | Bli**tz** |
| Medi**z**in | je**tz**t |
| kur**z** | |

### The **w, f, ph,** and **v**

The German **w** is pronounced like the English *v* as in "visit." The German **f** and **ph** are pronounced like the English *f* as in "fellow."

| | |
|---|---|
| **W**ein | **f**ahren |
| **w**ollen | **F**ernseher |
| sch**w**er | **Ph**ysik |
| ein**w**erfen | Pam**ph**let |
| lang**w**eilig | Philoso**ph** |

The German **v** is pronounced like the English *f* as in "fellow." In some words of foreign origin, however, the German **v** is pronounced like the English *v* as in "visit."

| **f** SOUND | **v** SOUND |
|---|---|
| Vater | Vanille |
| vergessen | Vase |
| wieviel | Villa |
| Volk | Universität |
| völlig | Offensive |

## The **b, d,** *and* **g**

If **b, d,** or **g** stands at the beginning of a word or syllable, it is pronounced just like the English "boy," "dog," or "girl." Whenever these letters are at the end of a word or syllable, or are followed by **t** or **s**, they are pronounced like *p, t,* and *k* respectively as in "pig," "toy," or "kid."

| FRONT **b** | END **b/p** | FRONT **d** | END **d/t** | FRONT **g** | END **g/k** |
|---|---|---|---|---|---|
| lieben | lieb | deutsch | Land | Geburt | Tag |
| aber | ab | dann | und | vergessen | Flug |
| verboten | Urlaub | drinnen | Sand | Gold | fliegt |
| Bus | lebt | gedient | verwandt | gibt | lügt |
| Band | Krebs | Gedanke | (Bads) | egal | (Schlags) |

## The **ig** *and* **ng**

If **ig** occurs at the end of a word or syllable or in front of a consonant, it is pronounced like the German **ich.** The German **ng** is pronounced like the English *ng* as in "singer."

| | |
|---|---|
| hungrig | bringen |
| langweilig | gingen |
| wenig | hängen |
| Ewigkeit | Wohnung |
| Heiligtum | Heizung |

*The* **pf, ps,** *and* **kn**

Both consonants are pronounced in the **pf, ps,** and **kn** combinations.

| | | |
|---|---|---|
| **Pf**effer | **Ps**ychologie | **Kn**ie |
| **Pf**osten | **Ps**eudonym | **Kn**opf |
| **Pf**licht | **Ps**alm | **Kn**abe |
| A**pf**el | **ps**t! | **kn**urren |
| To**pf** | Ra**ps** | ge**kn**ackt |

## Additional guidelines

Some additional guidelines for proper German pronunciation that may be helpful include the following.

1. The German **j** is pronounced like the English *y* as in "young."

   jetzt          jung          Jugend

2. The German **y** is pronounced like the German **ü.**

   Physik          System          Psychiatrie

3. The **ck** is pronounced lik *k*, and the preceding vowel is always short.

   E**ck**e          Sa**ck**          Gepä**ck**

4. The German **qu** is pronounced like the English *k* plus *v*.

   **Qu**alität          **qu**er          **Qu**ark

5. The ending **-tion** is pronounced *tsion*, with two distinct vowel sounds, the second one long.

   Na**tion**          Sensa**tion**          Reak**tion**

## Word stress and sentence intonation

Aside from learning these phonetic guidelines, you will need to pay close attention to word stress and the intonation of the sentence.

Word stress in German is relatively simple. Most non-compound words put the stress on the first syllable or stem syllable: **mórgen, géstern, stéhen, Besúcher, Gespräch.** If the word is of non-German origin, this rule frequently does not apply: **Studént, Literatúr, Physík, Natión, Philosóph.** In compound words the stress lies on the first word or first stem syllable: **Aúfschrift, Déutschland, Férnseher, Gepäckträger, Verkéhrsunfall.** However, these rules do not always apply, so listen closely to your instructor and the tapes.

Sentence intonation is much more difficult. It is directly related to the syntax of the sentence. In an affirmative statement, for instance, the intonation is quite different from that in a question. Compare the intonation of the following sentences.

Karl geht in die Schule.        Geht Karl in die Schule?

Wohin geht Karl?

In addition, the stress of an individual word can change the meaning of a sentence significantly. There is a great difference between **Karl géht in die Schule** and **Karl geht in die Schúle.** In the first sentence we are told Karl *walks* to school, he does not drive. In the second sentence we learn that Karl goes to *school* and not anywhere else. Again, listen very carefully to your instructor and the tapes of the Lab program whenever new syntactical constructions are introduced, in order to learn the intonation properly.

After learning all the German sounds and stress patterns, practice saying the following sentences.

| | |
|---|---|
| Wann kam Tante Anna? | *When did Aunt Anna come?* |
| Nach dem Tee gehen Peter und Werner an den See. | *After tea(time) Peter and Werner go to the lake.* |
| Liebe Lili, willst du wissen, wie ich dich liebe? | *Dear Lili, do you want to know how much I love you?* |
| Bitte, gib dem Spieler am Klavier noch ein Bier! | *Please give the piano player another beer.* |
| Mein Sohn, dort oben ist das Telefon. | *My son, the telephone is up there.* |
| Morgenstunde hat Gold im Munde. | *The early bird catches the worm.* |
| Nach dem Essen sollst du ruhen oder tausend Schritte tun. | *After dinner you should rest or go for a short walk (lit. do a thousand paces).* |
| Mädchen, möchtet ihr nicht in der Küche weiche Brötchen essen? | *Girls, don't you want to eat some soft rolls in the kitchen?* |
| Unser Koch kocht auch gut nach einem Kochbuch. | *Our cook also cooks well by following a cookbook.* |
| Zehn Zigeuner ziehen zehn Zentner Zuckerrüben. | *Ten gypsies are pulling ten hundredweights of sugar beets.* |

**TRANSLATIONS OF
CONVERSATIONS**

Colloquial language cannot be translated literally. The English below is the colloquial equivalent of the German conversations; it does not attempt to translate word for word.

## Chapter 1: A Piece of Information

JUDY Good morning. I'm looking for the Institute of German Language and Literature.

MR. KELLER Adenauer Street number one. It's right over there.—Are you from the United States?

JUDY Yes, I'm from Buffalo, New York. My name is Judy Miller.

MR. KELLER And now you're studying here in Germany?

JUDY Yes, I'm studying German and sociology.

MR. KELLER That's interesting.

JUDY I'm looking for a book by Kafka.

MR. KELLER What's the name of the book?

JUDY *Amerika.* I hope it's here.

MR. KELLER I'm not sure. The card catalogue is right over there.

JUDY Thank you for the information. Good-bye.

MR. KELLER You're welcome. Good-bye, Miss Miller. Good luck!

## Chapter 2: On the Phone

KLAUS Schönberg speaking.

MONIKA Klaus, this is Monika. Excuse me, do you have a moment?

KLAUS Of course! Why?

MONIKA We have a record player now. It's brand new.

KLAUS Really? Great!

MONIKA I find its sound simply fantastic. Do you perhaps have a record by Peter Alexander?

KLAUS Unfortunately, I have no record by Alexander, but I have a few jazz records, for instance by Louis Armstrong.

MONIKA Great! Do you know the record "Please, with Whipped Cream" by Udo Jürgens?

KLAUS No, is it a new one?

MONIKA No, it's not new, but I really like the record.

KLAUS Wonderful! I'll be right over. So long, Monika.

MONIKA So long, Klaus. See you later.


## Chapter 3: Bus or Taxi?

*Tempelhof Airport, Berlin. Robert has just arrived in West Berlin. He picks up his luggage and leaves the terminal. Outside, taxis are waiting. He asks a cab driver for information.*

ROBERT Good morning. Excuse me, is there a bus from here to the Kurfürstendamm?

TAXI DRIVER Not directly from here. But do you see the bus stop over there? Take bus number eight!

*A bus number eight is just leaving.*

ROBERT How often does the bus to the Kurfürstendamm run?

TAXI DRIVER Just a moment. I believe, every fifteen minutes.

ROBERT Really?

TAXI DRIVER But take a taxi! Hop in!

ROBERT Thank you. I'm not in a hurry and I don't have enough money for a taxi. Thanks for the information.

TAXI DRIVER You're welcome.

*After fifteen minutes a bus number eight arrives and Robert boards it. The bus is full.*

ROBERT Are you going to the Kurfürstendamm?

TAXI DRIVER No, no. Get off quickly and take bus number fifteen.— Get in, please. Move on! Move to the rear, please!

*The bus driver shuts the door.*

ROBERT (*to himself*) Next time, I'll take a taxi.

# Chapter 4: The Student Room

*Heinz lives in Cologne but is studying in Marburg. He is looking for a room. He reads the newspaper and then goes to a rental agency. There he talks with Miss Schell.*

MISS SCHELL Good morning. May I help you?

HEINZ I'm a student here in Marburg and I'm looking for a room.

MISS SCHELL How much would you like to pay per month?

HEINZ About two hundred marks per month.

MISS SCHELL One moment, please. How about a room right by the University? It costs two hundred and forty a month, heat included.

HEINZ That's not particularly cheap. Does that include cooking facilities?

MISS SCHELL Yes, I'm sure.

HEINZ Does the room have a shower or a bath?

MISS SCHELL No, but it has a wash basin.

HEINZ And how about the toilet?

MISS SCHELL It's right by the room.

HEINZ Not bad! What's the address, please?

MISS SCHELL Mrs. Becker, Lindenstraße five. Near Hindenburg Square.

HEINZ Thank you! How much do I owe you?

MISS SCHELL Eight marks. (*She brings the student a form.*) Please sign this form and give it to Mrs. Becker. (*Heinz signs and pays.*)

HEINZ Many thanks! Good-bye!

*Heinz goes home.*

# Chapter 5: In Court

DISTRICT ATTORNEY Now please tell us, Mr. Steinhoff, how did the accident happen?

STEINHOFF Well, I went to a party at the home of some friends.

D.A. What did you drink?

STEINHOFF We drank wine, beer, or orange juice.

D.A. I see. And naturally you drank orange juice.

STEINHOFF I think so.

D.A. How is that? I don't understand. The police stopped you and took a blood test.

STEINHOFF That's right.

D.A. Did you really drink only orange juice?

STEINHOFF Perhaps somebody mixed in some vodka, but I didn't notice anything.

D.A. Mr. Steinhoff, have you forgotten already? You damaged public property!

STEINHOFF Oh, you mean the tree?

D.A. Yes, how did that happen?

STEINHOFF A Volkswagen passed me and I quickly turned to the left.

D.A. But Mr. Steinhoff, the tree was on the right.

STEINHOFF Then I probably didn't see it.

D.A. Why not, Mr. Steinhoff?

STEINHOFF I have no idea.

D.A. Then I'll give you the answer. Unfortunately, you had too much orange juice in your blood.

## Chapter 6: The Rolls

*George and Sybil had a date for nine a.m. in a stand-up coffee bar. George is fifteen minutes late.*

SYBIL Here you are at last! Where have you been?

GEORGE Hi, Sybil. I'm sorry. I really meant to be on time.

SYBIL What happened again?

GEORGE I looked for a parking place a long time and couldn't find one.

SYBIL That's nothing new.

GEORGE Finally I parked the car on the sidewalk in front of the bakery.

SYBIL Go on.

GOERGE I was just about to get out when a cop came along. "You can't park here. Drive on," he said.

SYBIL But you know you can't park there.

GEORGE "Only for a few minutes," I begged him. But the guy showed no pity and was about to give me a ticket.

SYBIL But why did you want to go to the bakery?

GEORGE Well, I was supposed to bring some rolls.

SYBIL And where are they?

GEORGE The rolls? Good Lord, I forgot all about them!

## Chapter 7: The Vacation Trip

*Jutta and Kurt have been married for fifteen years and have two children, Walter, 12, and Claudia, 10. They are making plans for the family vacation. They would like to take a vacation trip with the children.*

JUTTA Listen, Kurt, we must make plans now for our vacation.

KURT (*reading the newspaper*) There's ample time for that.

JUTTA Not at all. In two months you'll have your vacation.

KURT (*drops the newspaper*) Agreed. But where shall we go? Unfortunately, we have hardly any money left for vacation.

JUTTA Well, we certainly can't stay at home. The children, for instance, would like to see the South of France.

KURT What, the South of France? That's too expensive. Why don't we drive up to the North Sea, perhaps to Westerland?

JUTTA But you know very well that traveling within Germany isn't cheap either. Besides, it'll probably be raining up there again.

KURT Then we'll take umbrellas instead of bathing suits.

JUTTA Don't be so cynical. After all, we must do something for the children.

KURT Of course. But during our vacation I'd like to have some rest. Southern France is so far away and one gets so tired while driving.

JUTTA Well after all, I can drive too, can't I? So how do you feel about Southern France?

## Chapter 8: Looking for the University

*Fritz and Rudi, two friends who are university students, arrive in a Volkswagen in Münster, Westphalia, coming from Bielefeld. They are heading toward the railroad station. They stop on a street and ask a passer-by for information.*

FRITZ Excuse me, how do we get from here to the University?

PASSER-BY To the University? That's very simple. Do you see the fountain up ahead at the end of the parking lot?

FRITZ Oh, yes.

PASSER-BY There you turn immediately to the right and keep going until you get to the Klosterstraße.

FRITZ You mean right up there ahead, behind the fountain?

PASSER-BY Hm, yes. But be careful! At the Klosterstraße you must turn to the left.

RUDI (*studying a city map*) Will we pass the cathedral?

PASSER-BY No, the cathedral is straight ahead. But that way is no good. It's a pedestrian mall.

FRITZ But at the Klosterstraße we turn to the left?

PASSER-BY You'll have to. You'll see, it's a one-way street. After that you'll come to an intersection.

FRITZ All right.

PASSER-BY But after the intersection you drive on to the end of the Schützenstraße.

FRITZ And then?

PASSER-BY Then you better ask someone else.

FRITZ Many thanks.

PASSER-BY You're welcome.

FRITZ (*to Rudi*) Hey, did he say go to the right or straight ahead up there at the corner?

RUDI I haven't the slightest idea. Go straight ahead. Don't worry, we'll find the University. They say it's a palace.

## Chapter 9: Should We Go to the Movies?

*Heinz is a film enthusiast. He calls up his friend Karl Zimmermann, and tries to convince him to go to a movie that night.*

KARL Zimmermann speaking.

HEINZ Hi, Karl. This is Heinz. So you're home at last. I called you an hour ago, but didn't get an answer.

KARL Well, I was at Professor Dietrich's seminar. Toward the end he let a student go on talking, though we were all practically asleep.

HEINZ That's nothing new. When I was in his seminar a year ago, that happened every week. But listen, do you feel like going to the movies?

KARL Of course I do, but I've got a date already.

HEINZ Don't kid me! You've absolutely got to see the Faßbinder film at the Odeon, if you're really interested in the art of the film.

KARL That's all fine and dandy, but I can't be in two places at the same time.

HEINZ Right! So I'll pick you up as soon as you've eaten. Okay?

KARL But Heinz, tonight I'm seeing *Faust* with Margret. Do you understand?

HEINZ Why didn't you say so in the first place?

KARL Because you keep right on talking.

HEINZ Okay, then, have fun! But don't turn your date into a Gretchen tragedy!

## Chapter 10: The Rate of Exchange

*Mr. and Mrs. Kohler, German Americans, are on a vacation trip through their old homeland. They flew from Chicago to Frankfurt two days ago and meanwhile have rested up from their flight. They enter the breakfast room of their hotel and sit down at a table. They have just ordered their breakfast and begin to talk.*

MRS. K. Look, someone left his newspaper.

MR. K. I don't think so. It must belong to the hotel. Do you see the papers on the table over there? They are there for the guests.

MRS. K. Of course. I've got to get used to the customs over here again.

MR. K. Just a moment. I'll get myself the *Frankfurter Allgemeine.* Which newspaper would you like to look at?

MRS. K. The *Süddeutsche*, please. We must by all means look up the exchange rate of the dollar.

*Mr. Kohler goes to the table and comes back with both newspapers.*

MR. K. I hope the rate hasn't dropped any more. Unfortunately, for us Americans the Economic Miracle has its dark side.

MRS. K. Fantastic! It says here: "Dollar recovers on the Frankfurt Exchange."

MR. K.  Good. We'll go to the bank as soon as we're finished eating, and change a few more traveler's checks.

*One hour later in front of the bank.*

MRS. K.  How many marks have we gained now for two hundred dollars, in comparison with yesterday's rate of exchange?

MR. K.  Just a minute! I'm computing it.—Good Lord—five whole marks! That may be just enough for the taxi back to the hotel.

## Chapter 11: Long Hair

*Mrs. Eichendorff is a working mother. Her son Jürgen, aged 16, is a pupil at the municipal Gymnasium. He is changing clothes to go to a small birthday party for his good friend Paul, the son of rich parents.*

JÜRGEN  *(calling from upstairs)* Hey, Mom, what shall I wear?

MOTHER  By all means, a clean shirt and your new tie.

JÜRGEN  Which new tie? Oh, that dull tie that Uncle Emil gave me! But what suit shall I put on?

MOTHER  The dark blue one, of course. Why do you even ask? And don't forget to put on clean socks that match.

*After a short while Jürgen comes downstairs.*

JÜRGEN  How do I look?

MOTHER  Fairly acceptable. But put on your warm overcoat and a hat. It's cold out.

JÜRGEN  No, no—I won't be cold. And anyway, I don't want to go walking around like a mobile clothes hanger.

MOTHER  Wait a minute! Didn't you say you wanted your hair cut a little?

JÜRGEN  Are you out of your mind? In cold weather my long hair keeps me nice and warm. Be seeing you!

## Chapter 12: The Discothèque

*Jutta Jünger (22) is a chemistry student in Cologne. Hansjörg Braun (23) studies sociology. They are friends and happen to meet downtown.*

JUTTA  Hansjörg! Hansjörg! Hello, Hansjörg! Can't you hear me? Hansjörg!!!

HANSJÖRG  What? How's that? Oh Jutta, it's you—hello!

JUTTA  How are you? What's new?

HANSJÖRG  Nothing new—the usual. I'm reading and writing, and I'm late again with a seminar paper. You know me well enough.

JUTTA  But where are you coming from now?

HANSJÖRG  Beg your pardon?

JUTTA (*shouting*) Where you're coming from? From the university library?

HANSJÖRG What? Yes, from the Jimmy Discothèque. There's a great band playing there now—"The Singing Vampires."

JUTTA Why aren't they called the "Howling Vampires"? You can hardly hear any more.

HANSJÖRG So what? That way I won't hear every noise. By the way, the Vampires sing several good hits of considerable sociological and political interest.

JUTTA You don't say! But why don't these people ever invite Biermann?

HANSJÖRG What's that? You want to invite me for a beer?

JUTTA Oh, forget it! Let's go! We'll drink something refreshing over there. Swallowing will do your hearing some good.

HANSJÖRG What did you say?

## Chapter 13: After the Lecture

*Werner is a physics student at a German university, and his friend Helga is in the fourth semester of medicine. Both are 23 years old. Helga arrives in the student cafeteria out of breath. There she finds her friend. He is sitting in front of his meal, half dreaming.*

HELGA Werner, so here you are!

WERNER Yes, of course. Where else? It's already—(*looks at his watch*)—twenty after twelve and high time we had lunch.

HELGA But we had agreed to meet at a quarter to twelve in front of the lab building, and to eat downtown.

WERNER But hadn't we agreed on that for tomorrow?

HELGA No, for today.

WERNER Then I've sure made a mistake. How dumb of me!

HELGA I should say so!

WERNER Please don't be mad at me. Sit down. I've already got lunch for both of us.

HELGA Okay, but we'll eat downtown tomorrow. Our seminars don't start until 4:30 p.m. anyway.

WERNER Agreed. But you know, the lecture by Professor Schürmann this morning was fabulous—clear and entertaining.

HELGA Honestly? An entertaining math lecture certainly is something unusual.

WERNER But Professor Schürmann really has a good sense of humor.

HELGA Then I'll come with you to the lecture tomorrow.

WERNER What for?

HELGA Otherwise, you'll forget our date again.

## Chapter 14: The Psychologist

*Franz and Ferdi are students at the University of Vienna. Franz is in the second semester of psychology and Ferdi in the first semester of Germanics. They live in a small rented apartment and are on their way home from the university.*

FRANZ We must hurry to get home quickly.

FERDI Why so fast? First I'd like to have something sweet in the café over there.

FRANZ Again? But I want to give you the psychology test that we discussed yesterday in the seminar.

FERDI So I'm to play guinea pig again? What's the name of the test you're so excited about this time?

FRANZ (*excited*) It's a Thematic Apperception test.

FERDI What? That sounds horrible. What have you psychologists dreamed up this time?

FRANZ Very simple. We show you a picture whose meaning you have to interpret. In the process, your personality expresses itself.

FERDI You already know my so-called "personality."

FRANZ Who knows? Maybe it's much deeper than I think.

FERDI Oh really? That could be interesting.

FRANZ Imagine: on a test sheet you see a man who stands in front of a picture, dreaming. What's in the picture and what's he thinking about?

FERDI Hm, very simple. The picture is a still life—a big piece of Sachertorte, and the man is thinking: "Boy, am I hungry!"

## Chapter 15: The Abitur

*Anita, Anton, and Wolfgang are three last-year students at the Gymnasium who are about to take the Abitur exam. For almost three months they have been studying together three times a week to prepare for the exam. One evening they talk with one another during a break.*

ANTON Listen, my head is swimming. That's a really mean math problem we solved there.

WOLFGANG You should say, "that Anita solved for us."

ANTON True. If we could only take the Abitur together as a group, then we'd pass with flying colors.

ANITA A fantastic idea! Then I would take on mathematics, and Anton could write the English composition for us.

WOLFGANG And me?

ANTON Don't make a fuss! You know German literature backwards and forwards.

WOLFGANG Maybe. But I'd rather write my own poem than comment on a hackneyed quote out of a Schiller poem.

ANTON Ha, ha—his own poem! Listen to that, Anita! The teachers would certainly confer the Nobel Prize on him for his poem.

WOLFGANG You see, Anita, he's laughing at me again! Anton, unfortunately you have no imagination.

ANTON "Imagination"! Don't make me laugh!

WOLFGANG If the teachers had more poetic sensitivity, they'd leave more room for our own thoughts and feelings.

ANITA Once again, what's this all about? Don't quarrel. None of us can take any more stress. Why don't we go to our discothèque afterward?

WOLFGANG Great! But promise me not to give a lecture about the physics of sound on the way home!

## Chapter 16: Hitchhiking

*Ray is an American student of German descent, studying at the Free University of Berlin. He is standing at the city limits of West Berlin near the Berlin Wall, at an exit leading to the DDR. In his hands he holds a piece of cardboard on which he has written "To Hamburg." Monika and Freddy approach in an Opel and stop in front of him.*

MONIKA *(leaning out of the car)* Hello. What are you waiting for?

RAY What am I waiting for? A friendly soul who'll take me to Hamburg.

MONIKA To Hamburg? But what's written on that piece of cardboard of yours?

RAY What's written on it? "To Hamburg," of course.

FREDDY But look at the sign from the front!

RAY *(laughing)* Oh, how dumb of me! I had it upside down. Most of the drivers must have laughed about it when they saw me. But nobody was willing to stop.

FREDDY Some of them must have thought you spoke an exotic language. But hop in!

MONIKA Yes, do! You're lucky. As it happens, we're driving to Hamburg.

RAY *(gets into the car)* Great! Many thanks!

*A little later in the car.*

MONIKA Why did you decide to go to Hamburg?

RAY We have our semester break. I simply threw an arrow at a map of Germany, and I'm going where the arrow hit.

MONIKA Did you also have the map upside down?

RAY No, luckily not, otherwise I probably wouldn't have met such a nice person as you.

FREDDY Easy now—no cupid's arrows!

## Chapter 17: The Stein of Beer

*Joseph, who works for a German firm in New York, finds himself in his home town of Munich on a business trip, and gets together with his old friend Franz in a beer hall.*

FRANZ Did you have a pleasant flight over the Atlantic?

JOSEPH The usual. People ate and drank a lot and, as always, they showed some old film.

FRANZ Could you rest a little?

JOSEPH Oh no! I was always awakened by crying children or passengers walking around.

FRANZ Too bad, but that can't be helped.

JOSEPH True, it's like in a hospital. You go to sleep only to be immediately awakened again.

FRANZ Well, it's not as bad as all that. You need to be cheered up. (*To the waitress:*) Two steins, please.

*The waitress brings two enormous mugs of beer.*

FRANZ To hell with it! Look at this stein of beer!

JOSEPH What's the matter?

FRANZ Two or three centimeters of foam. The big fraud in the pitcher! The stein should be lengthened by two centimeters. More room for beer and foam!

JOSEPH Well, it's not as bad as all that! Do have a drink! We've got to cheer you up!

## Chapter 18: The Mystery Writer

*A group of young people are going to a rock concert. But Gerd's brother Franz doesn't want to go with them.*

ANITA Gerd, where's your brother? Isn't he coming with us?

GERD He says he wants to stay home because he doesn't think much of rock concerts.

HILDEGARD He's probably reading a long novel again. He has a real bent for literature.

GERD Nonsense! He wants to see a detective story on TV.

BERTHOLD What, your brother? I wouldn't have expected that of him.

GERD Oh yes! He claims that one learns something about real life from them.

HILDEGARD Anita, did you hear that? Gerd, tell your brother he ought to come with us sometime—*then* he'd learn something about real life!

BERTHOLD Hilda, don't be so conceited!

GERD By the way, Franz says he wants to become a mystery writer himself. He says there's a lot of money in it.

ANITA He's thinking of money again! Incidentally, what's he doing with his ticket?

GERD He gave it to me and told me to sell it at the entrance for double its price.

BERTHOLD You see, Hilda, Franz understands something about real life!

## IMPORTANT STRONG AND IRREGULAR WEAK VERBS

### Strong verbs
*1st principal part*

| INFINITIVE | PRESENT | PAST | PAST PARTICIPLE |
|---|---|---|---|
| | | *2nd principal part* | *3rd principal part* |
| backen (*to bake*) | bäckt | backte (buk) | gebacken |
| befehlen (*to command*) | befiehlt | befahl | befohlen |
| beginnen (*to begin*) | | begann | begonnen |
| beißen (*to bite*) | | biß | gebissen |
| betrügen (*to deceive*) | | betrog | betrogen |
| beweisen (*to prove*) | | bewies | bewiesen |
| biegen (*to bend*) | | bog | gebogen |
| bieten (*to offer*) | | bot | geboten |
| binden (*to bind*) | | band | gebunden |
| bitten (*to request*) | | bat | gebeten |
| blasen (*to blow*) | bläst | blies | geblasen |
| bleiben (*to remain*) | | blieb | ist geblieben |
| braten (*to fry*) | brät | briet | gebraten |
| brechen (*to break*) | bricht | brach | gebrochen |
| eindringen (*to penetrate*) | | drang ein | ist eingedrungen |
| empfehlen (*to recommend*) | empfiehlt | empfahl | empfohlen |

| 1st principal part | | 2nd principal part | 3rd principal part |
|---|---|---|---|
| *INFINITIVE* | *PRESENT* | *PAST* | *PAST PARTICIPLE* |
| entscheiden (*to decide*) | | entschied | entschieden |
| entweichen (*to escape*) | | entwich | ist entwichen |
| erschrecken (*to frighten*) | erschrickt | erschrak | ist erschrocken |
| essen (*to eat; used of humans*) | ißt | aß | gegessen |
| | | | |
| fahren (*to drive*) | fährt | fuhr | ist gefahren |
| fallen (*to fall*) | fällt | fiel | ist gefallen |
| fangen (*to catch*) | fängt | fing | gefangen |
| finden (*to find*) | | fand | gefunden |
| fliegen (*to fly*) | | flog | ist geflogen |
| fliehen (*to flee*) | | floh | ist geflohen |
| fließen (*to flow*) | | floß | ist geflossen |
| fressen (*to eat; used of animals*) | frißt | fraß | gefressen |
| frieren (*to freeze*) | | fror | gefroren |
| | | | |
| gebären (*to give birth*) | gebiert | gebar | geboren |
| geben (*to give*) | gibt | gab | gegeben |
| gedeihen (*to thrive*) | | gedieh | ist gediehen |
| gehen (*to walk*) | | ging | ist gegangen |
| gelingen (*to succeed*) | | gelang | ist gelungen |
| gelten (*to be worth*) | gilt | galt | gegolten |
| genießen (*to enjoy*) | | genoß | genossen |
| geschehen (*to occur*) | geschieht | geschah | ist geschehen |
| gewinnen (*to win, gain*) | | gewann | gewonnen |
| gießen (*to pour*) | | goß | gegossen |
| gleichen (*to resemble*) | | glich | geglichen |
| gleiten (*to glide*) | | glitt | ist geglitten |
| graben (*to dig*) | gräbt | grub | gegraben |
| greifen (*to seize*) | | griff | gegriffen |
| | | | |
| halten (*to hold*) | hält | hielt | gehalten |
| hängen (*to hang*) | | hing | gehangen |
| hauen (*to spank*) | | haute (hieb) | gehauen |
| heben (*to lift*) | | hob | gehoben |
| heißen (*to be called*) | | hieß | geheißen |
| helfen (*to help*) | hilft | half | geholfen |
| | | | |
| klingen (*to sound*) | | klang | geklungen |
| kommen (*to come*) | | kam | ist gekommen |
| kriechen (*to crawl*) | | kroch | ist gekrochen |
| | | | |
| laden (*to load*) | lädt | lud | geladen |
| lassen (*to let*) | läßt | ließ | gelassen |
| laufen (*to run*) | läuft | lief | ist gelaufen |
| leiden (*to suffer*) | | litt | gelitten |
| leihen (*to lend*) | | lieh | geliehen |
| lesen (*to read*) | liest | las | gelesen |
| liegen (*to lie*) | | lag | gelegen |
| lügen (*to tell a lie*) | | log | gelogen |

| 1st principal part | | 2nd principal part | 3rd principal part |
|---|---|---|---|
| *INFINITIVE* | *PRESENT* | *PAST* | *PAST PARTICIPLE* |
| messen (*to measure*) | mißt | maß | gemessen |
| mißlingen (*to fail*) | | mißlang | ist mißlungen |
| nehmen (*to take*) | nimmt | nahm | genommen |
| pfeifen (*to whistle*) | | pfiff | gepfiffen |
| raten (*to advise, guess*) | rät | riet | geraten |
| reiben (*to rub*) | | rieb | gerieben |
| reißen (*to tear*) | | riß | ist gerissen |
| reiten (*to ride*) | | ritt | ist geritten |
| riechen (*to smell*) | | roch | gerochen |
| ringen (*to wrestle*) | | rang | gerungen |
| rufen (*to call*) | | rief | gerufen |
| saufen (*to drink; used of animals*) | säuft | soff | gesoffen |
| saugen (*to suck*) | | sog | gesogen |
| schaffen (*to create*) | | schuf | geschaffen |
| scheinen (*to seem, shine*) | | schien | geschienen |
| schieben (*to push*) | | schob | geschoben |
| schießen (*to shoot*) | | schoß | geschossen |
| schlafen (*to sleep*) | schläft | schlief | geschlafen |
| schlagen (*to beat*) | schlägt | schlug | geschlagen |
| schleichen (*to sneak*) | | schlich | ist geschlichen |
| schließen (*to close*) | | schloß | geschlossen |
| schmeißen (*to fling*) | | schmiß | geschmissen |
| schmelzen (*to melt*) | schmilzt | schmolz | ist geschmolzen |
| schneiden (*to cut*) | | schnitt | geschnitten |
| schreiben (*to write*) | | schrieb | geschrieben |
| schreien (*to cry*) | | schrie | geschrien |
| schweigen (*to be silent*) | | schwieg | geschwiegen |
| schwimmen (*to swim*) | | schwamm | ist geschwommen |
| schwören (*to swear an oath*) | | schwur | geschworen |
| sehen (*to see*) | sieht | sah | gesehen |
| sein (*to be*) | ist | war | ist gewesen |
| singen (*to sing*) | | sang | gesungen |
| sinken (*to sink*) | | sank | ist gesunken |
| sitzen (*to sit*) | | saß | gesessen |
| spinnen (*to spin*) | | spann | gesponnen |
| sprechen (*to speak*) | spricht | sprach | gesprochen |
| sprießen (*to sprout*) | | sproß | ist gesprossen |
| springen (*to jump*) | | sprang | ist gesprungen |
| stechen (*to sting*) | sticht | stach | gestochen |
| stehen (*to stand*) | | stand | gestanden |
| stehlen (*to steal*) | stiehlt | stahl | gestohlen |
| steigen (*to climb*) | | stieg | ist gestiegen |
| sterben (*to die*) | stirbt | starb | ist gestorben |
| stinken (*to stink*) | | stank | gestunken |

| *1st principal part* | | *2nd principal part* | *3rd principal part* |
|---|---|---|---|
| INFINITIVE | PRESENT | PAST | PAST PARTICIPLE |
| stoßen (*to push*) | stößt | stieß | gestoßen |
| streichen (*to stroke, spread*) | | strich | gestrichen |
| streiten (*to quarrel*) | | stritt | gestritten |
| | | | |
| tragen (*to carry*) | trägt | trug | getragen |
| treffen (*to hit, meet*) | trifft | traf | getroffen |
| treiben (*to drive*) | | trieb | getrieben |
| treten (*to step, kick*) | tritt | trat | getreten |
| trinken (*to drink; used of humans*) | | trank | getrunken |
| tun (*to do*) | | tat | getan |
| | | | |
| verbergen (*to hide*) | verbirgt | verbarg | verborgen |
| verderben (*to spoil*) | verdirbt | verdarb | verdorben |
| vergessen (*to forget*) | vergißt | vergaß | vergessen |
| verlieren (*to lose*) | | verlor | verloren |
| verschwinden (*to disappear*) | | verschwand | ist verschwunden |
| verzeihen (*to forgive*) | | verzieh | verziehen |
| | | | |
| wachsen (*to grow*) | wächst | wuchs | ist gewachsen |
| waschen (*to wash*) | wäscht | wusch | gewaschen |
| werben (*to advertise*) | wirbt | warb | geworben |
| werden (*to become*) | wird | wurde | ist geworden |
| werfen (*to throw*) | wirft | warf | geworfen |
| wiegen (*to weigh*) | | wog | gewogen |
| winden (*to wind*) | | wand | gewunden |
| | | | |
| zwingen (*to compel*) | | zwang | gezwungen |

## Irregular weak verbs and modals

| | | | |
|---|---|---|---|
| brennen (*to burn*) | | brannte | gebrannt |
| bringen (*to bring*) | | brachte | gebracht |
| | | | |
| denken (*to think*) | | dachte | gedacht |
| dürfen (*to be allowed to*) | darf | durfte | gedurft |
| | | | |
| haben (*to have*) | hat | hatte | gehabt |
| | | | |
| kennen (*to know*) | | kannte | gekannt |
| können (*to be able to*) | kann | konnte | gekonnt |
| | | | |
| mögen (*to like to*) | mag | mochte | gemocht |
| müssen (*to have to*) | muß | mußte | gemußt |
| | | | |
| nennen (*to name*) | | nannte | genannt |
| | | | |
| rennen (*to run*) | | rannte | ist gerannt |

| *1st principal part* | | *2nd principal part* | *3rd principal part* |
|---|---|---|---|
| *INFINITIVE* | *PRESENT* | *PAST* | *PAST PARTICIPLE* |
| sollen (*to ought to*) | soll | sollte | gesollt |
| | | | |
| wenden (*to turn*) | | wandte (wendete) | gewandt (gewendet) |
| wissen (*to know*) | weiß | wußte | gewußt |
| wollen (*to want to*) | will | wollte | gewollt |

**COMMON UNITS OF
MEASUREMENT**

## Measures and weights

1 ounce = 28 grams
1 pint *or* 16 oz. = 0.47 liter
1 quart *or* 2 pts. = 0.95 liter
1 pound *or* 16 oz. = 0.45 kilogram
1 ton *or* 2,200 lbs. = 1,000
   kilograms
1 hundredweight *or* 100 lbs. = 45
   kilograms

1 inch = 2.5 centimeters
1 cubic inch = 16 cubic centimeters
1 foot *or* 12 inches = 0.3 meter
1 yard *or* 3 feet = 0.9 meter
1 mile = 1,609 meters *or* 1.6
   kilometers
1 square mile = 2.6 square
   kilometers

## Maße und Gewichte

¼ Liter = 8.45 ounces *or* 0.53 pint
½ Liter = 16.9 ounces *or* 1.06 pints
1 Liter = 2.1 pints *or* 1.06 quarts *or*
   0.26 gallon
1 Hektoliter = 210 pints *or* 106
   quarts *or* 26 gallons
1 Pfund *or* 500 g *or* ½ Kilo = 1.1
   pounds
1 Kilogramm (Kilo) *or* 1,000 g *or* 2
   Pfd = 2.2 pounds
1 Zentner *or* 100 Pfd *or* 50 kg = 110
   pounds *or* 1.1 hundredweight

1 Tonne *or* 1,000 kg = 2,200 pounds
   *or* 1.1 tons
1 Zentimeter *or* 10 mm = 0.4 inch
1 Kubikzentimeter = 0.06 cubic
   inch
1 Meter *or* 100 cm = 39.5 inches *or*
   3.3 feet *or* 1.1 yards
1 Kilometer *or* 1,000 m = 1,100
   yards *or* 0.62 mile
1 Quadratmeter = 10.8 square feet
   *or* 1.2 square yards

## VERGLEICHS-
## THERMOMETER

CENTIGRADE    FAHRENHEIT

DIE THERMOMETER

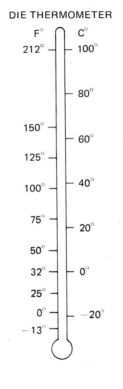

$$°C = \frac{10°(F - 32)}{18} \qquad °F = \frac{18°C}{10} + 32$$

DIE ENTFERNUNG

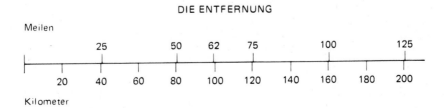

GRÖNLAND
(dän.)

NÖRDLICHES

EISMEER

Barentssee

Nordkap

Murmansk

Weißes
Meer

Archangelsk

ISLAND

kjavik

N
O
R
W
E
G
E
N

S
C
H
W
E
D
E
N

F
I
N
N
L
A
N
D

Bergen

Oslo

Stockholm

Göteborg

Helsinki

Leningrad

Russische S.F.S.R.

Moskau

Wolga

Estnische
S.S.R.

Lettische
S.S.R.

Riga

Litauische
S.S.R.

Minsk

Weißrussische
S.S.R.

Kiew

S
O
W
J
E
T

U
N
I
O
N

ATLANTISCHER OZEAN

Schottland
GROSS-
BRITANNIEN

Nordirland
Glasgow

Dublin
IRLAND

England

Wales

Birmingham

London

NORDSEE

DÄNEMARK

Kopenhagen

OSTSEE

R.S.F.S.R.

Hamburg

Berlin

Warschau

P O L E N

Krakau

Ukrainische S.S.R.

NIEDERLANDE

Amsterdam

DEUTSCHLAND

Brüssel
BELGIEN

Bonn

Frankfurt

Prag

TSCHECHOSLOWAKEI

Odessa

Moldauische
S.S.R.

Der Kanal

LUXEMBURG

Rhein

München

Wien

Budapest

Cluj

Paris

Bern
SCHWEIZ

ÖSTERREICH

UNGARN

RUMANIEN

FRANKREICH

Loire

Lyon

Turin

Mailand

Zagreb

Belgrad

Bukarest

Schwarzes
Meer

Golf von Biscaya

Bordeaux

Po

JUGOSLAWIEN

BULGARIEN

Donau

Bilbao

Marseille

ANDORRA

I
T
A
L
I
E
N

Adriatisches Meer

Sofia

TÜRKEI

RTUGAL

Madrid

Barcelona

Korsika

Rom

Tirana
ALBANIEN

GRIECHENLAND

SPANIEN

Tajo

Valencia

Balearen

Sardinien

Neapel

Sevilla

Gibraltar
(br.)

M I T T E L L Ä N D I S C H E S

Palermo

Sizilien

Athen

Kreta

abat
AROKKO

Oran

Algier

Tunis

MALTA

M E E R

Bengasi

TUNESIEN

A L G E R I E N

Tripolis

L I B Y E N

A F R I K A

ATLAS

Deutschland · Österreich · Schweiz

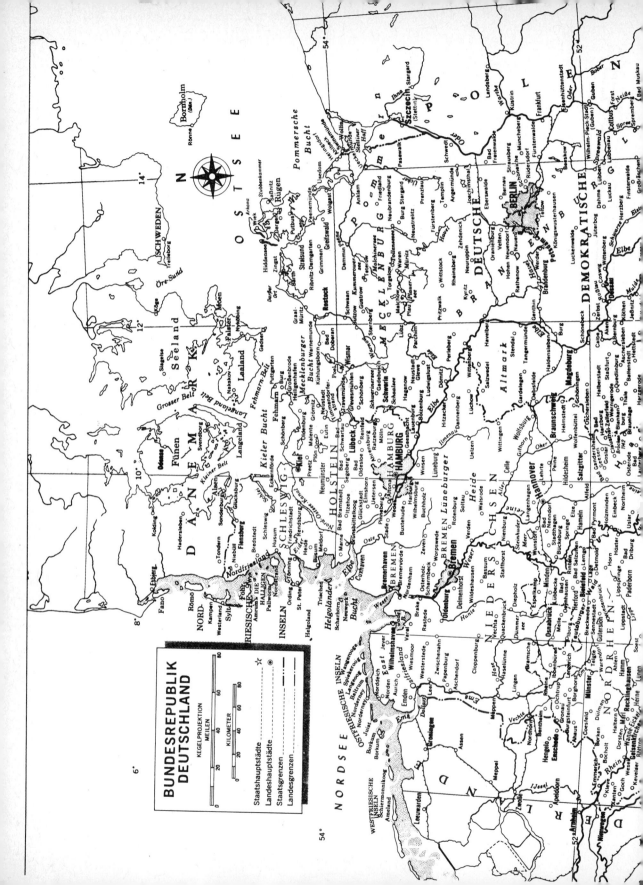

BUNDESREPUBLIK
DEUTSCHLAND

KEGELPROJEKTION

MEILEN

KILOMETER

Staatshauptstädte ☆
Landeshauptstädte ◉
Staatsgrenzen
Landesgrenzen

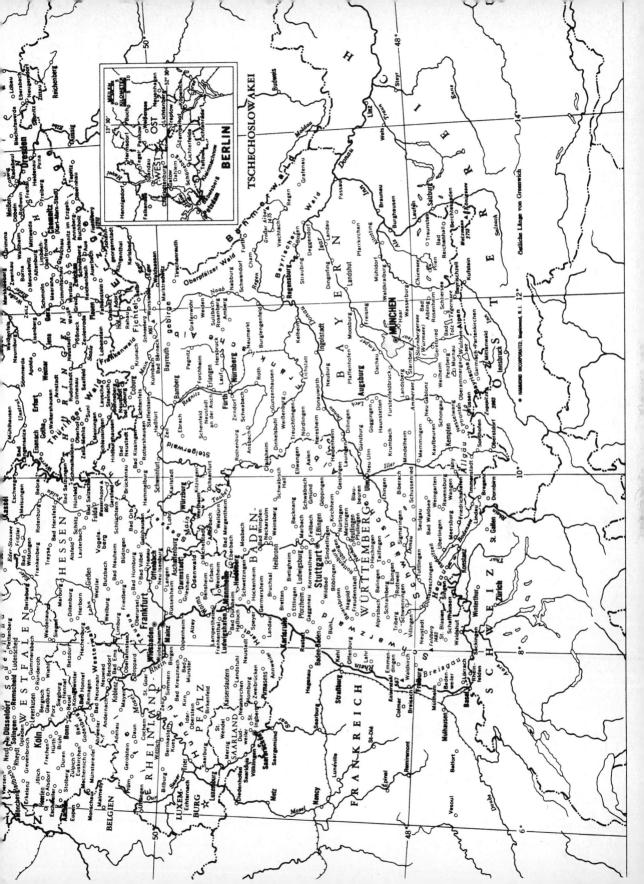

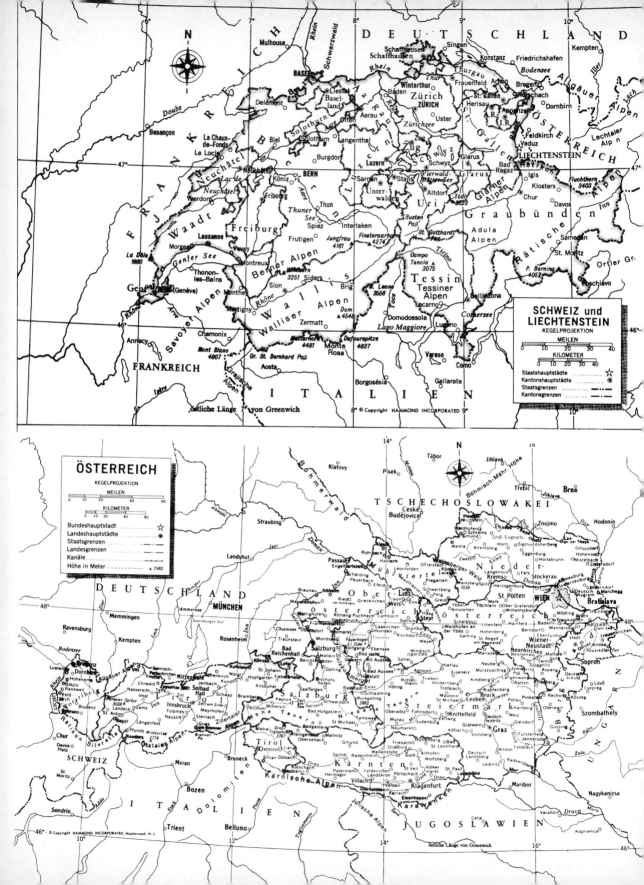

# VOCABULARY

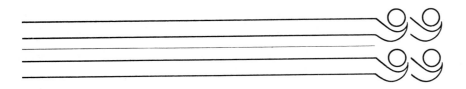

## A

der **Abend, -e**  evening (0)*

das **Abendessen, -**  supper, dinner (4)

**aber**  but (2)

**ab·fahren (fährt ab), fuhr ab, ist abgefahren**  to leave, to depart, to drive off (3)

**ab·helfen (hilft ab), half ab, abgeholfen**  to remedy (+ *dat.*) (17)

**ab·holen**  to come or go for, to come or go get (9)

das **Abitur**  Abitur, the final German examination covering all secondary-school studies (15)

**ab·machen**  to arrange, to agree upon; **abgemacht**  agreed, it's a deal (13)

die **Abstammung, -en**  origin (16)

**abwesend**  absent (15)

**acht**  eight (0)

**achtzehn**  eighteen (0)

**achtzig**  eighty (0)

die **Adresse, -n**  address (4)

**akzeptieren**  to accept (13)

der **Alkohol**  alcohol (2)

**alle**  all (10)

die **Allee, -n**  avenue (16)

**allein**  alone (8)

**allerdings**  indeed (13)

**alles**  all (3); **— schön und gut**  that's all fine and good (9)

die **Alpen** (*pl.*)  the Alps (7)

**als**  than (7); **—** (*conj.*)  when, as (9)

**also**  therefore (9)

**alt**  old (2)

(das) **Amerika**  America (1)

der **Amerikaner, -**  American (male) (1)

die **Amerikanerin, -nen**  American (female) (2)

**amerikanisch** (*adj.*)  American (12)

**an**  on, upon (8)

die **Analyse**  analysis (14)

**andere**  others (10)

der **Anfang, -e**  beginning (8)

**an·fangen (fängt an), fing an, angefangen**  to begin (10)

**an·geben (gibt an), gab an, angegeben**  to brag, to show off (18)

**angenehm**  pleasant (17)

die **Angst, -e**  fear (15)

**an·halten (hält an), hielt an, angehalten**  to stop (3)

der **Anhalter, -**  hitchhiker (16)

**an·kommen, kam an, ist angekommen**  to arrive (at a place) (3)

**an·kündigen**  to announce (6)

**an·rufen, rief an, angerufen**  to call (by phone) (9)

**anstatt**  instead of (7)

sich **anstellen**  to make a fuss (15)

die **Antwort, -en**  answer (5)

**antworten** (+ *dat.*)  to answer (7)

**anziehen**  to pull or put on (clothes) (9)

der **Anzug, -e**  suit (clothes) (9)

der **April**  April (0)

die **Arbeit, -en**  work (5)

**arbeiten**  to work (1)

die **Arbeitslosigkeit**  unemployment (15)

die **Archäologie**  archeology (14)

**arm**  poor (11)

der **Arm, -e**  arm (12)

die **Armee, -n**  army (14)

die **Art, -en**  kind, sort (13)

der **Atem**  breath (13)

der **Athlet, -en**  athlete (8)

der **Atlantik**  Atlantic (17)

**auch**  also (2)

**auf**  on, upon (8)

**auf·bauen**  to rebuild (14)

**auf·führen**  to stage (17)

die **Aufführung, -en**  performance (14)

**auf·geben (gibt auf), gab auf, aufgegeben**  to give up (8)

**aufgeregt**  excited (14)

---

* Numbers after entries identify the chapter in which a word first occurs; an entry followed by (0) first occurs in the Preliminary Chapter.

**aufgeweckt** bright (17)

**auf·halten (hält auf), hielt auf, aufgehalten** to stop, to hinder (16)

**auf·heben, hob auf, aufgehoben** to lift, to pick up, to preserve, to keep (10)

**auf·klären** to clear up (18)

**aufmerksam** attentive (6)

**auf·passen** to pay attention (to), to be careful (of) (8)

**auf·regen** to excite (18)

der **Aufsatz, ⸚e** written composition (15)

**auf·wachen** to wake up (*oneself*) (17)

**auf·wecken** to wake up (*someone*) (17)

das **Auge, -n** eye (9)

der **August** August (0)

**aus** out of, from (1)

sich **ausdenken, dachte sich aus, ausgedacht** to think up (14)

der **Ausdruck, ⸚e** expression (9)

**ausdrücken** to express (9)

**ausgeben (gibt aus), gab aus, ausgegeben** to spend (money) (7)

**aus·gehen (mit + *dat.*), ging aus, ist ausgegangen** to go out with (18)

**aus·halten (hält aus), hielt aus, ausgehalten** to endure, to bear, to stand (15)

**aus·kommen (mit + *dat.*), kam aus, ist ausgekommen** to get along with (18)

die **Auskunft, ⸚e** information (1)

sich **ausruhen** to rest up (17)

**aus·schlafen (schläft aus), schlief aus, ausgeschlafen** to get a good night's sleep (9)

**außer** except (+ *dat.*) (4)

**außerdem** besides (5)

**außerhalb** outside of (+ *dat.*) (7)

**aus·steigen, stieg aus, ist ausgestiegen** to get out (of a vehicle), to get off (3)

**aus·tragen (trägt aus), trug aus, ausgetragen** to carry out, to hold (games) (17)

**authentisch** authentic (18)

das **Auto, -s** car (3)

die **Autobahn, -en** freeway (11)

der **Autostop, -s** hitchhiking; **per —** **reisen** to hitchhike (16)

## B

die **Bäckerei, -en** bakery (6)

das **Bad, ⸚er** bath (4)

die **Badehose, -n** bathing trunks (7)

das **Badezimmer, -** bathroom (4)

der **Bahnhof, ⸚e** railroad station (4)

die **Bahnhofshalle, -n** railroad station hall (8)

**bald** soon (5)

die **Band, -s** band (orchestra) (12)

die **Bank, -en** bank (10)

der **Bart, ⸚e** beard (11)

der **Bauch, ⸚e** stomach (12)

der **Baum, ⸚e** tree (5)

der **Baustil, -e** architectural style (16)

**bedeuten** to have the meaning, to mean (4)

die **Bedeutung, -en** meaning (14)

sich **beeilen** to hurry (11)

**beeindrucken** to impress (9)

sich **befinden** to be (located) (10)

**befreien** to free, to liberate (7)

**begeistert (von + *dat.*)** enthusiastic (about) (14)

die **Begeisterung, -en** enthusiasm (14)

**beginnen, begann, begonnen** to begin (12)

**behaupten** to claim (18)

die **Behauptung, -en** claim (18)

**bei** near, at (the place of) (4)

**beide** both (10)

das **Bein, -e** leg (12)

das **Beispiel, -e** example; **zum —** for example (2)

**bejahen** to assent, to answer in the affirmative (18)

**bekannt** well known (6)

der **Bekannte, -n** acquaintance (12)

**bekommen, bekam, bekommen** to get, to receive (5)

**belagern** to lay siege to (14)

**belehren** to instruct (18)

**beliebt** popular, well liked (18)

**bemerken** to notice, to observe (18)

**bemerkenswert** remarkable (13)

das **Benzin** gasoline (6)

**bequem** comfortable (11)

der **Berg, -e** mountain (8)

das **Bergsteigen** mountain climbing (8)

der **Bergsteiger, -** mountain climber (8)

der **Bericht, -e** report (6)

der **Beruf, -e** profession (13)

die **Berufsaussichten** (*pl.*) professional prospects (15)

**berühmt** famous (16)
**beschädigen** to damage (5)
**beschäftigen** to occupy, to employ (9)
**beschäftigt** busy (15)
die **Beschäftigung, -en** activity, occupation (7)
**beschreiben, beschrieb, beschrieben** to describe (14)
**besetzen** to occupy (14)
**besichtigen** to visit (a place), to tour (17)
**besonders** especially (8)
**besprechen, besprach, besprochen** to talk over, to discuss (14)
**besser** better (5)
**besteigen, bestieg, bestiegen** to climb (8)
**bestellen** to order (3)
**besuchen** to visit (5)
der **Besucher, -** visitor (16)
**betrachten** to consider (9)
das **Bett, -en** bed (4)
**bevor** (*conj.*) before (9)
**bewegen** to move (8)
die **Bewegung, -en** movement, exercise (8)
der **Beweis, -e** proof, evidence (18)
**bezahlen** to pay (4)
**bezeichnend** significant, typical (17)
die **Beziehung, -en** relationship (13)
die **Bibliothek, -en** library (1)
das **Bier, -e** beer (2)
**bieten, bot, geboten** to offer (17)
das **Bild, -er** picture (14)
**billig** cheap (4)
die **Biologie** biology (14)
**bis** until, as far as (2)
**bitte** please (0); — **schön** you're welcome (8); — **sehr?** may I help you? (4)
**bitten** (**um** + *acc.*) to ask for (3)
**bitter** bitter (16)
**blau** blue (11)
**bleiben, blieb, ist geblieben** to stay (5)
**blind** blind (16)
**blitzen** to lighten (7)
der **Blödsinn** nonsense (18)
die **Blume, -n** flower (7)
die **Bluse, -n** blouse (9)
das **Blut** blood (5)
der **Boden, ⸚** ground, soil, land (7)
**böse** (+ *dat.*) angry (with) (13)
**brauchen** to need (8)
**braun** brown (11)
**breit** broad (11)

**brennen, brannte, gebrannt** to burn (5)
der **Brief, -e** letter (5)
**bringen, brachte, gebracht** to bring (4)
das **Brot, -e** bread (4)
das **Brötchen, -** roll (4)
die **Brücke, -n** bridge (10)
der **Bruder, ⸚** brother (8)
der **Brunnen, -** fountain (8)
die **Brust, ⸚e** chest, breast (12)
das **Buch, ⸚er** book (1)
die **Burg, -en** castle (10)
der **Bürgersteig, -e** sidewalk (6)
das **Büro, -s** office (8)
die **Bundesrepublik Deutschland (BRD)** West Germany, Federal Republic of Germany (6)
der **Bunker, -** bunker (17)
der **Bus, -se** bus (3)
der **Busfahrer, -** bus driver (3)

## C

das **Café, -s** café, coffeehouse (3)
die **Chance, -n** chance (13)
die **Chemie** chemistry (12)

## D

**da** there; — **drüben** over there (1)
**dabei** in so doing (12)
der **Dank** gratitude (3)
**danke** thank you (0)
**danken** (+ *dat.*) to thank (10)
**dann** then (3)
**das** that (1)
**daß** (*conj.*) that (9)
der **Deckel, -** top, lid (16)
**dein** your (10)
**denken, dachte, gedacht** to think (3)
**denn** for, because (9)
**deshalb** therefore (5)
**deutsch** (*adj.*) German (11)
**Deutsch** German (1)
(das) **Deutschland** Germany (1)
**deutschsprachig** German language (*adj*) (18)
der **Dezember** December (0)
**dicht** dense (11)
**dick** fat (8)
der **Dienstag** Tuesday (0)

**dieser** this, that (10)

das **Ding, -e** thing (2)

**direkt** directly, right (4)

**dirigieren** to conduct (14)

die **Diskothek, -en** discotheque (10)

**diskutieren (über)** to discuss (1)

der **Dom, -e** cathedral (8)

**donnern** to thunder (7)

der **Donnerstag** Thursday (0)

das **Doppelbett, -en** double bed (4)

**doppelt** double (18)

das **Dorf, ⸗er** village (10)

**dort** there (3)

sich **drehen** to turn (16)

**drei** three (0)

**dreißig** thirty (0)

**dreizehn** thirteen (0)

das **Drittel, -** one third (13)

**drittens** in the third place, thirdly (11)

**du** you (*sing.*) (1)

**dumm** stupid; **zu —** too bad! how dumb (of me) (13)

**dunkel** dark (11)

**durch** through (7)

**durchschauen** to see through (a person) (10)

**dürfen, durfte, gedurft** to be allowed to (6)

**durstig** thirsty (8)

die **Dusche, -n** shower (4)

**E**

die **Ecke, -n** corner (4)

die **Ehe, -n** marriage (13)

die **Ehescheidung, -en** divorce (13)

**ehrlich** honest (13)

das **Ei, -er** egg (4)

**eigen** own (15)

**eigentlich** really, actually (5)

die **Eigenschaft, -en** characteristic, attribute (17)

die **Eile** haste; **— haben** to be in a hurry (3)

**ein, eine** a (0); **— paar** a few (2)

**ein·atmen** to breathe in (8)

die **Einbahnstraße, -n** one-way street (8)

der **Eindruck, ⸗e** impression (9)

**eindrücken** to press in, to crush (9)

**einfach** simple (8)

der **Eingang, ⸗e** entrance (18)

**einige** some (10)

der **Einkauf, ⸗e** purchase, errand (8)

**ein·laden (lädt ein), lud ein, eingeladen** to invite (12)

**einmal** once; **— in der Woche** once a week (3)

**eins** one (0)

**ein·schlafen (schläft ein), schlief ein, ist eingeschlafen** to go to sleep (9)

**ein·steigen, stieg ein, ist eingestiegen** to get in or into (a vehicle) (3)

die **Eintrittskarte, -n** admission ticket (18)

**einundzwanzig** twenty-one (0)

der **Einwohner, -** resident, inhabitant (7)

**elegant** elegant (11)

**elf** eleven (0)

die **Eltern** (*pl.*) parents (8)

das **Ende** end (8)

**endlich** finally (3)

**eng** narrow (11)

(das) **England** England (1)

der **Engländer, -** Englishman (1)

die **Engländerin, -nen** Englishwoman (1)

**Englisch** English (1)

die **Entdeckung** discovery (18)

**enthalten (enthält), enthielt, enthalten** to contain (14)

der **Enthusiast, -en** enthusiast (9)

sich **entscheiden** to decide (16)

**entweder ... oder** either ... or (15)

sich **entwickeln** to develop (12)

die **Entwicklung, -en** development (12)

die **Epoche, -n** epoch (16)

**er** he (1)

**erfahren (erfährt), erfuhr, erfahren** to experience (17)

die **Erfindung, -en** invention (12)

sich **erfrischen** to refresh oneself (12)

**erhalten (erhält), erhielt, erhalten** to receive (9)

sich **erheben, erhob, erhoben** to rise (10)

sich **erholen (von** + *dat.***)** to recover (from) (10)

**erinnern (an** + *acc.***)** to remind (of) (10)

sich **erinnern (an** + *acc.***)** to remember (10)

**erkennen, erkannte, erkannt** to recognize (5)

sich **erkundigen (nach** + *dat.***)** to make inquiries about (10)

**erleben** to experience (10)
**erleichtern** to make easier, to relieve (17)
**erreichen** to achieve (6)
**ersetzen** to replace (9)
**erst** only (12); **erst -** first (13)
**erstaunlich** surprising (18)
**erstens** in the first place, firstly (11)
**erwarten** to await, expect (11)
**erzählen** to tell (a story) (5)
der **Erzähler, -** narrator (11)
**es** it (1)
der **Esel, -** jackass (16)
**essen (ißt), aß, gegessen** to eat (2)
das **Essen, -** meal (4)
das **Eßzimmer, -** dining-room (10)
**etwas** something (5)
**euer** your (10)
(das) **Europa** Europe (4)
der **Europäer, -** European (7)
**exotisch** exotic (16)

**F**

**fabelhaft** fantastic (15)
die **Fabrik, -en** factory (10)
**fahren** to drive (3)
das **Fahren** driving (6)
der **Fahrer, -** driver (6)
das **Fahrrad, ⸚er** bicycle (6)
die **Fahrt, -en** drive (6)
der **Faktor, -en** Factor (9)
die **Fakultät, -en** faculty (15)
der **Fall, ⸚e** case; **auf jeden —** by all means, in any event (14)
**fallen (fällt), fiel, ist gefallen** to fall (10)
**falls** in case (9)
die **Familie, -n** family (7)
die **Farbe, -n** color (11)
**fast** almost (1)
**faul** lazy (8)
der **Februar** February (0)
der **Fehler, -** mistake (13)
**feiern** to celebrate (17)
der **Feind, -e** enemy (14)
der **Felsen, -** rock, cliff (10)
das **Fenster, -** window (4)
die **Ferien** (*pl.*) vacation (7)
der **Fernsehapparat** television set (8)

das **Fernsehen** television (7)
**fertig** finished, ready (14)
das **Fest, -e** festival (17)
das **Feuer, -** fire (3)
der **Film, -e** film (9)
**finanziell** financial (15)
**finden, fand, gefunden** to find (1)
der **Finger, -** finger (12)
der **Fisch, -e** fish (4)
das **Fleisch** meat (4)
**fliegen, flog, ist geflogen** to fly (11)
**fließen, floß, ist geflossen** to flow (10)
der **Flug, ⸚e** flight (17)
der **Flugplatz, ⸚e** airport (3)
das **Flugzeug, -e** airplane (10)
der **Fluß, ⸚sse** river (6)
**folgen, ist gefolgt** to follow (10)
**folkloristisch** folkloric (17)
die **Form, -en** form (9)
das **Foyer, -** lobby (9)
die **Frage, -n** question; **eine — stellen** to ask a question (13)
**fragen** to ask (3); **— (nach + *dat.*)** to ask for (4)
(das) **Frankreich** France (1)
der **Franzose, -n** Frenchman (1)
die **Französin, -nen** Frenchwoman (1)
die **Frau, -en** woman, wife, Mrs. (1)
das **Fräulein, -** young lady, Miss (1)
**frei** free (3)
der **Freitag, -e** Friday (0)
die **Freizeit** leisure time (7)
**fremd** foreign (18)
sich **freuen (über + *acc.*)** to be glad, happy (about) (10)
der **Freund, -e** friend (male) (2)
die **Freundin, -nen** friend (female) (2)
**frieren, fror, gefroren** to freeze (11)
**frisch** fresh (11)
der **Frühling, -e** spring (season) (0)
das **Frühstück, -e** breakfast (4)
**führen** to lead (14)
**fünf** five (0)
**fünfzehn** fifteen (0)
**fünfzig** fifty (0)
**für** for (1)
**furchtbar** horrible (5)
**fürchterlich** terrible, horrible (14)
der **Fuß, ⸚e** foot (12); **zu — gehen** to go on foot

der **Fußgänger, -** pedestrian (8)

die **Fußwanderung, -en** hike;
    **Fußwanderungen machen** to go on
    hikes (8)

## G

**ganz** quite, completely (2); —
    **recht** that's right (9); **—e 5 Mark** a
    whole five marks (10)

der **Garten, ∸** garden (4)

der **Gärtner, -** gardener (7)

der **Gast, ∸e** guest (10)

das **Gasthaus, ∸er** inn, small hotel (4)

das **Gebäude, -** building (10)
    **geben (gibt), gab, gegeben** to give; **es**
    **gibt** there is, there are (4)

das **Gebiet, -e** region, area (10)
    **geboren werden** to be born (13)

der **Gebrauch, ∸e** use, usage (10)

der **Geburtstag, -e** birthday (13)

der **Gedanke, -n** thought (15)

das **Gedicht, -e** poem (15)
    **gefährlich** dangerous (2)
    **gefallen** (+ *dat.*) to please, appreciate
    (10)

das **Gefühl, -e** sense of touch, feeling,
    sentiment, emotion (9)
    **gegen** against (7)

die **Gegend, -en** region, area (17)

die **Gegenwart** present time (10)
    **geheim** secret (17)
    **gehen, ging, ist gegangen** to go; **zu Fuß**
    **—** to go on foot, walk; **das geht**
    **nicht** that doesn't work (3)

das **Gehör** sense of hearing (12)
    **gehören** (+ *dat.*) to belong to (10)
    **gelb** yellow (11)

das **Geld, -er** money (3)
    **gelingen, gelang, ist gelungen** (*impers.* +
    *dat.*) succeed (10)

das **Gemüse, -** vegetable (4)
    **gemütlich** jolly, good natured, cozy (11)

die **Gemütlichkeit** coziness (17)

die **Generation, -en** generation
    **genug** enough (3)
    **genügen** (*impers.* + *dat.*) to suffice (10)

die **Geologie** geology (14)

das **Gepäck** luggage (3)

    **gerade** just, exactly (3)
    **geradeaus** straight ahead (8)
    **gering** slight (13)
    **gern** gladly; **etwas — haben** to like
    something (2)

der **Geruch** sense of smell (12)

das **Geschäft, -e** business firm (10)

das **Geschäftshaus, ∸er** store (16)

die **Geschäftsreise, -n** business trip (17)
    **geschehen** to happen (9)

die **Geschichte, -n** history, story (11)
    **geschieden** divorced (13)

der **Geschmack** sense of taste, good taste
    (12)

die **Gesellschaft, -en** society, company (13)

das **Gesetz, -e** law (13)

das **Gesicht, -er** face (10)

das **Gespräch, -e** conversation, discussion (9)
    **gestern** yesterday (0)
    **gesund** healthy (2)

die **Gesundheit** health (2)

der **Gewinn** profit, gain (12)
    **gewinnen, gewann, gewonnen** to win, to
    gain (10)

sich **gewöhnen** (**an** + *acc.*) to get used to,
    become accustomed to (10)
    **gigantisch** gigantic (8)

der **Gipfel, -** peak (8)

die **Gitarre, -n** guitar (2)

das **Glas, ∸er** glass (7)
    **glauben** believe, think (2)
    **gleich** directly, right away (1); **gleich-**
    same (13)
    **gleichzeitig** simultaneous, at the same
    time (9)

die **Glocke, -n** bell (14)

das **Glück** luck (1)
    **glücklich** happy, lucky (15)

der **Gott, ∸er** God (9)

das **Gras, ∸er** grass (16)
    **grau** grey (11)
    **groß** big (4)
    **großartig** magnificent (15)

die **Großmutter, ∸** grandmother (8)

der **Großvater, ∸** grandfather (8)

der **Grund, ∸e** reason (13)
    **grün** green (11)

die **Gruppe, -n** group (15)

der **Gruß, ∸e** greeting (5)
    **grüßen** to greet (5)

**gut**  good (0)
die **Güte**  goodness; **meine —**  my goodness (10)
das **Gymnasium**  German highschool (11)

## H

das **Haar, -e**  hair (10)
**haben**  to have (2)
**halb**  half; **es ist —** (neun)  it is half past (eight) (0)
**halten** (hält), **hielt, gehalten**  to stop (3); **— für** (+ *acc.*)  to take for, to consider (16); **— von** (+ *dat.*)  to think (about), to feel (about) (7)
die **Haltestelle, -n**  (bus or train) stop (3)
die **Hand, ⸗e**  hand (10)
**häufig**  frequent (13)
die **Hauptstadt, ⸗e**  capital (17)
das **Haus, ⸗er**  house (4)
der **Haushalt, -e**  household (13)
**heben, hob, gehoben**  to lift (10)
der **Heimweg, -e**  way (or return) home; **auf dem —**  on the way home (15)
das **Heimweh**  homesickness; **— haben**  to be homesick (15)
die **Heirat**  marriage (13)
**heiraten**  to marry (13)
**heiß**  hot (0)
**heißen, hieß, geheißen**  to be called (1)
die **Heizung, -en**  central heating (4)
**helfen** (hilft), **half, geholfen** (+ *dat.*) to help (10)
**hell**  light, pale (color) (11)
das **Hemd, -en**  shirt (9)
der **Herbst**  fall, autumn (0)
**herein·bringen, brachte herein, hereingebracht**  to bring in (5)
der **Herr, -en**  man, gentleman, Mr. (1)
**hervor·heben, hob hervor, hervorgehoben**  to point out (18)
**herzlich**  cordial (5)
**heute**  today (0); **— abend**  this evening (1)
**heutzutage**  nowadays, these days (5)
**hier**  here (1)
der **Himmel, -**  sky (11)
das **Hindernis, -se**  obstacle (8)
**hinein·mischen**  to mix in (5)
**hinter**  behind (8)

der **Hit, -s**  hit (song) (12)
**hoch, hoh-**  high (13)
das **Hochhaus, ⸗er**  high-rise building (10)
die **Hochzeit, -en**  wedding reception (13)
**hoffen**  to hope (1)
**hoffentlich**  hopefully (5)
**holen**  to fetch, to get (9)
(das) **Holland**  Holland (6)
**hören**  to hear (3); **— auf** (+ *acc.*)  to listen to (8)
die **Hose, -n**  trousers, pants (9)
das **Hotel, -s**  hotel (3)
**hübsch**  pretty, attractive (4)
der **Hügel, -**  hill (10)
der **Humor**  humor (13)
der **Humorist**  humorist (14)
**hundert**  hundred (0)
**hungrig**  hungry (8)

## I

**ich**  I (1)
die **Idee, -n**  idea (11)
die **Ideologie, -n**  ideology (12)
das **Idol, -e**  idol (12)
**ihr**  you (*fam. pl.*) (1)
**illustrieren**  to illustrate (7)
**immer**  always (2); **— noch**  still, yet (6)
**imposant**  imposing (14)
**in**  in (1)
die **Industrie, -n**  industry (6)
die **Inflation, -en**  inflation (7)
**informieren**  to inform (1)
**innerhalb**  inside of, within (7)
das **Institut, -e**  institute (1)
der **Intellekt**  intellect (9)
**interessant**  interesting (1)
das **Interesse**  interest (12)
**interessiert**  interested (9)
**international**  international (12)
die **Interpretation**  interpretation (9)
**interpretieren**  to interpret (14)
**intervenieren**  to intervene (7)
die **Invasion, -en**  invasion (12)
**inzwischen**  meanwhile (10)
**irgendein**  some, any (17)
sich **irren**  to be mistaken, to make a mistake (13)
der **Irrtum**  mistake, error (13)

## J

**ja** yes (1)
die **Jacke, -n** jacket (9)
das **Jahr, -e** year (4)
das **Jahrhundert, -e** century (14)
**jährlich** annually (4)
der **Jahrmarkt, ⸚e** annual fair (17)
der **Januar** January (0)
**je . . . desto** the (more) . . . the (more) (13)
**jed-** each, every (10)
**jemals** ever (8)
**jemand** someone (5); — **anders** someone else (8)
**jetzt** now (1)
der **Journalist, -en** journalist (6)
die **Jugend** youth (11)
der **Jugendliche, -n** the youth (12)
der **Juli** July (0)
der **Junge, -ns** boy (4)
die **Jungen** (*pl.*) young people (4)
der **Juni** June (0)
die **Justiz** justice, law (18)

## K

der **Kaffee** coffee (2)
**kalt** cold (0)
der **Kamerad, -en** comrade, chum (11)
die **Kanone, -n** canon (14)
der **Kapitalismus** capitalism (13)
die **Karte, -n** card (2)
die **Kartoffel, -n** potato (4)
der **Katalog, -e** catalogue (1)
die **Katastrophe, -n** catastrophe (14)
der **Kater** hangover (*sl.*) (17)
**kaufen** to buy (2)
**kaum** hardly (7)
**kein** no, not a, not any (2)
der **Kellner, -** waiter (17)
die **Kellnerin, -nen** waitress (17)
**kennen** to know (someone or something), to be acquainted with (2)
der **Kerl, -e** guy, fellow (6)
das **Kind, -er** child (1)
das **Kino, -s** movie theater; **ins — gehen** to go to the movies (9)
die **Kirche, -n** church (4)

der **Klang, ⸚e** sound (2)
**klar** clear (13)
die **Klasse, -n** class (1)
**klassisch** classical (12)
das **Klavier, -e** piano (2)
das **Kleid, -er** dress (9)
die **Kleidung** clothing (11)
**klein** little, small (11)
**klug** intelligent, bright (1)
der **Koffer, -** suitcase (4)
die **Kohle, -n** coal (11)
der **Kollege, -n** colleague (male) (12)
die **Kollegin, -nen** colleague (female) (12)
**komisch** comical (16)
**kommen, kam, ist gekommen** to come (1)
**kommentieren** to comment (15)
der **Kompromiß, -sse** compromise (12)
**können (kann), konnte, gekonnt** to be able to (6)
**konservativ** conservative (15)
**konventionell** conventional (13)
das **Konzert, -e** concert (14)
der **Kopf, ⸚e** head (12)
das **Kopftuch, ⸚er** scarf (9)
der **Körper, -** body (12)
die **Körperbewegung** physical activity (8)
**kosten** to cost (4)
**krank** ill, sick (2)
das **Krankenhaus, ⸚er** hospital (17)
die **Krankheit, -en** illness, disease (8)
die **Krawatte, -n** tie (9)
die **Kreuzung, -en** intersection, crossroads (8)
der **Krieg, -e** war (6)
der **Krimi, -s** thriller (18)
der **Kriminalfall, ⸚e** criminal case (18)
der **Kritiker, -** critic (18)
der **Krug, ⸚e** pitcher (17)
der **Kuchen, -** cake (3)
die **Kultur, -en** culture (9)
**kulturell** cultural (16)
sich **kümmern um** (+ *acc.*) to take care of; to worry about (10)
die **Kunst, ⸚e** art (9)
der **Künstler, -** artist (14)
**kurz** short (11)
**kürzlich** recently (5)
der **Kuß, ⸚sse** kiss (15)

## L

lachen  to laugh (11)

das **Land, ⸚er**  land, country (7)

die **Landkarte, -n**  map (16)

die **Landschaft, -en**  countryside, landscape (10)

**lang, lange** (*with respect to time*) long, for a long time (5)

**langsam**  slow (3)

**langweilig**  boring (11)

der **Lärm**  noise (8)

**lassen (läßt), ließ, gelassen**  to let, to let go (3)

**laufen (läuft), lief, ist gelaufen**  to run, go (by foot) (3)

die **Laune**  mood (17)

**laut**  loud (12)

das **Leben**  life (7)

**ledig**  single, unmarried (13)

**legal**  legal (15)

**legen**  to lay, to put (10)

der **Lehrer, -**  teacher (15)

die **Leibesübung, -en**  physical exercise; **Leibesübungen machen**  to take physical exercises (8)

**leicht**  easy, light (8)

**leiden, litt, gelitten**  to suffer (15)

**leider**  unfortunately (2)

**leise**  quiet, soft (voice) (12)

**lernen**  to learn (11)

**lesen (liest), las, gelesen**  to read (3)

**letzt, -**  last (11)

die **Leute** (*pl.*)  people (7)

**liberal**  liberal (13)

das **Licht, -er**  light (16)

**lieb**  dear (5)

**lieben**  to love (12)

**liegen, lag, gelegen**  to lie, be situated (4)

die **Limonade, -n**  lemonade (12)

**links**  left, on the left; **nach —**  to the left (3)

**literarisch**  literary (18)

die **Literatur, -en**  literature (1)

**los; was ist —**  what's going on?; **nur —** go on, fire away; **der Teufel ist —**  all hell is let loose (15)

**lösen**  to solve (13)

**los·fahren (fährt los), fuhr los, ist losgefahren**  to depart (15)

**los·gehen, ging los, ist losgegangen**  get under way, begin (15)

**los·lassen (läßt los), ließ los, losgelassen**  let loose, let go (15)

**los·machen**  to loosen, to disengage, get away from (15)

die **Lösung, -en**  solution (13)

die **Luft, ⸚e**  air (6)

die **Lust**  desire, joy; **— haben**  to be in the mood, feel like (doing something) (9)

## M

**machen**  to make (3)

die **Macht, ⸚e**  power (14)

das **Mädchen, -**  girl (1)

der **Magen, ⸚**  stomach (16)

der **Mai**  May (0)

das **Mal, -e**  occasion, time; **zum ersten —**  for the first time (14)

**man**  one, you, we, they, people (6)

**mancher**  many a, several, some (10)

**manchmal**  sometimes, once in a while (2)

der **Mann, ⸚er**  man (1)

die **Mannschaft, -en**  team (8)

der **Mantel, ⸚**  coat (9)

die **Mark**  Mark, the unit of German currency (4)

der **März**  March (0)

das **Maß, -e**  moderation; **das — ist voll**  my patience is exhausted; **das geht über alle Maßen**  that exceeds all bounds; **das — vollmachen**  to fill the cup to the brim; **in hohem Maße**  to a high degree; **in großem Maße**  to a large extent; **in gewissem Maße**  to a certain extent; **in vollem Maße**  amply, completely; **— halten**  to know one's bounds; **nach —** tailored (17)

die **Maß**  stein (16)

die **Masse, -n**  mass, crowd (16)

die **Mathematik**  mathematics (14)

die **Mauer, -n**  wall (16)

die **Medizin**  medicine (13)

das **Meer, -e**  sea (11)

**mehr**  more (6)

**mehrere** several (10)
**mein** my (10)
**meinen** to mean (5)
die **Meinung, -en** opinion; **meiner —
nach** in my opinion (13)
**meistens** mostly, for the most part,
generally (6)
der **Mensch, -en** human being, man (2)
**menschlich** human (13)
**merken** to notice (5)
der **Meter, -** meter (13)
**mieten** to rent (7)
die **Milch** milk (4)
die **Million, -en** million (0)
das **Minimum** minimum (18)
die **Minute, -n** minute (3)
**mit** with (3)
**mit·bringen, brachte mit, mitgebracht** to
bring along (6)
das **Mitglied, -er** member (8)
**mit·machen** to go along (with
something) (15)
**mit·nehmen** to carry with, to carry
along (7)
der **Mittag, -e** noon (4)
das **Mittagessen, -** lunch, dinner (4)
die **Mitte** middle (11)
das **Mittelalter** middle ages (10)
die **Mitternacht, ⸚e** midnight (13)
der **Mittwoch** Wednesday (0)
die **Möbel** (*pl.*) furniture (5)
**mögen (mag), mochte, gemocht** to like
to (6)
**möglich** possible (3)
die **Möglichkeit, -en** possibility (9)
der **Moment, -e** moment (2); **— mal** just a
moment (3)
der **Monat, -e** month (4)
**monatlich** monthly (4)
der **Montag** Monday (0)
das **Monument, -e** monument (16)
der **Mord, -e** murder (18)
**morgen** tomorrow (0)
der **Morgen, -** morning (0)
**morgens** in the morning(s) (6)
**müde** tired (7)
der **Mund, ⸚er** mouth (12)
das **Museum, Museen** museum (16)
die **Musik** music (12)
**musikalisch** musical (12)

der **Musiker, -** musician (14)
**müssen (muß), mußte, gemußt** to have
to (6)
der **Mut** courage (14)
die **Mutter, ⸚** mother (8)
die **Mütze, -n** cap (11)


**N**

**nach** after, to (referring to cities and
countries) (4)
**nachdem** (*conj.*) after (9)
**nachher** later (15)
der **Nachmittag, -e** afternoon (8)
**nachmittags** in the afternoon (9)
die **Nachricht, -en** news (5)
**nächstes Mal** next time (3)
die **Nacht, ⸚e** night (13)
**nahe** near (13)
die **Nähe** proximity; **in der —** in the
neighborhood, nearby (10)
sich **nähern** to approach (17)
die **Nase, -n** nose (12)
die **Nation, -en** nation (8)
die **Natur** nature (8)
**natürlich** naturally, of course (2)
**neben** next to, by (8)
der **Neffe, -n** nephew (8)
**nehmen (nimmt), nahm, genommen** to
take (3)
**nein** no (1)
**nennen, nannte, genannt** to name, call
(10)
**nett** nice (5)
**neu** new (2)
**neun** nine (0)
**neunzehn** nineteen (0)
**neunzig** ninety (0)
**nicht** not (1)
**nicht mehr** not any more (6)
die **Nichte, -n** niece (8)
**nichts** nothing (4)
**nie** never (5)
**niemand** nobody (12)
**noch** yet, still (4)
die **Note, -n** grade (15)
**nötig** necessary; **etwas — haben,** to
need something
die **Nummer, -n** number (3)

**nun** now (10)
**nur** only (2)

## O

**ob** whether (9)
**oben** up, above (7)
das **Obst** (*sing. only*) fruit (4)
**obwohl** (*conj.*) although (9)
**oder** or (0)
**offen** open (9)
**öffnen** to open (1)
**oft** often (3)
**ohne** without (2)
**ohnehin** anyway (15)
**ohne . . . zu** without (8)
das **Ohr, -en** ear (12)
der **Oktober** October (0)
der **Onkel, -** uncle (8)
die **Oper** opera (6)
der **Orangensaft, ⸚e** orange juice (5)
das **Orchester** orchestra (17)
**organisieren** to organize (17)
der **Ort, -e** place, spot (9)
der **Osten** East (13)
(das) **Österreich** Austria (1)
der **Österreicher, -** Austrian (male) (1)
die **Österreicherin, -nen** Austrian (female) (1)

## P

der **Palast, ⸚e** palace (8)
der **Pappdeckel** piece of cardboard (16)
der **Park, -s** park (7)
**parken** to park (6)
der **Parkplatz, ⸚e** parking place (6)
die **Partei, -en** party (political) (8)
die **Party, -ies** party (5)
der **Passagier, -e** passenger (17)
der **Passant, -en** passer-by (8)
**passen** to fit; **zueinander —** to be compatible, to suit each other (13)
**passieren, ist passiert** (*impers. + dat.*) to happen (5)
**passiv** passive (18)
die **Pause, -n** intermission (9)

die **Person, -en** person (7)
die **Persönlichkeit, -en** personality (14)
**pflanzen** to plant (7)
die **Phantasie** imagination (15)
die **Physik** physics (13)
der **Plan, ⸚e** plan (7)
die **Platte, -n** record (2)
der **Plattenspieler, -** record player (2)
der **Platz, ⸚e** place, square (7)
**Platz nehmen (nimmt), nahm, genommen** to take (have) a seat (3)
**plötzlich** suddenly (1)
**poetisch** poetic (15)
die **Politik** politics (1)
**politisch** political (12)
die **Polizei** police (3)
der **Polizist, -en** policeman (6)
**populär** popular (6)
die **Popularität** popularity (7)
**praktisch** practical (15)
der **Präsident, -en** president (4)
**prima** great! super (*sl.*) (16)
das **Problem, -e** problem (2)
die **Produktion** production (12)
**produzieren** to produce (12)
der **Professor, -en** professor (9)
das **Programm, -e** program (1)
**protestieren** to protest (3)
das **Prozent, -e** percent (12)
die **Prüfung, -en** examination (15)
der **Psychologe, -n** psychologist (14)
die **Psychologie** psychology (14)
**psychologisch** psychological (14)
das **Publikum** people, audience (public) (6)
der **Pulli, -s** sweater (9)
der **Pullover, -** sweater (9)
**pünktlich** punctual, on time (6)

## Q

die **Qualität, -en** quality (7)

## R

das **Rad, ⸚er** wheel, bicycle (6)
das **Radfahren** bicycling (6)
**radikal** radical (15)
die **Rate, -n** rate (13)

das **Rathaus,** **̈er** city hall (10)
   **rauchen** to smoke (2)
der **Raum,** **̈e** room (1)
   **rechts** right, on the right; **nach —** to the right (3)
   **recht haben** to be right (7)
   **reden** to talk (5)
   **reduzieren** to reduce (18)
   **rege** busy, lively (17)
der **Regenschirm, -e** umbrella (7)
die **Regierung, -en** government (7)
   **regnen** to rain (0)
   **reich** rich (11)
das **Reich, -e** empire (16)
die **Reihe, -n** row (16)
die **Reise, -n** trip, journey (7)
   **reisen** to travel (4)
der **Reisescheck, -s** travelers check (10)
das **Restaurant, -s** restaurant (9)
   **restaurieren** to restore (10)
das **Resultat, -e** result (5)
   **richtig** right (5)
die **Richtung, -en** direction (8)
das **Risiko, -s** risk (12)
der **Rock, ̈e** skirt (9)
der **Roman, -e** novel (18)
   **rot** red (11)
die **Routine, -en** routine (7)
   **rückwärts** backwards (15)
   **rufen, rief, gerufen** to call (11)
die **Ruhe** rest, peace (7)
   **ruhig** quiet, still (16)
der **Russe, -n** Russian (male) (1)
die **Russin, -nen** Russian (female) (1)
   **russisch** Russian (*adj.*) (11)
(das) **Rußland** Russia (1)

## S

der **Saal, Säle** hall, large room (9)
   **sagen** to say (3)
der **Salat, -e** salad (4)
der **Samstag** Saturday (0)
die **Sandale, -n** sandal (9)
der **Sänger, -** singer (12)
   **sauber** clean (17)
   **säubern** to cleanse, clean up (6)
   **schaffen** to create (15)
der **Schatten, -** shadow, shade (14)

   **schauen** to look (10)
der **Schauspieler, -** actor (9)
die **Scheidung, -en** divorce (13)
   **scheinen, schien, geschienen** to shine, to seem (7, 9)
   **schenken** to give (a present) (11)
das **Schild, -er** sign (4)
das **Schlafzimmer, -** bedroom (5)
der **Schlager, -** hit, popular song (12)
   **schlecht** bad (0)
   **schließlich** finally (6)
der **Schlüssel, -** key (4)
der **Schmutz** dirt (6)
   **schmutzig** dirty (6)
der **Schnee** snow (11)
   **schneiden, schnitt, geschnitten** to cut (11)
   **schneien** to snow (0)
   **schnell** fast, quickly (3)
der **Schnurrbart, ̈e** mustache (11)
   **schon** already (5)
   **schön** beautiful (0)
   **schreiben, schrieb, geschrieben** to write (5)
der **Schriftsteller, -** writer (18)
der **Schuh, -e** shoe (9)
der **Schüler, -** pupil, student (11)
   **schwach** weak (2)
die **Schwäche, -n** weakness (2)
   **schwarz** black (11)
die **Schweiz** Switzerland (1)
der **Schweizer, -** Swiss (male) (1)
die **Schweizerin, -nen** Swiss (female) (1)
die **Schwester, -n** sister (8)
   **schwierig** difficult (7)
   **schwimmen, schwamm, ist geschwommen** to swim (8)
   **sechs** six (0)
   **sechzehn** sixteen (0)
   **sechzig** sixty (0)
der **See, -n** lake (6)
die **See** ocean, sea (7)
die **Seele, -n** soul (14)
   **sehen (sieht), sah, gesehen** to see (3)
   **sehr** very (2)
das **Sehvermögen** sight (12)
   **sein (ist), war, ist gewesen** to be (1)
   **sein** his (10)
   **seit** since, for (in reference to time) (4)
   **seitdem** since (time) (9)
die **Seite, -n** side (16)
der **Selbstmord, -e** suicide (16)
das **Semester, -** semester (15)

die **Sendung, -en** broadcast (18)

der **September** September (0)

die **Serie, -n** series, serial (18)

der **Sessel, -** armchair (4)

sich **setzen** to sit down (10)

    **sicher** certain (1)

    **sie** she, they (1)

    **sieben** seven (0)

    **siebzehn** seventeen (0)

    **siebzig** seventy (0)

    **singen, sang, gesungen** to sing (12)

    **sitzen, saß, gesessen** to sit (8)

das **Skilaufen** skiing (5)

    **so** so (6); thus (7)

    **so ... wie** as ... as (6)

    **sobald** as soon as (9)

die **Socke, -n** sock (9)

    **so daß** so that (9)

    **sofort** immediately (4)

    **sogar** even (6)

der **Sohn, ⸚e** son (8)

    **solange** as long as (9)

    **solch, solche** such a (9)

der **Soldat, -en** soldier (16)

    **sollen** to be supposed to (6)

der **Sommer, -** summer (0)

    **sondern** but, on the contrary (9)

der **Sonnabend** Saturday (0)

die **Sonne, -n** sun (8)

der **Sonntag** Sunday (0)

    **sonst** otherwise (13)

    **sooft** as often as, whenever (9)

die **Sorge, -n** worry (11)

    **sorglos** carefree (15)

    **sozial** social (13)

der **Sozialismus** socialism (13)

die **Soziologie** sociology (1)

    **soziologisch** sociological (12)

der **Spaß, ⸚e** fun (6)

    **spät** late (0)

    **später** later (9)

das **Spiel, -e** play, game (17)

    **spielen** to play (2)

der **Sport** sport(s) (8)

der **Sportclub, -s** sport club (8)

der **Sportler, -** sportsman (14)

die **Sprache, -n** language (1)

    **sprechen (spricht), sprach, gesprochen** to speak (2)

    **springen, sprang, ist gesprungen** to jump (8)

der **Staat, -en** state (7)

das **Stadion, Stadien** stadium (17)

die **Stadt, ⸚e** city (4)

    **städtisch** municipal (11)

die **Stadtmitte** city center (4)

der **Stadtpark, -s** municipal park (7)

das **Stadttheater, -** city theater (7)

    **stark** strong (2)

    **statt·finden, fand statt, stattgefunden** to take place (17)

    **stehen, stand, gestanden** to stand (3)

    **steigen, stieg, ist gestiegen** to climb (13)

die **Stelle, -n** place, spot (15)

    **stellen** to put, set (4)

    **sterben (stirbt), starb, ist gestorben** to die (14)

die **Steuer, -n** tax (7)

der **Stil, -e** style (12)

    **stimmen** to be correct (17)

der **Stock** (*sing.*), **Stockwerke** (*pl.*) floor, story (of a building) (11)

die **Straße, -n** street (1)

die **Straßenbahn, -en** tram (6)

der **Streik, -s** strike (15)

    **streiken** to strike (15)

sich **streiten, stritt, gestritten** to quarrel (15)

der **Stress** stress (15)

das **Stück, -e** piece (3)

der **Student, -en** student (male) (1)

die **Studentin, -nen** student (female) (1)

    **studieren** to study (1)

das **Studium, die Studien** study (15)

der **Stuhl, ⸚e** chair (4)

die **Stunde, -n** hour (1)

    **stündlich** hourly (4)

die **Subvention, -en** subsidy (18)

    **suchen** to look for (1)

der **Süden** South (7)

die **Suppe, -n** soup (4)

    **süß** sweet (14)

die **Symphonie, -n** symphony (14)

## T

der **Tag, -e** day (1)

    **täglich** daily (4)

das **Tal, ⸚er** valley (10)

die **Tante, -n** aunt (8)

    **tanzen** to dance (12)

die **Tasse, -n** cup (3)

der **Täter, -** culprit (18)
**tätig** employed, occupied, active (13)
**tatsächlich** indeed (5)
**tausend** thousand (0)
das **Taxi, -s** taxi, cab; **— fahren** to go by cab (3)
der **Tee** tea (3)
der **Teil, -e** part (9)
**teilen** to divide (13)
das **Telefon, -e** telephone (2)
**telefonisch** by telephone (18)
der **Tennis** tennis (2)
die **Terrasse, -n** terrace (11)
der **Test, -s** test (psychological) (14)
**teuer** expensive (4)
der **Teufel, -** devil (9)
das **Theater, -** theater (9)
das **Theaterstück, -e** theater play (9)
das **Thema, Themen** theme, subject (9)
die **Theorie, -n** theory (14)
**tief** deep (11)
der **Tisch, -e** table (4)
die **Tochter, ⸚** daughter (8)
die **Toilette, -n** toilet, bathroom (4)
**toll** mad, crazy; fabulous (*sl.*) (12)
das **Tor, -e** gate (16)
der **Tourist, -en** tourist (4)
die **Tradition, -en** tradition )9)
der **Traum, ⸚e** dream (14)
**träumen** to dream (12)
die **Trauung, -en** wedding ceremony (13)
**treffen (trifft), traf, getroffen** to meet, to hit (5)
**treiben, trieb, getrieben** practice, work at; **Sport —** to engage in sports, go in for sports (8)
die **Treppe, -n** staircase (3)
**trinken, trank, getrunken** to drink (2)
**trotz** in spite of (7)
**tschüs (tschüß)** so long (2)
**tun, tat, getan** to do (6)
die **Tür, -en** door (1)
der **Turm, ⸚e** tower (16)
die **Turnübung, -en** gymnastic exercise (8)

## U

**üben** to practice (8)
**über** above, over, about (concerning) (8)

**überall** everywhere (6)
**überhaupt** at all (10)
**überholen** to pass (5)
**übermorgen** day after tomorrow (10)
**überreden** to persuade (9)
**übertreiben** to exaggerate (18)
**üblich** usual (12)
die **Übung, -en** practice (8)
die **Uhr, -en** clock, watch; **wieviel — ist es?** what time is it? (13)
**um** at (with time of day), around (7)
**um . . . zu** in order to (8)
**umso besser** so much the better (15)
der **Umzug, ⸚e** parade (17)
**unabhängig** independent (13)
**unbedingt** absolutely, definitely (13)
**und** and (0)
der **Unfall, ⸚e** accident (5)
**unfreundlich** unfriendly (11)
**ungefähr** approximately (4)
**ungelöst** unsolved (18)
**ungesund** unhealthy (2)
**ungewöhnlich** unusual (13)
**unglaublich** unbelievable (12)
das **Unglück** misfortune (14)
**uniformiert** in uniform (16)
die **Universität, -en** university (1)
**unrecht haben** to be wrong (13)
**unser** our (10)
**unter** under (8)
**unterbrechen (unterbricht), unterbrach, unterbrochen** to interrupt (18)
**unterdrücken** to suppress, to oppress (9)
die **Unterdrückung** suppression (9)
die **Untergrundbahn, -en (U-Bahn)** subway (14)
sich **unterhalten (unterhält), unterhielt, unterhalten** to converse, have a good time (10)
**unterschreiben, unterschrieb, unterschrieben** to sign (4)
**unterstützen** to support (9)
der **Urlaub** leave, vacation (7)

## V

der **Vater, ⸚** father (8)
die **Verabredung, -en** date, appointment (9)
**verändern** to change (1)

**verantwortlich** responsible (12)

**verbessern** to improve (7)

**verbinden, verband, verbunden** to join, unite, combine (9)

**verdienen** to earn, to deserve (6)

die **Vergangenheit, -en** past (10)

**vergessen (vergißt), vergaß, vergessen** to forget (3)

der **Vergleich, -e** comparison; **im — mit** by comparison with (10)

das **Vergnügen** fun; **viel — !** have fun! (9)

**vergnügt** happy, gay (18)

**verheiratet** married (7)

**verhöhnen** to mock, deride (15)

der **Verkehr** traffic (11)

**verkehrt** wrong, topsy turvy, upside down (11)

**verlängern** to prolong, lengthen (17)

**verlassen (verläßt), verließ, verlassen** to leave behind (3)

**verlieren, verlor, verloren** to lose (5)

das **Vermittlungsbüro, -s** rental agency (4)

**verneinen** to deny, answer in the negative (18)

**verschieden** different (15)

**verschmutzen** to pollute (6)

die **Verschmutzung, -en** pollution (6)

**versetzen** to transfer, remove to another place; **in eine bessere Laune —** to cheer up (someone) (17)

**versprechen (verspricht), versprach, versprochen** to promise (15)

sich **versprechen (verspricht), versprach, versprochen** to make a slip of the tongue, to misspeak oneself (15)

**verständlich** understandable (15)

**verstärken** to strengthen (14)

**verstehen, verstand, verstanden** to understand (5)

**versuchen** to try (8)

die **Verzeihung** pardon, excuse (2)

**viel** much (1)

**viele** many (4)

**vielleicht** perhaps (2)

**vielversprechend** very promising (15)

**vier** four (0)

**viertel** quarter; **es ist — vor (vier)** it is a quarter to (four); **es ist — nach (vier)** it is a quarter past (four) (0)

**vierzehn** fourteen (0)

**vierzig** forty (0)

die **Violine, -n** violin (2)

der **Virus, Viren** virus (18)

das **Volk, ⸚er** people (9)

der **Volkstanz, ⸚e** folk dance (17)

der **Volkswagen, -** VW (5)

die **Volkswirtschaft** economy, political science (16)

**voll** full (6)

**von** (+ *dat.*) by, of, from, about (1)

**vor** (+ *dat.* or *acc.*) in front of, before (8); **—** (+ *dat.*) ago (9)

**voraus·sagen** to predict (18)

**vor·bereiten auf** (+ *acc.*) to prepare (15)

**vorgestern** day before yesterday (10)

die **Vorlesung, -en** lecture (13)

der **Vormittag, -e** forenoon (13)

**vorsichtig** careful (9)

**vor·stellen** to put forward, to introduce (9)

sich **vor·stellen** to imagine (14)

die **Vorstellung, -en** performance (9)

**vorwärts** forward (15)

**vor·ziehen, zog vor, vorgezogen** to prefer (12)

## W

die **Waffe, -n** weapon (18)

der **Wagen, -** car, carriage (6)

**wahr** true (8)

**während** while (9)

die **Wahrheit, -en** truth (8)

**wahrscheinlich** probable (5)

das **Wahrzeichen, -** landmark (16)

der **Wald, ⸚er** forest (8)

der **Walzer, -** walz (14)

**wandern** to hike (14)

**warm** warm (0)

die **Warnung, -en** warning (2)

**warten (auf** + *acc.*) to wait (for) (8)

**warum** why (2)

**was** what (1) **— für ein** what kind of (9)

das **Waschbecken, -** wash basin (4)

**waschen (wäscht), wusch, gewaschen** to wash (10)

das **Wasser** water (6)

**wechseln** to change (exchange) (10)

**wecken** to awaken (*someone*) (17)

der **Wecker, -** alarm clock (17)

der **Weg, -e** way; **auf dem —** on the way (14)

das **Weihnachten, -** Christmas (15)

**weil** because (9)

der **Wein, -e** wine (5)

**weinen** to cry (17)

der **Weinberg, -e** vineyard (10)

die **Weise** way, method; **auf diese —** in this way (18)

**weiß** white (11)

**weit** far (4)

**weiter** (+ *verb*) to (do) further, to go on (doing) (3)

**welch ein, welcher** which (2)

die **Welt, -en** world (7)

**wem** to whom (4)

**wen** whom (2)

**wenig** little; not much (8)

**wenige** (*pl.*) few (10)

**wenigstens** at least (6)

**wenn** if, when (7)

**wer** who (1)

die **Werbung, -en** advertisement (18)

**werden (wird), wurde, geworden** to become (7)

**werfen (wirft), warf, geworfen** to throw (16)

das **Werk, -e** work (of author, composer, etc.) (14)

**wessen** whose (11)

die **Weste, -n** vest (9)

der **Westen** west (13)

das **Wetter** weather (5)

**wichtig** important (7)

**wie** how, as; (1) like (7)

**wieder** again (3)

**wiederholen** to repeat (9)

die **Wiederkehr** return (11)

das **Wiedersehen** reunion; **auf —** goodbye (0)

**wieviel** how much (4)

sich **winden, wand, gewunden** to wind (10)

**wir** we (1)

**wirklich** really (1)

der **Wirt, -e** inkeeper (male) (16)

die **Wirtin, -nen** innkeeper (female) (16)

die **Wirtschaft** inn, management of affairs, mess (*pej.*), economy (16)

**wissen (weiß), wußte, gewußt** to know (a fact) (6)

die **Wissenschaft, -en** science (18)

**wo** where (1)

die **Woche, -n** week (4)

das **Wochenende, -** weekend (12)

**wöchentlich** weekly (4)

der **Wodka** vodka (5)

**wofür** what for (13)

**woher** where from (3)

**wohin** where to (3)

**wohnen** to reside, live (4)

das **Wohnhaus, ¨er** apartment house (16)

die **Wohnung, -en** apartment (14)

das **Wohnzimmer, -** living room (5)

**wollen (will), wollte, gewollt** to want to, intend to (6)

**woraus** out of what (14)

**worin** in which (16)

das **Wort, -e** word (4)

**wovon** of which (16)

**wünschen** to wish (12)

## Z

die **Zahl, -en** number (13)

der **Zahn, ¨e** tooth (12)

**zapfen** to tap (17)

**zehn** ten (0)

**zeigen** to show (4)

die **Zeile, -n** line (in a text) (18)

die **Zeit, -en** time (2)

die **Zeitung, -en** newspaper (3)

der **Zenith** zenith (14)

**zerreißen, zerriß, zerrissen** to tear up (14)

**zerstören** to destroy (14)

die **Zigarette, -n** cigarette (2)

die **Zigarre, -n** cigar (2)

das **Zimmer, -** room (3)

die **Zimmervermittlung, -en** rental agency (4)

die **Zitrone, -n** lemon (11)

**zu** to (referring to persons and public places) (3); **—** too (in excess of) (4)

der **Zucker** sugar (2)

die **Zueignung, -en** dedication (14)

**zuerst** first of all, at first (4)

**zufällig** accidentally (12)

**zufrieden** content (15)

der **Zug, ¨e** train (4)

**zuhören** (+ *dat.*) to listen to (10)

die **Zukunft** future (7)
  **zukünftig** future (*adj.*) (18)
  **zu·lassen (läßt), ließ, zugelassen**
    to admit (15)
  **zu·machen** to close (3)
  **zu·nehmen (nimmt zu), nahm zu, zu-**
    **genommen** to increase (12)
  **zurück·kehren** to return (13)
  **zurück·laufen** to run back (3)
  **zusammen** together (7)
  **zusammen·kommen, ist**

  **zusammengekommen** to come
    together, to gather (6)
der **Zuschauer, -** viewer, audience (18)
der **Zustand, ⸚e** condition, state (18)
  **zuviel** too much (2)
  **zwanzig** twenty (0)
  **zwei** two (0)
  **zweitens** in the second place, secondly
    (11)
  **zwischen** between (8)
  **zwölf** twelve (0)

## A

**about** über
**accident** der Unfall, ⸚e
on **account of** wegen (+ *gen.*)
**address** die Adresse, -n
**again** wieder
**against; I have nothing — you** ich habe
  nichts gegen dich
**ago** vor (+ *dat.*); **an hour —** vor einer
  Stunde
**air** die Luft, ⸚e
**airport** der Flugplatz, ⸚e
to **allow; to be allowed to** dürfen (darf),
  durfte, gedurft
**already** schon
**although** obwohl (*conj.*)
**always** immer
**America** Amerika
**around** um (+ *acc.*)
to **arrive** ankommen, kam an,
  angekommen
**art** die Kunst, ⸚e
to **ask** fragen; **to — for** bitten um (+ *acc.*)
**attractive** hübsch
to **awaken** (*someone*) wecken; (*oneself*)
  aufwachen

## B

**bad** schlecht
**band** die Band, -s
**bathroom** das Badezimmer, -; das Bad,
  ⸚er
to **be** sein (ist), war, gewesen
**beard** der Bart, ⸚e
**beautiful** schön
to **believe** glauben, denken
**best** am besten
**bicycle** das Fahrrad, ⸚er
**book** das Buch, ⸚er
**boy** der Junge, -n
**bus stop** die Bushaltestelle, -n
to **buy** kaufen
**by** von

## C

**cake** der Kuchen
to **call** (on phone) an·rufen, rief an,
  angerufen
**car** der Wagen, -
**careful** vorsichtig
**castle** die Burg, -en
**cheap** billig
to **cheer up** in eine bessere Laune versetzen
**child** das Kind, -er
**church** die Kirche, -n
**city** die Stadt, ⸚e
**city traffic** der Stadtverkehr
**class** die Klasse, -n
**coffee** der Kaffee
**cold** kalt
to **come** kommen, kam, gekommen
to **convince** überzeugen
**corner** die Ecke, -n
**country** das Land, ⸚er
**courage** der Mut; **to lose —** den Mut
  verlieren, verlor, verloren
**crazy** toll (*sl.*)
**cup** die Tasse, -n

## D

**dangerous** gefährlich
**date** die Verabredung, -en
**definitely** auf jeden Fall
to be **delighted** sich sehr freuen
**dense** dicht
**despite** trotz (+ *gen.*)
to **destroy** zerstören
**devil** der Teufel, -
**disc jockey** der Diskjockey, der
  Diskosprecher
to **discuss** diskutieren (über + *acc.*)
to **do** tun, tan, getan
to **drink** trinken, trank, getrunken
to **drive** fahren (fährt), fuhr, gefahren
**during** während

**E**

to **eat**  essen (ißt), aß, gegessen
**education**  die Erziehung
**eight o'clock**  acht Uhr
**emperor**  der Kaiser, -
**England**  (das) England
**enough**  genug
**enthusiastic**  enthusiastisch
**even**  sogar
**evening; this evening**  heute abend
**event; in any —**  auf jeden Fall
**every twelve minutes**  alle zwölf
  Minuten
**everything**  alles
**except**  außer (+ *dat.*)
**expensive**  teuer
**express** (*adj.*)  ausdrücklich

**F**

**face**  das Gesicht, -er
to **fall asleep**  ein·schlafen (schläft ein),
  schlief ein, ist eingeschlafen
**famous**  berühmt
**far**  weit; **as far as**  bis
**fifth**  fünfte
**film**  der Film, -e
to **find**  finden, fand, gefunden
**fire**  das Feuer, -
**first; the — thing**  das erste; **at —**
  zuerst
**for two months**  zwei Monate
  lang
to **forget**  vergessen (vergißt), vergaß,
  vergessen
**fortunately**  glücklicherweise
**France**  (das) Frankreich
**free**  frei
**freeway**  die Autobahn, -en
**friend**  der Freund (male); die Freundin
  (female)
**frightful**  schrecklich
**from**  aus, von
**in front of**  vor
**full**  voll
**furniture**  die Möbel (*pl.*)

**G**

**garden**  der Garten, ⸚
**German**  Deutsch
**German Democratic Republic**  Deutsche
  Demokratische Republik (DDR)
to **get out (of a vehicle)**  aus·steigen, stieg
  aus, ist ausgestiegen
**girl**  das Mädchen, -
to **give**  geben (gibt), gab, gegeben
to **go downstairs**  hinunter·gehen, ging
  hinunter, ist hinuntergegangen
to **go there**  hin·gehen, ging hin, ist
  hingegangen
**God**  der Gott, ⸚er
**goodbye**  auf Wiedersehen
**great** (*sl.*)  prima
**group**  die Gruppe, -n

**H**

**haircut; to get a —**  sich die Haare
  schneiden lassen
to **happen**  passieren, ist passiert
to **have**  haben
to **have to**  müssen (muß), mußte,
  gemußt
**health**  die Gesundheit
**highest**  höchst-
**history**  die Geschichte
to **hold games**  Spiele aus·tragen (trägt aus),
  trug aus, ausgetragen
to **be home**  zu Hause sein; **go home**  nach
  Hause gehen, ging, ist gegangen
**hotel**  das Hotel, -s
**how**  wie
to **hurry; to be in a —**  Eile haben

**I**

**ideological**  ideologisch
**ill**  krank
**industry**  die Industrie, -n
**information**  die Auskunft, ⸚e
to **interest**  interessieren

## J

**jacket** die Jacke, -n
**June** der Juni

## K

**key** der Schlüssel, -
to **know** (people) kennen, kannte, gekannt;
    **to —** (a fact) wissen (weiß), wußte,
    gewußt

## L

**language** die Sprache, -n
to **learn** lernen
at **least** wenigstens
to **leave** verlassen (verläßt), verließ,
    verlassen
**left; on the —** links
to **let in** hinein·lassen (läßt hinein), ließ
    hinein, hineingelassen
**letter** der Brief, -e
**library** die Bibliothek, -en
to **like to** (do something) gern (+ *verb*)
to **listen to** hören
**literature** die Literatur, -en
a **little** ein wenig
to **live at** wohnen bei (+ *dat.*)
**long** lang, lange (of time); **so —** tschüs;
    **for a — time** lange
to **look for** suchen
to **lose courage** Mut verlieren, verlor,
    verloren
**loud** laut
**lovely** hübsch
**luck; good —** viel Glück!

## M

**man** der Mann, ⸚er
**mankind** der Mensch, -en
**many** viele
**Mark; German mark** die Mark
**me** mich
to **mean** meinen

**member** das Mitglied, -er
**moment** der Moment, -e
**money** das Geld
**month** der Monat, -e
**mood; to be in the —** Lust haben
**morning** der Morgen, -
**mountain** der Berg, -e
**moustache** der Schnurrbart, ⸚e
**movie** das Kino
**Mr.** Herr
**Mrs.** Frau
**much** viel
**museum** das Museum, Museen

## N

**name** der Name, -n
**narrow** eng
**never** nie
**new** neu
**news** die Nachrichten (*pl.*)
**newspaper** die Zeitung
**nine** neun
**no** nein
**not** nicht; **— yet** noch nicht
**now** jetzt
**number** die Nummer, -n

## O

to **occupy** belagern
**often** oft
**old** alt; **— man** der Alte, -n
**Olympic Games** die Olympischen Spiele
    (*pl.*)
**on** auf
**opinion; in my —** meiner Meinung nach
**or** oder
to **order** bestellen
to **organize** organisieren
**our** unser
**overcoat** der Mantel, ⸚

## P

**pardon** Verzeihung
**parents** die Eltern (*pl.*)

to **park** parken
to **pass** überholen
  **past** die Vergangenheit
to **pay** bezahlen
  **people** die Leute (*pl.*)
  **performance** die Aufführung
  **perhaps** vielleicht
  **piece** das Stück
  **plan** der Plan, ⸚e
to **play** spielen
  **please** bitte
  **police** die Polizei (*sing.*)
  **political** politisch
  **polluted** verschmutzt
  **popular** beliebt
  **probably** wahrscheinlich
  **professor** der Professor
to **put on** (clothes) anziehen

## Q

**quickly** schnell

## R

  **railroad station** der Bahnhof, ⸚e
  **rain** der Regen
  **ready** fertig
  **really** wirklich
to **rebuild** restaurieren
  **recently** kürzlich
  **record** die Platte, -n
  **refreshing** erfrischend
  **region** die Gegend, -en, die Region, -en
to **repeat** wiederholen
to **replace** ersetzen
  **right; — away** gleich; **— over there** gleich da drüben
  **river** der Fluß, ⸚sse
  **room** der Raum, ⸚e, das Zimmer, -; **make — for** Platz machen für (+ *acc.*)
to **run** laufen (läuft), lief, ist gelaufen
  **Russian** (*adj.*) russisch

## S

  **said; it is —** man sagt
  **seat; to have a —** sich setzen

  **several** verschiedene
  **she** sie
  **short** kurz
to **show** zeigen
to **sit** sitzen, saß, gesessen
  **slow** langsam
  **sociology** die Soziologie
  **something** etwas
  **song** das Lied, -er
  **soon** bald
  **soul** die Seele, -n
to **sound** klingen, klang, geklungen
to **stay with** bleiben bei (+ *dat.*)
to **stop** halten (hält), hielt, gehalten
  **student** der Student, -en, die Studentin, -nen
to **study** studieren
  **subway** die Untergrundbahn, -en (U-Bahn)
  **such** solch ein
to **support** unterstützen
  **surely** sicher

## T

to **talk** sprechen (spricht), sprach, gesprochen
  **tax** die Steuer, -n
  **taxi driver** der Taxifahrer, -
  **television** das Fernsehen; **— set** der Fernsehapparat, -e
to **tell** sagen
  **tennis** das Tennis
  **terrible** schrecklich
  **thank you** danke; **thanks a lot** vielen Dank
  **there is; there are** es gibt (+ *acc.*)
  **thing** das Ding, -e
  **time** die Zeit, -en
  **tired** müde
  **to** nach, zu
  **today** heute
  **tomorrow** morgen
  **tonight** heute abend
  **too (much)** zu (viel)
  **tourist** der Tourist, -en
  **train** der Zug, ⸚e
to **travel** reisen
to **try** versuchen
  **two hundred** zweihundert

# U

**unfortunately** leider

# V

**vacation** die Ferien (*pl.*)
**very** sehr
**Vienna** (das) Wien
to **visit** besuchen

# W

to **walk** (on foot) zu Fuß gehen; **to —
 around** herum·laufen (läuft herum),
 lief herum, ist herumgelaufen
to **want to** wollen (will), wollte, gewollt
**war** der Krieg, -e
**water** das Wasser, -
**we** wir
to **wear** tragen (trägt), trug, getragen
**weather** das Wetter

**weekend** das Wochenende,
**welcome; you are —** bitte
**well-known** bekannt
**what about** worüber
**when** (past) als; **—** (if) wenn
**where** wo; **— (to)** wohin
**whether** ob
**while** während
**who** wer
**whom** wen
**whose** (*rel. pr.*) dessen
**why** warum
to **wish to** mögen (möchte), mochte,
 gemocht
**with** mit; **— what** womit
**within** innerhalb (+ *gen.*)
to **work** arbeiten
to **write** schreiben, schrieb, geschrieben

# Y

**young** jung; **— people** junge Leute, die
 Jugend

# INDEX

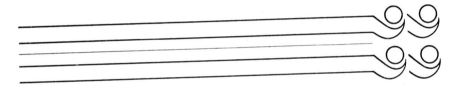